Jimmy and Rosalynn Carter

Jimmy and Rosalynn
Carter

THE GEORGIA YEARS, 1924–1974

E. Stanly Godbold, Jr.

OXFORD
UNIVERSITY PRESS

2010

OXFORD
UNIVERSITY PRESS

Oxford University Press, Inc., publishes works that further
Oxford University's objective of excellence
in research, scholarship, and education.

Oxford   New York
Auckland   Cape Town   Dar es Salaam   Hong Kong   Karachi
Kuala Lumpur   Madrid   Melbourne   Mexico City   Nairobi
New Delhi   Shanghai   Taipei   Toronto

With offices in
Argentina   Austria   Brazil   Chile   Czech Republic   France   Greece
Guatemala   Hungary   Italy   Japan   Poland   Portugal   Singapore
South Korea   Switzerland   Thailand   Turkey   Ukraine   Vietnam

Published by Oxford University Press, Inc.
198 Madison Avenue, New York, New York 10016

www.oup.com

Oxford is a registered trademark of Oxford University Press

Library of Congress Cataloging-in-Publication Data
Godbold, E. Stanly.
Jimmy and Rosalynn Carter : the Georgia years, 1924–1974 / E. Stanly Godbold, Jr.
p.   cm.
Includes bibliographical references and index.
ISBN 978-0-19-975344-4 (hardback)
1. Carter, Jimmy, 1924-   2. Governors—Georgia—Biography.   3. Carter, Rosalynn.
4. Governors' spouses—Georgia—Biography.   5. Georgia—Politics and government—1951-   I. Title.
F291.3.C37G63 2010
973.926092'2—dc22   2010010362

1 3 5 7 9 8 6 4 2

Printed in the United States of America
on acid-free paper

TO JEANNIE

ACKNOWLEDGMENTS

MY APPROACH to researching this biography has been to combine traditional manuscript and documentary analysis with the use of oral history. I spent many years reading through Carter's currently open presidential and governor's papers. I searched repositories where there are papers of other Georgia politicians, United States Cabinet members, and other people closely associated with Jimmy and Rosalynn Carter. In selecting subjects for interviews, I chose representatives from the major eras of the Carters' lives. I combined these with dozens of oral histories collected by the White Burkett Miller Center at the University of Virginia, the Jimmy Carter Presidential Library, and Georgia State University. Since the oral histories are filled with contradictions, I gave priority to interviews conducted nearest to the events they described or with persons intimate with the Carters. I adhered as closely as possible to the contemporary written source as the final arbiter of conflict.

To acknowledge adequately the people and institutions who assisted me would require a book in itself. Jimmy and Rosalynn Carter granted me interviews and answered questions by letter, and he freely gave me access to various collections of his papers. When I first visited the Jimmy Carter Presidential Library and Museum in Atlanta in August 1990, I never dreamed I would become so familiar with its collections, its people, and its ambience. As the weeks there stretched into months and years, the place did become home. Don Schewe, Martin Elzy, David Alsobrook, Jay Hakes, and Robert Bohanan introduced me to the collections and remained faithful advisers throughout. The very special people who worked in the research room, at the front desk, and with the Museum, earned more thanks and credit than I'll ever be able to deliver. They include Susan Ament, Bettie Joe Brown, Charlaine Burgess, Jim Dougherty, Betty Egwinike, Gary Foulk, Kathy Gillespie, Jim Herring, Juanita Jones, Yolanda Logan, Shelia Mayo, Ceri McCarron, Mary Anne McSweeney, Sylvia Naguib, Bert Nason, Sonia Robinson, Keith Shuler, Sara Saunders, Dave Stanhope, Chuck Stokely, Jim Yancey, and others. Likewise, at the Georgia Archives in Atlanta, I received generous help from Ed Weldon, Bob White, Dale Couch, Gail Miller DeLoach, Howard Hancock, John Harvey, Andy Phrydas, Peter Schinkel, Joanne Smalley, Bill Young, and others. Kathy Shoemaker and others at the Manuscript, Archives, and Rare Book Library of the Robert W. Woodruff Library at Emory University rendered invaluable aid. The reference librarians at Lander University in Greenwood, South Carolina, who assisted me include Dan Lee, Betty Williams, and others.

The Gerald R. Ford Foundation gave me a grant to conduct research in the Gerald R. Ford Presidential Library in Ann Arbor, Michigan. While there, I found Geir Gundersen, Helmi Raaska, and others particularly helpful. Archivist Sherrie Fletcher at the Ronald Reagan Library and Professor Michaela Reaves of California Lutheran University assisted in acquiring the Carter materials at the Reagan Library. Director David Alsobrook, who transferred from the Carter Library, and Supervisory Archivist Warren Finch at the George H. W. Bush Presidential Library rendered me good advice and assistance in accessing the Carter materials in their collections.

My home university, Mississippi State, gave me sabbatical leaves and financial assistance. The following students performed ably as research assistants: David Gleeson, Richard Haydel, Kevin Hall, Qiming Han, Todd Herring, David Hirsch, Todd Holden, Tony Iacono, Craig Piper, John Selman, Brian Schneider (California Lutheran University), Ryan Semmes, Kenneth Vickers, and others. Professional historians George Robson and Scott McMurry helped on occasion with both primary and secondary research. The John C. Stennis Oral History Project at Mississippi State University assisted with my interviews and travel budget. Colleagues and students invariably showed interest, asked good questions, and offered suggestions and encouragement.

The scholars from around the world who sometimes worked beside me at the Carter Library, or participated in discussions at conferences, were helpful with their criticisms and suggestions. Carl Biven of Georgia Tech shared ideas, books, lunches, and evenings with his family. Russell Motter ran up quite a telephone bill from Hawaii and, later, Houston, talking to me about the Carter era. Annette Wise is both an encyclopedia of information about the Carters in Plains and an excellent photographer.

In Atlanta, Richard McMurry, a distinguished Civil War historian, provided me with a place to stay, discussed the project with me in many restaurants, and finally read every word of the manuscript. Linda Matthews, Head of Manuscript, Archives, and Rare Book Library in the Robert W. Woodruff Library at Emory University, gave me many useful research leads. At the Library of Congress, Connie Cartledge, Mary Wolfskill, and Paul Chestnut assisted me. Louise J. Godbold, my mother, and John Glass read early drafts of the manuscript and made useful suggestions.

Thanks, too, go to the staffs of the Oral History Research Office Collection at Columbia University; the James Earl Carter Library at Georgia Southwestern University, the Lake Blackshear Regional Library, the Sumter County Historical Association, and the Sumter County Courthouse, all in Americus; the Early County Courthouse and the Blakeley Public Library; and the National Park Service in Plains. Mitchell Memorial Library at Mississippi State University, with its very helpful staff and excellent collections, proved a fine base from which to conduct research.

The people who gave me interviews include Rick Allen, Jimmy Carter, Rosalynn Carter, Morris W. H. Collins, Jr., Juanita Edmundson, Dan Edwards, Marty Franks, Rod Goodwin, O. M. Harrelson, Mary Finch Hoyt, Howard Jones, Billie Larson, Jackie Lassiter, Edmund Muskie, Tip O'Neill, Abraham Ribicoff, John and Julia Saunders, Gary Sick, Scott Singletary, "Miss Allie" Smith, Rear Admiral James R. Stark, U.S. Navy (ret.), Gordon C. Stewart, India Thompson, Stansfield Turner, and Cyrus Vance. Jan Handy and Jane Thorne shared with me the printed memorabilia they saved from the Carter era. Steve Hochman, Assistant to President Carter, asked good questions over several lunches and arranged some of my introductions and interviews. Kenneth H. Thomas, Jr., of Decatur, granted me access to his voluminous research into the Carter, Gordy, Smith, and Murray family genealogies.

The scholars and journalists who have written about the Carters and the Carter presidency whose works are cited in the notes have provided information and inspiration for this work. This biography is built on the numerous works of scholars, journalists, politicians, archivists, and others who have created and managed the primary and secondary sources that made it possible. Scholars who read and criticized all or part of the manuscript include Professor Carl Biven of Georgia Tech University; Dr. Phil Chase, Senior Editor of the Papers of George Washington, at the University of Virginia; Professor Ruth Currie of Warren Wilson College; Dr. Martin I. Elzy, retired Assistant Director of the Carter Presidential

Library; Professor Laura Kalman of the University of California at Santa Barbara; Professor Gordon McKinney, Director of Appalachian Studies at Berea College; Professor Richard McMurry; Leo Ribuffo, Distinguished Professor at George Washington University; Rear Admiral James R. Stark, U.S. Navy (ret.); Professor T. Adams Upchurch at East Georgia State University; Professor Kenneth Vickers of Martin Methodist University; and a very perceptive anonymous reader for Oxford University Press.

Fred C. Smith, a professor of history at Lambuth University, read every word and made many useful suggestions. Susan S. Wansbrough, a journalist turned attorney in Dallas, took time from her own busy schedule to lend a helping hand, as she frequently does for so many others. Susan Ferber, Executive Editor at Oxford University Press, graciously extended indispensable assistance from the acquisition of the manuscript through the production process. Her colleagues, too, gave excellent and punctual assistance. Remaining mistakes in fact or judgment are the author's alone.

Our cat Maurice (1990–2007) made many a trip across the keyboard of the word processor, napped on every page of the manuscript, and contributed long hours of serene companionship. My wife Jeannie and stepdaughter Heidi accepted without complaint the often difficult challenge of living with someone who spent extended time away from home in libraries and archives and even more time cloistered in a forbidden study with stacks of papers and books and Maurice. During the good times and the bad, their love and support never wavered. Jeannie, especially Jeannie, made the creation of this book possible.

CONTENTS

The Carters and the Smiths

WHEN JIMMY AND ROSALYNN CARTER left their home in the Georgia governor's mansion in April 1972 for a trip to Brazil, they had no idea what a unique emotional adventure awaited them. Their host suggested a visit to an ancient Confederate cemetery and chapel near Americana. An unusual historical site, Americana was the surviving community settled by defeated Confederates who fled the United States at the end of the Civil War. Of the approximately twenty thousand who fled to Brazil, all vanished except those at the small settlement they nostalgically called Americana. They attempted to recreate their familiar plantation society in a country that protected the institution of slavery and welcomed the émigrés. Their lives there were harsh, causing some to leave, others to die or simply blend into the local population. Since Brazil, a strict Catholic country, would not allow Protestants to bury their dead in its cemeteries, they created their own *campo,* or field, near Americana, buried their dead there, and built a small chapel adjacent to it.[1]

The surviving self-exiled southerners became independent farmers whose progeny remained in Brazil but retained their language, their American and southern identities, and their long, often sad memories. Several hundred of them went four times a year to visit the Confederate burial ground and the tiny nondenominational Protestant chapel. The altar at those times was draped with the flags of Brazil, the United States, and the Confederacy. In time, their descendants erected a plain Confederate memorial bearing only the family names of the first refugees. One of them was an ancestor of Rosalynn Carter.[2]

When several hundred descendants of the Confederate expatriates heard that the governor of Georgia, his wife, and press secretary Jody Powell were coming to the cemetery, they rushed to greet them. They drew a large, crude circle on the ground, writing "WELCOME" in the dirt, and marked where the governor's helicopter should land. The Georgia visitors seemed a bit surprised by the warm welcome until they looked into the faces of the Brazilians and saw the southern faces of their ancestors. Both Rosalynn and Jimmy were intensely moved by the sight of the monument draped with a tattered Confederate flag, the chapel, the cemetery, and the courage, suffering, and faith of those lonely Americans who had fled their own homeland. Their descendants, standing before the Carters in that isolated spot more than a century later, might have been their neighbors in Georgia. Carter at first felt sad that they had left their own country, where they might have had a better life had they been able to accept the South's defeat in the Civil War. As Carter addressed the crowd, he saw how intently they listened, then noted that both Rosalynn and Jody were choking back tears. He paused, attempting to control his own tears, as his speech evolved into a sermon and a prayer. He gave thanks for the Christian spirit of those ancient rebels, then joined Rosalynn to bury a time capsule near the chapel. Fifteen years later, when Jody Powell remembered the event and tried to make sense of it, he thought that maybe they had "been touched so deeply" because "we discovered a part of ourselves that we hardly knew existed."[3] The moment ended, and Carter promised to tell their story when he got back home, then boarded the plane for Atlanta with Rosalynn and his entourage.[4]

Returning to their glamorous world as governor and first lady of Georgia, and later as thirty-ninth president and first lady of the United States, the Carters resumed their lives as modern southerners who despised the taint of slavery and racial discrimination in their history. They were devout Protestants—he Baptist and she Methodist—whose ambition and talents had driven them to seek and win the highest political office in their state and their country. As a political couple and international humanitarians, their public reception vacillated from adulation to hatred to unending controversy. As actors on the world stage for more than three-quarters of a century, they sought to institutionalize a world radically different from the one the folks buried in that cemetery near Americana had clung to. Remaining rooted in their past by genetic and cultural heritage, they were as determined as their ancestors to seek a new world—not by fleeing, but by changing the one they had inherited.

The purpose of this two-volume biography is neither to praise nor condemn but to challenge the popular image that the man from Plains was either saint or sinner, for he was neither. It also elevates his wife, Rosalynn Smith Carter, to the place of equal partner in his life and career, which he insisted she deserved. The story of one is the story of the other. One of their close friends in 1976 said, "You can't really understand Jimmy Carter unless you know Rosalynn."[5]

This volume, which covers their lives from birth to the end of his governorship, and the second one to follow are drawn from more than two decades of research in the presidential library, the state archives, and other repositories where manuscripts, recorded interviews, public documents, or other materials directly related to the Carters are located. It is also based on original, unpublished interviews with a wide variety of participants in the Carters' story. Despite all that has been written and said about them, much of it mythological, this book offers substantially more information about their prepresidential years. Presented in a format more factual than interpretative, it reveals a man who was scarcely the peanut farmer of popular myth but was the heir to a sizeable fortune and built, with the collaboration of his wife, a lucrative agribusiness. Growing and processing cotton was as important as growing peanuts in their business. Using much of their own money, they rode the changing politics of the South into the Georgia governor's office. Carter's shocking announcement that the time for racial discrimination in Georgia had ended attracted national attention.

Politicians to the core, the Carters skillfully moved from state to national politics by gaining control of the national Democratic party in 1974. Rosalynn sat quietly but knowingly on the stage behind her husband as he announced his candidacy for president of the United States on December 12, 1974. He was not solely the product of the indomitable mother, "Miss Lillian," who became so well known during the presidential years. His formative years were shaped by his relatively unknown, ambitious, nurturing father, "Mr. Earl," who set high standards for his firstborn son. Behind the facade of shy housewife, Rosalynn Smith Carter was a bright and shrewd businesswoman who helped build their family fortune and a brilliant political strategist. Vitally involved in their elections to the governorship in 1970 and the presidency in 1976, she shared every adventure, surprise, and defeat with her husband.

When they were unable to prevent their crushing defeat in their fight for reelection in 1980, the Carters comforted each other and soon emerged triumphant as cochairs of the Carter Center, a private humanitarian institution committed to "waging peace, fighting disease, building hope."

The story of the Carters and the Smiths is the story of America from the early settlement of colonial Virginia to the culture of backwoods Georgia on the eve of the Great Depression. It is also the story of the American South, which emerged differently from the rest of the country as it imitated the British pattern of social life, imported and enslaved millions of Africans in order to gain the highest yield possible from its vast acreage and long growing season, and developed a culture and political viewpoint incompatible with the rest of the nation. The path to wealth and power for ambitious southerners lay through agriculture, and the ancestors of Jimmy and Rosalynn Carter seized that opportunity.

The first Carter in America, Thomas Carter, Sr., arrived in Virginia as an indentured servant in 1637. After completing the years of his servitude, he and his progeny became prosperous through acquiring land and slaves and through marriage. Five generations later, Thomas's descendant Wiley Carter (1798–1864) was an illiterate frontiersman with landed wealth in Georgia, a colorful character who epitomized life on the southern frontier and exhibited family characteristics that would survive through many generations. He married good women, sought wealth through agricultural pursuits, showed minor interest in community service, and had a vicious temper. In 1843, while serving as deputy sheriff, he murdered his neighbor, Carrol Usry, in a dispute over ownership of a slave and in defense of his wife's honor in reaction to a disparaging remark Usry had made. At his trial the next year, a jury found him not guilty. His wife died five years later; he married the widow Sarah Chestnut Wilson, and in 1851 they set out for Sumter County, which was destined to become the home of the thirty-ninth president.[6]

By 1860, Wiley had become prosperous on his plantation about twelve miles north of Plains. He produced 147 bales of cotton that year, owned farm implements valued at $400, and possessed personal and real property worth $43,500.[7] That year, his son Littleberry Walker Carter (1832–1873), the fifth of eleven children, moved with his young family to be near his father.

Both the burden of history and the weight of family tradition fell heavily on Littleberry. At the beginning of the Civil War in 1861, he and three of his brothers—William Archibald, Wiley, Jr., and sixteen-year-old Jesse Taliaferro—enlisted as privates in Captain A. S. Cutts's Sumter Flying Artillery. In 1863, they fought at Sharpsburg, Maryland, and Gettysburg, Pennsylvania, and a year later in the South's victorious Battle of the Crater near Petersburg, Virginia.[8]

When their father died on December 6, 1864, these Carter brothers were with their company in Virginia; he left Littleberry $24,052.91 in inflated Confederate currency.[9]

Like his ancestors, Littleberry Carter rose in fortune and esteem, despite the physical devastation and political chaos of post–Civil War Georgia. He owned a peanut farm near Americus and was a partner in a business in town, an enterprise that caused him to fall heir to the violence that had dogged his father. On November 21, 1873, his business partner, Daniel P. McCann, murdered him during an argument over gambling receipts from a machine they owned, known as a "flying jenny." Littleberry was forty-two; his grief-stricken widow died on the day of his funeral. McCann fled to South America and never returned. Littleberry's estate sold for a pittance during the depression of 1873–1874, the flying jenny bringing $20.75. He and his wife left four orphans.[10]

Littleberry's oldest son, Billy (grandfather of the president), then fifteen, moved with his siblings to Plains of Dura, where their aunt and uncle could care for them. Settled in the 1840s in one of the state's best farming areas, Plains of Dura lay in Sumter County, eleven miles west of Americus. The village home of farmers who owned land in counties to the north, west, and south of Sumter, Plains also attracted a doctor, businessmen, preachers, and craftsmen. They named the settlement for the Babylonian meadow described in the Book of Daniel where King Nebuchadnezzar II built his golden image and cast Shadrach, Meshach, and Abednego into the blazing furnace for refusing to bow down to the idol. By remaining faithful to their own God, the three Israelites survived their trial by fire unharmed.[11] The citizens shortened the name to Plains, incorporated it in 1884, and in 1885 moved it a mile south, near the recently built Americus, Preston, and Lumpkin Railroad.

Before the town relocated, Billy had moved about fifty miles southwest to Early County. With a small inheritance, good opportunity, and hard work, during the 1890s he acquired 450 acres, three sawmills, a cotton gin, a store, and a ten-acre vineyard, from which he produced and sold three thousand gallons of wine per year. He and his wife, formerly Nina Pratt, from Abbeville, South Carolina, and their four children lived in the town of Arlington. Billy then built them a seven-room house for his large family in the Rowena community that faced the railroad tracks and stood in the shade of two giant oak trees.

Billy was a hard worker and a tough character. Once when the flues at his cotton gin clogged, Billy decided to go inside the boiler to clean them himself. He wrapped himself in burlap sheets, soaked them with water, and to the amazement of his hands and spectators, walked into the blistering-hot boiler and cleaned the flues, emerging unharmed. On another occasion, when he accidentally cut his knee deeply, he used a needle and thread to sew up the cut himself and went on with his work.[12]

Nina was not so tough. When she became ill with malaria in the swampy, mosquito-infested environment, her adoring husband built her and the children another house thirty miles to the north in Cuthbert. He commuted between Rowena and Cuthbert by train. The children were Ethel, born in 1887, William Alton in 1888, Lula in 1891, James Earl in 1894, and Jeannette in 1904. For Nina and Billy, however, the Georgia frontier, where the law was lax and murder was common, posed tough challenges. On September 3, 1903, when she was pregnant with their fifth child, her husband, like his father before him, was murdered.

Will Taliaferro killed Billy Carter in an argument over a piece of furniture. When Taliaferro vacated a store he had rented from Carter, he took with him a thread cabinet. Carter accused Taliaferro of theft, became very angry, and confronted him at Taliaferro's new store. They fought with bottles, breaking them and cutting each other severely. Billy drew a small pocketknife and cut Will across the abdomen with sufficient force to eviscerate him. Holding his organs in with his left hand, Will reached behind himself with his right hand, fetched his .32-caliber pistol, and shot Billy in the head. Both men were badly wounded. Nina rushed to Rowena in a horse-drawn buggy, brought her husband back to Cuthbert by train, and there watched him suffer miserably and die, despite their doctor's care, on September 4.[13]

Taliaferro recovered from his wounds and faced charges of voluntary manslaughter. In the October 1903 term of the Early County Superior Court, the judge declared a mistrial because the jurors could not agree on a verdict. At a second trial the next year, the jury acquitted him.[14]

Four months after her husband died, Nina gave birth to their fifth child. Nina's brother-in-law, Jeremiah Calvin Carter, sold her property for a substantial sum, and she moved to Plains. Still immersed in agriculture, she bought thirteen hundred acres of land in nearby Webster County. She rented the land and moved in early 1904 with her five children into a small, stylish Victorian house on Thomas Street, directly behind the site where the Methodists built their church in 1910.[15] She lived well on her husband's estate, and her elder son William Alton worked at a general store until about 1915, when he opened his own store on Main Street. Ruled by the land, the desire for money, austere religion, and the memory of his murdered father, Nina's son James Earl Carter, father of the future president, was ten when the family moved to Plains.

Rosalynn Smith Carter's ancestry, likewise tied to the land of Georgia, was embedded in the history of the South. Her people were not violent; they were better bred and more educated and pious than the Carters. Notable characteristics of Rosalynn's ancestors included their tenacity, quiet demeanor, willingness to serve their communities, closeness to the land, and religion.[16] Rosalynn's great-great-grandfather, George Lynch Smith, a North Carolinian, moved to Georgia in 1807 as a frontier missionary, broke with the Disciples of Christ Church, and founded his own Methodist church near Richland.

His son Tenderson, born in 1815, became a farmer in South Georgia in the 1830s. His handsome son Wilburn Juriston Smith (b. 1858)—doctor, farmer, and Methodist—married the very pretty and serious-minded Sarah Eleanor Bell in 1893. The second of their eight children, Wilburn Edgar (father of the future first lady), born November 20, 1896, inherited his father's good looks. He was twenty-two when his father died in 1918. His widowed mother, "Mama Sallie," moved into Plains and later lived in her granddaughter's childhood home. She died in 1951.[17]

For more than three centuries, as the Carters and Smiths made their way by happenstance into South Georgia, none of them could have known that the eventual union of their families would hurl them and Plains upon the world stage. Growing up in the 1930s in rural southwestern Georgia, Jimmy and Rosalynn were part of a society that was becoming fluid, as the Great Depression and the looming World War II began to change it. These events challenged the very heritage of the South by forcing its natives to scrutinize their economy, class structure, race relations, and post–Civil War isolation from the rest of the country and the world. It was both a society dying and a society being born, painful events that in the South produced some of the world's greatest creative writers, who attempted to explain in the most elemental human terms how the present must be reconciled with the past. Among them, William Faulkner of Oxford, Mississippi, became one of Carter's favorite authors, and Carson McCullers of Columbus, Georgia, one of Rosalynn's. Faulkner used characters from his native Mississippi to suggest how people, rich and poor, powerful and weak, black and white, male and female, shared a common humanity with each other and all peoples of the world. McCullers's mentally and physically handicapped people rose above their infirmities to become productive members of their families and society. From their changing South and its writers, Jimmy Carter and Rosalynn Smith acquired an optimistic world view in which human beings might break free of inhibiting shackles, and, as Faulkner states in his Nobel Prize acceptance speech, not only "endure" but "prevail."[18] Together, Jimmy and Rosalynn Carter hoped to help make it happen, for themselves, their state, their country, and the world.

CHAPTER ONE

A Boy in Archery

EARL INSISTED THAT HIS FIRSTBORN SON be named James Earl Carter, Jr. Most babies of that time and place were born at home, but since the baby's mother worked for Dr. Sam Wise, he allowed her to deliver her baby at his hospital in Plains. The first American president to be born in a hospital, Carter arrived at 7 A.M., Wednesday, October 1, 1924, weighing eight and a half pounds. Lillian Carter kept a baby book in which she recorded some of the details of his first months. He would be called "'Jimmy' now—but later of course t'will be 'Jim,'" she said, having no inkling of his future. Well-connected with affluent people, the family received a bounty of baskets, blankets, bootees, dresses, rattles, socks, a quilt, and $5 cash. The infant "smiled" at one month, "laughed out loud" at two and a half months, wore "short clothes" and said "Dad-da," "Bye-bye," and "Hey there" at six and a half months. At nine months he could stand alone.[1]

The infant boy had two powerful parents standing behind him. His father, James Earl Carter, who was ten at the time he moved with his mother and siblings to Plains, grew up fast. Driven by a family ambition to succeed, he was, according to his older brother Alton, a hardworking "hustler."[2] After attending high school in Plains, he entered Riverside Military Academy in Gainesville, northeast of Atlanta. That school enforced a rigid code of discipline for boys, many of whom had behavioral problems.[3] Earl joined Company A of the cadet corps during the 1910–11 session. The 1911 yearbook listed him as "Early Carter" of the "South Georgia Crackers" for the school year and simply as "Carter" in the summer Naval School and Camp.[4]

With a tenth-grade education, then the equivalent of high school, Earl Carter had more formal schooling than any of his ancestors, and he was as anxious as they had been to become financially successful. From age seventeen through nineteen, immediately after he left Riverside, he sought his fortune in Texas, where he sold "pressing irons," cast-iron flatirons that women used to iron clothes. In 1913 he returned to Plains and invested his savings first in an icehouse and later a laundry.[5]

After the United States entered World War I, Earl registered for the draft on June 5, 1917, requesting an exemption on the grounds that he had to support his mother, but his sisters remembered that he did not want to leave a young woman with whom he was in love. The army denied the exemption and inducted him on October 1, 1917. He was, according to his draft board, twenty-two, of medium height, stout, with blue eyes and light hair, a farmer and a clerk at his brother Alton's store. Earl served in Company I, 121st Infantry Regiment, and rose from private first class to sergeant, but he never left the country. He attended officer training school at Camp Lee, Virginia, where, on August 6, 1918, the army discharged him. He later accepted a commission as second lieutenant in the Georgia National Guard.[6]

Earl returned after World War I to an agricultural boomtown, where, according to his brother Alton, he transformed all that he touched into gold. In the 1920s, Plains had banks, churches, drugstores, a funeral home, a hospital, a hotel, a consolidated high school for whites, and another school for blacks. Earl seized the chance. He bought timber and farmland, worked beside hired black laborers in his fields, and dabbled in other business ventures. He bought and sold peanuts and in time entered the insurance, fertilizer, grocery, and mercantile businesses. When the Georgia Seed and Supply Company in Americus went bankrupt, Earl bought its stock cheaply, then opened his own grocery and mercantile store in Plains. In 1923, he bought seven hundred acres of good farmland in Webster County, borrowing $7,000, the only debt he ever incurred, which he paid off quickly.[7]

Already wealthy at age twenty-nine, Earl married Bessie Lillian Gordy on September 26, 1923. With brown hair flowing down to her waist, Lillian was twenty-five, a Methodist, vivacious, smart, and ambitious. She had moved to Plains from nearby Richland to work as a nurse at the Wise Sanitarium. Although she at first did not find Earl attractive, she listened to Dr. Wise's advice that Earl was likely to be very successful financially, and she did apparently grow to love him in what would become a rocky marriage. The groom dominated the wedding plans and their lives together. Their marriage took place at Earl's home, with only family members in attendance and his Baptist minister officiating. After an inexpensive, small reception at the groom's home, Lillian went back to work. As a symbol of her independence and continuing devotion to her father, she continued to keep her hair down to her waist, to please her father—until her first child, Jimmy, was born.[8]

Earl had married a strong woman in a political family. Lillian was the fourth of the nine children of James Jackson ("Jim Jack") Gordy and his wife Mary Ida Nicholson, a stern and intelligent woman. The Gordys, of Scotch-Irish descent, had moved into southwest Georgia a generation later than the Carters. The first, Peter, came from Maryland at the beginning of the nineteenth century, settling finally in Muscogee County in the 1830s on lands vacated by the Indians. Two of his grandsons died in the Civil War. Another, James Thomas Gordy, flourished in Chattahoochee County; he was a wagon master for the Confederacy and a private in Company B, Sixth Georgia State Militia, when his son Jim Jack was born in 1863. A Baptist and a farmer, he became a tax collector after the war.

Jim Jack—tall, dark, handsome, and stern—grew up with a keen interest in learning and a passion for politics. He was a Democrat and a Methodist. After their 1871 marriage, Jim Jack and Mary Ida moved to Richland, in Stewart County, where for twenty-one years he was postmaster. A nimble politician, he never held a public office but managed to keep his appointive job as postmaster under four presidents and both major political parties. Apart from his postmaster appointment, he owned a gasoline station and drove Oldsmobiles and Cadillacs. He knew the state's powerful politicians.[9]

When the state legislature met, Jim Jack journeyed to Atlanta to talk politics and run errands for those in power. He idolized Tom Watson, a schoolteacher and writer from Thomson who served one term as an innovative U.S. representative in the early 1890s. Jim Jack managed Watson's campaign in Georgia's Third Congressional District and allegedly suggested to him the idea for rural free delivery of the mail. An early advocate of reforms for blacks and farmers, Watson received the Populist party's nomination for vice president in 1896, and later for president. Jim Jack named one of his younger sons for him. When Tom Watson visited him at the post office, Lillian said, "It was just like Jesus dropping in." After losing an election in 1892, when some blacks voted against him, Watson became a notorious southern demagogue. He condemned Jewish citizens and African Americans alike and helped foment the kind of hate that fueled the

Ku Klux Klan. Jim Jack Gordy did not share those opinions and drifted away from him. Jack had at least one black friend whose company he relished. William D. Johnson, an African Methodist Episcopal (AME) bishop, often visited the postmaster and his daughter Lillian and may have had some influence on her belief that blacks should be treated equally with whites.[10]

Both Jim Jack and his wife Mary Ida were strict disciplinarians who reared their children to appreciate a larger world than Richland.[11] Lillian worshiped her father. She worked with him in the post office from the time she graduated from high school until she moved to Plains in 1921. She grew up on stories of state politics, the need for reform, and even the possibility that a Georgian might have a national political career. After her marriage, her father spent many hours with her and Earl, analyzing elections and telling his grandson Jimmy stories about Georgia politics. Jimmy was twenty-four when his grandfather died in 1948.[12]

Both the Gordys and the Carters welcomed baby Jimmy as a possible standard-bearer who might take forward their dreams of financial and political success. Earl Carter, swelled with pride, nicknamed his son "Hotshot." At this point, the family lived in rented rooms in a private home on Main Street directly across from the Methodist church. After an argument with the landlady about a pet dog, however, they moved to another house on the same street. Two years later, Earl bought a house on Bond Street, next door to what was to be the home of Rosalynn Smith.[13]

At twenty months, Jimmy contracted a disease that almost took his life. Like many young children in the area, he suffered from colitis, or uncontrollable bloody diarrhea. Lillian put him in the hospital, where she treated him herself with a slow-dripping, dense, cornstarch enema. The treatment worked. While enduring it, Jimmy cried for a pet goat. Head nurse Gussie Abrams, a friend of Lillian and Jimmy's godmother, brought one to visit him at the hospital and to have as a pet when he went home.[14]

Two months later in 1926, Lillian gave birth to Gloria. Nicknamed "GoGo" by their father, she resembled Jimmy but was physically larger and often had the advantage in their childhood fights. A rebellious child, she received more spankings from her father than Jimmy did. In 1929, after the family had moved to the country, a third child, Ruth, arrived. The apple of her father's eye, she was a pretty baby and later a pretty woman. A "curly-headed blonde," Ruth, in her father's opinion, was "prettier than Shirley Temple." When Ruth suffered with pneumonia and her family thought she would die, Earl stayed home and fed her liquids himself one drop at a time, held her up to the sunshine, and prayed with his wife and son until she got well. He called her "Boop-a-Doop," and she grew to adulthood convinced that she could do no wrong.[15]

In 1928, Earl purchased a farm in Archery, located two and a half miles south of Plains. The spacious, six-room house facing the railroad tracks became Jimmy's home until he left for college. Lillian set high standards for her children and established herself as someone who must be obeyed, but she was often an absentee mother. As a nurse, she sometimes worked twenty hours a day. She reared her children by memoranda, leaving so many notes on a desk for Jimmy and Gloria that they jokingly said that they thought the desk was their mother. "The strong memory in my mind," Jimmy said, "is coming home [from school] and Mother not being there."[16] They had household help, and Earl could easily come home form tending his fields and business to check on the children.

For a working woman, Lillian did the best she could to care for the children. She employed a series of African-American nannies, and she had other black servants who would draw water, build fires, clean the house, cook meals, and help with household chores. On weekends and special occasions, she photographed the children, cooked their favorite foods, and gave them parties. Sometimes she baked cookies and served them to Jimmy and his black playmates in the back yard. Just as her parents had reared her, she demanded that they read. They read at the table during meals, in the living room with their parents at night, and later alone in their bedrooms. When asked to tend to a chore, they sometimes begged to be excused on the grounds that they were reading.[17]

At Christmas, Lillian joined Earl, Jimmy, Gloria, and Ruth to search the farm for the perfect Christmas tree. She decorated it, shopped for gifts, cooked, and talked about the baby Jesus. One year when all three children were sick with the measles, she telephoned a radio station in Atlanta to ask for help. On Christmas morning, she and Earl carried the battery-powered radio into the sickroom. Soon they heard a popular entertainer, Little Jack Little, announce that he would sing especially for "Jimmy, Ruth, and Gloria." Then he burst into the popular saga of "Wooden Head, Puddin' Head Jones," who "didn't know beans from bones." The children perked up, bounced on the bed, and sang along, as their tearful parents watched. Despite the fact that the song had no relationship to the Christmas season, "Wooden Head, Puddin' Head Jones" became one of Lillian's favorite "Christmas carols."[18]

Lillian worked in Plains but was not of it. She sometimes skipped church, smoked cigarettes, and in the evenings sipped whiskey or wine with her husband. She played poker and attended wrestling matches and baseball games in nearby towns.[19] She kept the sizeable income she earned as a nurse and from the annual sale of pecans from their large grove. She was not a joiner. Standoffish, she offended some members of their Baptist church by caring for African-American patients. She never worried about being excluded from church functions, she said, because "We had too much money to be ostracized! ... we were the biggest contributors." A loving but distant mother, she was a powerful presence in her family.[20]

Earl became the nurturing parent to "Hot," "GoGo," and "Boop-a-Doop." Jimmy revered his mother, but he preferred to take naps with his daddy. Earl's own father had died when he was only nine, and he took an unusually passionate interest in rearing his own children. He made Jimmy feel proud the day they moved into the house in Archery. Since Earl had forgotten to bring the key, he boosted four-year-old "Hot" through a window with instructions to open the door from the inside. After settling into their new home, Earl sometimes roasted marshmallows or baked sweet potatoes in the open fire. He peeled a grapefruit, then handed sections to Ruth, Gloria, Jimmy, and Lillian, in that order, before eating some of it himself.[21]

Typical of the time, the house had no electricity or running water. It had porches on the front and back. Three rooms stood on either side of the hall that bisected the dwelling. To the right, ranging from back to front, there was a kitchen with a table for weekday meals, a dining room, and a living room. To the left of the hallway were three bedrooms, the front one for the girls, the middle for the parents, and Jimmy's at the back. All the rooms had high ceilings and plenty of large windows. Two chimneys with double fireplaces heated the front four rooms, and a wood-burning stove heated the kitchen. The tan clapboard house rested on brick pillars that provided plenty of room underneath for dogs, cats, chickens, and geese.[22]

About twenty yards behind the dwelling stood a fine privy with one hole for an adult to use and a lower, smaller one for a child. A servant swept the yard down to the bare dirt, and twice a year Earl hauled in fresh, white sand to spread over it.

A large mulberry tree provided hours of climbing fun, and an aromatic tree supposedly kept fleas from invading the house. A kudzu vine shaded the screened front porch, where the children often sat in a squeaking, wooden swing. A white picket fence on one side of the yard separated it from the cotton fields. Jimmy kept pet ponies in a lot behind the house. The children visited their Grandpa Gordy, who at one time lived in a house across the road, and they walked about a quarter mile down the dirt road to a swimming "hole."[23]

By the time the family moved to Archery, Earl had repaid his debts, acquired more land, and no longer worked in the fields himself. Since he owned his land and his home, had some cash, and could produce plenty of food, his family weathered the Great Depression that began in 1929 better than did many Americans. In 1934, he opened a peanut warehouse, where he stored peanuts he had bought for resale. He hunted, fished, and traveled, often taking Lillian with him on trips as far away as New York City.

At home, Earl and Lillian gathered their children around, told them about their journeys, and listened to them read aloud. Earl did not read as much as the others, but he encouraged Jimmy to collect books. Those works, gifts from his family and mother's friends, included a complete set of Guy de Maupassant's books, Edgar Rice Burroughs's Tarzan adventure stories, and a full set of the *Book of World Knowledge*. The late-nineteenth-century French author's realistic fiction, Burroughs's exciting tales set in Africa, and an encyclopedia introduced the farm boy to a world larger than Archery and whetted his appetite to know more.[24]

After supper, Earl supervised the children's homework and listened to their prayers. Before going to sleep, they practiced a ritual of goodnight kisses and calls of "I Love You the Goodest." In adulthood, they often signed their letters to each other, "ILYTG."[25]

Earl also handled the children's religious instruction and discipline. A devout Baptist, he took the children with him to attend church in Plains, while Lillian sometimes remained at home. At the age of eleven, Jimmy proudly declared himself to be a Christian and accepted baptism.[26] Despite his virtues, Earl had a mean temper that he did not always control.[27] When Earl called his son by his name instead of by his nickname, Jimmy knew that he was in real trouble. He got several whippings he never forgot. "Daddy used to whip my tail with spiraea," Jimmy said, recalling the flowering shrub with long, keen branches that grew by the front porch.[28]

"Mr. Earl," as the sharecroppers called him, often was as kind as he was strict, and Jimmy eventually came to recognize that his father's virtues outweighed his faults. In later memoirs, Carter revised his opinion of his father, indicating a bond of love and admiration that transcended the elder Carter's stern discipline. "My father was my hero," he wrote in 2004, a sentiment he routinely expressed in his mature reflections on his childhood.[29]

Earl believed in recreation. He dazzled Jimmy with his athletic skill. He built a dirt tennis court next to the house, and he challenged his children to defeat him at the game. They never could. In the early 1930s, Earl dammed a stream on his property to create a pond, and beside it he built the three-bedroom Pond House. He intended it to be both a safe recreational site for his adolescent children and a hunting and fishing retreat for himself and his buddies. Earl liked to dance; sometimes when his wife did not want to attend local dances with him, he took Ruth. He and Lillian gave parties, often large outdoor affairs at which they provided abundant food. At the end of the day, after the children were asleep, Earl shared a nightcap of bourbon with Lillian. Patrons and fans of baseball, he and Lillian made expensive trips to attend games, including those of her beloved Brooklyn Dodgers.[30]

Despite the good times Earl and Lillian enjoyed, their relationship was sometimes rocky. She admitted to her grown son Jimmy that his father was sometimes kinder to others than he was to her. After they married, she needed space to avoid his dominance, and she kept for herself the money she earned from the pecan harvest. He played poker, frequented the Americus Elks Club, and wanted her to go out every Saturday night with him and "raise hell." She did not enjoy dancing as much as he did, but she did not mind taking a few drinks. He may have cheated on her. She resented the way he danced with other women and sometimes argued with him after they returned home.[31]

Earl was the first of the Georgia Carters to take an interest in politics. Like most rural white Georgians during the depression of the 1930s, he was a "Talmadge man." Eugene Talmadge, the "wild man from Sugar Creek," posed as the little man's friend, a segregationist, an enemy of big business and cities, a devout Christian, and a colorful character; his promises and antics so thrilled his audiences that they elected him governor for two-year terms in 1932, 1934, 1940, and 1946. Earl disliked Talmadge's denigration of learning but had no complaint with his segregationist views. When Talmadge gave the commencement address at

Plains High School on April 24, 1933, Earl invited him to stay at his home, giving nine-year-old Jimmy the opportunity to hear about the governor's recent trip to Washington to attend the first inauguration of Franklin D. Roosevelt. The following year, when Talmadge sought reelection, Earl took Jimmy with him to hear "Ole Gene" regale an Albany crowd with his fiery speech, sample the barbeque, and listen to a band of fiddlers and a gospel quartet. Earl disliked Roosevelt's New Deal legislation because he thought it would meddle in the private lives and businesses of Georgians. He remained loyal to Talmadge, whose agrarian, populist rhetoric gave hope to hardworking farmers.[32]

Since Earl supported Talmadge but not Roosevelt, Jimmy learned that Georgia Democrats did not always agree with their national party. To get elected in Georgia, a candidate had to make populist promises to rural whites, and Earl held winners of the governorship in high esteem. While still a schoolboy, Jimmy told his friends that someday he would be governor of Georgia.[33]

Earl cultivated the friendship of local politicians, but he concentrated on his farm and his businesses. By 1953 he had acquired five thousand acres, much of it good cotton and peanut land. He owned a grocery store in Plains, sold seed and fertilizer, owned a small fire insurance agency, and developed his peanut brokerage business.[34] By the standards of his time and place, Earl Carter was a wealthy man.

Paternalistic, like the large slave-owning planters of the Old South and the millionaires of the North, Earl secretly dispensed favors to the poor. Comfortable with his racially segregated society, Earl did not go into the homes of blacks himself, but he paid for the supplies his wife took to them. "He had to be on my side," Lillian later remembered, "or he wouldn't have paid for the medicine and the clothes" that she gave to black people.[35]

Earl Carter never had the chance to explain his life and opinions. Since he died before Jimmy became famous, he escaped the interminable interviews about himself. Earl left no record of how he felt about the murder of his father, his fatherless childhood, his struggle for success, his opinion on race relations, or his attitudes and feelings toward his children. The recollections of his widow and children, other family members, friends, politicians and others, as well as the sterile details in public records, do not adequately recreate the inner man. Jimmy recognized him as the most powerful influence in his own life, and coming to terms with his father became his driving force. At the age of seventy, Jimmy wrote that he had finally come to understand that Earl was "the father who will never cease to be alive in me."[36]

The immediate world Earl created for young Jimmy was the 360-acre farm in Archery. There Jimmy developed habits, skills, and attitudes that later affected his public career. Earl expected "Hot" to rise early and work hard at a variety of jobs. In addition to cotton and peanuts, the farm produced vegetables, watermelons, pecans, corn, and sugarcane. Earl raised beef cattle, milk cows, sheep, hogs, chickens, and geese. The size and success of the farm allowed Earl to hire two hundred black laborers, work with seven competent black sharecropper families, and purchase fifty mules.[37]

Jimmy treasured one African-American couple, Jack and Rachel Clark, as dearly as any family members. The Clarks worked for wages rather than shares. Their neat, clean home, located just beyond the barn, became a haven for Jimmy. He spent the nights there when his parents were away, sleeping on a pallet on the floor near the fireplace in the living room. At the barn, Jack taught Jimmy about farm life.

Jimmy knew other black workers, but he did not became a part of their families. Fred and Lee Howard lived next door to the Clarks but never gained young Jimmy's confidence. Another man, Tump, fascinated Jimmy with his ability to lift five hundred pounds and to get to work earlier in the morning than anyone else. Richard and Virgil Johnson, Joe Ed Walker, Felton Shelton, and their families all worked the northern part of the farm and operated almost independently of the Carters. Willis Wright, one of Lillian's kidney patients, became so much a part of the Carter family that Earl consulted with him and felt comfortable leaving young Jimmy in his care. Earl sold Willis the farm on which he lived and helped him build a concrete block house. Since the sharecroppers supplied their own livestock and equipment, Earl gave them use of the land, two-thirds of the cash crops of cotton and peanuts, and one-fourth of the corn crop.[38]

Surrounded by black workers in the fields, the yard, at home, and at the Clark house, Jimmy liked their company. He witnessed their poverty and frustrations, and he absorbed some of their good qualities of character and spiritual richness. Although they loved the little white boy, like most blacks of their generation, they kept their true feelings about their poverty, their lack of class status, and their desire for equality with whites to themselves. Black families who sharecropped with Earl Carter enjoyed greater independence and profits than was typical of most southern sharecroppers, but they remained caught in the web of dependence on benevolent white landowners. Most sharecroppers found the system dehumanizing and yearned to break out of it.[39]

Earl operated a small, profitable, company store located just beyond the tennis court. He stocked overalls, shoes, shirts, home-cured meat, sugar, flour, canned goods, candy, tobacco, kerosene, gasoline, cheese, and castor oil. He opened the store only on Saturday afternoons when he paid the hands for their week's work. During the week, however, Jimmy sometimes reluctantly had to leave the midday dinner table to sell a customer a nickel's worth of whatever he or she wanted.[40]

The Carter farm was prosperous and self-sufficient. In addition to the store, it boasted a large, symmetrical barn, located northeast of the store, and a windmill that Earl ordered from Sears, Roebuck, and Company in 1935. It boasted a six-foot-deep concrete trench for dipping sheep and cows, who were herded through it when it was filled with a pesticide that would exterminate the vermin in their coats. A cane mill, two sheds, a garage, a storage house, a chicken yard, a fenced-in garden, a smithy, and a carpentry shop provided Jimmy opportunities to learn and to work. Later, Jimmy became a master craftsman, making furniture and other wooden items. He especially liked the barn, the center of farm life. Jack Clark presided there as a manager who knew and loved the operation of the farm better than did its white owner. Jack rang the huge farm bell "an hour before daylight" to alert owners and workers that it was time to get going.[41]

As Jimmy grew older and stronger, he assumed more difficult tasks. The fields of southwestern Georgia required many long workdays because there was a 245-day growing season and an average annual rainfall of fifty-three inches.[42] Insects relentlessly attacked crops, animals, and people. Fleas feasted on the blood of both animals and their owners, and the tormenting gnat became a regional legend. These tiny, dark grey, flying gnats traveled in swarms, attacking their victims around the eyes, mouth, and nostrils. During the summer "gnat season," people blew and fanned them vigorously away from their faces.

The exhausting work in cotton and peanut fields required physical stamina and a nearly superhuman ability to endure heat and humidity. In early summer, when the cotton plants matured and the blooms and bolls began to form, workers had to "mop" the cotton in order to poison the boll weevils, a chore Jimmy hated. He dipped a rag on a stick into a pail of a stinking, sticky, brown liquid mixture of molasses and arsenic and then applied the goo to the plants. When the bolls opened in late summer and early fall, Jimmy picked cotton, backbreaking labor for low pay in searing heat during the gnat season. He also used a mule to plow up peanut plants. That done, he endured more heat and gnats to help shake the dirt away from the nuts on the roots, then stack the whole plants with the nuts outward in a circular pattern around tall stakes that workers had placed in the fields. Stacking peanuts was a dirtier, hotter job than picking cotton.

Working after school, weekends, and summers, Jimmy stayed busy with his chores. He helped Jack Clark milk twelve cows and haul sugarcane to his father's steam-powered syrup mill. He plucked geese and packed the down, which his father sent away to be converted into comforters and pillows. When the dry goods came back, the Carters used the ones they needed and sold the rest. Jimmy turned potato vines and pruned watermelons. Earl allowed Jimmy free time on Saturday afternoons and Sundays after church. He did not compliment his son for a job done well, but he chastised him severely for a mistake or negligence.

During the hot months, Jimmy worked and played without wearing a shirt or shoes. He was small, skinny, and strong. He had big, clear blue eyes, light brown hair, slightly thickened lips, an oval face with nose and chin in decent, but not rugged, proportions. His thin skin freckled, burned, and peeled more easily than it tanned. He was a good-looking boy, but not handsome. His feet were too large in proportion to the rest of his body.

As a boy, and later as a man, Jimmy was "lonely" and "timid," words he used frequently throughout his life. He had a tree house in the backyard where he could read in solitude, and he loved pets. He cherished Bonzo, a Boston bulldog puppy, and he grieved almost uncontrollably when an automobile struck and killed him.[43] Later, he owned a favored bird dog, Sport, but no other pet ever quite took the place of Bonzo. His goat, which he named Old Gene Talmadge, after the governor, jumped on top of Earl's car one time too many, after which he mysteriously disappeared.

Jimmy had three ponies, Lady, Lady Lee, and Jolly, but the Shetland Lady was his favorite. He loved that pony, trained her to trot, to pull a cart, and to obey only him. Earl's exacting discipline, however, sometimes threatened Jimmy's beloved pony. Since Lady could not work to pay for her keep, Jimmy rode her on occasion, thus giving her credit for providing transportation. Sometimes he would be too busy to ride, and his father, angry about something, would menacingly ask how long it had been since he had ridden Lady.[44]

The black women who cared for Jimmy and his sisters were as intimate a part of his young life as were his parents and sisters. Annie Mae Jones lived with the Carters when Jimmy was six and seven. She went to work for Lillian at age thirteen, and according to Lillian, "stole me blind, but she loved my children and we loved her."[45] She did everything for the children, including cooking, cleaning, getting them to school, and loving them as if they were her own. When they became unruly, she attempted to frighten them into obedience. "I'm gonna call the Boogie Man," she would say when she wanted them to gather around her quietly. To keep them off the railroad tracks that ran in front of the house, she told them about a bloody ghost who walked the tracks. She sang folk songs and told them exotic tales in the dialect of her own African-American culture.[46]

Annie Lee Lester, another black nanny, sometimes found the eleven-year-old Jimmy to be a mischievous lad who attempted to frighten her. When he prepared to throw worms on her, or jumped into a pond and pretended to be drowning, she threatened to tell his father. Jimmy, who she said was "crazy about his father," begged her not to tell and thus escaped a whipping.[47]

Rachel Clark, Jack's wife, began to help the Carters when Jimmy was an adolescent. Jimmy was "a good-sized little boy," she said. Rachel maintained a serene dignity and aura of equality that the children learned to respect. She did not play games with the young Carters or frighten them. Illiterate but full of wisdom, she became Jimmy's closest friend.

Rachel remembered the Carter children as well-behaved and obedient. She liked having Jimmy stay at her spotless home and found him to be quiet and religious, a loner who liked to play with his dog and to read. He followed her around, often trying to help her. He picked cotton beside her, but she always picked more than he could. He told her about the times he went hunting with her husband Jack, talked about God with her, and asked her to pray for him. He never told her what he wanted to be; he "just was what he was," she said.[48]

Jimmy romanticized his adolescent relationship with Rachel and elevated her to a position almost equal to that of his father. After Rachel's death in 1987, he memorialized her in the poem "Rachel." In his list of the people most important in his life, and to whom he dedicated his volume of poetry, he listed Rachel fourth, after Earl, Lillian, and Rosalynn. He liked how she told him that God gave meaning to her life. She helped him to love nature, and when he was at her house, she made him feel that he "belonged" there. Jimmy thought she was a "queen," and later he sometimes went to see her when he was in Plains. They laughed, he said, and talked about the good times of old, and she told him what she thought he ought to do "in Washington, where I was working then."[49] Lillian did not remember Rachel being so important in her son's life, but she liked her and said that in Rachel's old age she gave her "a can of beer or something" every time they met.[50]

Second to Rachel, Bishop William Decker Johnson of the AME Church befriended his white Carter neighbors. Johnson and his brother, Francis M. Johnson, both African-American ministers, had founded the Johnson Home Industrial College in Archery. Begun in 1912, the college consisted of a sawmill and a planing mill that served the dual purpose of raising money and teaching skills to the students. There were three school buildings and a windmill, the latter suggesting atypical prosperity and comfort. In 1914, the Johnson brothers auctioned off lots to twenty-five black families, who formed the town of Archery. Five other houses in town belonged to the railroad, one of them occupied by the white foreman and his family, the other four by black workers. They were the only families in Archery in 1928 when Earl Carter moved his family to the farm. Bishop Johnson persuaded the railroad to allow the train to have a flag stop in Archery, which meant that if one wanted the train to stop there, one placed an upright flag near the track. Jimmy and his father occasionally attended the St. Mark's AME Church to hear the bishop preach and to listen to a visiting choir from Morris Brown College or some other black institution in Atlanta.[51]

At the Carter home, just a few miles from the church, however, there was tension between the black Johnsons and the white Carters. Lillian had fewer prejudices than Earl; when she welcomed the bishop's son Alvan at the front door, Earl discreetly departed by the back door. It was extremely rare in that place for black people to enter white homes except as servants. The bishop himself visited with Earl only in the yard.[52] As did many rural white youths, Jimmy had more black than white playmates. His closest black friend, A. D. Davis, was small in stature and a few years younger than Jimmy. A. D. hunted, fished, and boxed with the white boys. Often inseparable from Jimmy at the farm, he rode Lady, harnessed the goat to a wagon for playtime, sat in the kitchen to eat with Jimmy at mealtimes, and shared Jimmy's birthday celebrations. When they went to Americus together to attend a movie, however, Jimmy sat downstairs while A. D. climbed to the segregated seats in the balcony. A. D. quit school after the fifth grade and later worked at a sawmill to support his family. He remembered that Jimmy always took the dominant role. "Jimmy likes to star," he said.

Jimmy's white friends sometimes came to visit him, usually at the Pond House, but Jimmy rarely went to see them. They included the two Watson boys, sons of the railroad's section foreman, and Rembert Forrest, a schoolmate who rode horseback five miles to reach Archery. Rachel Clark thought that Jimmy "wasn't very close to nobody."[53]

White and black people in Archery occupied separate worlds. A. D., Annie Mae, and Rachel, no matter how close they were to Jimmy and his family, lived and worshiped in a segregated society. Black people knew their place, and whites did, too. In June 1938, Earl Carter, who was no racist according to his wife, allowed several dozen blacks to assemble in the yard and listen to the radio broadcast of the second boxing match between Joe Louis and Max Schmeling in New York City. Since the white Schmeling had defeated the black Louis in an earlier bout, their rematch had strong racial overtones. Standing outside under a mulberry tree, the neighbors listened to the radio Mr. Earl had placed in the living room window. When Joe Louis won, the black visitors politely thanked a disappointed Mr. Earl for letting them listen. Once they had crossed the road and the railroad to reach their own houses, they whooped and hollered for hours.[54]

Earl, like so many white southerners, viewed that match only as a contest between a black man and a white, but others saw it as a match between an American and a representative of Nazi Germany. From north to south, east to west, Americans—black and white, Jews, Indians, and Hispanics—screamed with delight and hugged each other when America's hero Joe Louis knocked out Germany's ambassador of anti-Semitism. One black writer declared that the happiest people in America were not blacks but Jews. W. E. B. Du Bois, the normally sedate black intellectual who led the early fight for racial equality, lost his composure in Atlanta and shouted, "Beat the hell out of the damn German bastard!"[55] Those few black people in Archery had millions of brothers and sisters, many of them nonblack, around the globe who needed someone to stand up for their rights.

Too young to be concerned with human rights, Jimmy passed much of his idyllic childhood outdoors. He fished, hunted, hiked, and swam. He collected arrowheads and old bottles, the beginning of lifelong hobbies. He sat beside streams, drifted down them in small boats, and traipsed through fields and woods alone or in the company of good dogs and good people. Those times did not stir him to a life of laziness, but, on the contrary, gave him inspiration and time to think.[56] The times Jimmy liked best were those when he went alone with Rachel. He marveled at how she fished six lines at once and knew where to find the best fishing holes. She let him earn his way by collecting the bait and carrying the fish. With her, he felt awed in the presence of a superior being. Jimmy struggled with the mosquitoes and yellow flies that attacked him but ignored Rachel. Otherwise, he went about his work undistracted by such other wildlife as rabbits, otter, wood ducks, and water moccasins.[57]

Jimmy took annual fishing trips with his father to more distant spots in South Georgia. Several times they went to the Okefenokee Swamp in the southeastern corner of the state, a vast land of "trembling earth" composed mostly of floating peat. They watched alligators and bears and sighted herons, egrets, ducks, pileated woodpeckers, bald eagles, and other birds. From the lake that formed the headwaters of the Suwannee River, Jimmy pulled largemouth bass and jack. Once he panicked when fishing with his father in the Little Saltilla, a stream several miles north of the Okefenokee. He had attached Earl's string of fish to a belt loop of his trousers, but the loop broke, dropping his father's entire catch back into the water. Fearing his father's response, the frightened boy began to cry, but his father hugged him and said there were many more fish in the river.[58]

Earl also taught Jimmy to hunt. Before he was old enough to handle a shotgun, Jimmy joined his father on early morning dove hunts, serving as pickup boy. Sometimes Earl let Jimmy carry one of his guns and gave him a cup of hot chocolate while the others drank coffee and liquor. At age ten, Jimmy acquired his own .22 Remington pump rifle and a bolt-action, four-shot .410 shotgun. When he was a bit older, his father allowed him to hunt with Jack Clark, his cousin Hugh, and other friends. While hunting alone for the first time, Jimmy fired into a covey of quail his dog had flushed from a grove of scrub oak trees near his house. He proudly picked up the bird he had killed and rushed to the blacksmith shop to show it to his father. As his approving smile vanished, Earl asked, "Where's your gun?" In his excitement, Jimmy had dropped it. He went back and found it.[59]

Nearer home, the railroad tracks in front of his house fascinated Jimmy. They provided him with hours of creative play and beckoned to a world beyond

Archery. He and his "Cousin Beedie," Alton's son Hugh, placed pennies on the tracks for trains to flatten, or they walked the rails when there was no train in sight. The train was pulled by a barrel-shaped engine and known as the "Butt-head." It consisted of three cars and transported mail and passengers from Columbus, Georgia, to Americus, Macon, and Augusta. The fare from Archery to Americus was 15 cents. Jimmy rode it occasionally, but he usually traveled in his father's pickup truck.[60]

Sometimes Jimmy walked the rails two and a half miles into Plains, a town of more than five hundred people. As the prosperity of the late 1920s yielded to the depression of the 1930s, the town declined 40 percent in population but remained the place where people from surrounding areas gathered. Trains came and went, hauling cotton, watermelons, and passengers. Religious revivals, political rallies, medicine shows, circuses, woodcutting contests, and games of marbles and checkers attracted Jimmy's attention. As a five-year-old boy, he walked the streets selling nickel bags of boiled peanuts his mother had sent to town with him. A few years later, he and Beedie sold hamburgers or three dips of homemade ice cream, either for a nickel.[61]

Jimmy spent every Friday night in Plains with his grandmother, Nina Carter. After her children grew up and left home, she did not like to spend nights alone. Thus, her grandsons took turns staying with her, Jimmy on Fridays. She played games with them, cooked their favorite foods, and made them feel special. They slept in the bed with her. Since she abhorred getting old, she made them call her "Mama" instead of "Grandmama."[62]

Jimmy's favorite relatives in Plains were his grandmother Carter, his cousin Beedie, and Beedie's father, Uncle Buddy (Alton) Carter, but there were others. He had an abundance of aunts, uncles, and cousins. Most of his relatives were hardworking, religious people content with their middle-class existence. There were a few who suffered from mental aberrations and alcoholism. Two first cousins on his mother's side had schizophrenia and bipolar disorder and had to be hospitalized. One of them, Linton Slappey, sometimes walked the streets of Plains, screaming obscenities and making such brutally frank comments about some of the citizens that Linton's father sent him back to the state's mental institution.[63] Two of his mother's brothers had serious problems with alcohol. A tower of stability, her sister Emily, nicknamed Sissy, helped rear Jimmy and later became an important member of his political team.

Jimmy's uncle Tom Gordy inspired him to become a Navy man. As a boy of eight and nine, Jimmy corresponded with his uncle, then a radioman on ships in the Philippines and China. Tom Gordy responded with descriptions of exotic places that fired the imagination of the young farm boy. He sent his uncle a "lucky piece." Tom promised to carry it "with me wherever I go," asked for a photograph of his nephew, and told him he would soon be leaving a port in the Philippines and going back to China.[64]

The next year, after a brief discussion of Santa Claus and Jimmy's new pony, Tom explained how he had communicated by code with a man many miles away on the battleship *Pennsylvania*. "Say, Jimmie how would you like to be able to send and receive messages from a little Practice Set?" Uncle Tom asked. His uncle promised to make him one when he returned home, but in the meantime asked the boy to drink his sweet milk and to write again soon.[65]

The next month, Tom wrote that he had intended to visit the tomb of Sun Yat-sen, the Chinese revolutionary hero who had united the nation in 1911 and briefly served as its provisional president, but had arrived on shore too late to do so. He explained that Sun Yat-sen was to the Chinese "like Washington is to the United States," except the Chinese revered him more than Americans regarded their president. Tom said he would be sailing from Nanking to Shanghai where he would buy souvenirs for the family.[66]

Tom filled his letter of May 20, 1933, with tales of his adventures in China. He had just returned from "way up the Yangtze River," he said, where he wished "Jimmie" could have been with him. He described four or five cities he had seen; "At Kiukiang we went up in the mountains and up above the clouds," he explained, riding in sedan chairs attached to long poles, which four Chinese men carried on their shoulders. "Felt funny when we had to go through a cloud," he continued, but "had a swell time." Nevertheless, it had been two and a half years since he had been home, and Tom very much looked forward to getting back to Georgia, where he would go fishing and "possum hunting" with his nephew.[67] Jimmy saved those letters, cherished the model Chinese junk Tom brought him, and dreamed of growing up to be like the uncle with a manly swagger who named one of his own sons for Jimmy.[68]

If children learn by observing adults, young Jimmy saw much to imitate in the lives of his Uncle Tom, his Uncle Buddy, and his father. Old enough to realize that making money pleased his father, he set out to do the same. As a child, he sold peanuts, hamburgers, and ice cream, and he saved his money. Earl helped him take advantage of the 1932 cotton surplus. At age eight, Jimmy had saved enough money from his peanut sales to buy five bales of cotton at 5 cents a pound, or $25 per bale, from a government warehouse. His father helped him transport it to Archery and store it in a shed. Some years later, as an enterprising teenager, he sold it for 18 cents a pound and used his profit to buy five tenant houses from the estate of a deceased undertaker. He rented them collectively for $16.50 per month; in 1949, when Jimmy was in the Navy, his father sold the houses to the tenants who lived in them.[69]

As he became a budding entrepreneur, Carter's changing relationships with his black childhood friends were the typical mark of the passage of a white boy of his generation and southern heritage into adulthood. As he and his black friends entered puberty, they understood that they could no longer be social equals in Sumter and Webster counties. Dating and marrying across racial lines was forbidden, and young white adults had many opportunities still unavailable to blacks. Bishop William Johnson died in 1936; his funeral attracted crowds of whites and blacks, including mourners from other states who drove Lincolns, Packards, and Cadillacs. Rachel Clark thought the large crowd came "from all parts of the world."[70] After the funeral, however, the white and black mourners went their separate ways.

Furthermore, the arrival of electricity at the farm revolutionized Jimmy's life and set him apart from poor blacks and whites. Because Earl Carter directed the local Rural Electrification Administration, his family became one of the first to benefit from electricity. Farmers gathered in Plains to talk with politicians and negotiate with power companies. Farm chores became easier, and the habits and style of family life changed, giving every member more independence. Less bound to the rising and setting of the sun, or the wishes of the group, Jimmy gained control of his schedule and environment.[71]

The outdoor privy became obsolete that year when Earl transformed a small closet in his and Lillian's bedroom into a bathroom. He installed a lavatory, rigged a small water tank over a commode so that it could flush, and put in a metal pan with a drain to the ground outside to serve as the base for a shower. The shower itself consisted of a bucket with holes punched in the bottom; the bather had to pour water into the bucket, then jump under it and bathe quickly before all of the water drained away.[72]

In that bathroom, Jimmy had one of his more memorable discussions with his father. Earl very authoritatively summoned "Jimmy," not "Hot," to the new room for a conference. Sitting on the commode with the lid down, Earl asked Jimmy to make him a promise. The terrified adolescent thought "he was going to tell me about sex or something like that." He was relieved to learn that his father, who smoked three packs of cigarettes a day, wished only to make Jimmy promise that he would not smoke before age twenty-one. After remaining faithful to his promise, at age twenty-one Jimmy took a puff on one cigarette, did not like it, and never smoked again.[73] The same year, 1936, Jimmy went on his first date, driving his father's pickup truck. He combed his hair, slicked it back, and brushed his teeth. At school, he wrote an essay entitled "Cleanliness," emphasizing the importance of clean teeth, hair, hands, skin, and minds. All were necessary, he thought, "to look good."[74] Apparently, he remembered nothing more about the date, or he was not inclined to tell it.

The next year, Jimmy's brother Billy was born, but the thirteen years that separated them kept the brothers from becoming close to each other until both were adults. Earl nicknamed his new son "Buckshot," spoiled him, and indulged him in a manner quite different from the way he had treated his firstborn son. At thirteen, Jimmy did not seem to mind the birth of a baby brother. Ready to take responsibility for himself, he turned his attention toward Plains, where he attended the seventh grade. Rachel Clark said he was "one [of] ours what we raised up...one of our boys."[75]

CHAPTER TWO

A Girl in Plains

BORN THREE YEARS LATER than the farm boy in Archery, Rosalynn Smith, too, was the oldest of four children. Growing up in Plains during the Great Depression, she began life in happy circumstances. Her mother Allie and her father Edgar went to Allie's parents' home about six miles south of Plains to await the arrival of their baby. At 6 a.m. on August 18, 1927, Rosalynn arrived, weighing six pounds, seven ounces. A month later, they moved back into their house on dusty Bond Street in Plains. A modest white clapboard structure with porches along the front and one side, it had a long hall from front to back that divided it into halves. A privy stood discreetly in the back yard, and it was located just four doors south of the railroad tracks and the future Carter Warehouse.[1]

Rosalynn's parents were not so colorful or successful as the Carters. Her father, Wilburn Edgar Smith, twenty-two when his father died, attended the Methodist church and enjoyed the esteem of his community, but he dropped out of school in Plains after the eighth grade. When he registered for the World War I draft, his reading and writing skills were so poor that a clerk had to complete the form for him. He was able to sign his name. Soon after he was drafted, however, the war ended, and he did not serve in it.[2] He farmed land that he and his brother inherited from their father, operated an automobile repair garage, and drove the school bus. One of the girls who rode his bus was Frances Allethea Murray. On June 20, 1926, after she had grown up and had studied home economics at Georgia State College for Women in Milledgeville, she married him.[3]

The Murrays were a bit feistier than the Smiths. They, too, had moved from North Carolina to Georgia. A private in a North Carolina regiment, Nathan Murray, of Onslow County, fought for independence from Great Britain.[4] His son Drury and Drury's wife, Susan, moved to Georgia, where in 1833 they bought a farm six miles southwest of Plains, which Rosalynn inherited.[5]

At age seventy-four, in 1860 Drury had amassed 1,360 acres of land in Sumter County and owned twenty-three slaves, whom he housed in two cabins. He died in 1862, but his son John William Fulwood Murray served the Confederacy in Company H, Thirteenth Georgia Infantry Regiment. He returned from Virginia to farm and to practice his Primitive Baptist faith until his death in 1920. His son John William Murray, born in 1871, better known as "Captain Murray" (d. 1966), farmed, served as justice of the peace, and attended Plains Baptist Church. He married Rosa Nettie Wise (1880–1941), a Lutheran active in her church's missionary society. Their neighbors and friends thought of them as extraordinarily good, gentle, kind, Christian people, shy and prosperous. Captain Murray did not have a temper, and one of his friends remembered that "to hear him pray…seemed like he was talking face-to-face with God." The Captain and Rosa began their life together on the Murray family farm, where they had only one surviving child, Allethea, born December 24, 1905.[6]

Captain Murray and his wife lived to see their daughter grow up, marry Edgar Smith, convert to his Methodist faith, and present them with grandchildren. Allie and Edgar named their first child Eleanor Rosalynn, for her grandmothers. Rosalynn looked like her grandmother Smith, her "Mama Sallie."[7]

At ages two and three, Rosalynn acquired brothers Jerry and Murray, and when she was almost ten her sister Allethea Lillian was born. By then, the family had become close friends with Lillian Carter and named their infant daughter for her. Neither impoverished nor wealthy, the Smiths enjoyed a simple, loving lifestyle in a comfortable home with plenty of good food, good-quality clothes, and adequate medical care. Both parents were willing to work to support their children. Their semirural environment and agricultural and domestic skills enabled them to weather the Great Depression of the 1930s.

Edgar was well prepared for fatherhood. When his father died, he had assumed the role of head of the family. He insisted that his five younger brothers attend the Methodist Church with him. A school dropout himself, he helped his siblings finish high school.[8] Nine years older than his wife, Edgar worshiped Allie. He had first dated her when she was in the ninth grade and had waited five years for her to come of age to marry. He enjoyed his family immensely. At five feet, eleven inches, he was slender, with black hair, blue eyes, and deeply tanned skin. When he came home in the afternoons, he picked up Allie, kissed her, and swung her around the kitchen in view of the children.[9]

Edgar worked at a variety of jobs. With his brother Oliver, he farmed more than one hundred acres of land they had inherited from their father. Located adjacent to his and Allie's backyard, the land was good for cotton, peanuts, and wheat. The Smiths owned several mules and had the help of one ten-ant farmer, George Merritt, who was also a "Holy Roller preacher."[10] Edgar worked on weekends as a clerk in Alton Carter's mercantile store, operated a garage, and sometimes drove the hearse for the local undertaker. Neither Edgar nor Allie had much interest in politics, although Edgar did serve briefly on the Plains City Council.[11]

The jobs for which the town remembered Edgar best were his driving the school bus and operating an automotive repair garage. Edgar was responsible for two school buses, which he kept in good running condition, stockpiling spare overhauled engines and other parts. The buses were old Model-T Fords with wooden bench seats and curtains instead of glass in the window openings. Since there was no antifreeze then, on cold nights the drivers had to drain the radia-tors and refill them the next day. They cranked them with a hand-turned lever, then traveled twenty-five or more miles over red clay roads.[12] Edgar liked the children.

Edgar's garage stood on the corner of Bond and Main streets across the street from Earl Carter's mercantile and grocery store. Edgar walked over to visit with Earl, drank Cokes with him, and planned hunting trips. Once Rosalynn was old enough to attend school, she walked from her house past her father's garage, from which he could see her travel safely across the railroad tracks and Main Street to the schoolhouse.[13]

From early childhood, the Smith children learned that Edgar expected them to attend the Methodist church and complete college degrees. Both he and Allie warned them not to smoke cigarettes or drink liquor. Edgar smoked, an addic-tion his wife deplored.[14]

Rosalynn's memories of her father were happy ones. She recalled how he entertained his children with tricks, stories, turning cartwheels, and even bak-ing a cake. She liked to watch him shave in the kitchen in the mornings and smoke his pipe in the evenings. She waited for him to return from work or from his frequent hunting and fishing trips. She laughed with him when he laughed aloud at *Amos 'n' Andy* on the radio, and it amused her to watch him tap his foot to the music of the Grand Ole Opry. She never forgot the day he embarrassed her severely when she mistakenly came home from school at recess instead of lunchtime. He sent her back to suffer the humiliation of her classmates' laughter. Sometimes she felt a little afraid of him, but mostly she remembered how much he loved her and her mother.[15]

Edgar and Allie shared the discipline of their children, assigning chores and making them obey rules. Both parents believed in talking to their children first, and then, if that did not work, a good spanking.[16] Allie believed in tough love, but she was devoted to her family.

Allie had graduated in 1925 with a two-year teacher's diploma from Georgia State College for Women in Milledgeville, but she married a month after her graduation and had her first baby fourteen months later. She never taught, but she earned some money sewing for others. She kept her house tidy and dressed her daughters in fine homemade clothes. Rosalynn would sometimes draw a sketch of a dress she saw in a store window in Americus and hand it to her mother to make. Allie tended her flower and vegetable gardens, and she placed hot meals on the table three times a day. Her only servant, a washerwoman, picked up the family's dirty clothes and returned them clean, ironed, and folded.[17]

Unlike Lillian Carter, Allie Smith was always home for her family. From her, Rosalynn learned the value of organization and hard work. She could not have had a better example of loyalty to and love for a husband. Her parents worked together and emphasized the values of religion and education. Neither parent seemed to harbor any ambition for Rosalynn beyond that of being like her mother. Rosalynn grew up thinking that she would marry a local man and settle into a lifestyle like her mother's. Her life took very different turns from what her family expected, but Jimmy said that if Miss Allie had not reared Rosalynn the way she did, he would never have become president.[18]

One of the first indications of what her husband later called Rosalynn's "strong will" appeared in her relationship to her siblings. She loved her little brothers and sister and escaped many of the harsher aspects of sibling rivalry that sometimes tormented the Carters. She took full advantage of her position as the oldest child. All of them called her "Sister," a nickname that recognized her authority.[19]

Before starting school, Rosalynn played mostly with boys, since no other little girls lived on her street. She played kick the can, hide-and-seek, and cops and robbers with her two brothers and other boys. Her childhood games often involved competitive teams, with Rosalynn being the only girl in the group, and she played to win. Jerry conceded that Rosalynn bossed the rest of them around, sometimes using "fierce looks and threats to tell Mom."[20]

Rosalynn also played with paper dolls, often asking her mother to make clothes for them. She liked to sit on a kitchen counter and "help" her mama cook and to keep herself neat and clean. Her mother thought that as a child Rosalynn was "independent" and "thoughtful" of other people; she liked to be alone and read books.[21] Her reading filled her head with dreams of fantastic adventures. She especially liked *Heidi, Hans Brinker,* and *Robinson Crusoe,* books set in far-away places and with genuinely good heroes and heroines who triumphed over great odds to help desperate people.

In her real world, Rosalynn's childhood escapades took place mostly in her backyard, not the woods and streams that held such an attraction for young Jimmy Carter. Her yard, however, seemed enormous. There she could romp and play with her brothers and friends in a world of natural beauty. In one area, a vegetable garden provided tomatoes, eggplant, corn, cucumbers, okra, melons, and beans of several kinds. The flower beds filled with zinnias, petunias, hollyhocks, roses, and crepe myrtles decorated the yard with brilliant colors from early spring until late summer. The children played under the scuppernong arbor and ate the sweet grapes directly from the vine when they ripened in August. Fig, pear, and pecan trees provided treats, shade, and opportunities for climbing. When the pomegranates ripened, the children liked to eat the tart meat and sometimes throw the seeds at each other. They enjoyed the outdoor company of pet dogs, cats, and rabbits. The family had chickens, a milk cow, a few pigs, and several mules, all of whom Edgar kept in neat barns and pens at the back edge of the yard.[22]

Since the Murrays, Wises, Smiths, and Bells lived in close proximity to each other, Rosalynn grew up with a large extended family. "Mama Sallie" was her grandmother Smith, her daddy's widowed mother who lived with them until Rosalynn was fourteen. When Edgar invited his mother to live with his family, it pleased no one. Twenty-six years younger than her late husband, she had a long and dependent widowhood. Edgar provided her with two rooms at the back of his house, one of which was a kitchen, where she prepared and ate her meals separately from his family. Ill-tempered and impatient with his children, she sometimes scolded Rosalynn. Since Rosalynn did not like her, she sometimes deliberately irritated her and provoked the scolding. Rosalynn later blamed Mama Sallie for causing her almost pathological shyness. Mama Sallie attended church and PTA meetings, but Edgar and Allie's children all seemed relieved when she moved out in 1941.[23]

In contrast, Rosalynn's grandfather, Captain Murray, her "Papa," became her idol. She, her brothers, and younger sister visited him and his wife on weekends at their farm, but Rosalynn especially loved it when he came to visit them in town on Saturdays.[24] She stood on the dirt road in front of the house waiting for him. He gave her a nickel, and they walked together into town, where she bought a whole bag of candy at one of the grocery stores. Her Papa talked to her about religion, prayed, read his Bible, and attended the Baptist church.[25]

Papa Murray encouraged Rosalynn to love her own Methodist church, where she participated in programs for her age group. She studied the Bible and believed that God would reward or punish her according to her actions. Her exposure to religion was biblical and fundamentalist, but the heritage of her denomination was rooted in concrete historical events. It was rational and private, and it did not require that its adherents express their commitment in terms of being "born again."

In a small town where the church was the center of the community, members of one Protestant denomination mixed freely with those of the others but remained loyal to their own churches. The Methodists and Baptists were the two largest groups in Plains, and they frequently joked about one another. In terms of doctrine and social standing, with the Methodists being more permissive and formal than the Baptists, there was a subtle tension that ran deeply through the lives of their adherents. Fifty years after their marriage, and forty-three after Rosalynn joined the Baptist church, Jimmy liked to joke that Rosalynn still had a lot of the Methodist in her.[26]

Except for the churches, the railroad depot, and the school, Rosalynn did not particularly like Plains. The town held none of the fascination for her that it did for Jimmy Carter. She grew up four doors from Main Street. She could walk anywhere she wished, or sometimes, with her hair in pigtails, she rode her bicycle. She especially liked to watch the trains come and go. Some businesses closed during the depression, leaving empty buildings, which she found depressing. At the Suwanee Swifty store, where her mother sometimes sent her to buy meat, she watched the men sit around a wood-burning stove and play checkers. The owner often teased her, which angered her and caused her to run home.

Rosalynn felt confined by the town. Her parents told her that she would have to leave Plains to attend college. The town had no movie theater, no library, and no recreation center, and she abhorred the lack of privacy endemic to small town life. She appreciated the friendly neighbors and the churches, but she wanted more from life than she could ever find in such a small, isolated place.[27]

Unlike Jimmy, then growing up among black people in Archery, Rosalynn lived unequivocally on the white side of a racially segregated society; her friends and playmates were white. In the streets and stores of Plains and on her father's and grandfather's farms, she knew black people, but she had no close personal association with them. Unaware of racial prejudice that had been a part of her society since its genesis, she treated blacks kindly but without realizing that they and the outside world were already challenging the status quo.

Rosalynn's carefree days of childhood ended when she was thirteen. In the summer of 1939, Edgar and Allie suddenly allowed Rosalynn to attend a church camp and sent the other children to stay at the Murray farm. While they were gone, Edgar entered the hospital, where he was diagnosed with incurable leukemia. On their return, the children could see that their father was very ill. He attempted to reassure them, but Rosalynn noted that he did not go to work very often and became increasingly pale. Through eighteen agonizing months, his body wasted away, and he sometimes writhed in excruciating pain that necessitated morphine shots.

Rosalynn attempted to make him comfortable. She brushed his hair, read detective stories to him, and joined other family members to pray for him. The children cheered him with daily reports of their activities. Just to be near him, Rosalynn prepared her school lessons in his room. The preacher visited often, and the town nurse, Lillian Carter, gave Edgar injections. One day in October 1940, Edgar and Allie summoned the children to his sickroom. With tears running down his face, Edgar explained that he would not recover and that his greatest regret was that he would not live to see all four of his children go to college. The family could do nothing but wait, as family and friends and Nurse Lillian visited every day.

The night Edgar died, October 22, 1940, Lillian had taken Rosalynn home to the Carter farm in Archery. Rosalynn and Ruth were childhood friends, and Miss Lillian thought it would be helpful to give Rosalynn a break from her desperately sad home. Whether Jimmy was home that night and if he and Rosalynn saw each other, no one remembers. Jimmy was sixteen and interested in older girls, not friends of his little sister. And Rosalynn was too preoccupied with her family's crisis to think of anything else. In the middle of that night, Lillian, after receiving a telephone call, awakened the thirteen-year-old girl and took her back to her own home in Plains, where her father lay dead.

Mama and Papa Murray came to the family's aid. They helped plan the funeral at the Methodist church and the subsequent burial in the Lebanon Cemetery, located about halfway between Plains and the Carter farm. Papa paid Edgar's debts and rented out his farm; Mama stayed at the house with Allie and the children until she died eleven months later in September 1941.[28]

Despite the deaths of her father and her grandmother, Rosalynn resumed the normal life of a teenager and high school student. Edgar had little money and only a negligible pension, but Allie inherited the house and the farm debt-free. At thirty-four, with four children aged four through thirteen, Allie went to work, sewing for hire, selling milk and butter, working in the school lunchroom, and finally taking a job at the post office.[29] The boys took newspaper routes, and Rosalynn worked in a beauty parlor. All the children stayed in school. Allie kept the environment and standards of their home unchanged, and soon she got more help from her father.

When Rosalynn was fourteen, Papa Murray moved in with the family. His wife's death had left him alone on the farm. To make room for him, Allie moved the crotchety "Mama Sallie" to a home that Edgar's brothers and sisters provided for her. At seventy, Papa remained vigorous and helpful. A substitute father, he did not boss Allie or discipline the children. Rosalynn loved having his company.[30] She seemed mature beyond her years, and with a mind of her own, she may have acquired her passion for learning from her grandfather.

Rosalynn's childhood was vastly different from Jimmy's. Their parents had little in common. Rosalynn's were introverted, usually at home, always together, and not particularly ambitious or pecuniary. Black people had no role in their inner circle. The extroverted Carters drank liquor and smoked cigarettes and traveled in other states. They were rarely together, often absent from home, rampantly ambitious, determined to make money and keep it, and eager to push their children out into the world. They depended on African-American women to rear their children and black laborers to work their land.

The Smiths and the Carters, both good families sharing the same time and place, were a study in contrasts, but their oldest children had some things in common. Rosalynn was the oldest child, and her next two siblings were boys. Jimmy was the oldest in his family, and his next two siblings were girls. Despite strict traditional roles of what was expected of boys and girls, the gender line in their lives was not always absolute. Both were fond of solitude and liked to read. They had similar values and religious faiths. They attended the same school and studied with the same teachers.

CHAPTER THREE

School Years

JIMMY CARTER AND ROSALYNN SMITH attended all eleven grades at the only school for white students in Plains. Jimmy enrolled from 1930 until he graduated at age sixteen in 1941; Rosalynn from 1933 through 1944. The small enrollment and intimate involvement of the school with the community meant that teachers, parents, and students had personal relationships that nurtured learning. In addition to the basics of reading, writing, spelling, and arithmetic, dedicated teachers taught the fine arts, music, world and national history, government, home economics, typing, and shop. The principal administered corporal punishment to unruly students. A local boy could, Principal Julia Coleman told her students, as did her counterparts in hundreds of schools across the country, become president of the United States.[1]

The school building dominated the small town. Built in 1921, it was a long, red brick structure with tall steps and six massive, white columns at its two-story entrance. A large foyer provided access to the wings, the library, the auditorium, and the upstairs area. A steam boiler provided heat for the building in the winter, but there was no air conditioning or screens for the hot months.

To the left of the foyer was the principal's office, occupied alternately by Julia Coleman or Young Thompson Sheffield. "Miss Julia" tended to emphasize the intellectual life of the school, while "Y.T.," a pillar of the community, coached basketball, taught mathematics, and administered corporal punishment. On the rare occasions when Jimmy got a paddling, Sheffield summoned him to the office, told him to bend over, grasp a bookshelf, and receive five to ten whacks from a wooden paddle on his "rear end."[2]

Directly across from the principal's office, a small library contained a good map collection that fascinated Rosalynn in the eighth grade, a small collection of books, and a few more books borrowed temporarily from the Sumter County library.[3] The auditorium at the back of the foyer provided the only meeting place for citizens of Plains. For the students, it was the site of daily chapel, special programs, and graduation ceremonies.

Since he lived in the country, Jimmy rode a small, primitive school bus to Plains. In the spring and fall, he went barefoot and dressed in simple clothes.[4] Earl paid his sister, Ethel Slappey, who lived a short distance from the school, 5 cents per day to make hot lunches for Jimmy at her house. When Gloria entered school two years after Jimmy, he ran along beside her to their aunt's home for lunch, but he avoided telling his friends that she was his sister; he thought she was so "country" that she would embarrass him.[5]

In elementary school, Jimmy liked books and teachers.[6] His first-grade teacher remembered him as a bright, cooperative boy, but he shocked her one day by offering to give her his mother's diamond ring. When she refused the gift, he assured her that it would be all right because his father could buy his mother another one.[7] He sailed through the combined second and third grades, where he gazed every day at a reproduction of the famous Gilbert Stuart portrait of George Washington but learned almost nothing about Abraham Lincoln. In the third grade, Jimmy won a prize for reading more books than any other student in his class. He thought his fourth-grade instructor "the prettiest teacher we ever had," but he forgot her name.

Jimmy made friends. They included Bobby Logan, Rembert Forrest, Billy Wise, and Richard Salter. Occasionally he spent the night at one of their houses, and sometimes he invited one of them to Archery for skinny-dipping or fishing in one of his favorite streams.[8]

One day when he was in the sixth grade, the teacher was out of the room when some students threw papers from her desk into the trash can. She accused Jimmy, but he denied it. She ordered him to retrieve the papers and threatened to give him a bad grade. Refusing her order, he went home and told his daddy, who was then a member of the school board. After Earl talked with the teacher, Jimmy removed the papers from the trash, but he always insisted that he was innocent. The next year Mr. Sheffield gave him a paddling for getting into a "terrible fight" with his friend Bobby Logan in the boys' bathroom about a girl whom both liked. Except for occasional low marks in "deportment," no doubt the result of such mischievous behavior as that fight and the wastepaper episode, he made good grades. By the end of his sixth year, he earned an "A" in all of his courses except music, in which he made a "B". He also received an "A" in conduct.[9]

In 1936 Earl had accepted an appointment to the Sumter County school board, a position that recognized his prestige in the community. Outspoken about national politics and its local impact on Georgia, Earl condemned both Franklin and Eleanor Roosevelt. He disliked the president's call to help farmers by reducing production and his meddling in state politics. Eleanor Roosevelt's sympathy for black people provoked him. Earl had more reason to dislike Roosevelt, for he did not reappoint Jim Jack Gordy as Ridgeland postmaster. Lillian was likely miffed by the political snub, but, more seriously, it left her father so impoverished that he had to move near his daughter and her family. Young Jimmy might have learned more about politics from his grandfather as a result, but Earl and Lillian were relieved when almost a year later Gordy became deputy sheriff in Columbus.[10]

Earl did, however, take advantage of the New Deal programs that buttressed farmers and small businessmen. Unlike most of his neighbors, he had some money, and he bought land cheaply and fenced it as pastureland to collect a $10-per-acre government subsidy. He also earned pay and granted favors to his family and friends as director of the local Rural Electrification Association. He liked to discuss local and national politics, but Jimmy probably understood little more than that politics affected his family in some way.

In the seventh grade, the year he began to wear shoes to school, Jimmy studied music theory and learned how to play the harmonica and the guitar. Although he had scant musical talent, he developed an interest in music of all kinds. An avid reader, he became more interested in the classics and read many of them the year before Miss Julia Coleman assigned them to his eighth-grade class.

The eighth grade, presided over by the awesome Miss Julia, marked entry into high school. She directed the daily chapel meetings, sometimes served as principal, and dominated the first year of high school. Unmarried, Julia Coleman gave her life to her students. She was the daughter of a Baptist minister and a schoolteacher and had graduated from Bessie Tift College in Forsyth, Georgia, in 1908. What dreams this pretty, feisty young woman might have had that never came true she kept to herself. While a college student, she broke a leg, and that accident left her permanently crippled. She also suffered a retinal hemorrhage that nearly blinded her in one eye. She grew into a heavy, mature woman who tucked her wavy hair harshly under a net or pulled it up into a stern-looking bun. Every day she pinned a fresh flower on her dress at the cleavage of her generous bosom, and she kept a vase of fresh flowers on her desk. To her "pet" Jimmy and dozens of other students who came under her influence, she was a beautiful person.

During the summers in the 1920s Julia had attended courses in music, drama, and the arts at Lake Chautauqua, New York, where she met Eleanor Roosevelt. Later, when Eleanor Roosevelt was first lady, she invited Julia to the White House. Julia drank tea with the first lady and spent several days in Washington learning about the history and government of the nation, knowledge she later shared enthusiastically with her students. Julia corresponded with the first lady, inviting her to come to Plains to inspire her students, but Mrs. Roosevelt never visited.[11] Miss Julia sometimes required students to build models of the White House, and many of them must have been awestruck by the fact that their teacher had actually been in the building and conversed with the first lady.

Miss Julia had her favorite students, including some with learning or discipline problems whom she tried to help, and bright ones like Jimmy whom she pushed to learn more than the routine courses required. If a student showed interest in something the school did not offer, such as journalism, she helped that student learn it anyway. She drilled her students in art, literature, poetry, and classical music. They wrote and produced one-act plays, and they memorized passages from the Bible, poems, and Lincoln's Gettysburg Address. She coached them in debates on contemporary social and political issues, including whether the United States should aid Great Britain in its conflict with Nazi Germany.

Under Miss Julia's guidance, Jimmy won the "Great Books Contest" by reading more assigned books than anyone else, one of which was Leo Tolstoy's *War and Peace*. Although at first disappointed that it was not about cowboys and Indians, he later said it influenced his presidential thinking that common people, not aristocrats and rulers, determined the well-being of a nation. Miss Julia lived to see Jimmy inaugurated as governor of Georgia, but she died before he immortalized her in his inaugural address on January 20, 1977.[12]

Jimmy's extracurricular activities in high school included basketball, the Future Farmers of America, for which he helped construct a separate club building behind the school, and almost anything that had to do with books. He could not play baseball because the season conflicted with his spring farm work. The school was too small to field a football team. After the wooden gymnasium burned, Jimmy and his basketball teammates had to play in the nearby town of Preston. Since Jimmy and Billy Wise were the last boys to use a forge in the shop that was housed in the gym, town gossip accused them of having caused the fire. Jimmy always denied it.[13]

Jimmy became better known for his membership in the Book Lovers Club, whose members read such works as Shakespeare's *King Lear,* Victor Hugo's *Hunchback of Notre Dame,* Thomas Hardy's *Return of the Native,* Lew Wallace's *Ben Hur: A Tale of the Christ,* and John Muir's *Story of My Childhood and Youth.* Every Friday afternoon, he and the other boys on the debate team debated the girls on contemporary issues.[14]

During his high school years, Jimmy kept a busy schedule outside school. He worked long hours on the farm, taking on increasingly difficult tasks. He hunted and fished, rode his pony, pursued the entrepreneurial ventures of his earlier life, and participated in youth activities at his church. On occasion, he went with other teenagers to Magnolia Springs, about two miles from Plains, which boasted a swimming pool, a pavilion, and a juke box. He favored parties at his family's Pond House, however, where he exercised more control over who attended and what they did. Since his father was wealthy by local standards, the family drove pickups, Oldsmobiles, and Buicks.[15]

A "man about town" with the high school girls, Jimmy took them to Americus to the movies, to dances, to parties at the Pond House, to Magnolia Springs, to church, or simply to Godwin's Drug Store in Plains for a fountain drink after school. At thirteen, he found a soul companion in the book-loving, straight-A student Eloise Ratliff. Nicknamed "Teenie," this dark-haired beauty stood five feet three inches tall. She welcomed his attention at first but decided that he was too tight with his money; she dropped him for an older boy named Lonnie Taylor, who was tall and handsome and had his own Austin car. Jimmy dated Ann Montgomery, an accomplished pianist, and Betty Timmerman. Betty's parents were friends with Earl and Lillian; her mother agreed with Miss Lillian that their black neighbors deserved better treatment from whites. Jimmy and Betty once attended services at a black church. Their families and friends, including Rachel Clark, thought Betty was the girl Jimmy would marry.[16]

In 1940–41, his senior year, Jimmy ranked first academically in his class, but he squandered his opportunity to become valedictorian. He had friends among the brightest students, including Billy Wise, Bobby Logan, and Teenie Ratliff. He and his male friends suffered with "senior fever," a common attitude among students about to graduate, who often do foolish things at the very end of their school years. These boys had all been in school during the Great Depression of the 1930s; since fewer trains passed through Plains in those years, the town seemed more isolated and dull. Furthermore, the war that had begun in Europe in 1939 increased their desire to get out of Plains, even if only to Americus. Restless, impatient, and according to legend perhaps duped by Teenie's new boyfriend, Jimmy joined other boys in an April Fool's Day prank. Although Mr. Sheffield learned in advance that the boys intended to cut school that day and threatened severe punishment if they followed through with their scheme, they defied him. They went to Americus, attended a "picture show," toured the Coca-Cola plant, and then had the local newspaper publish a story about what a good time they were having. Jimmy got his first lesson in the power of the press. Back in Plains, he found his father and Y. T. Sheffield waiting for them. Earl restricted Jimmy to the school and to the yard in Archery for thirty days. Y.T. paddled them and gave them zeroes for that day's work.[17] The zeroes cost Jimmy the top position in his class. He graduated on June 2, 1941, second in a class of twenty-six. As she and her boyfriend had hoped, Teenie Ratliff became valedictorian.

On graduation day, however, Miss Julia allowed Jimmy, Billy Wise, Doris Cosby, and Richard Salter, all members of the debate team, to give a presentation entitled "Building for Today and Tomorrow." She wrote Jimmy's speech, "The Building of a Community," which the local newspaper said gave the audience much pleasure. He went back to the farm, and the next fall, he became a day student at Georgia Southwestern College, a two-year school in Americus.[18]

After Jimmy graduated, Rosalynn spent three more years attending Plains high school. She made nearly perfect grades. Well-dressed and quiet, she was protective of her younger brothers and sister.[19] Since her mother, "Miss Allie," had attended the same school, Rosalynn had to live up to that intimidating image. She also had to walk past her father's garage every day going to and from school.

Rosalynn loved her school years. In the first grade, she learned to make change at the toy store. In her elementary years, she went barefoot like the boys, and she acquired girlfriends, including Ruth Carter. After school Rosalynn often visited

Ruth in Archery, but she rarely saw Jimmy there. Ruth knew that her mother Lillian admired Rosalynn, and she liked having for her closest friend a girl older than herself.

In the seventh and eighth grades, Rosalynn's innocence as a young girl sheltered by family and church gradually shaded into her life without a father in a war-torn world. She joined the 4-H club to learn to be a homemaker. At about age thirteen, she wrote a poem about Christmas that emphasized equally the birth of Christ and the exchange of gifts.[20] Her faith deepened, and she worked harder at her studies, as she planned to fulfill her father's dream for her to attend college. Allie towered over her daughter, sheltering and pushing her, and enabling her to develop a balanced adolescent personality that was both serious and fun-loving.

Rosalynn could be mischievous. Despite Miss Julia's eminence, Rosalynn sometimes giggled at the aging woman's appearance and bad eyesight. Rosalynn could not help getting tickled when Miss Julia, attempting to water the flowers on her desk with a pitcher, sometimes missed the vase entirely and poured the water on her desk.[21] Julia, however, was an unusual model for her female students. Not only had she been to the White House and met a first lady of the United States, back home in Plains she had risen to a position of authority unknown to most other women.

Usually Rosalynn led a studious and exemplary life. When World War II began in 1939, her seventh-grade teacher, Thelma MacArthur, urged her students to read newspapers, listen to radio addresses, and observe current events. Rosalynn became fascinated and frightened by an intriguing and menacing world.[22] Miss Julia said that girls could pursue the same careers as boys and were not restricted to homemaking and teaching. Well-rounded, Rosalynn played softball and basketball. She loved to dance. She took piano lessons, sang in the choir, and served as president of the Methodist Youth Fellowship.[23]

She also maintained an active social life. She listened to popular music on the radio and jitterbugged with her brother Jerry in their living room. She went with a youth group from her church to Magnolia Springs to swim and square dance, and she attended parties Ruth gave at the Carter Pond House. Several boys, including Robert Mills and Ross Oliver, liked her; she went out with them, and others, once or twice, then dropped them. When one telephoned, she stepped out into the front yard so that her mother could tell the spurned suitor truthfully

"She's not in the house right now." Before Jimmy, she never found one she liked enough to date more than a few times.[24]

Since World War II was fought during Rosalynn's high school years, they were quite different from Jimmy's. Rosalynn excelled in all of her classes, including home economics and typing, but she took a serious interest in the war, government, and geography. After one of her teachers talked about the battles, Rosalynn went to the library to locate the sites on the maps. She longed to see the world. She read the casualty list of men from the area that Miss Julia posted in the library. Students demonstrated their patriotism by buying government bonds and war stamps. In chapel, they prayed for the soldiers, sang patriotic songs, and pledged allegiance to the flag. On certain days, as a member of the Victory Corps, Rosalynn wore a khaki skirt, long-sleeved shirt, black tie, and a private's hat when her group drilled like members of the armed forces. Classes did not meet on a special holiday, Ration Day, which Rosalynn sometimes celebrated by going home with Ruth Carter to play leapfrog with her and others in the Carter front yard.

Rosalynn excelled at mathematics, science, and drawing pictures of airplanes. She became particularly interested in machinery, perhaps owing to her late father's occupation, and the sense of power and mastery one might feel from operating it. She sometimes envisioned herself as a great artist, a stewardess, or an architect.[25]

The war changed life in south Georgia. Letters came back from foreign countries; the world came to Plains in ways more vivid than anyone alive there at the time had ever imagined. The school and the churches blended patriotism and religion. At school the students concluded their prayers "in Christ name." There were no Jews in town, and any non-Christians who might have lived there remained silent. Flags typically adorned the pulpit areas of the churches, and the pledges, songs, and prayers of the people sounded the same as those the youth repeated at school. Although Sunday school teachers taught that freedom of religion in America was sacred and the separation of church and state crucial to preserve it, neither the teachers nor the students seemed burdened by the fact that the way they lived contradicted what they believed.

In 1944, Rosalynn graduated first in her class of fifteen. As valedictorian, she managed to overcome her almost pathological shyness to deliver her first major public address. Well researched and organized, it revealed an unusually mature understanding of the contemporary world for a seventeen-year-old girl. Declaring that "no nation is stronger than its people," she emphasized the heritage of freedom, the importance of education, the need for successful businesses, and the necessity of religion. When the unfortunate war ended, she said, the United States would have to compete with other countries in a changed economic environment. She urged her classmates to apply "the human touch" as they carried on "the great tradition of freedom in the country we love."[26] Years later, when Jimmy teased her, she could remind him that *she*, unlike him, had been first in her class and had written her own speech.[27] She spent the summer at home on Bond Street before entering Georgia Southwestern College.

When Rosalynn graduated from high school in 1944, Jimmy was already at the Naval Academy, but he did not go there directly from high school. His father wanted him to go to West Point, but Jimmy's hero was his Uncle Tom Watson Gordy, a Navy man. Because of the depression, Earl, who was more tight than poor, pressured Jimmy to attend a school where he could get his education at taxpayers' expense. Earl himself had attended the Riverside Military Academy and had served in the Army during World War I. He did not resist Jimmy's preference for the Naval Academy, for he understood that attendance at an academy would save Jimmy from being drafted and possibly assigned to a combat zone. Jimmy wrote the Naval Academy for catalogs and worried whether he could pass the physical examination or meet the requirement to be appointed to attend the Academy by his Congressional Representative. Earl asked Stephen Pace, the Democratic representative from his district, to make the appointment. Since Jimmy did not receive it by the time he finished high school, he enrolled at Georgia Southwestern College.[28]

With only two hundred students, the majority of them female owing to the military draft, Georgia Southwestern boasted one classroom building, a gymnasium, and two dormitories. About the time Jimmy entered in September 1941, it improved its English courses and its library, added a physical fitness program, and operated a farm that provided vegetables, milk, pork, and beef to feed resident students. The college provided debating, musical, religious, and fraternal organizations. The cost to attend for three academic quarters, or nine months, was $204. Jimmy commuted by truck from Archery as a day student, except for one quarter when Earl allowed him to live in a dormitory to escape the house where his baby brother, Billy, then about four years old, interfered with his studying. Jimmy excelled in introductory English, social science, chemistry, and trigonometry, and he did well in physics, but he got a "C" in solid geometry. Mathematics remained his most difficult subject throughout his college years.[29]

Even as a day student, Jimmy participated fully in college life. He sometimes stayed overnight in a dormitory with his friend Bobby Logan, hosted a picnic for fellow students at the Carter Pond House, and played on the school's basketball team. He joined the "Ingenuity, Fidelity, and Trustworthiness" fraternity, as they called themselves, and the "Investors," who sponsored an annual school dance.

He pursued the girls, especially Betty Timmerman and Marguerite Wise. He dated Bobby Logan's sister and others before he became strongly attracted to Marguerite. The daughter of Dr. Bowman Wise, with whom Lillian worked, Marguerite was petite, studious, and pretty, very much like Rosalynn Smith. A favorite of both Jimmy and his mother, Marguerite might have become the future Mrs. Jimmy Carter had not her mother intervened. Mozelle Wise did not think Jimmy good enough for her daughter, and the romance ended painfully for him.[30]

After the Japanese attacked Pearl Harbor on December 7, 1941, Jimmy emphatically informed his classmates that he would become a submarine commander. Only three days after that attack, the Japanese captured his cherished Uncle Tom Gordy on Guam and imprisoned him until September 1945. When Germany declared war on the United States, pictures of the hated Adolf Hitler sometimes appeared on campus. The beginning of the war in the Pacific and in Europe, made personal by the fate of his uncle, stoked Jimmy's determination to attend the Naval Academy, but he still had to wait for the political appointment and undertake additional academic preparation at the Georgia Institute of Technology.[31]

CHAPTER FOUR

Annapolis

AS THE SUMMER OF 1942 ended, a frightened seventeen-year-old Jimmy Carter left his home in Archery to go live in Atlanta. In July of that year, Representative Stephen Pace had appointed him to the Naval Academy. Since Pace had already used his five 1942 appointments, however, Carter had to wait another year before entering Annapolis. The Academy advised him to improve his preparation by attending the Georgia Institute of Technology in Atlanta to study general engineering and to enroll in the Naval Reserve Officers Training Corps.[1] At Georgia Tech, Carter studied hard, coped with homesickness, and missed the social life he had enjoyed back home.

Earl thought Jimmy was not spending enough of his allowance on social activities; both he and Lillian occasionally visited their "little country boy," as his mother called him, and allowed him to come home frequently. From school, Jimmy often visited his Aunt Sissy Dolvin in nearby Roswell. He liked his roommate, Robert Ormsby, who shared 308 Knowles Hall with him, but Ormsby was more interested in fraternity life, and the two boys did not become particularly close. Ormsby later became president of the Georgia Lockheed Corporation.[2]

At Georgia Tech, Jimmy attended football games but mostly concentrated on preparing for the Naval Academy. He made "As" in navigation, engineering drawing, first quarter elementary Spanish, and American government; "Bs" in naval history, analytic geometry, mathematics, and heat, electricity, sound, and light; a "C" in second quarter Spanish; and a "D" in his persistent bugaboo, differential calculus. He ranked in the top 10 percent of his class and met the academic requirements for admission to the Naval Academy. One of his Georgia Tech professors remembered him as a dedicated, but not outstanding, student, who was quiet in class and kept to himself.[3]

Jimmy returned to Archery until June 26, 1943, when he joined his fellow appointee Evan Mathis of Americus to board a train for Washington, D.C. Months earlier, Earl had signed papers giving permission for his son, a minor, to enter military service. After Jimmy's noon departure, Earl drove to pick up his friend Raymond Sullivan, went to an isolated pond, and drank whiskey until dark. Taking her own automobile, Lillian drove alone to a different pond, where she fished and wept. As she and Earl released their firstborn son, whatever pride and ambition they felt for him was sorely tempered by loving parents' unspeakable anxiety.[4]

After reaching Washington, Jimmy and Evan transferred to a bus for the remainder of the trip to Annapolis. The next day, June 28, both boys passed the dreaded physical examination. Jimmy was three months short of his nineteenth birthday, and at five-feet, six inches, he weighed 130 pounds.[5] Then they toured the campus and attended a movie. They marveled at Bancroft Hall, a building larger than the nation's Capitol, which had been named for George Bancroft, the historian and nineteenth-century secretary of the Navy. In that building they would sleep, eat, pick up their mail, and buy their necessities. The five upper floors, or "decks," as the navy called them, housed plain, uniform dormitory rooms, where, because of the war and the large enrollment of twenty-six hundred students, the midshipmen slept three to a room. The administrative offices were located on the first and second floors; support services and a six-hundred-foot mess hall filled the basement.

Jimmy and Evan found academic buildings, a large chapel, an armory, a gymnasium, a hospital, and separate officers' quarters. Everywhere loomed motifs of the sea, and the buildings were decorated with nautical artifacts. The same day, President Franklin Roosevelt signed an order reducing the course of study at the Academy from four years to three, which meant that Jimmy, a member of the class of 1947, would graduate in 1946. Two days later, June 30, Jimmy was officially sworn into the Navy.[6]

Near the end of his second day, Jimmy proudly wrote his "Dear Folks" on United States Naval Academy letterhead that it was "not so bad—yet" and that he was "not ready to come home." He drew illustrations of how he was supposed to wear his cap and recounted the necessity to snap to attention and say

"Midshipman Carter, 4th Class, Sir," whenever an upperclassman entered the room. He confessed that he had a cold and had been to sick bay twice, but he would get better, and urged them to "continue writing." He signed it, "Love, J." Soon, he advised them not to refer to him by his childhood nickname "Hot," and he told his sister Gloria not to write to him in pencil on lined notebook paper, because that would indicate to his friends that his sister lacked sophistication.[7]

The Academy intended to wean the new arrivals quickly from parents, girl-friends, attachment to region, and any other impediments to becoming loyal Navy men. With Jimmy, however, it had a tough case. He remained close to his family and suffered severe homesickness. At first he roomed with Evan at 3315A Bancroft, but they were soon assigned to different companies, Jimmy's being the Thirteenth. During the first week at meal time, he indulged in "some very good arguments about the Civil War, as most of us were from the South, and... one of the ensigns was from the North." It made him especially happy to meet several boys from Georgia, who "spooned on me," or dropped all pretense of rank, shook hands, and treated him like an equal. "The boys from Georgia really help each other out a lot." On the last day of July, a boy from Newnan, Georgia, passed an evening talking about "mostly women, as do all the other Ga. boys." Plebes were not allowed to date, and the Navy strictly controlled dances and social events.[8]

Six weeks after his arrival, Jimmy wrote to his family that it was "Over 5 months to Xmas. Hope I can stand it." Greatly disturbed when he was unable to receive a telephone call on August 22 because it was "after taps," he was relieved on August 25 when "I finally talked to my folks—Billy, Ma, & Daddy. Daddy said he was through with taking up peanuts." Although he had broken up with Betty Timmerman before going to the Academy, Jimmy was glad she sent him her picture.

One weekend early in November, Earl went to Annapolis to visit his son. After a brief visit on Friday night, the next day father and son ate lunch, went to a movie, and walked around town and the yard. "I was really glad to see him," Jimmy told his diary, "& enjoyed hearing about home. Billy has the mumps, he said." On Sunday, Jimmy and Evan dined with Earl, showed him Bancroft Hall, and "talked a lot" before the senior Carter departed.[9]

When upperclassmen hazed the stoic southerner, Jimmy responded with a fixed gaze from his cold, clear blue eyes. The large grin that covered his face when he was nervous, or secretly happy if he witnessed a tormentor's misfortune, got him into trouble. "My main trouble was that I smiled too much," he wrote, confessing that his superiors told him to "wipe it off." For the slightest infraction, he might be forced to eat his meals beneath the table, eat sitting in a nonexistent chair, receive twenty-seven whacks on his "tail" with the handle of a large serving spoon, or run laps. Near the end of his first year, he wrote that like most plebes, he was getting "reckless now" and had been beaten "with a serving spoon twice at noon for wiping a smile off to the class of '45."[10]

When a Yankee ordered Carter, like other Georgia boys, to sing "Marching through Georgia," the battle song that General William T. Sherman's troops sang as they pillaged the state near the end of the Civil War, Jimmy refused. He felt no loyalty to the Confederacy and sometimes attempted to disguise his accent, but he loved his home state and bristled at the order. The older student demanded three times that Jimmy sing the song, and three times Jimmy said, "Sir?" The angry tormentor insisted that Jimmy sing it every night; every night Jimmy refused until his "rear end was getting in worse & worse shape." Finally, an upperclassman from Arkansas intervened and stopped the torture. Carter, who was innately stubborn and resented being typed as a modern-day Confederate rebel, never sang "Marching through Georgia."[11] His stubborn refusal to do something he thought wrong recalled his denial in Plains of having thrown the teacher's papers in the trash can and foreshadowed a personality trait that impacted his decision making.

Carter also had good times that first year at the Academy. He attended movies regularly. He thought *The Constant Nymph* "stank," but he enjoyed *Thank Your Lucky Stars, Mr. Lucky, Action in the North Atlantic,* and *Heaven Can Wait.*[12] At the end of the day, the students staged "happy hour," a time when upperclassmen demanded that plebes sing for them and harassed those who had not learned the songs properly. Jimmy despised the hounding, but sometimes he had fun. He genuinely enjoyed the night he sang "Catalina Magdalena Reubensleiner Wallendiener Hogan Bogan Logan Was Her Name." The zenith of his fun came at Halloween when an upperclassman put him "in charge of a super–happy hour, with dire threats if it isn't good."

Jimmy threw himself into the assignment with gusto. He helped write, vamped, and starred in a costumed drama that spoofed his own Thirteenth Company, much to the merriment of the other midshipmen. Jimmy filled six pages in his diary, more space than he gave any other single event that year, with an animated description of how he had played the lead role of "Fearless Fosdick," a character from the popular Dick Tracy comic strip. In Jimmy's version, Fearless Fosdick "muttered over a horrid brew," rode his sword like a witch on a broomstick, "flitting" and "swooping" along the stage, and caught plebes with liquor and women. After it ended, Jimmy reported drily that the "happy hour tonight was swell." Actor, writer, and humorist, Jimmy immersed himself in that production with such zest that it seemed as though he had found his niche in life.[13]

Jimmy participated fully in athletic and recreational opportunities. He attended compulsory chapel every Sunday morning, prepared himself and his room for inspection, and braced himself to get "fried" if he made some mistake. He ran track, played lightweight football, wrestled, boxed, swam, and sailed. He pushed himself to the maximum physical limit for a young man of his small size. He injured his foot during a cross country run and on various occasions suffered minor bruises and strains. In 1945, he fell and broke his right shoulder during a wrestling bout. When not playing, he became an enthusiastic spectator at the Academy's games.[14]

Jimmy found academic life at times interesting and at times tedious, but generally less difficult than the classes he had taken at Georgia Tech. During his plebe year, he studied "Bull," "Dago," "Steam," "Skinny," and "Math," the Navy's slang names for English composition and literature, foreign language, marine engineering, chemistry and physics, and mathematics. Except for the foreign language, the Academy determined the curriculum. Since companies at the Academy were organized according to the language they studied, Carter, who selected Spanish, went into the Thirteenth. Placing midshipmen who studied the same language and curriculum in the same company facilitated their assembling and marching in formation to class. Jimmy's new roommate Don Andrews, who held a degree in civil engineering from Iowa State University, and upperclassman Joe Marzluff helped him with his studies.[15]

Although Jimmy liked literature,[16] late in his plebe year he became exhausted with the reading and complained that he was "bilging on Bull." Georgia Tech had prepared him well for his Spanish, engineering, and science courses, but mathematics remained difficult. On February 6, he wrote: "We've been having permutations & combinations in math & I don't get that stuff at all. My math average has really dropped. I've had the best profs yet in my subjects but we change tomorrow & I'll probably get the usual sorry plebe profs." Jimmy ended the year with high grades, and some of his classmates thought that he excelled without having to spend much time studying.[17]

During that year, Carter got his first glimpse of foreign dignitaries. On his nineteenth birthday, October 1, 1943, he participated in a dress parade for the sultan of Saudi Arabia. "He looked just like a Sultan should look, & was interesting. Rated 19 guns," Jimmy wrote. Less impressed the following May, Jimmy complained that he and the others had had to parade on a hot day in blue winter uniforms while "Some Peruvian president gave the Admiral a darned medal, & we stood out in the sun for a long time while they made speeches, etc."[18]

By the end of his first year, Carter had become, as the Academy intended, a "Navy man." He had endured the humiliation of hazing that was designed to prepare him to handle stress and command others. He had the equivalent of a sophomore-level college education. He had learned to drill, stand watch, handle small arms, and identify many types of ships and airplanes, both friendly and hostile. He learned to pilot the two-seat scout seaplane, the OS2U Kingfisher, and the "old, slow, reliable PBY" Catalina that Navy pilots used to rescue people at sea, but he chose an elite career in submarines. After Carter won the Democratic nomination for the presidency in 1976, he wrote a former upperclassman: "Your training of me as a plebe has paid off—so far!"[19]

At the end of his plebe year, Carter boarded USS *New York* for his first summer cruise. An ancient battleship 565 feet long, propelled by eight steam boilers, she had been launched on October 30, 1912. After service in the Atlantic during World War I, she and her sister ship *Wyoming* had escorted President Woodrow Wilson to Europe in 1918 to negotiate the Versailles peace treaty.[20] While cruising the Caribbean on board *New York* during the summer of 1944, Carter learned to bathe and wash clothes in saltwater, skimp on food and sleep, survive in tight spaces with no privacy, and to man a 44mm antiaircraft gun. He had his first brush with danger when his ship sighted a German submarine, zigzagged violently to escape, and suffered a broken propeller in the process. What annoyed him most, however, was cleaning the trough-shaped urinal that splashed saltwater as the ship rolled and lurched.[21]

Without the hazing, Carter's second and third years became easier and too busy for him to continue keeping a diary. His training was 30 percent scientific, 30 percent cultural, and 40 percent professional. He drew $780 per year, with a monthly spending allowance ranging from $3 at the beginning of his tenure to

$12 at the end of it. He enjoyed the strict regulation of virtually every minute of his day, the summer cruises, extracurricular activities, and the Navy's athletic events.[22]

When his sister Gloria entered training in the Cadet Nurse Corps at Mt. St. Agnes School in Mt. Washington, Maryland, Jimmy got to visit her and their parents. After a year, Gloria married Everett Hardy and moved with him to San Antonio, Texas.[23] By then Jimmy had outgrown his embarrassment about his "country" family. On one occasion when Earl and Lillian visited him at the Academy, one woman haughtily said to Lillian, "My dear, what a beautiful tan you have. Did you get it at the beach?" Responding quickly, Lillian looked disgusted and said, "No, I got it in the cotton patch." Jimmy later told his mother, "Mom, I've never been so proud of you in my whole life."[24]

Jimmy attended the Protestant chapel at the Academy because it was the most convenient place for him to worship during his first year. But he missed his Baptist church so much that he decided to go off campus. Soon, he was teaching a Sunday school class in a local Baptist church, a practice he would continue through the other stages of his life.[25]

Unlike most white men at the Academy, Jimmy befriended Wesley Brown of New York, the only black midshipman. Five previous African-American midshipmen had been unable to endure the racism, hazing, and violence directed at them long enough to receive their commissions. Jimmy related easily to black people, enjoyed their friendship, and particularly hated the image of white southerners as racists. He deplored the fact that other students gave Wesley "hell" because he was black.[26] Other southern midshipmen vehemently disapproved of Jimmy's actions.

Jimmy did not find Wesley a threat or a competitor but relaxed in his company, ran cross-country with him, and apparently did not mind when Wesley always won.[27] He enjoyed an easier relationship with the black underclassman than he had with most of his white peers. On one occasion when an upperclassman ordered plebe Brown to do so many pushups that he was badly shaken, Carter approached his friend, put his arm around him, spoke kindly to him, and then went his separate way. An unidentified midshipman who witnessed the event called Jimmy "a God damn nigger lover."[28] Unmoved, Carter maintained his composure and his friendship with Brown.

The Navy neglected no aspect of Carter's mental, physical, or social development. He learned the rules of etiquette, how to make public speeches on short notice, and how to dance.[29] The Navy also trained him to be what Mr. Earl wanted him to be, namely, a leader, a commander, and a "hotshot" among his peers. Prepared to command and to be commanded, Carter avoided sharing his private feelings with other men. He was secretive about his plans and ambitions, and he prepared to defeat in open competition any who challenged him. Nonetheless, he enjoyed the camaraderie of a few friends.

By the end of his senior year, Jimmy had become a member of a congenial group consisting of Bob Scott, Al Rusher, Blu Middleton, and Lou Larcombe. Jimmy engaged them in conversation on subjects ranging from piano music to weaponry, but he revealed little of his inner feelings.[30] Thirty years after they graduated, one of his classmates, Francis Hertzog, then an ophthalmologist, compared him to the Confederacy's General Robert E. Lee. Hartzog thought Jimmy might even exceed Lee in self-control and utilization of his mind and his strong character. He noted that Carter was a "loner" who did not make close friendships, nor did he need them.[31]

Carter was at the Academy on April 12, 1945, when news of Franklin Roosevelt's death fifty miles from his hometown stunned the nation. In Plains, the high school held a memorial service during which Miss Julia played "Ave Maria" and gave an address entitled "The Abundant Life." Four months later, while on maneuvers in the North Atlantic, Carter heard the flat, calm voice of his new president and future hero. Harry Truman announced that the United States had dropped atomic bombs on Japan. The war ended two days later, just as Carter's service in the Navy and the nuclear age were beginning.[32]

While Jimmy was at the Academy fulfilling his childhood dream, Rosalynn remained in Plains or in nearby Americus. She lived at home and commuted to college by riding with a neighbor from Plains. By majoring in interior design, she pursued her interest in architecture and foreign cultures as well as the domestic arts. At the end of her two-year course, she intended to follow her mother's example and enroll at the Georgia State College for Women in Milledgeville.[33]

As an Academy man, Jimmy had already embarked on a life that no girl of Rosalynn's place and era could hope to experience. Through the pages of his plebe diary, Jimmy Carter, a youth of eighteen and nineteen, revealed his dreams to himself alone. He wanted to be a writer and an actor, a real-life Fearless Fosdick who not only single-handedly solved the problem of evil but also presented his case to the world with words and actions that were clever, amusing, and convincing. Despite some difficult courses and a tendency to exaggerate his abilities, he had a good memory and the ability to master a wide range of academic and technical subjects. He missed and deeply loved his family and his home. And he needed a girlfriend.

CHAPTER FIVE

Navy Couple

IN THE HOT, DUSTY SUMMER OF 1945, people in Plains talked about the heat, the crops, and the war, unaware of an event on Main Street that three decades later would catapult their town onto the world stage. Jimmy Carter, the twenty-year-old eldest child of a prominent local family, was visiting his hometown before returning for his final year at the Naval Academy. As he drove down Main Street in a Ford car with a rumble seat, accompanied by his sister Ruth and her boyfriend, he glanced toward the Methodist church. There he spied a pretty young woman loitering on the steps.[1] Petite Rosalynn Smith, with her large, warm, intelligent eyes, exuded a seductive shyness that captivated the Academy man. Graduated as valedictorian of her class at Plains High School, she had completed one year at a nearby junior college. Jimmy stopped the car, not knowing that Ruth and Rosalynn had conspired to set up the meeting. He invited Rosalynn to attend the movie at the Rylander Theater in nearby Americus that night. She accepted.

Rosalynn was seventeen and Jimmy twenty that night in 1945 when they had their first date. His white Navy uniform dazzled her, and he thought her ravishing in her blue dress that buttoned all the way down the front. Immediately after their first date, Jimmy told his mother that he had met the woman he intended to marry. Lillian disapproved. "Jimmy, she's just a little girl! She's Ruth's friend," she argued. Lillian thought that Jimmy was so much more sophisticated than "naive" Rosalynn Smith of Plains, Georgia.[2]

Rosalynn's father lacked the powerful personality and wealth of Earl Carter, and neither her mother nor any other woman in Plains could equal Miss Lillian. Yet, connected by blood to the Wises, Murrays, Bells, and Smiths, her pedigree, ever so important in a small southern town, was superior to that of the Gordys and the Carters. Because her father died when she was young and her mother remained imprisoned in shyness, Rosalynn had no influential, potent adults to push her into the world. What she had was a robust spirit, a vigorous will, an inquisitive intellect, an energetic mind, an unspoken ambition, a quiet faith, and a tough ability to succeed at whatever she undertook.

It would take Jimmy a decade of marriage to realize the complements to his life-style that Rosalynn brought to their union. On their first date, he saw a very pretty, smart, seductively shy girl who smiled at him. Rosalynn did not fall so quickly for him, but she later confessed that she had fallen in love with a picture of him in his uniform. She realized that the man in that uniform, who now said he loved her, had begun to see that world about which she only read and dreamed.[3] The young lovers exchanged a flurry of letters, a correspondence that did not mention the major events of the day, but consisted of, according to Carter, "intimate love letters."[4]

World War II ended shortly after their courtship began. Rosalynn did not want Jimmy to go to war, but she remained reticent. He teased her about falling in love with his uniform, and he pretended to date other women. On at least one occasion, Jimmy did go out with another woman, and he suggested that Rosalynn see other men. When she reciprocated with letters about nonexistent boyfriends, he bristled, but they soon put aside their jealousies and committed to each other.[5]

When Jimmy returned home on his Christmas leave in 1945, he and Rosalynn sang Christmas carols before open fires and attended church and parties together. Rosalynn beamed beside Jimmy in his dress blue uniform. He teased her mercilessly, a Carter family trait indicating affection, but not always graciously received. On Christmas Day, Jimmy invited her into the Carter family; he gave her a silver compact engraved with the "ILYTG" family signature, "I Love You the Goodest," and he proposed. She rejected him but left the matter open for consideration. Only eighteen and in her second year of college, she had promised her father on his deathbed that she would attend college. She had already completed her application to Georgia State College for Women. She did not know clearly enough whether she loved Jimmy, or only his uniform and the ticket he offered to the world.[6]

In February 1946, Rosalynn went to Annapolis with Jimmy's parents, and while there she agreed to marry him. They set the date for July but decided to keep their plans secret until nearer his graduation the following June. They were uncertain about how Jimmy's family would react, and Rosalynn dreaded telling her mother that she had decided to marry instead of continuing her education.[7]

Soon after Rosalynn returned to Plains, Jimmy sent her a copy of *The Navy Wife*, a manual of more than two hundred pages that advised girlfriends, fiancees, and wives what to expect and how to act if they married Navy men. Before mailing it, Jimmy deleted, underlined, and annotated certain passages. He transformed a dry, somewhat silly, manual into a love letter. As a senior, he told her, he could ride in an automobile and take her out to dinner during June Week of his graduation. "You, darling," he wrote in the margin of a passage about "The Natural Girl":

> To begin with she is easy on the eyes. Her pretty soft brown hair has a semblance of a natural wave, her features are good, she has pretty teeth and a ready smile. She is slim and has a willowy figure. She dresses well, and knows how to wear her clothes. She is adaptable, is understanding, and can make the best of regulations and conditions as she finds them. She is a good cheery companion, an *excellent dancer,* never catty, has good manners....

Jimmy informed Rosalynn that at a brief ceremony following his graduation, "Mother and sweetheart" would "divide honors by each putting on one shoulder mark." He struck through an outdated passage that said ensigns were not allowed to marry for two years after graduation, and he deemphasized all references to long separations married couples could anticipate. "After a year or so I'll have Navy Wings, I hope," he wrote at that chapter title. After he spent a year at sea, they would live in southern port towns, he noted.

As for the chapter entitled "Engagements and Weddings," Jimmy underlined the title and wrote, "Darling, this part is up to you. Whatever you want is what I want. What we've already decided is what I think is best, but we can always change our minds. I love you." The chapter that described the "Business of the Naval Household," Jimmy said, "is a good chapter to know—we can work it out together." He underscored the passage that said "no one could be so ignorant as to marry a naval officer for his money." He commented that he would be slightly better off financially than most beginning ensigns, "although not much. Do you mind starving with your poor ensign?" On his $164 monthly pay, his $1,500 in savings bonds, and her $50 monthly government allowance, Jimmy did not think they could afford a car. Beside the passages that gave practical advice on how to acquire the necessary secretarial and business skills to operate the household, Jimmy wrote: "You'll really have to do all of this, I guess." When furnishing their bedroom, however, Jimmy emphatically marked that they would *not* need sheets for *twin* beds.[8]

Rosalynn was ecstatic. She tucked her application to the Georgia State College for Women into a book and forgot about it.[9] She could hardly wait until June Week, the gala six-day graduation celebration at the Academy, when she would return to Annapolis and help Miss Lillian put the shoulder boards on her fiance.

Meanwhile, the young couple revealed their wedding plans to their families and braced themselves for the responses. Allie Smith thought so highly of Jimmy Carter and his family that she did not try to persuade Rosalynn to change her mind. The Carter family responded quite differently. Since Gloria lived in Texas with her new husband, and Billy was only nine, neither cared much about Jimmy's marriage. Lillian, Earl, and Ruth, however, did not respond favorably. Although Lillian liked Rosalynn, she thought she was too young and nonaggressive. Earl feared that Rosalynn would be an impediment to "Hot's" career. Ruth quit speaking to her good friend who was about to become her sister-in-law, and it took many years before they spoke again.[10]

Ignoring the Carter family's reservations, the engaged couple looked forward to his graduation. On June 5, 1946, President Harry Truman appointed Carter an ensign in the United States Navy. Jimmy signed an oath to discharge his duties properly and "to support and defend the Constitution of the United States."[11] On June 11, in a grand ceremony at Dahlgren Hall, the midshipmen received their diplomas and commissions, then tossed their hats into the air. Moments later, Rosalynn stood on one side of Jimmy, Miss Lillian on the other, as they pinned the boards on his shoulders. He graduated number 60 in a class of 822.[12]

At 3 P.M. on Sunday, July 7, 1946, Jimmy and Rosalynn were married in the Plains Methodist Church. They sent no invitations, had no attendants, and hosted no reception. Their families and friends attended in sufficient numbers to fill the three-hundred-seat church. Rosalynn treated herself to a store-bought dress, a navy blue and white ensemble, knee length, sleeveless, with matching full-brimmed white hat, white gloves, and navy blue shoes. She wore a corsage of purple-throated orchids. Jimmy wore his dress white uniform.

The bride and groom arrived late. Whatever the reason for their tardy beginning, Carter harbored a lifelong abhorrence for tardiness on his part or that of anyone associated with him. On his wedding day, he grabbed Rosalynn by the hand and almost dragged her up the steps as the pianist played the wedding march a second time. Hand in hand, Jimmy and Rosalynn walked down the aisle together and exchanged vows in a simple Methodist ceremony.[13] No one gave her away.

Following a weeklong honeymoon at Chimney Rock, North Carolina, the mundane beginning of the young couple's Navy career lacked the excitement Rosalynn had anticipated. In Norfolk, Virginia, they rented an apartment at 1009 Buckingham Avenue, and the eighteen-year-old bride confronted the realities of Navy life. While her husband was at sea four or five days a week on board *Wyoming,* she stayed home alone and ran the household. She went with him to Philadelphia for a few weeks, where he attended radar school, but there, too, she found that her role was to maintain a base to which he could return on weekends for their reunions. They read books, listened to classical music, and studied Shakespeare. Their young lives were a cycle of weekly separations and happy reunions.[14] Despite their meager income, one weekend they splurged on a fine dinner, then attended a performance of Sigmund Romberg's operetta *The Student Prince.* Both loved the music and the live performance.[15]

On August 6, 1946, Carter had reported for service on *Wyoming* with youthful enthusiasm.[16] He served the experimental gunnery ship as electronics and photographic officer, earning $6 per day, plus $1.40 subsistence and $2 rent allowance. Like *New York,* on which he had trained at the Academy, *Wyoming* had also escorted Woodrow Wilson to Paris, but by this time it was an antiquated training ship. It was scrapped in 1948.[17]

On July 3, 1947, four days short of their first anniversary, Rosalynn gave birth to a son. She was nineteen and Jimmy only twenty-one when they became the parents of John William Carter, whom they nicknamed Jackie. Rosalynn had remained close to her grandfather, her Papa Murray, and she wanted to name her son for him. Earl complained bitterly because the infant had not been named for Jimmy and himself.[18] Encumbered tending her ill father, Rosalynn's mother could not go to her teenaged daughter in Virginia. Rosalynn thus depended on help from other Navy wives, Jimmy when he was at home, and her own instincts.[19]

Jimmy was happy with his little family, but he found his work as Electrical Gunnery Officer on *Wyoming* boring. He wanted to advance his education. He applied for a Rhodes scholarship to study political science and history in England for a year. He promised his commanding officer that he would not resign from the Navy during his tenure at Oxford University and that he would serve the Navy for three years after completing his studies.[20] A finalist for the scholarship, he became severely depressed when he did not receive it.[21]

Instead of going to Oxford, Carter accepted an assignment as aide to the executive gunnery officer on the battleship *Mississippi*. Similar to *Wyoming* and *New York*, *Mississippi* had been launched during World War I, but unlike them, it played an important role in the Pacific during World War II. During Carter's time aboard, it was a weapons trials ship that later in 1952 had the honor of firing the world's first antiaircraft guided missile.[22] But Carter lost interest in antiquated ships and looked forward to a career in submarines. His stable, quiet, reclusive personality fitted him for submarine life.

Carter received orders in April 1948 to report to the Naval Submarine School in New London, Connecticut.[23] Rosalynn enjoyed New London because Jimmy attended school all day and returned home every night. They went to the movies, cared for Jackie, and socialized with other Navy couples. They became friends with a Peruvian couple, Manolo and Maria Piqueras, and the four of them practiced Spanish and English together.[24] They took a mail-order commercial art course, studied *A Treasury of Art Masterpieces,* and learned to use charcoal, watercolors, and oil paints.[25] They occasionally expressed an interest in politics, and Jimmy alone among his group supported Harry Truman for the presidency in 1948.

In December, the Submarine School graduated Carter with distinction, third in a class of fifty-two. The Navy ordered him to Pearl Harbor, Hawaii, home base of USS *Pomfret* (SS 391).[26] The Carters bought their first car, a new 1948 Studebaker, and drove it to Plains for Christmas. Both families gathered at home for the holiday. Gloria, her husband, and her small son, William Hardy, Jr., had traveled from San Antonio to be with the Carters, and Rosalynn's brother Jerry was home from Georgia Tech.[27]

For the first three months of 1949, Jimmy and Rosalynn lived separate lives. She remained in Plains with Jackie and the two families when Jimmy reported for duty. He drove to Los Angeles, from which the Navy flew him to Hawaii and sent his car by surface transport. He served on *Pomfret* off the coast of China. One horrifying night, he was standing watch on the deck of the surfaced submarine when a huge wave swept over him, tore his hand free from a guardrail, lifted and engulfed him in its swirling dark waters, and then deposited him atop *Pomfret's* gun thirty feet aft. Since the storm knocked out the sub's radio and left some debris floating on the surface near Midway Island, the families at Pearl Harbor thought their sailors had been lost at sea. Rosalynn, waiting in Plains, knew nothing of the episode until she rejoined Jimmy.[28]

In March 1949, Rosalynn and Jackie flew to San Francisco, where after a short rest, they sailed on *USS Breckenridge* to Pearl Harbor.[29] Jimmy met them at the pier in April, and for the next fifteen months they indulged in joyful living. They ate native fruits, wore leis around their necks, danced the hula, and listened to Jimmy play "In a Little Grass Shack" on a ukulele. On April 12, 1950, Rosalynn gave birth to their second son, whom the hospital nurses nicknamed "Chip." They kept the nickname but yielded to Mr. Earl and named the baby James Earl Carter III.[30]

A young father in his midtwenties, Jimmy combined his happy family life with a blossoming Navy career. On *Pomfret,* from December 1948 through February 1951, he gained experience in several areas of submarine operation: engineering, supply, gunnery, communications, electronics, and sonar. His commander found him to be "an outstanding officer" whose "timely suggestions and cooperation" contributed to "the excellence of this ship."[31] He became intimately acquainted with every detail of the submarine as it participated in war games in the Yellow Sea. During the games, Carter and his fellow sailors simulated actual combat in which they were pitted against their own compatriots playing the role of the enemy; it was Carter's only experience in "combat." In May 1949, the Navy awarded him the China Service Medal and in June promoted him to lieutenant, junior grade.[32]

The next year, his commander reported, "LTjg Carter has just qualified in submarines," adding a few months later that Carter's "remarkably high native intelligence" and "moral and military character" made him an outstanding officer.[33] Rather than drinking coffee and playing poker with other officers, Carter frequently retreated to his bunk and read. He earned the respect of his peers and his men, but he did not become buddies with them. Some thought of him as a "seaman who never quite got over being seasick"; others said he was an arrogant southerner who refused to mingle, but all agreed that he was a skilled officer who "could run men with authority and machines with stubborn engineering application."[34] In June 1950, at the beginning of the Korean War, the Navy ordered *Pomfret* to San Diego.

A military man in the midst of the Korean War and the subsequent Cold War, Carter began to understand how military and diplomatic affairs might govern his life. From June 25, 1950, until the warring parties reached a truce on July 27, 1953, United Nations troops, which came largely from the United States, fought with the aid of Chinese communists, to stop North Korea's invasion of South Korea. The division of Korea left the East and West facing each other across a Demilitarized Zone at the thirty-eighth parallel. The United States supported the South, the Soviet Union the North, positioning the Americans and the Soviets in a cold war with each other. Acting as if they were at war against each other, they did no actual fighting with each other, but they entered a race against each other to become the most powerful nation in the world. As a submariner, Carter was in a branch of the service that became vitally embroiled in that race.

Rosalynn, who cared more about where she and her children lived than war and politics, reluctantly left Pearl Harbor for San Diego. Traveling with a four-month-old baby and a three-year-old child in a drafty old Navy transport to Los Angeles, she went ahead of Jimmy. Once he joined her, they took a train to San Francisco to pick up their car, and then drove down the coast to San Diego. The rapid influx of Navy personnel into the city made it difficult to find a decent house. They settled for one controlled by a nosey landlady in an impoverished Mexican neighborhood. Since Jimmy was frequently at sea, Rosalynn found herself alone again and often frightened. Earl and Lillian visited them, but Rosalynn was relieved when after a few months in San Diego the Navy sent Jimmy back to New London.[35]

Jimmy's dissatisfaction with his assignment in San Diego was not as deep as Rosalynn's. He learned that his Uncle Tom Gordy's first wife, Dorothy, lived in California with her new husband and children. Three years after the Red Cross and the Navy had informed her that her husband, then a prisoner of the Japanese, was presumed dead, she had married an old friend, not knowing that Tom was still alive. The pious Gordy family treated her as an adulteress, but she escaped their ire by moving to the West Coast with her new husband. When Tom showed up alive at the end of the war, Jimmy, who idolized him, seemed to be the only member of the family willing to forgive Dorothy. Tom recovered from the trauma of his four years in a Japanese prison camp, remarried, and settled in Florida. He kept in touch with his and Dorothy's children, but he never spoke of her again. Thus, Jimmy did not know what to expect when he went to visit her. She welcomed him warmly, gave a party, and seemed very happy that "at least Tom's nephew came."[36]

Jimmy's reunion with his aunt was fleeting, however, for the Navy soon transferred him. Commander R. C. Smallwood, Jr., thought Carter's detachment from *Pomfret* "a definite loss to this ship," but Jimmy could hardly contain his excitement about being able to do the final engineering work for SS *K-1* (later renamed *Barracuda*), the Navy's new submarine that it intended to use to ambush enemy submarines.[37] After a long drive in their Studebaker, the Carters again reached New London. Jimmy worked during the day and, avoiding opportunities for bonding with other officers, usually rushed home to Rosalynn and their sons at night. He and Rosalynn became Yankees fans, enjoyed the beauty of the New England countryside, and on Rosalynn's birthday, August 18, 1952, added a third son, Donnel Jeffrey, to their family. Rosalynn and the three boys were able to go to Provincetown, Massachusetts, with Jimmy when *K-1* began sea trials off the coast of Cape Cod. They could sit at their breakfast table and watch the submarine in action. Rosalynn found time to read *War and Peace* and to go sledding with Jimmy and the boys. When the tests ended, the entire Carter family returned to New London.[38]

As prospective engineering officer on *K-1*, Jimmy directed the final assembly of its long-range listening sonar, planned procedures it would use at sea, participated in testing, and helped train senior officers who would command it. A deep-diving boat, *K-1* gave Jimmy the experience he needed to be eligible to command a submarine, although he was not yet high enough in grade for such an appointment. He was protective of his engineering crew, lived in very tight quarters on board with them, and once said he loved "the unreserved masculine" life in which he and his men were isolated from the rest of the world. At *K-1*'s commissioning ceremony, Jimmy stood proudly on board with five other officers, an easygoing officer who had worked in the engine room with his men. One of them recalled: "He was stern, but he got the job done."[39] Most of them could not recall his having been close friends with anyone, but he remained on the fringes of their social lives, smiling, and willing to help.[40]

In June 1952, after he wrote a thesis about sound bearings, Carter earned promotion to lieutenant. According to Commander F. A. Andrews, Carter's thesis and his record qualified him to command submarines. Andrews went on to describe Carter as "without doubt the most outstanding individual within his age and rank group that I have observed."[41]

Carter developed a leadership style on *K-1*, attempting to earn respect and to lead by example. For example, when British officials at Nassau refused to allow a black sailor from *K-1* to attend a shore party, Carter refused to attend, and the other officers followed his example. When Jimmy told his father about the episode, Earl took the officials' side. Thereafter, the two silently disagreed on the subject of race relations.[42]

Following his success on *K-1*, Carter applied for admission to the Navy's small, highly select group of nuclear engineers. Spearheaded by Admiral Hyman George Rickover, the Navy in 1949 had decided to experiment with nuclear propulsion for ships. It had contracted with Westinghouse to build a power plant for *Nautilus,* a submarine whose nuclear reactor would heat water into steam, and with General Electric to build a plant whose reactor would heat liquid sodium to power *Seawolf.* Both projects were well under way by 1952 when Carter applied for the program.[43] He submitted to a two-hour interrogation by Admiral Rickover.

More influential on the youthful future president than anyone except his parents and Rosalynn, Rickover instructed Carter in tenacity and stoicism. Like Mr. Earl, Rickover demanded perfection and rarely complimented anyone for a job well done. He intimidated most Navy officers. Some who later enjoyed distinguished naval careers simply could not or would not tolerate his abusive interviews. At the end of a grueling interview, one bright Academy man told Rickover that he was not prepared to sacrifice his freedom for the Navy's atomic submarine program, after which Rickover ordered him out of his office.[44] Another left the room angrily a few minutes after his interview began, informing the admiral that "not even God can treat me that way."[45]

Sweating coldly during his session with Rickover, Carter was well equipped by temperament, his life as James Earl Carter, *Junior,* experience on the family farm, and his first year at the Naval Academy to deal with the inevitable verbal abuse. He thought he had impressed Rickover with his knowledge of a broad range of topics, but Rickover fired back questions he could not answer. When

Rickover asked where he ranked in his Naval Academy class, Jimmy proudly, but inaccurately, said, 59 out of 820. Stone-faced, Rickover asked Lieutenant Carter if he had done his best. Jimmy almost lied to him, but thought better of it and said not always. "Why not?" Rickover retorted. Jimmy pondered the question forever and later used it as the catchphrase for his public career.[46] Rickover accepted him immediately.

Rarely have two unrelated men been so alike in thought, personality, and even physical appearance as Hyman G. Rickover and James Earl Carter, Jr. Twenty-six years apart in age, they were small, wiry, physically and mentally strong men whose commitment to duty drove them into innovative, patriotic careers for which they often did not receive recognition. Never close, both were loners willing to confront any obstacles that fell across their chosen paths. Striving to build the world's best Navy, Rickover endured slow promotions and political controversies to pursue his goals tenaciously into his old age. As a senior citizen, he reaped the reward of being able to chat comfortably in the White House with the president he had once terrorized.[47]

Born August 24, 1898, to Jewish parents in Russian-dominated Poland, young Hyman Rickover and his family had lived in fear of persecution. After immigrating to New York City in 1904, Abraham Rickover moved his wife and children to Chicago, where he worked as a tailor. His son Hyman grew up with an intense patriotism for the country that had saved his family. Graduating from the Naval Academy in 1922, Rickover, like Carter after him, ranked in the top quarter of his class. He shunned sports and dating, and his lack of simple social and political skills repelled his classmates. He earned a master's degree in electrical engineering at Columbia University. During World War II, he served with such distinction that the Navy promoted him to captain. His struggle to win appointment as rear admiral, mired in politics and personal discrimination, partly because he was Jewish, ended successfully in February 1953. Undaunted, Rickover set about persuading his country to develop nuclear-propelled ships.[48]

After entering Rickover's nuclear submarine program in 1952, Carter moved his family into an apartment on Duanesburg Road in Schenectady, New York. He studied nuclear physics and reactor technology at Union College, the basis for his claim to be a nuclear engineer, and assisted General Electric workers in building the prototype nuclear reactor for *Seawolf*. For eleven months, he worked with them in a mammoth steel structure near the Knolls Atomic Laboratory.[49] Jimmy traveled regularly from Schenectady to Atomic Energy Commission meetings in Washington. In Hanford, Washington, he learned about the use of plutonium in atomic power, and he observed the experimental reactors for the *Nautilus* prototype in Idaho. An expert on nuclear reactors, Carter had no fear of a meltdown or nuclear accident. He believed that nuclear energy was the hope of the future.[50]

When the reactor core in a nuclear plant near Chalk River, Canada, melted down, Carter joined the team of experts who visited the site. To prevent the escape of radiation, the core had to be disassembled. The team practiced on a duplicate of the disabled reactor. Wearing protective clothing, each man remained inside for only ninety seconds, the time during which scientists calculated he would absorb the maximum amount of radiation his body could tolerate for a year. Reminiscent of his grandfather Billy Carter, whom he never knew, but who had wetted himself down to enter a fiery furnace and clean the flues at his cotton gin in Rowena, Georgia, Jimmy took his turn of one minute and twenty-nine seconds in the disabled reactor. Completing their mission, the young men joked about the possibility of being sterile or dying early, but none of them suffered any ill effects from his ninety seconds inside a nuclear reactor.[51]

For his work on *Seawolf*, Carter earned Admiral Rickover's highest praise. Rickover reported that Carter did "an excellent administrative job" setting up the training program for the crew, made "excellent progress in learning the technical aspects of nuclear engineering," and worked well with the Atomic Energy Commission. "His leadership of the men assigned and his cooperation have been outstanding," Rickover wrote in 1953 when recommending him for promotion.[52]

The adjectives Carter chose to describe Rickover described himself perfectly: "stern, brilliant, dedicated, innovative, nonconformist." Resorting to his characteristic use of hyperbole, Carter said that Rickover, in his opinion, was "the best engineer who has ever lived on earth." Before retiring at age eighty-four, Rickover explained how to use nuclear energy for peaceful as well as military pursuits, converted the Naval Academy's curriculum to favor engineering programs, thumbed his nose at several generations of politicians, and "justified many times over" Jimmy Carter's "confidence in him."[53]

Carter sometimes felt that Rickover, like his father, pushed him too hard, and he turned to art to release the frustration and creativity he almost never expressed verbally. In Connecticut, his first painting depicted a very gray landscape with three trees bent low by the wind, one more tree standing tall, a small body of water, a boat, and a mountain. He gave the painting to his mother.[54] Whether that landscape expressed his inner feelings about his relationship to his siblings, his self-image, or a sublimated psychic bleakness or represented nothing more than his replication of a real scene is a matter of conjecture. A need for artistic expression became a relatively unknown part of his psyche. His love for classical arts, which he had first learned from Miss Julia, remained with him while he adjusted the nuts and bolts of a killer submarine.

At home, Rosalynn managed the family budget, cared for the babies, and loyally supported his career. The constant separations and reunions that Navy life entailed seemed to bond them more closely to each other. Together, they shared love for their three young boys, painted, and studied Spanish and art. They attended the Protestant chapel services on the Navy bases, where Jimmy often taught Sunday School, but Rosalynn remained a Methodist and Jimmy a Southern Baptist.

As southerners in exile, Jimmy and Rosalynn no longer related to their past in the same way. Jimmy could go home again; that was the one thing Rosalynn did not want to do. Neither Jimmy nor Rosalynn knew what his next move in the Navy might be, but Rosalynn loved that lifestyle. Jimmy liked the Navy, but he had remained an outsider, and his love for his home, opportunity to make money in agribusiness, and desire for a career in politics and literature continued to fire his imagination. When he received a telephone call from his mother telling him to come home because his father was dying, he was ready to go. Rosalynn was not.

CHAPTER SIX

The Shadow of Mr. Earl

DESPITE ROSALYNN'S PROTESTS and Admiral Rickover's steely touch, the shadow of Mr. Earl again fell over Jimmy. After Earl Carter died in 1953, Jimmy alone among his heirs was capable of managing his father's business. Eleven years had elapsed since he left Plains for Annapolis. Neither Jimmy nor Rosalynn imagined that he would cut short his Navy career to return home. In the 1940s, Earl Carter had increased his wealth and expanded his influence in the community more than his children knew. He owned more than five thousand acres in Webster and Sumter counties, much of it planted in lucrative crops such as cotton and peanuts. He also operated a thriving seed and fertilizer warehouse and owned a small fire insurance agency in Plains. He and Lillian sold the farmhouse in Archery after Jimmy left home and moved with nine-year-old Billy into a new two-story, brick home beside the paved road in Plains.[1]

A shrewd businessman, Earl Carter ranked among the area's more powerful men. During the growing season, he furnished credit to both black and white farmers, some of whose debts he never attempted to collect. Although a segregationist, Earl believed he treated blacks fairly.[2] An anonymous "Big Daddy" who sometimes used a mediator to hide his philanthropy, he distributed goods and money to destitute black and white families alike. Living in a world of her own as the community's beloved nurse, Lillian had little knowledge of how her husband operated his businesses, but she did know that he could be kind and generous. After his death, his incredulous children encountered many people who stepped forward in grief to mention their appreciation of his benevolence.[3]

After he became financially secure, Earl devoted more time to community service and to politics. A director of the Rural Electrification Association since

1937, he attended its 1948 meeting in Chicago.[4] Rotarian, Mason, Elk, Lion, and Baptist, he served on the Sumter County Commission and became a permanent fixture in the prominent male cliques of Plains and Americus.[5] On his appointment to the Sumter County School Board in 1936, a position he held until his death, he successfully led a movement that built the county's first school for black children.[6]

Previously content to support politicians who understood his agricultural interests, Earl decided in 1952 to enter politics himself. He had earlier supported Eugene Talmadge, the "wild man from Sugar Creek," whose short stature, disheveled hair, horn-rimmed glasses, red galluses, and impassioned oratory immortalized him as one of the South's premier demagogues. Staunch segregationist and "friend" of rural Georgians, "Ole Gene" demanded low taxes, cheap automobile license plates, and inexpensive utilities while quietly supporting the economic interests of the elites against whom he raged. He posed as the friend of both the "little man" and the businessman.

As governor, Eugene Talmadge attacked academic freedom in the state's colleges and universities and temporarily cost them their accreditation. Rabidly ambitious, he told Georgians in 1946 that they had only three friends, namely "God Almighty, Sears Roebuck, and Gene Talmadge." His tax reductions, however, mostly benefited wealthy Georgians, trucking companies, and textile mills. In part, by whipping poor, uneducated white constituents into a frenzy with race-baiting rhetoric, he won the governor's office in 1932, 1934, 1940, and 1946. Earl Carter found Talmadge's stand on every issue except education appealing.[7]

"Ole Gene" had plenty of competition. In 1942, attorney Ellis G. Arnall gained support from those outraged by Talmadge's vilification of higher education, and won the governorship. During four years in office, he promoted education, supported a new state constitution that allowed eighteen-year-olds to vote, abolished chain gangs, and established a merit system for state employees. Eugene Talmadge returned to defeat him in 1946 but died before his inauguration. Because the Talmadge forces knew that the gravely ill Gene might not survive the election, they put up his son Herman as a write-in candidate.

In a comic, chaotic scene, three men then claimed to be governor of Georgia. On his father's death, Herman claimed the governorship on the basis of his write-in votes, seized the governor's office, and changed the locks on the doors. Melvin E. Thompson, who had been elected lieutenant governor, set up a rival governor's office downtown. The incumbent Ellis Arnall, arguing that the state constitution mandated that the current governor remain in power until the new one was duly elected and inaugurated, refused to relinquish the position even though Talmadge had seized his office. Two months later, the state Supreme Court awarded the post to Thompson. Two years later, in 1948, Herman Talmadge won the election for governor.[8]

As happened elsewhere in the South, the rural, antibusiness, antiintellectual segregationists usually won elections. Under Georgia's county unit system, they had a real advantage. Each county had two, four, or six "unit votes," depending on its population, and these votes went to the candidate who won the largest number of popular votes in the county. The rural populations thus exercised disproportionate power in the state legislature; local bosses, who controlled the white electorates in the counties, dictated who the representatives would be.[9]

During Arnall's governorship, however, a growing coalition emerged of liberals and urbanites, many of them war veterans, who wanted reform. One of them, J. Frank Myers, a young Navy pilot, returned from World War II to his home in Sumter County and then became a student leader at the University of Georgia Law School. After graduation, he settled into law practice in Americus and began a political career. He won a seat in the state legislature in 1949 and vigorously opposed Governor Herman Talmadge.[10]

When Myers announced his bid for reelection in 1951, Governor Talmadge asked Earl Carter to run against him. Earl, who did not like Myers and the changes he represented, agreed. Each candidate campaigned by traveling about the county talking to friends. Twelve-year-old Billy went along with his father and handed out campaign cards. Earl got 2,177 votes to Myers's 1,936. He won because he believed in racial segregation and the county unit system; he remained a Talmadge loyalist. During Earl's short service in the legislature, he helped establish an agriculture extension center near Plains and served on the State Trade School Committee. When the governor gave the commencement address at Plains High School on June 2, 1953, he stayed with Earl and Lillian.[11]

In the 1940s and early 1950s, with Jimmy away in the Navy, Earl's family changed. Assuming that Jimmy would continue his naval career, Earl spoiled young Billy and became closer to him than he had ever been to his eldest son. Earl led Billy to believe that he would eventually take over the family businesses. While in high school, Billy became active in the Future Farmers of

America, and he went to Atlanta with his father to work as a page while Earl served in the state legislature.[12] An intelligent youth who liked to read, Billy lacked ambition, and he did not get the push from his father that drove his brother Jimmy.

Gloria's life had not been easy. Her parents had disapproved of her 1945 marriage to William Everett Hardy. After four years, she returned home divorced and penniless, with a young son whom she had nicknamed "Toadie." Gloria then attended business school, worked as an accountant and bookkeeper, and finally became an art teacher. A week before her father's death, she married Walter Spann, a wealthy local peanut farmer, who adopted her son and made it possible for her to quit work. Gloria wrote poetry, painted, and rode motorcycles, becoming a den mother to biker groups.[13]

Ruth left Georgia State College for Women after two years and married Robert Stapleton, a veterinarian who had graduated from Auburn University. She moved with him to Fayetteville, North Carolina, where he entered a partnership with her first cousin, Willard Slappey. There she became the mother of three children and enjoyed an affluent lifestyle, but she remained close to her daddy and distant from her former friend Rosalynn. In the early 1950s she appeared to be a contented mother and wife, but the death of her father in 1953 pushed her into a serious depression. The birth of a fourth child left her so seriously depressed that she withdrew from her children, her church, and all of her social activities. Seeking help, she attended a religious retreat in Minnesota. Eventually her problems became so overwhelming that she entered three years of intensive psychotherapy, from which she emerged a devout Christian, determined to commit her life to evangelism.[14]

Happier than her children in the early 1950s, Lillian liked living in town and remained close to her husband and interested in politics but had no interest in his business affairs. Content to pass her time with work, reading, and occasionally attending local literary and "Stitch and Chat" club meetings, she settled into a comfortable existence with Earl as her anchor and support.

In the winter of 1953, the news that Earl, then fifty-nine, had terminal pancreatic cancer shocked his family. Emotionally devastated, Lillian knew that both she and Billy depended on Earl financially. Still a teenager, Billy faced losing a beloved father before he was ready to be independent. Ruth's closeness to her father had not changed with her marriage, and Gloria had returned home to seek his help. Jimmy alone had an independent life away from Plains. He wept when he learned of Earl's looming death.[15]

Jimmy had played down his rural Georgia background, but as his father lay dying, he began occasionally to talk to some of his fellow sailors about his family's Georgia "plantation" with its fifteen hundred dependents who without his father would not have the means to live.[16] In reality, the Carter farm was a large operation that supported the family very well and employed more than two hundred black laborers who in turn supported their own families. Lillian could not operate the business herself, Billy was too young, and the girls were preoccupied with husbands and children. When she called Jimmy in Schenectady, she told him that he must come home.[17]

Jimmy visited Plains without Rosalynn and spent many hours with his father. The two men became reacquainted. As he learned about how much his father enjoyed the esteem of the community, Jimmy reevaluated his own career. He concluded that his father had lived a more productive and happy life than he could ever hope to have in the Navy. He noted, too, how his father refused to give in to the cancer and tried to lift everyone's spirits. People came to the Carter house to bring food and give thanks to the dying man. Jimmy saw nothing now of the stern disciplinarian who had reared him on the Archery farm, but he did glimpse the intense love between his mother and father as Lillian quietly went about caring for Earl.[18]

Earl died at home at 9:30 A.M. on July 22, 1953, with his wife and children around him. At the moment of his death, Annie Mae, Jimmy's childhood nanny, lifted Earl from the bed and cuddled him in her arms.[19] Lillian and Gloria retreated to the back sitting room to receive well-wishers, but Billy fled the house, crying hysterically. Jimmy and Ruth set out across the county in an automobile to notify Earl's friends who did not have telephones. One large black man named Ed dropped his head and sobbed on the steering wheel of his tractor when he heard the news.[20] The funeral service took place in the Plains Baptist Church three days later. Both the Baptist and Lutheran ministers officiated, an indication that the deceased was a man of distinction. Earl's family buried him in Lebanon Cemetery, a few miles south of Plains.[21]

It was midsummer and Earl had already extended credit to his customers for that crop year. Since he kept many of his business transactions in his head, his grief-stricken heirs depended on the goodwill of the debtors to pay what they owed. Lillian declined an offer to serve the remainder of Earl's term in the state legislature, but she did agree to complete his term on the school board.[22]

Earl had understood his family members and their needs quite well. He left an estate valued at about $400,000. He left to Lillian the Pond House and the ten acres of land on which it stood, all his town real estate, and the lucrative income from his government bonds—"Said Bonds and Real Estate to be sold at her death or her Marriage and divided Equally among my Four Children or their heirs." He designated funds for Ruth's and Billy's educations if they had not yet attended college, and he left $500 and his fire insurance agency to his faithful executive secretary, Nell Walters. Earl directed that the remainder of his property, including five thousand acres of farm- and timberlands, be sold and the proceeds divided equally among his wife and children. He appointed Jimmy his executor.[23]

Stunned by this new image of his father as a benevolent, secret philanthropist, Jimmy faced the most important emotional and professional crisis of his life. He had to decide how to carry on and expand the work of his demanding late father within the context of a lifestyle both comfortable and rewarding for Rosalynn and himself. Earl also left him a financial and political inheritance. Coming to terms with his father became a lifelong journey for the then twenty-nine-year-old son.

Earl Carter's death also confronted Jimmy with immediate, practical problems. The grieving, helpless faces of his family, and the awesome responsibility that now seemed to be his alone, posed a challenge. For prompt solace, he had inner strength, his Christian faith, his family, and especially Rosalynn. His strong, typically southern emotional attachment to the land of his childhood and his fierce determination to succeed made his decision easy.

While trying to comfort her husband, Rosalynn confronted a conflict of her own. She did not agree with Jimmy's decision to return to Plains. She resented it, argued against it, and even talked about divorce. Nevertheless, Jimmy stubbornly announced that he would resign from the Navy and go home. The opportunity afforded him the chance to develop three of the driving themes of his and his father's lives—to be his own boss, to make money, and to do good deeds.

Getting released from the Navy required time and political help. Since Carter was one of only two nuclear engineers completing *Seawolf*, he was more important to the Navy than the typical lieutenant. On August 17, he submitted his resignation to the secretary of the Navy. Because of his father's death, he said, he had the responsibility "of caring for the financial and personal interests of my mother and young brother...and several other families" who were dependent on his father's business.[24] His commanding officers noted that he was in good health, did not owe any money to the United States, and had always received top ratings and recommendations for promotion. The manager of the Schenectady Branch of the U.S. Atomic Energy Commission rather plaintively observed that Carter was undergoing training as a "prospective engineering officer" for *Seawolf* and that his resignation would leave the group with only one trained officer until the next summer.[25]

Carter sought help from Georgia's two senators and his own representative. Senator Richard B. Russell, Jr., merely asked that Carter's reasons be accepted and he be released from the Navy. Senator Walter F. George, who lived near Plains, noted that farmers in the area probably owed Earl Carter's estate more than $100,000, his businesses supplied "one-third of Sumter County," and the "only possible person to continue is his son, Lieutenant James E. Carter." Representative E. L. "Tick" Forrester of Georgia's Third District informed the chief of naval personnel that he "personally" knew that many farmers in Sumter County "were wholly dependent upon the late Mr. Carter and it is vital to that section of Georgia that his work be carried on." Forrester understood perfectly the relationship between white landowners and black laborers in his district.[26] On October 2, Jimmy received his release from active duty, and on October 10 he accepted an appointment as lieutenant (junior grade) in the United States Naval Reserve.[27]

The long shadow of Mr. Earl, at least in Rosalynn's mind, fell across their lives like prison bars. He would determine their future in ways they could not have imagined as they prepared to return home. Jimmy had a new image of his father, a new sense of opportunity, and a better understanding of the role of politics in his and his father's affairs. He was much like his father, who had returned from World War I to seek his fortune in the land of his youth.

Rosalynn saw it quite differently. The man in the Navy uniform she had married for both love and the adventure of taking her to the places she had seen only on maps now said he would put aside that uniform and take her back to that place she had left seven years earlier.

CHAPTER SEVEN

The Emergence of Rosalynn

A VERY ANGRY ROSALYNN did not want to return to Plains. Her husband had not asked her opinion about his career change, and she was trapped with three small children and no career of her own. She threatened to divorce Jimmy, but she packed sullenly while her ebullient husband bounced off to New York City to pick up his honorable discharge. Rosalynn and the children drove the family automobile from Schenectady to Washington, D.C., where Jimmy met them. When baby Jeff got a glimpse of his father standing near the Washington Monument, he became excited, fell in the car, and cut his tongue seriously enough to necessitate a frantic trip to the Children's Hospital.[1]

The next day, the young family visited "Tick" Forrester, the congressman who had written the letter that helped Carter gain release from the Navy. When Forrester, a small, arrogant man, condemned black people and berated residents of public housing projects, he caused Rosalynn to feel even more apprehensive about their return to Plains. She and Jimmy had black friends; they disagreed strongly with typical southern politicians and those whites who would preserve a segregated society that discriminated against blacks. The young Carters, who had no jobs and little money, expected to live in a public housing project in Plains. Rosalynn sat in stony silence for the remainder of the trip. She did not smile when Jimmy, on their arrival, cheerfully announced, "We're home."[2]

Settling into their new lives came easily for Jimmy, but Rosalynn required months to adjust. Visits with her mother and Miss Lillian made her feel that she and the children were in the way. She, Jimmy, and the children, ranging in age from one to six, lived with Miss Lillian for a few unhappy days until they could move to their own apartment. They found a public housing complex that rented to whites at $30 per month. Jimmy liked the fact that the apartment at 9-A Paschall Street was so cheap, and Rosalynn gave a relieved sigh that she had a place of her own.[3]

For weeks, Rosalynn remained gloomy. She put up bookshelves and set up the apartment, but she did not visit with the other wives and mothers who lived there. She cared for her children, but she withdrew from other family members. Jimmy tried to comfort her and to convince her that they had made the right move. Rosalynn feared domination by her mother and mother-in-law and disliked the small town bereft of recreational and cultural facilities. Her mother gently reminded her that Plains was a friendly place where everyone knew each other and that people were beginning to gossip about her aloofness. Rosalynn then mustered a smile when she passed old friends and neighbors, determined to show more interest in the town and its people, and decided that she could reclaim the independence and dignity she had enjoyed as a Navy wife.[4]

In Plains, one's social status depended on one's church. During the Navy years, Rosalynn had attended chapel with her husband and children, but she had kept her membership in the Plains Methodist Church. In the male-dominated society of Plains, however, a wife was expected to join her husband's church. At a revival service in 1954, Rosalynn dutifully agreed to join Jimmy's church. She made her decision, she said, because she thought it was important for all members of a family to attend the same church. She argued bitterly with the minister's wife, who insisted that Rosalynn deny her Methodist baptism by sprinkling and submit to the Baptist immersion. Rosalynn asserted her independence and refused to deny her Methodist baptism, but she acquiesced to immersion, and joined that church out of love for her family. Forty years later, Rosalynn admitted, "I joined the Baptist church with Jimmy, but I'm still a Methodist at heart."[5]

Finding a suitable place to live remained a problem for the Carters. In the fall of 1954 they rented Bobby Montgomery's house, a comfortable home near the Baptist church, but they could stay there only a year until the Montgomerys returned from Florida. In September 1956 they rented the Ed Stewart place, a large, wooden house built in 1840 and located on the Old Preston Road toward Lebanon Cemetery and Archery. As children they had thought it was haunted and walked around it through the woods rather than risk passing in front of it. Freed from childhood fears, Jimmy and Rosalynn repaired the roof, walls, and shutters themselves and added a modern kitchen.

The spacious dwelling with its large yard filled with blooming magnolia trees and camellia bushes, surrounded by a peach tree farm, gave Rosalynn the freedom she needed to begin to enjoy her new life in Plains. The house was cold and drafty in the winter but afforded the Carter boys space for pets and play. Seven-year-old Jack removed bricks from beside a chimney and discovered a secret room four feet deep and six feet wide. His parents speculated that it might have been a hiding place for Yankee soldiers during the Civil War, perhaps escapees from the notorious prison at Andersonville. Legend had it, too, that some Union soldiers had died there and their ghosts haunted the place. Amused by such stories, Jimmy and Rosalynn relaxed in the privacy of the old house and its large yard. They tried to buy the place, but the owner would not sell.[6]

Rosalynn's attitude about returning to Plains began to change. She and Jimmy nurtured their boys and pursued their own interests in art and literature. Since high school, when they both had come under the strong influence of Julia Coleman, they had appreciated art. In the Navy they had begun to paint. In the yard of their "haunted" house, together they set up easels under sunny skies and painted landscapes. Driven, creative people, in their new environment they found common bonds and ambitions. The relaxation and satisfaction they found in painting together would remain with them, and it foreshadowed a partnership in their business and public lives.[7]

Literature and poetry ranked higher than art in the young couple's lives, but Jimmy dug deeper than Rosalynn in search of meaning. He often found himself sitting on sacks of fertilizer in his downtown warehouse waiting for customers. To pass the time, he read an anthology of modern poetry.

In 1954, Carter discovered the work of Dylan Thomas. At first intrigued and disturbed by Thomas's poem "A Refusal to Mourn the Death by Fire of a Child in London," Carter finally saw the meaning in the last sentence: "After the first death there is no other." At his desk in the warehouse office, he diagrammed Thomas's sentences, searching for hidden meanings, and savored the Welshman's words.[8] Thomas, who died the same year as Earl, wrote about his love of humanity and praise for God. More important, he left the unfinished "Elegy" about his own dead father in which he wrote: "Until I die he will not leave my side." Carter discovered Thomas's poetry at the right moment for it to help him reconcile his own life with that of his late father.[9]

Carter especially liked to read novels and essays about the South. James Agee's *Let Us Now Praise Famous Men,* the poignant account of poor, struggling tenant farmers in Georgia during the Great Depression, became his favorite book. Although Carter had not been as poor as the people Agee described, the book reminded him of his childhood.[10]

Carter's favorite southern novelist, William Faulkner, became the South's first winner of the Nobel Prize for literature. Carter read all the Faulkner novels himself and to his children. He found within them the saga of the South's history from the decade before the Civil War through the 1950s. Through generations of family history, much of it fractured and unlovely, Faulkner chronicled in inimitable style the verities of the human heart, both divine and human forgiveness for sins, and the endurance and triumph of humanity in its black and white southern manifestations. Jimmy Carter thought that Faulkner "accurately analyzed . . . the fallibility of human beings and the basic weaknesses of mankind, and has encapsulated those struggles between good and evil, pride and humility, achievement and failure, perhaps better than any other Southern writer."[11] Those words that Carter used to describe Faulkner paint a self-portrait of himself. Although he never verbalized it at an early age, the creative vein in his own personality made Jimmy want to be a writer as well as an artist. Carter, his family, his ancestors, and his native society were precisely the kind of materials from which Faulkner created some of the world's greatest literature.

Meanwhile, Rosalynn read Carson McCullers. A native of nearby Columbus, McCullers portrayed in her books and stories a pantheon of the South's physically and mentally broken, alienated people who somehow managed to survive and to prevail. In *The Heart Is a Lonely Hunter, Member of the Wedding,* and *Ballad of the Sad Café,* Rosalynn found many of the types of people to whom she later would dedicate her public career. "I was moved by the compassion and understanding with which she wrote about her characters, almost all of whom were handicapped or alienated and lonely," Rosalynn said. She also found in McCullers's novels dozens of Faulknerian characters who, despite being social outcasts, managed to live meaningful and useful lives. Many of the stories were set only a few miles from where she had grown up and now lived.[12]

Although quite different in education, training, experience, and tastes from most of his neighbors, Carter adjusted easily to life in Plains. He blended into male hunting and fishing groups and into the agricultural and business world of his father. To be considered "a man" in his part of the country, one had to own dogs and to hunt. Jimmy loved to go hunting with the other men, and he could joke, curse, and drink with the best of them, but he did not get drunk.[13]

Jimmy intended to expand his father's operations and become the best agribusinessman in Georgia. He assumed that Rosalynn, like the other wives of Plains, would help him as soon as she was ready. He thrived on competition, and in his warehouse business he got plenty of it from Oscar Williams and his sons Frank and Albert. The Williams men had grown up three miles northwest of Plains on a farm similar to the Carters' in Archery. Oscar Williams owned and operated the Plains Cotton Warehouse, which bought and stored cotton and sold fertilizer and farm supplies.[14]

Williams's firm predated Earl's warehouse and was a larger operation when Jimmy first went into business in Plains. Despite what Jimmy called "a hot competition," the two families dealt with each other in a "friendly fashion." Deacons in the Baptist church, they called each other "Brother Frank, Brother Albert, and Brother Jimmy," but they were intensely competitive in business. Taking a personal interest in his customers, Carter offered friendlier service rather than the cheaper prices of the rival Williams family. Too small an operator to start a price war with the Williamses, Carter took his customers into his family. Sometimes he took several of them home unannounced to lunch. Rosalynn liked to prepare lunch and took a personal interest in the business and its clients.[15]

By mutual consent of the other family members, except Billy, Carter gained the controlling interest in his father's estate. He bought Ruth and Gloria's portions, making it possible for him to set up a private corporation of which he and Rosalynn owned 60 percent, Lillian 23, and Billy 17. Jimmy and Rosalynn became comanagers. Lillian, who had never been involved in her husband's businesses, did not like it when Jimmy declared Rosalynn an equal partner. Billy resented his older brother taking over a legacy that his father had reared him to think would be his.[16]

In 1954, when Carter filed his annual report as an inactive member of the Navy Reserves, he modestly described himself as someone who operated a "warehouse and farms," supervised up to twenty employees, provided "banking loans to local farmers," and earned an annual salary of $3,600. With each year, until his last report when he left the reserves in 1961, his financial accounts became more glowing until he confessed to being the owner-manager of ten large farms, a storage warehouse, a peanut-shelling plant, a grain elevator, a fertilizer distributorship, financier for at least one hundred farmers, and supervisor of fifty employees. He left unanswered the question about his annual salary.[17]

The young Carters used their substantial inheritance to build their wealth in less than a decade. In 1953, they could do nothing more than collect debts owed Earl. The next year, they earned only $200 from selling bags of fertilizer. Fiercely determined to succeed, Carter consulted more experienced farmers and his Uncle Alton—"Buddy"—who had been like a father to him since Earl had died.[18] Alton Carter farmed and operated a general store on Main Street; he also had looked after Jimmy's grandmother Carter until her death in 1939. What Uncle Buddy did not know Jimmy learned from the county agent and his own research. He read magazines and books and took courses at the Coastal Plain Experiment Station in nearby Tifton.[19] He planted a new variety of slash pine tree on his land near Preston, which eventually came to be named for him and became a Georgia timber crop.[20]

Both Carters kept busy; Jimmy walked the streets in khaki pants and work shoes like other farmers.[21] In 1955, Rosalynn began keeping the books for the Carter Warehouse. Jimmy tried to teach her, but "Jimmy didn't know how to keep books," she exclaimed. She borrowed accounting textbooks from a friend who taught the subject at a nearby vocational school and taught herself. She had a talent for business and enjoyed the challenge of keeping three sets of books on the family's nitrogen, peanut, and warehouse businesses.[22] She knew the financial details of the family operation better than Jimmy, studied the tax laws, and often instructed him about what they could and could not afford to do. She made herself an indispensable partner in the business and on occasion ran it alone when Jimmy went away to pursue religion and politics.

Rosalynn worked long hours, especially during the harvest season. She managed the budget for both the business and the family, putting her $300 monthly salary into a joint checking account with Jimmy's salary and doling out pocket money to him as he asked for it. Jimmy did physical labor, recruited customers, learned the latest techniques for planting cotton and peanuts, raised certified peanut seeds, and designed modern machinery. Rosalynn and Jimmy's partnership worked, as each complemented the labor of the other.[23]

By 1962, when they were still in their thirties, the Carters embarked on a streak of financial success. Lucky to have entered business in the prosperous 1950s and to have been given a generous start by Earl, in a dozen years they developed their farms and warehouse into a multimillion-dollar operation. Although they treated their black workers kindly, the availability of cheap black labor enhanced their profits. One employee, Calvin Blackmon, remembered, "I liked Mr. Carter. I thought he was a good man. And Lordy, I sacked a lot of peanuts."[24]

Instead of buying and reselling certified peanut seeds, Carter raised the seeds himself. He bought three more acres in downtown Plains and in 1959 expanded his warehouse at the corner of Main and Bond streets. He added a peanut-shelling and drying plant, which he designed and built with the help of P. J. Wise, and processed his and his neighbors' peanuts. In 1959 he joined the Georgia Crop Improvement Association, Inc., an organization for those who sold certified seed. He served as its president in 1961 and 1962 and became known throughout the state. By 1960, Carter's Warehouse was the third largest business in its tax district, ranking behind the convalescent home and the Williams family's cotton warehouse. The Carters were well positioned to pull ahead of their rival; in the following decade they could anticipate grossing about $2.5 million each year.[25]

Pull ahead they did the next year, when they added a $300,000 cotton gin. Since the Carters raised hundreds of acres of cotton, as well as peanuts, they could gin their own as well as that of the neighbors. Both producers and processors of the region's two major money crops, as well as suppliers of seeds and fertilizers, Jimmy and Rosalynn owned the largest agribusiness in town. With the help of Billy, still a minor partner, the Carters built a corn mill and, more important, added a liquid nitrogen business when that compound became the newest form of fertilizer. Indeed, Jimmy and Billy were featured on the cover of a leading farmers' magazine for their use of the most modern equipment and techniques on their extensive farms. But it was Jimmy and Rosalynn who owned majority interest in the business and masterminded its financial success. By 1970, the couple who had returned from the Navy with few assets in 1953 earned $137,000 in a good year, and by 1976, their personal assets topped $800,000.[26]

Rosalynn, when she was not at the warehouse, cared for their three sons, Jackie, Chip, and Jeff. She worked at the warehouse in the mornings, leaving Jeff, who was too young to attend school, with a young black woman. Once Jeff was in school, Rosalynn often spent time alone on the back porch with the newspaper and a cup of coffee before going to the warehouse. She went home at noon to prepare lunch for the family. After school, she allowed Jack and Chip to visit the warehouse, play on the bags of fertilizer, or ride in the big trucks with their daddy. Although black women sometimes helped her at home, especially with Jeff, Rosalynn did not turn her children over to nannies as Miss Lillian had. From time to time, the two grandmothers, aunts, and uncles also helped.[27]

Jimmy's sisters did not share the new life Jimmy and Rosalynn found in Plains. Ruth Carter Stapleton retreated into her life in North Carolina, and Gloria Spann became a "motorcycle queen."[28] Her son "Toadie," an emotionally unbalanced boy, hated his mother and stepfather. As a preteen, he smoked, drank, stole his Uncle Billy's car, and got suspended from school. After neither psychiatrists nor Jimmy's prayers helped, Jimmy invited him to live for a few weeks with his family. "Toadie" taught Chip, age nine, to smoke, drink, and curse, and he later confessed that he liked to peep at his Aunt Rosalynn when she changed clothes. Jimmy ordered him out of the house but allowed him to work at the warehouse. A few years later, "Toadie" disappeared, resurfacing in California as a criminal and drug addict.[29]

Billy resented his older brother's paternalism and developed a severe case of sibling rivalry. In 1955, immediately on graduation from high school, he joined the Marines, married his teenage girlfriend, Sybil Spires, and left Plains. He later returned for two years but soon departed to attend Emory University. Although intelligent, he lacked discipline and drank too much. Owing to poor grades, Emory dismissed him after three years. Billy then drifted about the country with his wife and children, working at odd jobs. He retained his 17 percent interest in the family business and eventually returned to Plains, where he and Sybil reared their six children. An alcoholic, he worked with Jimmy at the warehouse and on the farms. He operated his own service station, which became a town meeting and drinking place.[30]

Plains was not large enough for both Jimmy's mother and his wife. Lillian discovered a very different Rosalynn who returned from the Navy. Rosalynn had no intention of lapsing into her youthful dependence on her family and in-laws. After she and Lillian had lived in the same house for a few days, Lillian said bluntly that there was "no house big enough for two women to live together." When pressed by journalists in 1976, Lillian declined to discuss Rosalynn, but she did reveal: "Rosalynn loves me as much as I love her."[31]

The two women could not have been more different. Rosalynn shared everything with Jimmy from the rearing of the children to the operation of the business.

Jimmy elevated her to a position in his life that Lillian could never have imagined with Earl. Lillian felt alone after her husband died and her youngest son had left town. Rosalynn had a full life in Plains, which Lillian seemed to resent. "Either she or I had to go," she remembered pointedly; "So I left."[32]

Lillian accepted a job as housemother for the Kappa Alpha fraternity at Auburn University in Alabama. She drove away from Plains in a new white Cadillac, because Jimmy did not want anyone to think that she had taken that job because she needed the money. Although she enjoyed the work and the company of the students, the loud Saturday night parties got on her nerves so badly that it became the job of one of the brothers "to talk [Miss Lillian] out of quitting every Sunday morning."[33] Six years later, she resigned to become the administrator of the Blakely Nursing Home in a small town about forty miles southwest of Plains. Embarrassed to discover that many of the home's residents were younger than she, Lillian quit after two years and passed her time in Plains, visiting her family, going on religious retreats, and taking vacations with relatives.[34]

Jimmy continued to develop a busier and fuller life in Plains. In 1955, he joined the Plains Lions Club, an organization that helped the blind. "Lion Jimmy" rose through every office of the local chapter to become district governor in 1968–69. Under his leadership, the Lions built a swimming pool in Plains, promoted charities, and erected street signs. The Lions had 208 clubs in Georgia, and Carter visited them all. He became so influential among them that he helped organize the National Collegiate Athletic Association Peach Bowl and thus achieved statewide recognition. Rosalynn shared the activities of the Lions, attended state meetings in Atlanta with him, and found that she could live in Plains and sometimes enjoy the urban culture and excitement of Atlanta as well.[35] Jimmy loved Plains and Sumter County. When the Georgia Power Company sponsored a "Better Hometown Contest," he helped Plains win it. He taught Sunday school and became a deacon and a scoutmaster. He accepted appointments to the Sumter County hospital, library, and school boards, thus becoming well known in Americus. He formed extensive business and political connections and used his position as president of the Georgia Planning Association to get state money for the county.[36]

Carter joined more and more organizations. He chaired the Sumter County Future Farmers and Homemakers of America Committee in 1956, presided at state Lions Club meetings, and hosted a Plains Baptist Brotherhood fish supper.

He and Rosalynn were active in the school's PTA, and she taught a children's Sunday school class and served as a Cub Scout den mother.[37]

Rosalynn had forgiven Jimmy for bringing her back to Plains and went everywhere with him. As Earl and Lillian had done, the two hosted dinner parties and dances at the Pond House. Unlike Earl and Lillian, they did everything together. They took a speed-reading course, dancing lessons, played golf, went fishing, and attended stock car races in South Carolina and Florida. Calling themselves the "Three Musketeers," they became friends with John and Marjorie Pope (and later Betty Pope, after Marjorie's death and John's remarriage) and Billy and Irene Horne. The couples spun around the dance halls of Albany and Americus on Saturday nights. They liked to jitterbug, rumba, waltz, and square dance. To join the Sumter Squares, they had to promise to use deodorant and not eat onions on the evenings of the dances. They went to Cuba and New Orleans to fish and listen to jazz. In New Orleans, Rosalynn confessed, she and Jimmy drank wine at lunch for the first time.

Although heavy drinking and even some adultery characterized their social group, Jimmy and Rosalynn rejected the adultery and drank in moderation. They joined the country club in Americus and generally associated with wealthy people. Frantically busy with her family, the business, and the party circuit, Rosalynn came to realize that she was having more fun than she had had in the Navy.[38] Now she and her husband were big fish in a steadily growing pond.

Jimmy and Rosalynn returned to Plains at the beginning of a decade when race relations and the civil rights movement dominated American politics. The Carters held attitudes different from those of the majority of their white neighbors. Jimmy had grown up among black people in Archery, his mother cared for blacks as well as whites, and both he and Rosalynn had associated with blacks as equals in the Navy. At his warehouse one day, Carter let a black woman with a wagonload of peanuts she wanted to sell go ahead of white male farmers. The farmers bristled at the idea of letting a black person, even a female, go ahead of whites.[39] In 1954, the first full year the Carters were back home, the U.S. Supreme Court ruled in *Brown v. Board of Education* that African Americans had the constitutional right to full integration into public schools. Racial integration had existed in the armed services since President Truman had mandated it in 1947, but now the Court challenged the social mores and economic traditions of much of the nation, including Plains and Sumter County.

White southerners responded to the *Brown* decision with a plan for "massive resistance." By hastily building separate but equal schools for black students, they hoped to block integration. A member of the Sumter County Board of Education from December 1955 until January 1963, and its chairman from 1960 through 1962, Carter faced the issue head-on. Like so many southern politicians and businessmen who feared change, he attempted to improve the plight of black students within a segregated society. In 1956, when he learned that white students rode buses while black students walked, he supported a controversial motion to relocate the black school more conveniently for black students, but it would mean black and white students would walk the same streets at the same time. When whites protested, he agreed to move the school a greater distance from the white school to "avoid friction" between the races in Leslie and De Soto, rural communities in Sumter County. He later changed his mind, arguing for the original site because it would be more cost-efficient and promising to "minimize simultaneous traffic" of white and black students.[40] His critics later used the episode to argue that he had yielded to white pressure for the move to prevent the integration of the schools.[41] Carter may have thought that the white protesters would be overruled, or he may have simply yielded to them to keep the peace.[42]

In the late 1950s, Carter tried to improve education for African Americans within a segregated framework. He belonged to that large group of southerners who sometimes argued that their best chance to prevent integration was to make blacks' facilities truly separate but equal. Carter sought to provide better transportation for African-American students. He got the board to approve running water both for the Plains school and the Negro elementary school in Leslie and to purchase a used piano for the black high school. After he became chairman of the board in 1960, he bought four new typewriters for the white school and transferred four old ones to the "Colored High School." His copious notes on the minutes of the School Board meetings indicate that the "Negro schools" had met the requirements for accreditation by November 6, 1961, and that despite a financially lean year, he was considering possible improvements at "Negro H.S. Athletic field."[43]

Carter did not demand integration or openly defy the traditions of his region. The first black children did not enter Sumter County's previously all-white schools until 1965, eleven years after the *Brown* decision. By then, the national civil rights legislation had been implemented and accepted sufficiently that

Sumter County escaped volatile disturbances such as those that occurred in 1957 in Little Rock, Arkansas, and elsewhere in the late 1950s and early 1960s.

Carter dealt with other matters related to the school budget, hiring teachers, and improving curricula. Since he and Rosalynn had three sons in the school, they had a personal interest in how it operated. "We would like for Jackie," Jimmy wrote with reference to his oldest son, "to have 4 years English, math and science and in addition 4 years social studies, 2 years language, ½–1 year typing, plus spelling & phys. ed."[44]

Nevertheless, the race issue engulfed the state in debate about the schools. Governor Herman Talmadge had threatened to abolish the state's public schools before he would allow them to be integrated. His successor in 1958, Ernest Vandiver, was elected to office under the campaign slogan "No, not one!"—a promise he intended to keep that there would be no racial integration in Georgia.

In 1955, less extreme white southerners who favored nonviolent resistance to the integration of the races had organized the White Citizens Council. Beginning in the Mississippi Delta, the movement swept across the South, reaching Plains at the time the Carter business began to flourish. In Plains, the police chief and the Baptist minister joined others to visit the Carters at their office. When the Carters refused to join, the visitors offered to pay the $5 membership fee and threatened to boycott their business if they did not. Jimmy, with a flash of his famous temper, tore up the membership application and flushed it down the toilet. The miffed whites organized a boycott, but it had little impact on the Carters' business. The all-white country club in Americus, however, expelled them.[45]

Determined to protect his thriving business, Carter felt he could not afford to become identified with those who favored absolute equality between the races. His relationship with a Christian coalition that had built an interracial and socialistic farm in 1942 about four miles from the Carter Warehouse became shrouded in controversy. Called Koinonia (Greek for fellowship), the farm had been established by Clarence Jordan, a white Baptist minister from Georgia who held a doctorate in New Testament Greek and an undergraduate degree in agriculture. He and his wife Florence returned from a missionary assignment in Burma to move into a small house on the 440-acre farm on the Dawson Highway (GA 49). Committed to teaching poor blacks and whites how to farm, cook, sew, and generally improve their lives, Koinonia maintained its isolated, peaceful existence until the *Brown* decision in 1954. After *Brown*, it suffered violent attacks by white citizens who accused Jordan of advocating racial integration. Anonymous ruffians riddled the farm's sign with bullet holes, dynamited its roadside produce stand, chopped down its fruit trees, and fired bullets into the premises after dark.

Clarence Jordan remained calm, but increasing numbers of whites began to ostracize him in the 1950s. Parents of the children at Koinonia appealed to the Sumter County Board of Education, headed by Carter, to make the Americus schools admit their children. The board refused. No record survives that would reveal Carter's involvement in that meeting.[46]

Clarence Jordan was a jovial and decent Baptist minister who had been present at the revival service when Rosalynn had joined the Plains Baptist Church. Rosalynn liked him, and his presence at that service had made her passage under the water into the Baptist fold more tolerable. Jimmy, however, did not want to jeopardize his business by becoming too friendly with the hated Koinonia community. What relationship he had with Koinonia remains lost in the question of whether his or Florence Jordan's memory is correct. Florence recalled that Carter did not visit Koinonia or speak about it, but Carter claimed that he went there several times to try to sell them the products and services of his warehouse. He may have had communications with Clarence that Mrs. Jordan did not know about. Jordan, who bought his supplies wholesale, could not afford Carter's prices, but he did hire the Carter Warehouse to shell his seed peanuts.[47]

Rosalynn took a dramatic stand for justice toward Koinonia. When no one else would, she befriended Jack Singletary, a white man who had lived at Koinonia before buying his own farm at nearby Smithville. Jack retained his contact with Koinonia and endured the epithet "white nigger" from his neighbors. A graduate of the Naval Academy, he had served time in prison as a conscientious objector after World War II. Jimmy and Rosalynn did not know him at Annapolis, but they met him after they returned to Plains and openly supported him.[48]

Singletary had a young son who was terminally ill with leukemia, the disease that had taken the life of Rosalynn's father. Despite Singletary's relative poverty and tragic circumstances, the Plains Baptist Church and the majority of the area's white community shunned him. When the child died, Rosalynn took the family a baked ham and stayed for the funeral. The Plains Baptist minister feared he would be driven from town if he officiated at it, and neither he nor any other minister would conduct the service. Rosalynn joined the Singletary family and their friends for a simple burial at Koinonia with no officiating minister. After the burial, Rosalynn visited her Baptist minister and shamed him into going to the grave site and conducting a service. She stood up to the Baptist church, the segregationists, and many of the most prominent leaders of the county who wanted Jordan to close down his farm and leave the area.[49]

Jimmy and Rosalynn intended to stay in Plains. In 1961, they built their home on Woodland Drive. Designed by Albany architect Hugh Gaston and erected by master craftsmen, it is a large, brick, ranch-style house, the finest in Plains. Although other rising middle-class families built ranch-style houses, they did not employ architects, insist that the corners of the doors and windows fit so perfectly that they would not need moldings, or hang chandeliers in the dining room. The house had four bedrooms, living and dining rooms, a large den, a screened porch, and a garage. The two-acre lot had space for dog pens and a tennis court, and later a patio and a new garage. Jimmy made certain that the house did not have columns on the front in the antebellum style; it was thoroughly modern and convenient, with more than three thousand square feet of living space. Jimmy crafted some of the furniture himself, and Rosalynn was her own interior decorator.[50]

Their new home became the center of the Carters' family life. The boys now ranged in age from nine to fourteen. Jimmy demanded that they all be at the supper table sharply at six, but he allowed them to read and talk during the meal. Often he played games with them by setting up debates and arguing viewpoints he did not believe. When Rosalynn became confused and frustrated by the conversations, he lovingly teased her by saying, "Now, Rosie!"

A strict disciplinarian like his father, Jimmy spanked his sons with switches and paddles. Although he ordered them not to smoke cigarettes, they did so. When one child, refused to do things Jimmy's way, according to sister Ruth, "Jimmy just couldn't understand him." Jimmy worked hard at teaching them, however; he helped them with their homework. The oldest son, Jack, attended the Governor's Honors Program at Wesleyan College in Macon in 1964 and became a National Merit Scholarship finalist. Miraculously, he escaped serious injury in 1964 when a small pistol with which he and a friend were playing discharged and the bullet hit him in the neck.

Jimmy taught his sons to fish and hunt, took them to church and on vacations, replicating his own childhood with Earl. He and Rosalynn took them to the Florida coast often to fish and swim. One year, 1959 or 1960, they took a trip to Washington, D.C., camping along the way. When each boy reached age twelve, Jimmy required him to do hard physical labor at the warehouse and on the farm after school on weekdays and Saturdays. He and Rosalynn paid them for the work, but they were expected to buy their own clothes and to save money for college. Jimmy later confessed that he was too severe on them. Rosalynn was undoubtedly the more gentle parent.[51]

Less than a decade after their return to Plains, Rosalynn had emerged as an indispensable member of the family and community. She joined Jimmy in a campaign to build a consolidated county high school for the five hundred students then scattered in three different schools. As chairman of the Sumter County School Board, Jimmy analyzed studies of school systems and decided that Sumter County needed one model high school where students could study basic courses, use science laboratories, learn foreign languages, and take music education. Winning the vote to consolidate the schools became their passion.

The Carters lost the campaign, however, to the opposition that had been organized by Carter's cousin Hugh. People in rural areas voted against it because they did not want the school, which would be located in Americus, to be so far from where their children lived. Some opponents argued that consolidation would be an excuse for racial integration. Neighbors, relatives, and warehouse customers stopped speaking to Jimmy and Rosalynn. They heard the final vote announced at a high school basketball game they were attending. They stopped at the warehouse on their way home. A crude, hand-printed sign attached to the door proclaimed: "COONS AND CARTERS GO TOGETHER."[52] Angry but unbowed, Carter resolved to seek a higher office, and Rosalynn was ready to help him.

CHAPTER EIGHT

First Campaign

IN THE EARLY 1960S, Carter used his business and civic connections as an entree into politics. His mother thought he "got bored" with the agribusiness, but his minister warned him that the political life would not be easy.[1] Carter responded that he could serve more people as a politician than any minister could reach.[2] He got his first lesson in politics when he fought a pitched battle to become a deacon in his church. Because he had argued for the legal sale of alcoholic beverages in Sumter County, the church refused to elect him deacon. One old timer wryly noted that "Jimmy knew...the bootleggers." In 1962, however, the congregation overlooked the wicked ways of "Brother Jimmy" and elected him deacon.[3]

On October 1, 1962, his thirty-eighth birthday, Jimmy told Rosalynn that he planned to run for the state senate. Once she recovered from her surprise, Rosalynn liked the idea and soon discovered that she loved planning political strategy, campaigning, and winning, as much as she loved her home and business. Unbeknownst to both her and Jimmy, she was also very good at it, making it possible for their marriage to evolve into a political partnership rare in American history.[4] They entered politics at the time two changes revolutionized Georgia and the nation. The civil rights movement of the 1950s and 1960s gave unprecedented opportunities to African Americans and frightened many whites who did not want such changes, and the demise of the county unit system radically altered the election process in southwestern Georgia. The Carters sat out the former and took advantage of the latter.

The civil rights movement erupted with shocking force in nearby Albany, the largest city in the region. Students at the all-black Albany State College were joined by Martin Luther King, Jr., of Atlanta in massive protests demanding the integration of the city. Known as the Albany Movement, the effort failed, but it served notice that African Americans would no longer be complacent about their traditional place in Georgia society.[5] The Carters ignored the Albany Movement, but future politicians would need black votes to win.

The demise of the county unit system, the very system that had placed Mr. Earl in the state legislature in 1953 made it possible for his son to win a senate seat. On March 26, 1962, in the case of *Baker v. Carr*, the U.S. Supreme Court decreed "one man, one vote" the law of the land. The Court ruled that the Fourteenth Amendment protected equality in legislative apportionment and courts could accept cases that challenged whether states had equitably drawn their legislative districts. States like Georgia, where the system enabled white rule, faced a major upheaval. The county unit system had prevailed in Georgia since 1868, when the Republican-dominated legislature had written a constitution that called for indirect elections of state officers. Popular votes counted only within the county. Under the Reconstruction-era constitution, the eight largest counties, regardless of their population, each cast six votes. About thirty smaller ones each cast four, and more than a hundred had two votes each.[6]

The county unit system penalized minorities and cities. It was a convenient vehicle to nullify the ballots of the few African Americans who voted in the 1950s. By mid-twentieth century, Atlanta's densely populated Fulton County had less representation than the state's sparsely populated southwestern counties. In rural counties, such as Quitman, with small white populations, local bosses controlled the electorate and defied the law with impunity.

In Atlanta, unknown politicians and judges spoke out. On April 2, 1962, Morris Abram, an attorney from Fitzgerald in South Georgia, filed *Sanders v. Gray* in the North Georgia Federal District Court. James O'Hear Sanders, a defeated candidate for the state senate from the Georgia coast, sued James Gray, state chair of the Democratic party, and Ben Fortson, secretary of state, on the grounds that the county unit system had cost him the election even though he had received a majority of popular votes. Segregationist governor Ernest Vandiver, Democratic gubernatorial candidate Marvin Griffin, and Chairman Gray all stood fast in favor of the county unit system.

Because the U.S. Supreme Court had mandated judicial action, the North Georgia District Court appointed a panel of three federal judges to hear arguments in the case. Elbert P. Tuttle, senior judge on the court of appeals, chaired the group. Well known for his sympathy with civil rights groups, he welcomed the chance to dismantle a political system that discriminated against blacks.[7] Frank Hooper, the federal district judge for North Georgia, and Griffin Bell of Americus completed the panel. Tuttle and Hooper were expected to oppose the county unit system, but Bell refused to comment until he heard the argument from Sanders's attorney. When Abram attempted to inject the issue of black voters into the case, Bell declared it to be irrelevant. Bell, a distant relative of Rosalynn, was as notoriously loyal to the Democratic party as he was conservative. A "yellow dog" Democrat, he supported the party even if it nominated liberal candidates such as Kennedy. He had chaired John F. Kennedy's successful 1960 campaign in Georgia, and Kennedy had rewarded him with an appointment to the federal bench. On April 28, the judges decided in favor of James Sanders and thus demolished the county unit system.

The ensuing chaos split the Georgia Democrats into bitter factions, creating an opportunity for a new type of politician. When a panel of federal judges threatened to redistrict the legislature without legislative action, Governor Vandiver announced that he would call the lawmakers into special session to work out how that state would obey the federal mandate. In the vigorous debate over the governor's intention to call the special session, president pro tem of the senate, Carl Sanders, a candidate for the Democratic nomination for governor, agreed with Vandiver that the state should obey. Former governor Marvin Griffin—also, again, a candidate—wanted to defy the government and fight for the county unit system. Powerful U.S. Senator Richard Russell and his junior colleague Herman Talmadge, son of Ole Gene, threw their weight against the Vandiver-Sanders faction.[8]

The debate simmered until the Democratic primary on September 12, 1962. Garland Byrd, a former classmate of Jimmy at Georgia Southwestern and progressive on social issues, suffered a heart attack and dropped out of the race. The conservative former governor Marvin Griffin, who favored segregation and the county unit system, lost to the more progressive Carl Sanders. As the Democratic nominee, Sanders was assured of winning the governorship in the general election. Sanders announced that he would cooperate with incumbent governor Vandiver to redistrict both the house and the senate. On September 27, Vandiver called the legislature into special session to reapportion the senate. The legislature enacted a plan for redistricting, and Vandiver signed it.[9]

Georgia redrew some of its legislative district lines, added more counties to each district, and made the senate seats permanent instead of rotating them among counties within the districts. As a result, a senate seat became a greater prize than it had been under the old system. The new Fourteenth Senatorial District included Sumter, Webster, Terrell, Randolph, Quitman, Chattahoochee, and Stewart counties, which meant that it stretched from Americus west to the Alabama state line and encompassed most of the area in which Jimmy and Rosalynn and their many relatives owned property. Although Homer Moore of Richland had recently been elected to the senate seat, the addition of more counties to the district necessitated a new election.

Carter perceived a dual opportunity. The divisions within the state Democratic Party created the possibility for a newcomer to play the factions against each other for his own political gain. District Fourteen, which included Sumter and the six smaller counties, had no obvious candidate because Homer Moore had not built a constituency in Sumter or the more populated section of the new district. Carter seized his chance.[10]

The Carters analyzed the white power structure of their area. They had voted for Sanders and could expect the support of the governor-elect. With fast political maneuvers comparable to the twists and turns for which they had become known in the ballrooms and square dance halls of South Georgia, they molded their politics exactly as they had created their lucrative business. Carter said little about issues, and least of all about the divisive topic of race.

With the election only fifteen days away, Carter announced in the Americus newspaper that he believed himself to be "well qualified" to serve as state senator. The newspaper supported him, and his family and friends swung into action. Rosalynn designed a poster with Jimmy's picture and the words "CARTER" and "SENATOR" in letters bold enough to be seen at a distance. From the peanut warehouse she telephoned people whose names were on the Sumter County voters' list, asked for their support, and if they gave it, asked them to call others.[11]

Some friends, who joked that Carter was running for the senate to get off the school board, were delighted to help him. Billy Blair, whose father owned the local newspaper, provided media coverage. John Pope, a wealthy manufacturer of burial vaults, volunteered to help. Warren Fortson, an attorney whose brother

Ben was Georgia's secretary of state, passionately wanted Carter to win and had the legal savvy and political connections to help him do it.

The campaign itself became a family affair. Lillian, Gloria, and the two oldest Carter sons handed out cards. When not at the warehouse, Jimmy and Rosalynn devoted every spare minute to the campaign. Jimmy shook hands and talked to anyone who would listen, asked radio stations to interview him on the air, and made his first brief, nervous appearance on television at a station in Columbus. Since he was district governor of the Lions Club, members of fifty-four affiliates in southwestern Georgia knew him. His warehouse customers came from four of the seven counties in the district.[12]

Carter evaded controversial topics but campaigned for better education and good government. The same newspaper that carried the notice of his candidacy also reported that two people had been killed in a race riot the night before on the campus of the University of Mississippi after James Meredith had enrolled in that bastion of segregation. Carter did not mention that episode, which attracted worldwide attention, or comment on the first two black students who had been admitted to the University of Georgia under court order earlier in 1962. He remembered that he had lost the vote for a consolidated county school partly because so many of his relatives and neighbors thought it would be an integrated school. He took the high ground of government reform and personal honesty, but he soon learned that those issues would not determine the election.

Carter's opponent, Homer Moore, who had won the election before redistricting, announced that he would be a candidate in the new district. Active in his community and well liked, Moore, sixteen years older than Jimmy, was from Lillian Carter's hometown of Richland in Stewart County. A wealthy farmer, he owned a warehouse similar to Carter's and competed for some of the same customers. Since Moore did not operate a cotton gin, his economic rivalry with Carter was minimal, and the two men were cordial to each other.[13]

Although Moore seemed honest, the Carters soon found reason to accuse others involved in the election of mischief and fraud. On Election Day, Rosalynn's cousin Ralph Balkcom, school superintendent of Quitman County, called to tell her that a local boss planned to rig the primary election at the courthouse in Georgetown. Jimmy asked his friend John Pope from Americus and a reporter from the *Columbus Ledger-Enquirer* to go to Georgetown and observe the poll. The reporter apparently knew what was happening and had no intention of reporting it. Without assistance from the local press, Pope challenged the local boss, Sheriff Joe Hurst, who planned to control the Quitman County election as he had done for almost thirty years since he had served as county commissioner in 1935. A power broker in Atlanta, Hurst had served in the State Highway and Revenue departments, as commissioner of agriculture, and for one term in 1949 as state representative. He could deliver Quitman's two unit votes to the candidate of his choice. In 1962 he brazenly told Homer Moore's campaign manager, Sam Singer, that he intended to stuff the ballot box.[14]

Without shame or fear of the consequences, Hurst managed the voters and the votes to suit himself. Since blacks were prevented from voting by Jim Crow laws, he ignored them. A small group of educated whites would oppose him, but they could not determine the election. He had convinced the white people who received welfare payments that he controlled their checks. Fully involved in her husband's outrageous machinations, his wife used her position as welfare director to have welfare checks delivered to Hurst's post office box; Hurst then personally distributed them to the recipients. On Election Day, he and his helpers denied the secret ballot, told voters to strike Carter's name from the ballot, destroyed other ballots and registration rolls, and stuffed the box with up to six ballots at a time, many of them "cast" by dead people. When Pope protested, Hurst replied, "No one has ever told me how to run this county and especially no one from Sumter County."[15] There were only 333 stubs in the ballot book, but Moore carried the county by a vote of 360 to 136. Pleased with the results, Moore declared that he had the greatest respect for his opponent, who had carried only Sumter and Chattahoochee counties.[16]

Jimmy and Rosalynn refused to accept the results. He researched legal issues, and she analyzed the local politics. They called for a recount and hoped to prevent the state Democratic convention in Macon from certifying Moore as the party's candidate. Leaving Rosalynn to operate the warehouse, Jimmy went to Americus, where he began a vigorous campaign in the newspaper to expose the fraud. From there, he traveled to Macon with Pope.

In Macon, Carter and Pope found that no one was interested in the grievances of an obscure defeated candidate. The convention routinely endorsed the men who had been selected in the primaries. Besides, all eyes were focused on governor-elect Carl Sanders. A native of Augusta, Sanders was a sophisticated attorney, whom many believed to be fair. Jimmy had never met him and made no effort to do so after he learned that his mission to Macon lay in ruins.[17]

Returning home, Jimmy sought the help of Warren Fortson, his friend and attorney, who disliked crooked power brokers. Fortson had successfully handled a similar case when he had helped Tom Marshall win a contested election as superior court judge. Taking up Carter's case, Fortson collected thirty affidavits from people in Georgetown who said they had witnessed illegal activities at the polling place. Jimmy then stood on the courthouse steps in Georgetown and announced to a small, friendly group that he would both demand a recount and expose the fraud that had taken place three days earlier.[18]

Jimmy needed the help of attorneys, judges, and newspapers. His cousin Don Carter of the *Macon Telegraph* recommended investigative reporter John Pennington with the *Atlanta Journal,* a Sumter County native with a passion for justice. For his attorney, with Fortson's help, Jimmy chose Charles Kirbo, a Bainbridge native, who had become a partner in the prestigious Atlanta law firm King and Spaulding. Kirbo thought it too small a matter too far from Atlanta, but his former law partner Griffin Bell and his old University of Georgia classmate Don Carter urged him to help Jimmy. Kirbo found Carter "young," "tanned," and "timid," but since they were from the same part of the state, "I told him I was fixing to see what we could do."[19] Kirbo introduced Carter to David Gambrell, a junior member of the firm who would do most of the work.

Kirbo kept his eye on Carter. He was amazed at the man he had been asked to help. Later, Kirbo said he found Jimmy to be "an unusual person." He "exuded confidence," was "simple" but also "sophisticated." Likewise, Kirbo had never met a family quite like Jimmy's. They worked together, they "lived very simply," and they had "a lot of nice things, but he was tight and very careful with his money."[20] Carter had found a great legal friend in Kirbo and leaned on him heavily for advice. Kirbo liked to keep in the shadows himself, but he became Carter's number one adviser and behind-the-scenes confidant.

With Kirbo at their backs, despite a Hurst man's threat to burn Carter's warehouse to the ground, Jimmy and Rosalynn pressed for the October 22 recount. The recount committee consisted of Homer's representative, Sam Singer, Jimmy's representative, Billy Horne, and Mitchell County's senior superior court judge, Carl E. Crow. A tough and honest jurist who had once listened to the arguments of young attorney Charles Kirbo in Bainbridge, Crow was now an old man serving the Dougherty Judicial Circuit. He spit tobacco juice frequently, favored short testimonies, never showed emotion, and kept attorneys and their clients guessing until he announced his decisions.[21]

John Pennington published a series of searing articles in the *Atlanta Journal*. He decried an election in which "the poll manager told voters who to vote for" and in which a five-inch hole in the top of the ballot box made it easy to remove ballots. He discovered there were more votes than voters and dead persons and prisoners had cast ballots in alphabetical order. Numerous witnesses came forward to testify to the corruption, Pennington wrote. When Judge Crow appeared in Georgetown to examine the ballot box, he found the voting rolls and stubs missing and discovered 102 votes that had all been cast for Moore neatly rolled and bound with a rubber band.[22]

On November 2, 1962, sitting tensely and holding hands in the courthouse, Jimmy and Rosalynn listened to the proceedings. On that day, the Associated Press reporter referred to the bedraggled candidate as "Jerry" Carter in a front-page story carried by the Americus newspaper. The Associated Press reporter noted ominously that George D. Stewart, state Democratic secretary, had declined to comment and to act until he had heard from his subcommittee, which had not yet met. Meanwhile, the drama came to its conclusion in Georgetown.[23]

Kirbo, who had grown up virtually on the steps of the Bainbridge courthouse, was just seven years older than Carter, a graduate of the University of Georgia Law School, a World War II army veteran, and one of the best courtroom lawyers in the state. A slow talker, he had a sharp mind and knew the law. Speaking deliberately in an intimate conversational style, Kirbo, a large, clumsy man, talked about how under current Georgia law politicians could steal an election just like chicken thieves dragging a brush behind them to wipe out their tracks. He casually suggested to the immobile, cantankerous, spitting judge that since records did not survive to determine what ballots had been placed in the Georgetown box, that box should be thrown out entirely. Crow agreed with him; he slowly announced that the committee had voted two to one, Moore's representative being in the minority, that the Georgetown box should not be counted. If the decision were upheld by the state Democratic committee and the Georgetown Democratic Executive Committee, Carter would win the primary 2,811 to 2,746. Later that night, Carter, Warren Fortson, and other male friends drank deeply from a bottle of Old Crow bourbon.[24]

Carter still faced a long and uncertain route to the state senate. Kirbo traveled to Augusta to get governor-elect Carl Sanders to sign documents declaring Carter the Democratic nominee from the Fourteenth District. Unknown to Kirbo, his mission had been made easier by Brooks Pennington, a mutual friend of Sanders and Carter but no relation to the journalist. In 1962 when Carter had become president of the Georgia Crop Improvement Association, Pennington, owner of a large grass seed business near Augusta, had been elected president of the Georgia Seedman's Association, thus bringing the two men into a mutually beneficial business relationship. Carter had already called Pennington and asked him to intercede with Sanders. Likewise, J. B. Fuqua, chairman of the state Democratic committee, had signed papers declaring Carter the winner.

Sanders accepted the chairman's decision and was waiting for the papers when Kirbo arrived. Moore's attorneys appeared hours later, but Sanders told them that it was too late.[25] Sanders later said that he had signed the papers not only to break up the dynasty in Quitman County but also to "set an example, that we would not allow local Democratic committees to conduct the elections unless they were done fairly, openly, and within the provisions of the law."[26]

Meanwhile, Joe Hurst, as chairman of the Quitman County Democratic Committee, had filed an injunction that Judge Crow's decision be postponed until after further hearings. Moore, too, had good attorneys in the persons of Jesse Bowles and George Busbee. Moore announced that his name would be on the ballot for the general election. Although it was Sunday, Kirbo and Fortson filed an injunction against Hurst's committee, while Jimmy, Rosalynn, and a few friends raced from county to county stamping Jimmy's name on the ballots. The matter had to be settled the next day, Monday, before the general election the following Tuesday. Superior court judge Tom Marshall heard the case.

Judge Marshall himself had once won a contested election with the help of Kirbo and Fortson, but he had also been a classmate of Jesse Bowles, Moore's attorney. He called ordinaries from all seven counties to meet at the Sumter County Courthouse in Americus. When several of them declined to make the trip, Marshall ordered the sheriffs to bring them. At 6 P.M. on Monday, November 5, with the polls scheduled to open at 7 A.M. Tuesday, Judge Marshall decided that neither the name of Moore nor Carter should be on the ballot; the election should be entirely a write-in contest. The ordinaries in Sumter and Quitman counties, however, who thought Jimmy should have won, left his name on the ballot. Judge Marshall did not take action against them, nor did Moore ask him to do so.

Carter's friends ran a half-page advertisement in the *Americus Times-Recorder* on Election Day instructing his supporters how to vote for him in counties where his name was on the ballot and in counties where it was not. They reminded the voters that a vote for Jimmy Carter was a vote "for the Democratic ticket...and for good clean government." With Hurst barred from the election, the voters in Quitman chose Carter over Moore by 448 to 23. Plains went for him 201 to 28. He won by 3,012 to 2,182. Moore conceded, but he said he might change his mind and contest the results on the grounds that two ordinaries had defied the judge by leaving Carter's name on the ballot.[27]

Exhausted from the physical and emotional strain and the loss of more than ten pounds in two weeks, Jimmy went to bed for twenty-four hours thinking that the ordeal had ended. Moore, however, declared that he was "taking action" against the write-in vote and might call for a decision by the state senate at the beginning of its next session.[28] Carter did not know most of the senators or Peter Zack Geer, the lieutenant governor–elect. Moore knew them all, but he announced that he would withdraw his protest and thus allow Carter to be seated.[29]

Carter went to Atlanta to meet Geer, who as lieutenant governor would appoint the senate committees. When Geer explained that he had already filled most of the positions, Carter agreed to serve as secretary to both the Committee on Educational Matters and the Committee on Agriculture, both mundane, time-consuming jobs that no one else wanted. Carter asked no questions about his contested Fourteenth District election, but he froze when the lieutenant governor said that one contested race would have to be decided by a vote of the senate.

At a gala party at the Henry Grady Hotel on Sunday, January 13, the night before the session began, Jimmy and Rosalynn visited Geer, ostensibly for Rosalynn to meet him. As they reached his door, they passed a grinning Homer Moore just leaving, and Jimmy feared that his own election might still be in doubt. The next morning at the opening session, with Rosalynn sitting on the edge of her chair in the balcony, Jimmy knew for certain that he was a state senator only when the lieutenant governor called him to come forward to take the oath of office.[30]

CHAPTER NINE

Politics and Business

AFTER ATTENDING THE SENATE'S FIRST DAY, January 14, 1963, Rosalynn returned to Plains, but she had caught fire with the idea of a life in politics. Senator Carter drove the 134 miles each way from Atlanta to Plains on weekends, tended to business, spent time with his family, and attended church. The Georgia state senate met annually for forty working days, typically convening in mid-January, thus keeping Carter away from home about six weeks in the winter months while Rosalynn tended the business and the family.

In Atlanta, Carter stayed at the Piedmont Hotel, a quiet and sedate address where the resident politicians carried on lively discussions and avoided too much partying.[1] Carter arose early, walked to the Capitol, and took his seat before the time for opening prayer and roll call. A speed-reader, he kept his pledge to read every bill that came across his desk; some twenty-five hundred did. A few other senators, who were not speed-readers and respected his Navy and business careers, asked his advice. He worked five days, whereas most senators worked only four, and he visited department heads asking them to explain to him in great detail what they did.[2] He intended to be the best senator in Georgia. He bonded with J. B. Fuqua, Bob Smalley, Lamar Plunkett, Ford Spinks, Bobby Rowan, and others who had been elected in 1962 and who stayed at the same hotel. He made friends, observed those in power, and analyzed the alliances that might be useful to him. His old friend Bobby Rowan from South Georgia recalled that Carter "came to the state senate with destiny on his mind."[3]

Grateful to the governor for assuring his victory over Homer Moore, Carter supported the Sanders administration. Sanders attracted national attention for the reforms he brought to Georgia. He improved education and care for the mentally ill, reformed the prison system, condemned corruption in the Highway Department, and began to streamline the state government, all issues that Carter embraced.[4] As a new senator, Carter complained that the General Assembly "pushed bills through so fast" that "we didn't have time to study them."[5]

Carter's political style differed from that of the typical Georgia politician. Uncomfortable with the backslapping gregarious manner, he compensated with hard work. He resisted special interest groups such as insurance executives, bankers, teachers, doctors, and contractors, many of whom would inevitably resent being labeled special interest groups. He did, however, favor his own interests by cosponsoring a bill to regulate the sale and use "of agricultural limestone" and another to regulate advertising "displays and devices" adjacent to the interstate highways.[6]

Carter focused on educational matters. He wrote bills to improve the qualifications for county school superintendents, helped get five instead of three senators on the Governor's Commission to Improve Education, and attached an amendment to a bill that guaranteed that teachers' transportation allowances could not be reduced if student attendance declined.[7] That commission, chaired by Governor Sanders and consisting of twenty-five members drawn from the general assembly, education, and business, formulated a plan for education in Georgia.[8]

Carter's modus operandi did not impress all of his colleagues. The speaker of the house, George T. Smith, disliked him intensely. A friend of Governor Sanders, Smith recalled years later: "we in the House referred to him as the intellectual fool—absolutely no common sense—just, it was his way or no way . . . smart, but no common sense."[9] Carter remained loyal to the Democratic party and his constituents.

Back in Plains after the session ended, Jimmy found that Rosalynn had not only done a masterful job running the business but also turned her attention to politics. Thinking of herself as "more a political partner than a political wife," she liked the role, but she was not prepared for the fishbowl existence and the barrage of criticism that went with the public life.[10] She discussed politics and their future with Jimmy, but when he returned to Atlanta at the beginning of the next week, she remained in Plains. While at home, Jimmy rejoined her in the work of building the business, and they avoided controversies that might inhibit their entrepreneurial efforts.

When the civil rights movement came to southwestern Georgia in 1963, Carter remained silent. In the spring, the Student Non-Violent Coordinating Committee sent representatives into Sumter County, where Clarence Jordan welcomed them to Koinonia Farm. During the summer, black and white students, some from as far away as Connecticut, marched in the name of Christian charity through the streets of Americus proclaiming the need for racial integration. White citizens and law enforcement officers responded swiftly, beating several local blacks, giving impassioned speeches condemning integration, and arresting more than 250 African-American demonstrators. A small group of whites in Americus, including Carter's attorney Warren Fortson and others of his friends, sought a compromise, but Carter was not among them. He remained quietly uninvolved ten miles away in Plains. When Clarence Jordan died in 1969, Carter did not attend the funeral.[11]

Many people in Sumter County knew that the Carters, especially Miss Lillian, supported President John F. Kennedy and his brother Attorney General Robert F. Kennedy. When the Kennedy brothers pushed hard to integrate the South, some local whites began to identify the Carters with the Kennedys.[12] Both Jimmy and Rosalynn were stunned by the news of the assassination of President Kennedy on November 22, 1963, in Dallas, Texas. Chip, a student at Plains High School, became enraged when his teacher said "That's good" and his classmates clapped when they heard the news. He hurled his desk at the teacher and suffered the consequences of a three-day suspension. His parents did not scold him, although hurling a desk at a teacher for any reason might be considered serious misconduct.

As the nation and the world mourned the president, most white southerners thought his successor, Lyndon Johnson of Texas, would be sympathetic to their concerns. Many of them, however, including some of Jimmy's friends in Americus, became Republicans rather than declare their loyalty to the Democratic Texan. Jimmy and Rosalynn remained loyal to the national Democratic party. Luckily for them, the crop harvest season had ended, and their agribusiness had entered its winter dormancy, making a boycott of their business meaningless. The few threats they received proved harmless.[13]

At the time of the assassination and its aftermath, Carter was in the midst of his campaign for reelection to the state senate. He played it safe by proclaiming the popular gospel of improved education and economic vitality for southwestern

Georgia and avoiding issues of race and presidential politics. At Ellaville, he convinced a group of educators, as he had convinced himself, that they could reduce the dropout rate, send more students to college, and have a four-year college in Americus. "We farmers," he told a group of them on another occasion, should join the Farm Bureau, because it provides a "wonderful opportunity" to influence legislation.[14]

Once reelected, Carter organized the West Central Georgia Area Planning and Development Commission (WCGA) in 1964. In Atlanta, he had learned about a similar organization that was effective in North Georgia. He chaired a group in Americus that expressed interest in establishing the WCGA; he argued that such a commission would promote education, agriculture, mineral surveys, industry, and waterways. "We can cooperate among ourselves without forfeiting individualism," he said to an eager audience, many of whom resented the students from outside the South who marched in their streets. Financing, he reassured, would cost only about 10 cents per person.[15] As chairman and president of WCGA in 1964, he received federal grants from President Johnson's new social programs. His commission used those funds to launch the Head Start and Neighborhood Youth Group programs, restore an antebellum plantation and Indian village, promote tourism at the Andersonville Civil War prison site, transform Lake Blackshear into a recreational area, and study the potential use of the Flint River valley.[16] The WCGA also gave Carter a political pulpit more extensive than his own district and set him up to be elected the next year as chairman and president of the Georgia Planning Commission.

In January 1964, Carter returned to the state senate, where the Democratic Executive Committee appointed him to a group charged with rewriting the party's rules. In Atlanta he associated with men and women who were shedding their parochial viewpoints, and circulated in a city that was becoming increasingly integrated. His friends in the senate included young, idealistic members who had supported President Kennedy and wanted to change Georgia. Bobby Rowan of Enigma, Robert Smalley of Griffin, Lamar Plunkett of Unadilla, Billy Blair of Americus, and Janet Merritt of Plains became his closest allies.[17] In the company of congenial and intelligent people, Carter dropped his "loner" image and opened up to those who might understand and appreciate his viewpoints. He remained, however, a man in a hurry who did not suffer fools patiently.

About midway through the session, Carter and some of his colleagues took time to poke fun at his 1962 contested race in Quitman County. Bobby Rowan introduced a proposal to amend the state's election law to read that no person could vote in either the primary or general elections "who has been deceased more than three years." After an animated debate over whether survivors truly understood the intent of the deceased, the senate moved on to more serious means to change laws that had given men like Joe Hurst so much power.[18]

As chairman of the senate's Committee on Educational Matters, Carter publicly condoned racial equality for the first time. He worked with two black men who influenced his thinking and strategy. Horace Tate, the executive director of the state's Black Teachers Association, often attended Carter's committee meetings. Carter and Tate became friends as well as political allies. The lone black senator, Leroy R. Johnson from Atlanta's Thirty-eighth District, served on Carter's committee. The next year, Carter wrote him, with characteristic overstatement: "One of the most gratifying experiences I have ever had has been to serve with you in the Senate." A year later, Johnson returned the compliment, writing to Carter that he had represented his district well and "made an unusual contribution to the leadership" of the senate.[19]

Since two black friendships could not provide a political base from which Jimmy might advance his public career, the Carters sought others for personal and professional companions. They formed friendships with Marvin Shoob, William Gunter, and their wives. Shoob, a Savannah attorney and close friend of Carl Sanders, became the first of many Jewish allies, but many more Jewish Americans would later vacillate between skepticism and hatred for the mysterious Baptist politician from Georgia. Shoob and Carter stayed in Atlanta after the legislative session to draft the new party rules. Rosalynn and Janice Shoob often joined them for dinner. Gunter, a progressive attorney from Gainesville, had served in the legislature since the 1950s; he admired Carl Sanders. He and his wife, Betty Gail, were Presbyterians who liked to discuss with the Baptist Carters the possibilities of converting Christian faith into political action.[20] They noted that members of both Jewish and Christian faiths believed in a system of ethics and justice, but they often split on political issues.

During the brief 1964 session, Carter introduced legislation that established a program called the Minimum Foundation Program for Education Fund to aid poor public school districts. He supported legislation that provided free textbooks and free transportation to public schools. He voted to increase taxes on the sale of cigars and cigarettes. He favored more public safety officers, a lower sewer tax for the city of Hapeville, and a registration fee for trucks to "haul seasonal products grown in this state." He pushed through a resolution to amend the constitution to allow local county school superintendents to create the pool from which the governor would then appoint members of the state Board of Education.[21]

Carter returned home during spring planting season, but he enjoyed politics more than farming. Hoping for revenge on his old enemy Joe Hurst, Jimmy jumped into another contested election in Quitman County. In the spring of 1964, that county's Democratic executive committee refused to qualify Rosalynn's cousin Ralph Balkcom to run against Hurst for state representative. Again with the help of Warren Fortson, Carter got Balkcom's name on the ballot. Carter exposed Hurst's criminal activities, providing proof to the Federal Bureau of Investigation that Hurst operated a moonshine business, stole land from unknowing citizens, and had rigged previous elections. As a result, Hurst served time in a federal prison, his wife Mary took over his bid, and Balkcom won the house seat by twenty-five votes.[22]

Carter ran unopposed for reelection to the senate in 1964. His highly publicized effort to transform Georgia Southwestern into a four-year college made him so popular that no one dared oppose him.[23] Announcing his candidacy, he proclaimed his "primary interest" to be the university system of Georgia. He expected to achieve his goal of expanding Georgia Southwestern into a four-year institution not only to provide higher education nearer home for many young people, but for the prospective "cultural and economic benefit to our entire area."[24] Carter had a tough fight, for the Board of Regents enjoyed independence from Carter's Subcommittee on Higher Education. One of the regents, Howard H. "Bo" Callaway, an emerging major political rival and a Republican, fought Carter's plan because he wanted a four-year college in his own hometown, Columbus.[25]

Carter won. In a matter of months, the Board of Regents and the state legislature upgraded Georgia Southwestern to a four-year college. Carter served on the college's scholarship advisory committee, making speech after speech asking for money and bragging shamelessly about the college's faculty. He and Rosalynn attended its homecoming, where he served as marshal in a parade.[26] The comfort he enjoyed in Americus yielded to the fear and discomfort he felt at a special session of the legislature in Atlanta. Governor Sanders called the meeting in June

1964, responding to pressure from the federal government on the state legislature to consider passing a fair elections act and a revision of the state constitution. Carter delivered his first speech in the senate. He nervously spoke against the "thirty questions" that voting officers contrived to bar African Americans from the polls. Not even a "political science professor" at Emory University or at the University of Georgia could have answered them, he said. He concluded that "a black pencil salesman ... could make a better judgment about who ought to be sheriff than two highly educated professors at Georgia Southwestern College." Since he feared negative reaction to his remarks, he was relieved that neither the newspapers nor the senate journal published them. A dozen years later, as a candidate for president of the United States, he mentioned that speech, but there is no record of it from the time. He did manage, however, to get into the official record his resolution "commending the Plains High School baseball team for winning the State class 'C' Baseball Championship."[27]

When the house's recommendations for revising the election provisions of the state's constitution came to the senate, Carter had much to say and found himself on the winning side of the vote about half the time. He got his colleagues to approve an amendment that separated church from state. He voted with the minority against a state lottery, but he was in the majority opposed to writing an entirely new constitution and favoring constitutional regulation of local school systems.[28]

His comments on the separation of church and state later got Carter into trouble. He objected to the wording "Every man has the natural and inalienable right to worship God according to the dictates of his own conscience." Fearing that it implied every person should worship God, he substituted a phrase based on the Constitution of the United States: "No law shall be passed respecting an establishment of religion or prohibiting the free exercise thereof." In the final vote, he was one of only four senators to stand for his revision. Some of his political enemies later accused him of being an atheist.[29]

Reg Murphy, editor of the *Atlanta Constitution*, met Carter the same year and instantly disliked him. Politics aside, Murphy thought, "there is a man ... who will never be human enough to overlook the faults of anybody else."[30]

Returning to southwest Georgia in July 1964, Carter found a fractured political world. On July 2, President Johnson signed the Civil Rights Act, sadly noting that in doing so he would be delivering the South to the Republicans. Southern white segregationist Democrats scrambled to support Arizona Senator Barry

Goldwater, the Republican nominee for the presidency. With his promise of state rights, Goldwater won the support of thousands of Georgians, including former governor Marvin Griffin and Carter's friends John Pope and Stephen Pace, Jr. Howard H. "Bo" Callaway, a wealthy descendant of Americus pioneers, supported Goldwater and became Georgia's leading Republican.[31]

As the fall elections approached, Carter found himself in an advantageous position created by the chaos stemming from the controversy over civil rights. Running unopposed for reelection to the senate, he had a free hand to become involved as much, or as little, in the other elections as he saw fit. He supported his family's endorsement of the national Democratic candidates. Lillian and Gloria suffered ridicule for operating the local Johnson campaign headquarters in Sumter County. "Didn't bother me a damned bit," Lillian recalled; "stupidity is something I grew up with." When Chip went to school displaying an "I'm a Democrat" sticker, older boys roughed him up; his father advised him to pin the button back on and learn how to box.[32]

Carter focused on the Third District congressional race, where there would be a real contest between a Democrat and a Republican. At the Democratic convention, he nominated his old friend, former lieutenant governor Garland T. Byrd. Byrd won the nomination and faced the powerful "Bo" Callaway in the general election. A West Point graduate and a man of immense inherited wealth whose family had traditionally shown no regard for working people, Callaway was the very opposite of Carter. On behalf of the conservative Byrd, Carter attacked Callaway on virtually every topic except race. Carter failed, however, for Callaway easily defeated Byrd, thus becoming the first Republican congressman from Georgia since Reconstruction. Unwilling to accept his candidate's defeat, Carter decided privately that he would run against Callaway himself for that seat in 1966.[33]

Throughout the summer and fall of 1964, Carter kept a high profile. Using his position as chairman of the West Georgia Planning Commission, he delivered many speeches indirectly condemning Callaway. He did not reveal his own intention for 1966, but he supported causes that would win him votes. He promoted crusades to improve the community, taking care not to mention civil rights for blacks. "And I never have claimed to be one of the heroes of the civil rights movement," he said many years later; "I was not."[34]

The same newspapers that reported Carter's speeches also reported, sometimes in adjacent columns, gruesome stories about race relations. The *Americus*

Times-Recorder carried Associated Press stories about four Ku Klux Klan members in Athens, Georgia, who murdered a black educator and the first black students to enter a previously all-white elementary school in Mississippi. The Georgia story that captured the attention of the nation contained photographs of Atlanta restaurant owner Lester Maddox, axe handle in hand, driving blacks away from his business.[35]

Back in Atlanta in January 1965 for the beginning of the senate's session, Carter served on committees dealing with education, defense, veterans affairs, highways, agriculture, and natural resources. He persuaded Governor Carl Sanders to approve matching funds of $8,750 for his West Central Georgia Planning Commission.[36] He argued successfully for a law that would establish a state scholarship committee and the creation of a Georgia Higher Education Assistance Corporation to help students acquire money for college. He wanted counties and municipalities to have planning commissions, the state librarian to provide the senate with legal publications, and rural schools to become equal to urban ones. Boldly, he argued that state appropriations for schools in the South, including Georgia, should achieve the national median. "We need to do away with [a] defensive attitude," he declared. Georgians should compare themselves to the "nation, not [the] South. We must run fast just to stand still." Like a typical conservative politician, he declared that states must retain control of their school systems.[37]

Reforms, Carter said, could be accomplished without new taxes. He vigorously argued against any kind of financial excesses, such as an unneeded government building, expensive consultants, and needless state agencies. He opposed the governor on a $4 million appropriations bill by arguing unsuccessfully to delete $500,000 from it.[38] By the end of the session, he could legitimately claim a fiscally conservative record.

On March 4, 1965, Carter announced that he would be a candidate for the Third District seat in the U.S. House, held by "Bo" Callaway. Although Carter had been campaigning indirectly for almost a year through his work with the planning commission, a typical modus operandi he employed when seeking public office, he now openly bragged about his senate record. He boasted about granting more autonomy to city and county governments, improving education, reforming election laws, and saving the taxpayers money, most of them conservative issues that would appeal to working-class whites. Despite his exaggeration of his accomplishments, his colleagues voted him to be one of their most influential legislators.[39]

When the 1965 legislative session adjourned on March 12, Carter returned home dizzy with success. Governor Sanders noticed Carter's influence on the legislature and wrote him: "It was my personal pleasure to have been associated with you during the recent session."[40] When friends asked him the secret of his success, Carter replied that he was "stubborn" and "willing to work [his] head off" and "to consider the folks back home as well as what's best for the state."[41]

During that summer and fall, virtually every speech, every appearance, and every social occasion became a campaign event for Carter's 1966 race against Callaway. Carter gladly accepted Governor Sanders's appointment to attend the Southern Regional Education Board's annual work conference on higher education at Jekyll Island in late July. He used that forum to proclaim that the state must provide a low-cost college education for all Georgians who sought it. But when the same newspapers reported Sumter County's plan for the integration of its secondary schools, Carter's name was nowhere to be seen.[42] His diffidence in racial matters was Lincolnesque, in that it revealed nothing of where he actually stood on the burning issue of the day, and it was very politic.

In the fall, the *Columbus Sunday Ledger-Enquirer Magazine* published a feature story about the idyllic Carters at home. It portrayed Jimmy and Rosalynn in a euphoric mood, settled into their comfortable family and business partnership. They traveled with their three sons in Mexico, where they added to their collection of Indian artifacts. Rosalynn especially enjoyed their new home and her gardening. They talked with Jeffrey, age twelve, about dinosaurs, and with Chip, fifteen, about politics. They watched their eldest and brightest, Jackie, graduate from high school second in his class and prepare to enter Georgia Tech. Jimmy shot pool in the family room and played football in the yard with his sons. Rosalynn pursued her creative interests in art, ceramics, and drama. She served on the board of directors of the Sumter Players, a community drama group, and joined Jimmy in presenting to the public the image of a dedicated, loving, relaxed family. Jimmy was ecstatic about the article; he wrote to its authors that he was "very grateful" to them for helping him overcome the "cool" treatment he usually received from the district and state press.[43]

Carter had slyly cooperated with the author, intending to use that article in his fight against Callaway. While preparing the story, one of the authors advised Jimmy to look his "handsome best" for the photographer. She said she would "give about anything I own to see dear, little old 'Bo's' face when he picks up the paper and sees it." She continued, "He hasn't cornered the market on brains, looks, or appeal, and she hoped that the feature story would make that point."[44]

Carter needed the boost of a good press, for late in the summer of 1965 he and Rosalynn had faced a difficult political crisis. Mixed groups of blacks and whites tried in vain to establish a biracial committee in Americus and to integrate the leading churches there. When that news reached Plains, the Baptist congregation scheduled a meeting to discuss what to do. The Carters were in Roswell to attend a wedding when they heard about the meeting at their church. Jimmy wanted to go home to speak and to vote, but Rosalynn protested that they should avoid the confrontation and the threats of more boycotts against their business. "Brother Jimmy" won that argument, and in the presence of more than two hundred people he recommended that the congregation reject the other deacons' position that the ushers bar "Negroes and other agitators" from the church. The six people who voted for Jimmy's proposal included his wife, his mother, his two sons, himself, and an elderly man who had not heard the discussion. Although fifty-four members voted with the deacons, the majority simply declined to vote, which Carter later saw as a positive sign.[45]

Carter watched Sumter County fall under the control of segregationists and one of his friends get driven out of town. When the Sumter County Commission met to discuss a petition with two hundred names calling for the firing of Warren Fortson as the County's attorney, Carter attended the meeting. Another petition with one hundred names supported Fortson, but its weight and Jimmy's arguments had little impact. The commission transferred the county's business to other attorneys, and Fortson put his house up for sale and moved to Atlanta. He had committed no offense more serious than to remain a loyal Democrat and to favor a biracial committee to discuss the leading issue of the day.[46]

Politics did not interfere with Carter's business affairs. He appealed to the president of the Citizens Bank of Americus "to get all" of his and his mother's "farm land released from the collateral on the Small Business Administration (SBA) note." He argued that he had already paid $66,000 on the principal and that he had added enough new buildings and equipment, all paid for and valued at $76,834, to be sufficient collateral without the farmland. The Small Business Administration advised the local bank to deny his request, which it did, since it appeared to be for personal rather than sound business reasons.[47]

Angered by the denial, in December 1965 Carter gathered six partners and applied for a charter for a national bank to be built in Americus. He saw a good opportunity to enhance his considerable wealth by controlling the banking component of his agribusiness. He researched the requirements for such a bank carefully, then convinced J. G. Dariso, James C. Dixon, George B. Marcil, John M. Pope, Russell Thomas, Jr., and E. J. Wise to become his partners. As agent for the venture, Carter reported that on January 18, 1966, their application had been accepted by the regional comptroller of the currency. Their application promised an original capital of $600,000 and the sale of sixty thousand shares of stock. No one investor would be allowed to own more than 3 percent of the stock. The plan failed because the deputy comptroller of the currency believed the applicants did not demonstrate the need for such a bank.[48] Carter abandoned the idea, for he had decided to concentrate on a more important political battle.

When Carter returned to Atlanta in January 1966 for his final session in the senate, he had already made plans to run for Congress later that year. Building a record on which he could run for a higher office, Carter added service on the powerful Appropriations Committee and Agriculture and Natural Resources Committee to his other assignments.

During his final weeks in the senate, Carter vigorously opposed spending money for a driver's education program in the schools when, he said, his "little community doesn't have advanced math, foreign languages, and a lot of other mandatory courses." Y. T. Sheffield took offense at his exaggerated statement, and in an open letter reminded him that Plains High School offered Latin, Spanish, advanced math, and driver's education. "We would appreciate you not using Plains High School as an example unless you are sure of the facts," his former coach and principal reprimanded him. Carter claimed to have been misquoted, saying that he had been referring to other schools in his district.[49]

Unbowed, Carter, with votes on his mind, fiercely opposed salary increases for state supreme court and state court of appeals judges in favor of a uniform salary plan. He voted against special interest bills and for education and conservation measures. He voted with the majority against declaring nudism illegal, but he thought "open lewdness" should be a misdemeanor.[50]

Carter took a special interest in the federal Food and Agriculture Act of 1965. Armed with voluminous data, he made an impassioned plea to the national assistant deputy administrator of the State and County Operation of Agricultural

Stabilization and Conservation Service offices to enforce the Act. Passed on November 3, 1965, the Act extended an act from the previous year for four more years. It was the first multiyear farm program that provided commodity programs for feed grains and cotton and allowed farmers to reduce voluntarily their acreage of those and other crops in order to receive payments through price supports. The Act, Carter argued, protected farm prices and income, reduced surpluses, encouraged domestic use of farm products, and enabled U.S. farmers to compete in world markets.[51]

Carter felt some reluctance about ending his senate career in 1966, for he had come to love that legislative body and dreamed of ways he might improve it. He told Rosalynn that he might run for lieutenant governor, because that position would enable him to transform the senate into "a businesslike body... [that] would work."[52] He soon decided, however, that the office of lieutenant governor would not give him the power he wanted. His work analyzing the impact federal legislation had on him and on Georgia whetted his appetite to participate directly in making federal laws.

When Carter ended his senate career in March 1966, he had established a record on which he intended to run for Congress. He favored education, economic development, government reform, conservation, and fiscal conservatism. The Sanders administration accumulated a budget surplus, and Carter suggested a tax cut to return money to the people. Some journalists and senators found Carter difficult to understand, quick to cry that he had been "misquoted," petty, a nitpicker, and self-righteous, but none could deny that he had been a hardworking and effective senator.[53] Despite being labeled a "loner" by hostile journalist Reg Murphy, Carter developed friendships with progressive politicians who were wealthy small businessmen like himself.

CHAPTER TEN

Reach for the Governorship, 1966

AS CARTER DREAMED OF WINNING a national office, he believed life in the nation's capital might help Rosalynn and him retrieve part of the lifestyle they had enjoyed in the Navy and at the same time keep their roots in Georgia. Already successful in business, they had more time to invest in politics. Carter liked a challenge, and Republican Bo Callaway's campaign for reelection to the House of Representatives posed one he could not resist. Furthermore, that party's capitalization on racial turmoil to win elections angered him. Hoping to revive the strength of his own party, he welcomed a contest against someone he disliked, and there was no better opponent than Bo Callaway.

The year Callaway was elected to Congress had been a watershed year for the rise of the Republican party in the South. Senator Strom Thurmond of South Carolina had switched parties to join the Republicans, a move that endeared him to conservative southern Democrats. Many white southerners deplored President Johnson's endorsement of the civil rights acts. Callaway was among them; he defected to the Republican party, winning votes in 1964 from segregationist Georgia Democrats. The Republican presidential candidate, Senator Barry Goldwater of Arizona, carried the Deep South in 1964 but failed to defeat Johnson. Johnson's reelection caused thousands of southern Democrats to flock to the Republican party, as all across the old Confederate states the Democrats lost their grip on the "solid South."[1]

Callaway was "a staunch enemy of mine in every way," Carter said.[2] The rivalry between the two men was intense and personal as well as political. Like Carter, Callaway had a large Baptist following. In fact, Callaway's cousin, the Reverend Royall Callaway, a "premillennialist" who proclaimed to the impressionable boy that the Jewish people would return to Palestine and Christ would return to Earth to rescue his church from evil, had baptized Jimmy in the Plains Baptist Church in 1935.[3] In contrast to Carter, Bo Callaway had commanded a tank unit in Europe during World War II and enjoyed the status of a military hero; Carter had graduated from the Naval Academy and pursued a military career that did not involve combat. Economically and socially, the two men were also rivals. Callaway, heir to a textile fortune, had a proud family name much better known than Carter in Georgia. Both men were the same age and the rising leaders of their respective parties. As Carter's friend Philip Alston said, Jimmy "wanted to whip the Callaways."[4] A loyal Georgian—but not national—Democrat, Carter hoped to rid his district of the Republican representative.[5]

In preparation for the race, Carter turned to the University of Georgia. He asked Morris W. H. Collins, professor of political science and director of the Institute of Government there, to teach him about government. Sometimes Carter would go to Athens for private lessons, and sometimes Collins went to Atlanta. Collins remembered Carter as an enthusiastic student who left their sessions with stacks of books. The two men spent many hours together during the 1966 campaign, and Rosalynn often went with Jimmy to the Atlanta meetings. Carter learned about the mechanics of government, but he did not agree with his professor's more liberal political perspective.[6]

Seeking practical as well as academic knowledge, Carter went to Washington to consult Georgia's Democratic congressional delegation. He met Jack Flynt, James Mackay, Charles L. Weltner (who had voted for the Civil Rights Act of 1964), and Phil Landrum in their offices. He told them of his plan "to wage a most vigorous campaign" against Callaway and asked for their help. Although they knew little about Carter, they welcomed a viable Democratic opponent to their Republican colleague.[7]

Carter also called on Georgia's Democratic senators in Washington. He met Herman Talmadge and Richard Russell together in Russell's office "to discuss the political situation in our state." He speculated that "our Republican friend" Callaway would become a candidate for governor, and he was certain that the two senators would "take an active part to prevent our entire state government from being won by the Republicans."[8] Both men viewed the rise of Carter suspiciously; Russell even feared Carter might become a contender for his Senate seat. Three weeks before the Georgia Democratic primary, "Dick" Russell wrote to "Jimmy" that rumors that he, Russell, would not run for reelection were "completely false" and that "I wanted you, as a leader in our state, to know that they are baseless."[9] Carter wanted Russell's support, not his Senate seat.

Plunging into the campaign, Jimmy and Rosalynn took lessons to improve their memories, wrote letters asking for money and votes, and crafted speeches recounting his record as state senator and as chairman of the West Central Georgia Planning Commission. He spoke on courthouse steps, at women's group meetings, at dedications, at Honors Day at Georgia Southwestern, and at regional meetings of the Lions Club and other civic organizations.[10] The Carters avoided the topic of race, but Callaway played to white fears of mandated racial equality and asked members of the John Birch Society and the Ku Klux Klan, both extremist groups, for their votes. More seriously for the Carters, however, Callaway won support from wealthy former Democrats, including some of Carter's friends.

Carter vigorously denied any association with the hated national Democrats and President Johnson. He swung onto the coattails of Georgia's longtime, popular senator Russell, who had led the battle against national civil rights legislation. "My name won't be under Lyndon Johnson on the ballot," Carter declared. "I consider myself a conservative. I'm a Dick Russell Democrat."[11]

In May, the campaign took a bizarre twist when both Callaway and Carter dropped out of the congressional race to run for governor. The leading candidate, Ernest Vandiver, had suffered a slight heart attack and withdrawn, leaving former governor Ellis Arnall, who had been out of politics for eighteen years, and newcomer restaurateur Lester Maddox the principal contenders.[12] Bo Callaway stood a good chance to become Georgia's first Republican governor since Reconstruction.

Jimmy turned to his old friends Griffin Bell and Charlie Kirbo for advice. Bell advised him not to run for governor because he was not yet well known in the state, and Kirbo doubted that he had time to prepare for a statewide race.[13] Rejecting their advice, Carter decided to forfeit a sure win in the congressional race for the challenge of continuing the competition with Callaway and the chance to become governor.

Carter made his decision without consulting Rosalynn, but she shared his optimism and enthusiasm.[14] Others laughed or expressed dismay that he would drop out of the congressional race where he was a sure winner to enter one with an uncertain outcome. Some of his friends, including those who had contributed to his campaign, needed an explanation. Carter invited several of them to meet him and Rosalynn at the Holiday Inn in Albany for drinks. They did so, and one of them, who may not have been sober herself, noted that she had never seen "Rosalynn that zonkered from liquor."[15] Rosalynn could hardly contain her excitement about the campaign and the chance for a new lifestyle.

Carter joined a crowded field consisting of Ellis Arnall, Hoke O'Kelly, James Gray, Garland Byrd, and Lester Maddox in the battle for the Democratic nomination. Arnall, a well-known former governor from the Franklin Roosevelt era, had criticized the state's backwardness after World War II. Many blacks, who could vote because of recent federal civil rights legislation, found him an attractive candidate. O'Kelly, an elderly farmer and businessman and a perennial candidate from Gwinnett County, wanted to maintain the status quo, but few people took him seriously. Gray, a graduate of Amherst College and a native of Massachusetts, had a good reputation locally as editor of the *Albany Herald*. As the Talmadge candidate and an avowed segregationist, he expected to get the Vandiver votes. Carter's friend Garland Byrd had graduated from Georgia Southwestern and had had Jimmy's support in his 1964 race for the state senate, although his racial views were similar to those of Gray. In such a field, Carter, according to the *New York Times*, was indeed "a racial moderate."[16]

Carter and the other candidates made the mistake of not taking Lester Maddox seriously. Maddox, who had gained national notoriety by keeping blacks from entering his Pickrick Restaurant in Atlanta, had run unsuccessfully both for mayor of Atlanta and lieutenant governor of the state. Although he liked individual blacks and did not use violent or abusive language about them, he abhorred forced integration. He believed that segregation was the Christian way for both races. The son of a Atlanta blue-collar steel worker, Maddox had dropped out of high school after the eleventh grade, and later, with the help of his wife Virginia, prospered in the restaurant business. Since 1949 he had run a series of newspaper advertisements entitled "Pickrick Says," in which he inserted political comment. He favored state rights, free enterprise, and the Christian religion. Much like "Ole Gene" Talmadge, he posed as the "friend of the little man," quietly winning a following that would put him in the governor's mansion.[17]

Carter began to raise money for his campaign. He met with Hal Gulliver, Bill Gunter, and Bobby Troutman at the Riviera Motel on Peachtree Street in Atlanta.

After he told them that Kirbo had volunteered to put up $75,000, Gunter offered to raise more. Gulliver promised favorable articles in the *Atlanta Constitution*. Troutman, the son of Kirbo's partner at King and Spaulding, had served in the firm before leaving to make a fortune in real estate. Furthermore, he had roomed with Joseph Kennedy, Jr., at Harvard Law School, had helped manage John Kennedy's successful 1960 campaign in Georgia, and thought that Carter was "like Kennedy."[18]

The next day, Carter assembled his campaign committee and set up his Atlanta headquarters in Suite 562–64 of the Dinkler Motor Hotel. He chose his old friend Brooks Pennington, who had helped him win Governor Sanders's endorsement in 1962 and had served with him in the senate, to manage his campaign. The other members included Paul Broun of Athens, Robert Smalley of Griffin, Bobby Rowan of Enigma, and Ford Spinks of Tifton, all friends from his senate years. They recruited David Gambrell and Philip Alston, both prominent Atlanta attorneys. Sadly for Jimmy, John Pope had already committed to Callaway, Marvin Shoob had promised to help Arnall, and Warren Fortson had become too controversial to be of help. Shoob's wife, however, supported Carter.

Carter's followers included other friends in Americus, young people, a very few black leaders, and politically active female volunteers who wanted a progressive governor. Most of the Carter groups were 1960s idealists willing to make sacrifices to improve their society while seeking no personal gains.[19] Carter, as well as members of his campaign committee, was a more pragmatic politician than the visionaries who followed his star.

On June 12, 1966, with Rosalynn at his side, Carter announced formally before about one hundred enthusiastic supporters in a committee room at the state Capitol that he would be a candidate for governor of Georgia. About the same time, on the West Coast the Republican party chose actor Ronald Reagan as its candidate for governor of California.[20] As Carter's star rose in the east and Reagan's in the west, neither man could have imagined how they would clash in a contest for the presidency less than a score of years later.

In June 1966, however, most of the country paid little attention to either Reagan or Carter, for they were upstaged by African-American civil rights activist James Meredith being peppered with birdshot as he marched down a highway in the Mississippi Delta. The escalating war in Vietnam, the popularity of the

Beatles, and the announcement by Martin Luther King, Jr., that he planned a march in Chicago in August attracted much more attention than stories about obscure rising politicians.

Undaunted, Carter hired Gerald Rafshoon, a young, Jewish New York advertising expert, to create an attractive television image for him. Rafshoon had moved to Atlanta to seek his fortune; he seemed shocked that Carter could pronounce the word "Negro" correctly. After hearing one of Carter's commercials by a timid country singer who intoned "Jimmy Carter is his name," Rafshoon called Gulliver and told him that Carter needed help. Meeting Carter at the Dinkler Hotel, Rafshoon suggested a livelier, more positive advertisement: "There's a man they say can't win, they don't make the difference, YOU do; when he comes to town get out and meet him." Rafshoon thought he could transform the unimpressive speaker and unknown politician into a winner. Troutman, who contributed more money to the campaign than any other donor, paid Rafshoon's bill.[21]

Carter adopted Rafshoon's image of him as "a young man who has the best interests of the state at heart." He rejected all labels except "Georgian," "southerner," and "American."[22] He hoped to win votes from people who believed him to be what they wanted him to be. By being vague but sincere, he attempted to be all things to all people.

Since she had set her heart on moving to Washington, Rosalynn needed to adjust to the idea of life in Atlanta. She embraced Jimmy's plan and worked to make it come true. Leaving the warehouse in the care of Billy and Sybil, Rosalynn took the three boys, who were out of school for the summer, and moved to the Dinkler Hotel to work in the campaign. She often dashed up and down the stairs when the elevators were too slow to suit her. She handled most of the political correspondence. She made phone calls, distributed handbills, shook hands, and instructed their sons about how they could help.

Life on the campaign trail was not always easy for Rosalynn, who once suffered the indignity of being spat on by a Callaway supporter. She continued to care for her family, and she suffered a major personal loss when her beloved Papa Murray died that summer at the age of ninety-five. She and Jimmy took only enough time to attend his funeral, but her grief was deep.[23]

Returning to the campaign, Rosalynn received help from other family members. Gloria, Miss Lillian, and Lillian's sister Sissy Dolvin all pitched in. They recruited and organized volunteers, relied on their friends in Atlanta and South

Georgia, sought advice from Kirbo, and cheered Jimmy. Lillian traveled across the state giving extemporaneous speeches and charming her listeners with her personality and wisdom. Ruth arrived by train from Fayetteville, North Carolina, on Monday mornings, worked all week, then rode the train back home on Friday night. The campaign brought Rosalynn tighter into the Carter family circle.

Gloria operated the campaign headquarters in Plains. She sent checks, letters, newspaper editorials, invitations to speak, humorous commentary, and news from home to Jimmy and Rosalynn in Atlanta. On one occasion, after the Carter sons had returned to Plains to attend school, she advised Rosalynn: "The boys are FINE and working hard. Lots of love to you both, and just be so pretty as usual, and you'll be the best asset he's got!" Another time she sent them two telegrams from "NICE Republicans" and urged them to try to get "a bit of rest." She hoped they were getting "the stuff I'm mailing" but had the feeling "it is going to the cemetery" and signed her letter "Both TG," meaning I love you both the goodest.[24]

For the first time, Carter ran a well-organized and professional campaign. In addition to the family, he had a committee, money, and an advertising specialist.

Rosalynn participated in political discussions, examined sources of money, studied the electorate, and contemplated popular issues. Her Methodist-inspired commitment to social justice and help for the needy translated into a political agenda. Her logical, businesslike mind that had helped Jimmy transform a $25,000 business into a multimillion-dollar operation in less than a decade provided the anchor that her husband sometimes needed for his hotheaded enthusiasm. Both innovative, driven, and intelligent, they formed a winning partnership. Still shy in public, Rosalynn was not bashful at home; she spoke her mind to Jimmy, and he listened to her. Sometimes he took her advice, sometimes he did not, but all who glimpsed the inner circle knew that the term "Carter campaign" included Jimmy *and* Rosalynn.

Carter traveled from one end of the state to the other, shaking hands, making speeches, promoting himself, and avoiding controversy. When he talked about the plight of mental patients in the Central State Hospital, where one of his first cousins resided, his voice cracked with emotion, and he won the trust of many listeners.

Although most black voters had already committed to Arnall, Carter appealed to them at meetings at the Wheat Street Baptist Church and Morris Brown College in Atlanta. By explaining how they shared a common religious background, he began to build a rapport that would be crucial to his future elections. He attacked front-runner Arnall for misusing highway funds and for being a poor representative of the party.

Carter presented himself as honest and compassionate, with impeccable records in politics and business, and as one who lived an exemplary personal life. He worked long hours, skipping meals and sleep, and dropping twenty-two pounds to a very thin 130. John Girardeau, a law student at Emory University who drove for the candidate, found Jimmy both idealistic and practical, easy to anger, quick to forgive, and genuinely religious as he knelt in his underwear to pray beside his bed every night.[25]

Charles Kirbo, whose political savvy and legal skill, helped Carter win the state senate seat in 1962, emerged as his most important adviser. He invited wealthy people to meet the candidate and Rosalynn for a drink in the Piedmont Room of Atlanta's exclusive Driving Club, where financial decisions were made that could make or break a political candidate. David Gambrell, who, like Kirbo, was a partner at King and Spaulding, served as treasurer.[26] Kirbo and Bill Gunter introduced Carter to some of the most influential people in Atlanta. They included Bob Lipshutz and Conley Ingraham, attorneys who liked Carter's style; Phil Alston, an attorney and fund-raiser who disliked the ranting of Maddox and thought Arnall a "has been"; and Anne Chambers Cox, whose family published Atlanta's major newspapers.

Kirbo became the senior member of the team and the kingpin in Carter's 1966 campaign. He praised Carter's style and marveled at how he went out day after day, armed with a file box and a lunch prepared by Rosalynn, to speak to Rotary and Lions clubs, then made notes on what jokes he had used when and where. Kirbo, and virtually Kirbo alone among his advisers, saw how Carter talked to his customers, other farmers, and salesmen in the agribusiness. He told them that they held a wrong attitude toward black people, that he disagreed with them, and that they would have to adjust their notions, "in part on a religious basis." As a man speaking in such a fashion to his friends, he did not offend them and probably won their votes. "If anybody else had talked the way he talked," Kirbo said, "they would have told him to go to hell."

Kirbo counseled the young, inexperienced members of the team: Jody Powell, Hamilton Jordan, and later Jack Watson and Frank Moore, all of whom called him "Mr. Kirbo." He listened to their personal problems, gave them financial advice, and often spent three hours a day helping them bring order to a chaotic campaign. He lectured them on "loyalty vs. efficiency" and argued that the more competent they were, the greater the chance for victory. He had access to Carter, noting that the hardworking candidate, who was "not a worrier," rose above the din of the campaign.[27]

Younger than Kirbo, Thomas Bertram Lance joined the campaign as Carter's peer. President of the First National Bank of Calhoun in North Georgia and grandson of a Methodist circuit rider, Lance thought Carter was a good businessman with a sound philosophy of government. Politically ambitious himself, Lance had been educated at Emory, the University of Georgia, Louisiana State University, and Rutgers University. By virtue of his marriage to LaBelle David of Calhoun, he had entered the banking business and had become wealthy.

Both small-town boys, devoutly religious, successful in business, and zealous for public office, Lance and Carter bonded instantly. They first met each other under an oak tree at Berry College in Rome, Georgia, where they sampled barbecue that had been prepared to entertain the Coosa Valley Area Planning and Development Commission. Lance attended because his hometown of Calhoun might be affected by the commission's decisions, and because he wanted to offer his help to Carter.[28]

Hamilton Jordan, a twenty-year-old student from the University of Georgia, had taken a summer job spraying mosquitoes in his hometown of Albany, where he heard Jimmy address the Elks Club. An idealistic college student in the 1960s, "Ham" found Carter so different from other Georgia politicians that he volunteered to help. The nephew of Clarence Jordan, founder of Koinonia, Ham shared much of his uncle's visionary view of what could be done for poor people in the state. Carter hired him as a youth coordinator for the campaign, and Ham brought along his girlfriend, Nancy Konigsmark.[29]

Ham's talent for organization and understanding of politics, and his and Nancy's passionate interest in the youth-driven revolutions of the 1960s, served the candidate well. The young social rebels of the 1960s, who loathed Republican leader Barry Goldwater and denounced the war policies of Democratic president Johnson, found in Jimmy Carter a politician they could trust.

In the midst of the campaign, Hamilton's uncle Clarence Jordan died. Neither doctor nor coroner would risk the wrath of the people in Americus to make the short trip to the Christian commune. Millard Fuller, who would later found

Habitat for Humanity, hauled Clarence's body into town for an autopsy. Convinced that death had been from natural causes, he and friends quickly buried Clarence in a pine box in an unmarked grave at Koinonia. By the time Hamilton got the news from his mother, the funeral had already taken place. The purpose of Clarence's life and the tale of his rejection by the good people of Americus left an indelible mark on the energetic, and some said strange, young man from Albany who became one of Carter's most influential political advisers.[30]

Since Georgia's senators Russell and Talmadge spoke against Bo Callaway without endorsing Carter or any of the Democratic candidates, Brooks Pennington resorted to trickery to give Carter a higher profile. Pennington, a wealthy seedman from Madison, cosigned a note for $50,000 with David Gambrell, Philip Alston, and Bill Gunter to help finance the campaign. He asked his seed customers for contributions and accepted some that came from outside Georgia. Without consulting Russell and Talmadge, he printed thousands of postcards with a message from "the Concerned Friends of Dick Russell and Herman Talmadge," warning Democratic voters that if Ellis Arnall won, he would "mold" the Georgia party into the "image of the National Democratic Party." Pennington had some of the "Defeat Arnall with Carter" postcards mailed from Washington, D.C., and others from Talmadge's hometown, Lovejoy. Others meant to be mailed from Atlanta were set aside by friends of Arnall working in the Atlanta post office until after the election was over. Carter himself denied any knowledge of the post card caper.[31]

Those Georgia Democrats such as Troutman who wanted Carter to be "like Kennedy" were in the minority. Although Carter's youth and looks, like those of John Kennedy, appealed to female and young voters, those constituencies alone were not sufficient to elect him.

On the trail, Carter spoke freely about his religion, his family, his childhood pets, and his commitment to good government. When he and Rosalynn campaigned at Savannah Beach, Jimmy removed his shoes and rolled up his pants and waded into the water to shake hands with bathers. The mayor of Macon accused Rosalynn and Jack of violating a city ordinance by stopping traffic on Riverside Drive to hand out literature. Carter quipped that although his wife was pretty, he did not think "her beauty would stop Macon traffic at rush hour." What slowed the traffic, he suggested, was former governor Arnall's refusal to spend adequate highway funds in that county.[32]

Rosalynn campaigned with the three boys in shopping centers from early in the morning to late at night. She appeared on television and radio programs, visited towns small and large, and usually made a good impression with her youthful looks, incredible stamina, and genuine concern for people.[33]

Carter joked often, but he seriously announced a "blueprint" for sixty-three programs he would implement without a tax increase, a promise so grandiose it tested reality. It was typical of his hyperbolic speeches. His plan offered progressive reforms in education, crime prevention, mental health, and highway construction. If enacted, he claimed, it would bring political reform, triple the state's industry, and let Georgia keep "pace with the rest of the nation." When questioned, Carter promised that he would appoint qualified women and blacks to top state posts, but he did not volunteer such controversial information.[34]

Carter sent mixed signals about his stand on race relations, but he did occasionally advocate equal opportunity for blacks. Those statements got lost or ignored in the noise of political battle. He claimed the loyalty of "responsible Negro educators and churchmen" because of his "long interest in education." He declared that he spoke "to white people and Negroes" and that "as governor" he would "treat every citizen fairly."[35]

A riot in Atlanta's black Summerhill section in September made it impossible for Carter to avoid comment on the race crisis. After an Atlanta policeman shot and wounded a suspected automobile thief in that black slum, Stokely Carmichael, a well-known civil rights leader, drove through the streets in an old van urging residents to rise up and support black power. During the ensuing riot, sixteen people were injured and seventy-five arrested. Atlanta authorities arrested Carmichael for inciting the riot, which, Carter said, was precisely the correct thing for them to do. The specter of that race riot so close to the election added votes to Maddox's column.[36]

When polls midway through the campaign showed that he lagged behind Callaway, Arnall, Gray, and Maddox, Carter displayed his famous temper. He began an all-out attack on his opponents. He vigorously denied Byrd's charge that U.S. Attorney General Robert Kennedy, much hated by white segregationists, ran his campaign. "I do not know any of the Kennedys, and I am sure they do not know me," he told audiences in Brunswick and Covington.[37] He especially condemned Arnall, the man with whom he often agreed, as a corrupt, archaic, pork-barrel politician who would merely splinter the Democratic party. Carter claimed that he found many people "embarrassed and nauseated" by both Arnall's and Maddox's "clownish stunts." He railed at Arnall for calling him "Jimmy Who" and for inviting certain Georgians whom Arnall alleged were Communists "to go to Russia or go to hell." Carter condemned Arnall's vulgar language, his efforts to split the party, and especially his alliance with powerful, flamboyant banker Mills B. Lane.[38] He accused the other candidates of making false promises and lacking both the experience and skills to serve the people honestly.

Despite the friends he made, his aides' attempts to play both ends of the political spectrum, and his own hard work, Carter failed to win the Democratic nomination on September 28. The *New York Times* reported that Carter's "boyish smile," Kennedy looks, and "non-controversial statements" were not sufficient to gain victory. A pall settled over the Carter family in the Dinkler Motor Hotel as they learned on election night that Arnall had won 29.4 percent of the vote, Maddox 23.5 percent, and Carter 20.9 percent. Aunt Sissy, later recalled that "the gloom was terrible" and she began to cry. Sissy soon regained her composure, however, for she knew "Jimmy is the kind of loser who becomes more determined than ever to win."[39]

Carter declined to support either Arnall or Maddox in the runoff.[40] Arnall thought the race had polarized into a white-versus-black issue, which gave him little chance against Maddox. He also thought, and Carter later agreed, that many Republicans voted in the runoff for Maddox because they thought their candidate, Callaway, would have a better chance against Maddox than Arnall in the general election. An embittered Arnall complained that Carter had cut into his votes just enough to prevent him from winning without a runoff.[41] Carter had made a strong enough showing, however, that for Arnall to have won without a runoff he would have had to have gotten virtually all of Carter's votes. There was a runoff, and the colorful archsegregationist Lester Maddox won it.

In the general election in November, Carter supported the party but not the candidate. Maddox polled more votes than Callaway, but not the requisite 50 percent majority. Arnall, running as an independent, had drawn away just enough votes to deny either Callaway or Maddox a clear victory. On January 10, 1967, the Democratic-controlled General Assembly, acting under the state constitution, declared Lester Maddox governor.[42]

Humiliated by their loss, burdened with debt, and so depressed that they forgot to thank their supporters, Jimmy and Rosalynn returned empty-handed to

Plains. Miss Lillian said that Jimmy "cried like a baby." His cousin Beedie found him walking alone in the peanut field, dejected. On reflection, Jimmy refused to accept defeat. "A good loser is still a loser," he said, as he vowed never to lose again.[43]

Kirbo remained optimistic. He thought that Carter had been so well organized that it would only be a matter of time before he would win. He reported receiving letters from attorney friends congratulating him on the "outstanding job which you and your organization did for Jimmy Carter" and promising support the next time around.[44]

Likewise, after the election, Ralph McGill, editor of the *Atlanta Constitution*, wrote a private letter to Senator Robert Kennedy to explain that the future of the Democratic party in Georgia was not as dire as the Maddox victory might indicate. "Jimmy Carter, who ran third in the Democratic gubernatorial primary, is the best bet for the immediate future," he predicted. "In the primary the Negro vote went very heavily to Ellis Arnall," he explained, "but in the state Carter picked up quite a few Negro votes and he had much more of an appeal to the younger voter than did Arnall." Maddox won only because "Goldwater Republicans" crossed over and voted for him, while Negro voters stayed home. "Carter is a young south Georgian of fairly decent instincts and motives and is the best bet for a statewide campaign in the years ahead," he continued. "This could change, but presently, he is the best vote getter on the moderate side."[45]

McGill's assessment of Carter and the Democratic party in Georgia was accurate. Carter, however, still had a long way to go to win in his state. Since the Kennedy name aroused hostility among the white segregationists who comprised the majority of Georgia's voters, Carter vigorously denied any association with that famous New England family. The more progressive Georgians, however, nursed their wounds and bided their time until Carter could make a comeback.

In early November, Jimmy and Rosalynn returned to Atlanta to attend a fundraising dinner in their honor. The Dinkler Hotel canceled their bill for almost $5,000, but they still owed more than $4,000 on the campaign. The enthusiastic crowd cheered the Carters' declaration that they were not out of politics. Campaign manager Brooks Pennington announced that Jimmy really had not lost, because now, "They don't say Jimmy Who, they say Jimmy When—in 1968 or 1970?"[46]

Two weeks after his defeat, Carter called Hamilton Jordan to apologize for having left town in November without having thanked him, a call Jordan interpreted as a sure indication that Carter intended to try again in 1970.[47] Maddox appointed Carter to the state's Democratic Executive Committee, which gave him a solid base to remain a power in the party.[48] Carter's election team remained loyal to him and worked well with each other. Rosalynn sent handwritten notes to dozens of campaign workers who had labored "night and day to help Jimmy Carter become Governor," and Kirbo said he thought Carter would win in the near future.[49] Within a few weeks of his loss, Carter planned to try again in 1970. He used his contacts with farm organizations, meetings of the Lions Club, the area planning commission, his religious connections, and Rosalynn's thank-you notes to keep his name before the people and in the press.[50] But before he reentered politics, he reexamined his religious faith and enlarged his agribusiness.

CHAPTER ELEVEN

Born Again, Running Again

AT AGE FORTY-TWO, as Carter reeled from his loss to Lester Maddox, he encountered the profound religious experience that Southern Baptists call being "born again." His unplanned blend of religion and politics typecast him forever as a "born again" Christian politician and became a major issue in his public life. In Rosalynn's Methodist tradition, the concept of being born again is less prevalent, although her Sunday school teachers had ingrained within her a belief that a good Methodist must be committed to the improvement of her society. The Baptists, too, placed a major emphasis on missionary activities in foreign countries. Although the Carters' religious expressions were not identical, their goals were.

The person who delivered Jimmy's "born again" experience was Ruth, not Rosalynn. A vivacious woman who claimed to have received what she called "the gift of inner healing," Ruth had became a wealthy evangelist. She walked in the piney woods of Webster County with her older brother in the fall of 1966 and urged him to accept God's will for his life. That experience lived more in the memory of his sister than it did in his, but Jimmy admitted to her that he could give up anything in his life except politics.[1] Although Ruth counseled her brother during his spiritual crisis, it was Rosalynn who had to help explain her husband's religion. When Jews, Catholics, once-born Protestants, and skeptics asked what "born again" meant, both she and Carter had to answer.

Shortly after his talk with Ruth, Carter heard his pastor in Plains, Robert Harris, preach a sermon in which he asked, "If you were arrested for being a Christian...would there be enough evidence to convict you?" The question haunted Carter. He realized that he had spoken about Christ to only 140 people since he had left the Navy but he had bragged about himself to at least a quarter million people during the late campaign. He decided to display Christian love toward others, read and teach the Bible, and practice humility. Holding fast to his political ambition, he thought he felt God's call to politics.[2]

After Carter became a national politician addressing millions who did not understand his Southern Baptist heritage, he attempted to explain what he meant by being born again. Two decades after the experience, he thought it meant an "intimate melding" of his life "as a brother" with Jesus who shared God as "a mutual parent." Such intimacy with God did not bring perfection, but it enhanced "striving, stretching, and searching" in one's "new life." "It is a highly personal and subjective experience," Carter wrote, "possible only if we are searching for greater truths about ourselves and God."[3] More emotional than rational, such an experience seems best understood only by those who have known it themselves.

Rosalynn denied that Jimmy had slipped into a serious depression or had undergone some mystical experience. "I've heard people talk about Jimmy after he lost, having his 'experience' with Ruth and all. I don't remember any of that. He doesn't either," she said in 1976. She said he did walk with Ruth, but he just prayed, "developed a closer relationship with Christ," and decided to run again for governor. She ridiculed the idea that he had had a "mystical experience ... nothing like that ever happened."[4] Truth to tell, Jimmy's "born again" experience may have been as much a political as a spiritual rebirth.

Carter said nothing about it in his 1975 campaign autobiography other than that his church life had become more meaningful, and he had participated in several lay missions. In 1977 he denied that he had wept or gone into any kind of "emotional state," and he bemoaned the fact that so many people had "let their imaginations run wild" about his conversion experience. He expressed shock that some northerners thought he had had a "mystical experience."[5]

The conversion experience is an act of faith that is utterly private and virtually defies rational explanation. It is, to those who believe in it, however, quite real and motivational. Carter's "born again" feeling seems to fall into the category of "intensification experiences," which are characterized by the renewal of one's childhood beliefs. Typically, they occur near midlife to a proud and angry person who has experienced some intimate upheaval in his life that may take several years to resolve.[6] Carter was forty-two, proud, and angry, his ambition derailed by the 1966 defeat, when he became born again. His unabashed talk about his faith, his attempts to live by it, and his confession of failure all indicate that to him the renewal of his childhood beliefs was permanent and true. No religious phony, Carter used his faith as both crutch and challenge.

Carter read theology, a practice he had begun after the death of his father. From theologian Paul Tillich he learned that doubting one's God and one-self happens to human beings and is acceptable in Christian thought and that faith is a continuous search, not a final answer. From the existential-ist Soren Kierkegaard, best known for his advice to take the "leap of faith," Carter found courage to "bet his life" on "the God in Jesus Christ." Carter read Dietrich Bonhoeffer, who died in a Nazi concentration camp and had much to say about how comfort comes to the faithful. From orthodox theo-logian Karl Barth, Carter learned that the Bible, which was at the heart of the Christian faith, should not to be taken literally. Supplementing his reading of theology with a detailed study of the Bible, Carter believed in the power of God to create the universe and the creatures in it and the ability of a man to find God's plan for himself.[7]

Carter's search for a theologian who expressed what he needed to believe about life, politics, and religion led him to study the neoorthodox Reinhold Nie-buhr. During their senate years, Jimmy and his friend Bill Gunter discussed the link between religion and politics, and in 1965 Gunter loaned him *Reinhold Nie-buhr on Politics*. The essays traced the evolution of Niebuhr's political thought through several of his powerful books, including *Moral Man and Immoral Society* (1932), *The Children of Light and the Children of Darkness: A Vindication of Democ-racy and a Critique of Its Traditional Defense* (1944), and *The Irony of American History* (1952). Carter referred to the volume of essays as his "political Bible" and proceeded to read Niebuhr's sermons, books, and biography. Carter found his work a logical explanation of how one could be both politician and Christian. Man had the capacity for justice and making democracy possible, Niebuhr said, but the inclination for injustice made democracy necessary. Religion could be a source of error if it did not instill humility. Moral individuals, who sometimes erred, might pursue social justice in an unfeeling world, according to Niebuhr. He thought President Abraham Lincoln's pursuit of justice without claiming any knowledge of divine will the proper standard for a head of state. In essence, he verbalized ideas Carter cherished.[8]

Niebuhr became the favorite of many post–World War II Democrats, includ-ing southerners breaking away from the old racism that had defined their region. The theologian's warning to American leaders not to imitate their enemies seemed to demand perennial diplomatic and domestic reevaluation.[9]

As a young pastor of Bethel Evangelical Church in Detroit, Niebuhr sympa-thized with exploited automobile industry workers and became a Socialist. In 1928 he accepted an appointment as a professor of ethics at Union Theological Seminary in New York City, where he gradually abandoned his socialistic views, supported Roosevelt's New Deal, and became renowned as a teacher.

Politically active, Niebuhr became a founder of the Americans for Democratic Action and vice chairman of the New York State Liberal Party. Niebuhr thought that the kingdom of God might best be manifested on Earth through the strength of the Western democracies.[10] He approved the United Nations' reestablishing the nation of Israel in 1948, but he argued that the Palestinian Arabs deserved to enjoy the protection of the United Nations in designated areas of the new Jewish nation. "Justice must be the instrument of love," Niebuhr wrote, words Carter underlined in his copy of June Bingham's biography of the theologian.[11] Niebuhr did not find politics and principle contradictory, nor did he deny the importance of the indi-vidual's ability to decide which should prevail in case of conflict. Nations should practice humility, he said, and "moral man" could exist in an "immoral world."

Like Niebuhr, Carter found it impossible to divorce religion from political action. Carter believed in "realistic" morality and that politicians could bring jus-tice to a sinful world.[12] Carter found reconciliation, resolution, and promise in his religion and politics. Both Carter and Niebuhr understood that humans could not attain perfection, but they could be inspired to do their best. Carter's reading of Niebuhr seemed to lead him into a Machiavellian belief that in some cases the ends justified the means. If Carter were to become an instrument of justice on a large scale, he had first to get the power to make the world more just.

Less burdened with matters of religion and politics, Lillian looked for pro-ductive ways to pass her time and to put distance between herself and the young Mrs. Carter. To get needed "space," Lillian left town from time to time, first to become a house mother at Auburn University, and then in the spring of 1966 to join the Peace Corps.[13]

A sixty-seven-year-old grandmother at the time Carter lost the 1966 primary, Lillian was at the University of Chicago learning the Marathi language that she needed to work in a family planning program in Maharashtra, India. On arrival in New Delhi in December 1966, she sat beside two turbaned snake charmers.[14] When she reached her destination at Vikhroli, near Bombay, she recoiled from the poverty, disease, and wretched living conditions she encountered. She came to love the place and its people and accepted physical hardships she had never known before. On her seventieth birthday, August 15, 1968, she wrote that she had discovered "what life is really all about" in that remote place separated from all her material goods. She urged her children to "dare do the things . . . that have meaning for you."[15] Soon thereafter she returned to Plains, where she found that Jimmy and Rosalynn had entered a new world of their own.

If Rosalynn had hoped to have Jimmy to herself without other feminine distractions, she was happily disappointed on October 19, 1967, when she gave birth to Amy Lynn. Amy was born almost exactly nine months after Jimmy had lost his 1966 bid for the governorship. Since he and Rosalynn had always wanted another child, preferably a daughter, they were tearfully joyful at becoming parents again in their early forties, the age when many of their friends were about to become grandparents. Brothers Jeff, now fifteen, Chip, seventeen, and Jack, twenty, waited with their father to greet baby Amy when she emerged from the delivery room with her mother.[16] For Amy's first six months, Rosalynn took the warehouse books home, where she could both work and care for her daughter. She also handled political correspondence from home. She sometimes watched the birds, too, the beginning of a hobby she later taught Jimmy.[17]

Carter's relationship with his sons did not change. With them he mimicked Mr. Earl. Unable to give freedom to the young sons whom he loved, he attempted to mold them in his and Mr. Earl's image. He disciplined them, when they were children and teenagers, with extra work, a wooden paddle, and restrictions on their recreational activities.[18]

After Chip failed a Latin test, his livid father learned Latin himself, then taught it to Chip. The boys knew that their father would accept no excuse for failure. Jack transferred from Georgia Tech to Emory, protested the war in Vietnam as a poor man's fight, then dropped out of college and joined the Navy, all without parental approval. Soon he found himself off the coast of Vietnam as a buoy tender.[19] All three sons smoked cigarettes, an indulgence their father abhorred.[20]

During their political hiatus, Jimmy and Rosalynn resumed control of their booming agribusiness. Jimmy recruited customers and kept the business on the cutting edge of scientific progress. Billy owned 17 percent, worked for the business, and claimed his share of the profits. In the 1960s, the two brothers worked together comfortably and became emotionally close. They raised cotton, corn, and soybeans, and they took pride in their high-quality seed peanuts, cotton gin, warehouse, and peanut sheller.[21]

During the 1968 growing season, the Carter brothers excited the world of cotton production with an innovative technique of formulating and distributing fertilizer. In a fifteen-ton-per-hour formulating plant, they mixed liquid, suspension fertilizer according to a prescription they devised from analyzing soil samples from their cotton fields. Before spraying the land, the operator could add an herbicide or any other chemical to the mixture. The Carter brothers purchased a Tryco Floater, a large springless truck manufactured in Decatur, Illinois, that could roll across the fields at speeds up to twenty miles per hour. Equipped with a thousand-gallon tank and a thirty-three-foot boom with flow nozzles, it could treat twenty acres an hour. As owners of the formulating plant, the Carters offered to sell prescription fertilizer to the public. "The response last year was overwhelming," Jimmy grinned. He predicted even greater success the next year, and no doubt, as a politician, took pleasure in getting his story and pictures of himself and Billy on the cover of the Far West edition of *Cotton: The Magazine of Advanced Technology for Large-scale Producers.*[22]

Carter traveled in South Georgia, giving speeches, keeping his name and his opinions before the voting public. He addressed the American Legion in Americus, the PTA in Plains and Ellaville, and the Governor's Honor Program students in Macon. He chaired the Georgia Planning Commission, and he triumphantly announced that as a result of his initiative, the federal government would build a national historical park at Andersonville on the site of the Civil War prison camp. He spoke to Baptist groups, Civitan clubs, and Lions clubs. Often he spoke about advances in agricultural technology, but he repeatedly emphasized that community problems should be solved in the community by the people who understood them, not by federal intervention. He called for the Democratic party to be reorganized along lines that would increase local authority.[23]

Carter sometimes "witnessed" to strangers and, coincidentally, rehearsed his political style. In 1967 and 1968 he attended Baptist lay retreats in the North Georgia mountains. On January 28, 1968, he preached the Layman's Day sermon at his church in Plains. His notes indicate that he quoted Arnold Toynbee,

Aldous Huxley, Hyman Rickover, and—several times—Paul Tillich. Despite his avowed love of Niebuhr, Carter more often quoted Tillich. He believed that philosophers, theologians, and authors of the Bible had difficulty understanding God, but Jesus had taught his followers to "Be not conformed" to the world. They should pursue a "new dedication," as Paul had written in Galatians 2: "It is no longer I who live, but Christ who lives in me."[24] He avoided discussion of the nature of Christ.

In May 1968, Carter joined Project 500, which the Southern Baptist Mission Board established to found five hundred churches. One of four members of a team who traveled to Loch Haven, Pennsylvania, a coal-mining town, he went door to door for a week, identifying himself as a Georgia peanut farmer, "witnessing," and, he said, "feeling God near him.[25] Back in Plains, he sent the people he had visited in Pennsylvania letters and small gifts, admonishing them not to "become complacent with prosperity nor discouraged with failure." He reminded them that they were always in his prayers.[26]

At Thanksgiving 1968, Carter and three other men from Plains journeyed to Springfield, Massachusetts, for a weeklong mission trip. They worked with Spanish-speaking minorities to found a church that would hold services in their language. Carter watched Eloy Cruz, a muscular Cuban, talk a man out of committing suicide. Cruz explained that he used gentle hands for hard work, much as Jesus had done. Later, Carter sometimes drew an analogy between the way Cruz worked and a government that should exercise financial discipline and also deliver essential services to the afflicted. Back in Americus, Carter sponsored a Billy Graham Film Crusade that inspired 515 people to make "decisions for Christ."[27]

Jimmy's mother admitted that her son had "worked up North spreading the word," but she thought "Too much has been made of this religious issue. It's a private thing."[28] Carter, however, did not keep his religion private.

Carter's Christian faith instructed, but did not contradict, his politics. He believed in the separation of church and state, but he thought Christian faith should find expression in political action. As a traveling missionary he talked about the Bible, the life and teachings of Christ, the Holy Spirit, and the need to be saved. He avoided the divisive political issues of the day, especially the civil rights movement and the war in Vietnam. Very unlike Jesus, Carter coveted political power.

On her return from the Peace Corps, Miss Lillian became a popular public figure. In the fall of 1968, she gave speeches about her experience, often photographed with Rosalynn and Ruth and identified as the mother of politician Jimmy Carter. John Pennington, the journalist who had helped Jimmy in his 1962 contested senate race, published a feature story about her in an Atlanta magazine entitled "Grandmother with A Mission." Her sons welcomed her home with a new Pond House.

The Carter brothers hired Hugh Gaston of Albany, the architect who had designed Jimmy and Rosalynn's house, to construct a rustic-looking but modern house secluded from the country road by heavy woods. Every room afforded magnificent views of the woods and the pond.[29] The Pond House was also designed to be a meeting and entertainment place for a rising politician.

A straw poll in 1968 indicated that Carter could win the 1970 governorship over both former governor Carl Sanders and Republican Bo Callaway.[30] An unannounced candidate for governor, Carter addressed a meeting of the Georgia Press Institute in Athens in February and admitted he had not visited about three hundred Georgia communities "strictly to sell seed peanuts." A month later, he told the Rotarians in Americus that understanding local officials and facing "the future with courage" were necessary "to retain control over our own destiny." As if that comment did not reveal his conservatism adequately, he condemned student protests at public colleges and universities. He urged citizens to participate in government activities, and he said Georgia's cities must be given expanded sources of revenue. At Augusta in June, the state Lions convention awarded him the International Presidential Award for outstanding work as chairman of the Georgia Council of Governors.[31]

In October 1969, Carter went to Atlanta to accept the Georgia Youth Council's first annual Adult Recognition Award, and the next month he addressed the Americus-Sumter County Business and Professional Women's Club on the subject of how "neglected prenatal care contributed to illiteracy." He vigorously condemned a plan to dump nuclear waste in Georgia and decried the busing of students to meet federal guidelines for racial integration in the public schools. On February 19, 1970, Atlanta mayor Sam Massell named him Young Businessman of the Year.[32]

The Young Businessman of the Year had had the unusual experience the previous October of sighting an unidentified flying object. He described it as a "bluish," "reddish," and then "luminous" blob on the horizon near Leary, Georgia, in southeastern Calhoun County. He and ten of his fellow Lions, who were returning from their meeting, watched it for ten minutes before it disappeared. Four years later, on October 17, 1973, he officially reported it to the UFO Bureau in Oklahoma City. Long after his presidency, he still loved to tell the story. The myth that the CIA once told him while he was president that he did not have high enough security clearance to receive information they had about UFOs always amused him. Thus, he announced, tongue in cheek, that the CIA would not give him information about the UFO![33]

In 1969, however, Carter was more interested in his political future than solving the mystery of an unidentified flying object. In Georgia, he needed the support of Robert W. Woodruff, the powerful chief executive officer of the Coca-Cola Company, but Woodruff had supported Callaway and Sanders. To be accepted by Woodruff, one had to be invited to his Ichaway Plantation, near Newton, Georgia. Carter, who had not met him, wrote him forthrightly, asked to come and see him at the plantation and "talk about quail, bird dogs, and one or two other less important matters." Woodruff politely declined to allow him on the plantation but did agree to ask his office in Atlanta to set up an appointment.[34]

Preparing to announce his candidacy, Carter thundered to a group of Kiwanians in LaGrange that "Georgians are deeply conservative, but are not racists." By declaring himself to be a nonracist conservative, Carter could ask both Georgia whites and blacks for their votes. Since he knew that under the state constitution, incumbent Lester Maddox could not succeed himself when his term ended in 1970, he hoped to win some of Maddox's white followers and add others more congenial to his own viewpoint.

Covering as many bases as possible, Carter called himself "a conservative progressive." Georgians, he said, were law-abiding citizens, who believed in the "autonomy of the individual man" and that "those less fortunate have an equal right to opportunity." They were patriotic, religious people who should come up with their own programs for improving their state. They should avoid the state's traditional split into urban and rural blocs. They should "set standards high" and "never fear defeat." He condemned those who protested the war in Vietnam by saying, "I have a son in Vietnam and I wish the war there could be honorably ended." Referring to his own Navy service, he declared, "I was in Korea, but I felt

I had the support of the people." Although he had been in a submarine near the coast of Korea, he had not seen combat in that war.[35]

Carter's publicity adviser, Gerald Rafshoon, disapproved of some of his speeches. Rafshoon specifically suggested that he not say that he expected Maddox's followers to vote for him. Such statements, Rafshoon cautioned, would turn away moderate and liberal support and violate their plan that "we cannot label you." He recommended total silence on the subject of Maddox; "Let's face it Jimmy, he ain't gonna endorse you." Rafshoon denied being "an offended liberal" himself but urged Carter not to alienate suburbanites who liked him. He recommended a direct attack on Carl Sanders and "short, succinct" answers to tough questions. For example, if asked about the Kennedys, Carter should respond: "That's right, I have supporters who worked for John Kennedy. I also have supporters who worked for George Wallace, Herman Talmadge, Ellis Arnall, Lester Maddox, Rodney Cook, Sam Massell, and isn't that what Georgia is all about?" Rafshoon admitted that "you and I can wince at the corniness but look at the most popular television shows, (I know you don't but I do and so do the rest of us average Georgians)."[36]

Rafshoon helped Carter make a pitch for votes to groups and individuals who did not like each other. Clinging to the image of the peanut farmer, Carter declined to reveal his net worth.[37] In a glowingly optimistic interview with the *Americus Times-Recorder,* he announced that he had been campaigning for four years, had spent $20,000 of his own money to pay his 1966 debts, and that volunteers, not professional politicians, ran his campaign. He expected to prove that Sanders had removed control of the government from average citizens, to use every member of his family to help him win, and to "return the Georgia Democratic party back to Georgia Democrats." He went on to say that Georgia needed a governor who understood both the rural and urban areas of the state and the business community. Finally, he said: "We also need somebody to speak up for Georgians who have been neglected so badly in the past, and I honestly believe that I can fulfill these needs."[38]

On April 3, 1970, Carter walked into the old Supreme Court room in the Capitol with two-year-old Amy in his arms, his family following, and announced to the packed room, "I am a candidate for Governor of Georgia." The first Democrat to announce, he promptly attacked his probable opponent. Although he never spoke Carl Sanders's name, he assumed the wealthy former governor would be his major challenger. Thus, he declared, "Georgians never again want a governor who will use the tremendous power and prestige of the office for his own personal wealth." He did not criticize incumbent Lester Maddox, who under terms of the state constitution could not succeed himself as governor but could become lieutenant governor. Carter knew Maddox would likely be elected lieutenant governor; he thus diplomatically emphasized his own belief that the laws should be obeyed during the school desegregation crisis and that the school system should exist "for the benefit only of the children." The Carters then left the Capitol for Plains to attend a day of celebration in his honor.[39]

The mayor of Americus declared April 4 "Jimmy Carter for Governor Day." On that day in Plains, Jimmy and Rosalynn listened to the Americus High School band and to praise from local dignitaries. Cousin Hugh Carter, whom Jimmy had chosen to chair his campaign, proudly stood beside "Cousin Hot" and said, "Ladies and Gentlemen, I present to you the next governor of Georgia—Jimmy Carter." Three thousand guests consumed hundreds of pounds of barbecue as they gathered to cheer their county's first candidate for governor. "I've spent many days in Plains," Carter said to the enthusiastic crowd, "but this is the greatest day of all." Three weeks later, at the Rose Festival Parade in nearby Thomasville, he rejected the customary convertible and drove a tractor past thousands of spectators.[40]

CHAPTER TWELVE

A Conservative Progressive

THE CARTERS AND THEIR WORLD changed dramatically after 1966. The Carter sons grew up in an era of war, drugs, "free love," social protests, and rebellion. Demands for civil rights for African Americans and protests against the war in Vietnam had erupted across the nation, but not often in Georgia. In 1969 the Republican party, with the help of southern voters, placed Richard M. Nixon in the White House.[1] Not shy about expressing strong disapproval of Nixon, the Carters remained loyal to the Democratic party when they pondered how to appeal to voters who disagreed with them. Playing both sides of the fence, Carter posed as both "conservative and progressive," thus assuming a contradictory and confusing stance in his 1970 campaign.[2] He accepted the challenge of getting enough votes to win an election in a society splintered by debates over changing racial relations at home and a nationally divisive war abroad.

Confronted with a labyrinth of volatile race relations, the ambitious couple from Plains had to choose the right advisers and create a controversial winning strategy. The Civil Rights Act of 1964, the Voting Rights Act of 1965, and the murders of Senator Robert F. Kennedy and Martin Luther King, Jr., in 1968, made their task difficult. Sympathetic with blacks' demands for equality, the Carters knew that the majority of Georgia voters did not agree. The civil rights movement galvanized opposition in the streets and in the voting booth. To win the governorship of Georgia in such an atmosphere required evasiveness and vague semantics, as well as experience and knowledge of state politics. Carter emerged as a typical southern politician whose campaign rhetoric did not reveal the kind of governor he would be.

Likewise, the war in Vietnam, already nine years old and with no end in sight, had tainted American society and politics. Personally connected to the war through their son Jack, who was in the Navy, the Carters emulated the patriots of their own World War II generation. Carter condemned the leadership of presidents Lyndon Johnson and Richard Nixon, but he did not reprove American participation in the long, undefined Southeast Asia war, a position sure to find favor with many Georgia voters. He agreed with the late Martin Luther King, Jr., however, that it was a rich man's war and a poor man's fight. He lamented the fact that most of the men who went to war from his area were poor blacks, whose service indicated that racial inequality still prevailed in South Georgia.[3]

Change came more slowly to Georgia than to other states. Many white Georgians, led by Governor Lester Maddox, delayed implementing federally mandated racial equality. The martyred president John Kennedy and his brother Robert, as well as the slain Martin Luther King, Jr., had never been their heroes. Black Georgians, however, whose membership in the electorate steadily increased, believed that those men had given their lives for black liberation. The current social and political chaos had confounded the 1968 Democratic National Convention in Chicago; Carter had declined to attend it as a delegate for fear he might become identified with the liberal national Democrats.[4] Violent protests outside the hall and noisy ones within revealed a schism not healed by the nomination of Senator Hubert H. Humphrey of Minnesota.

The presidential election went to Nixon, but the majority of white Georgia voters supported Alabama's segregationist governor George C. Wallace. Running on the American Independent party ticket, he appealed to rural white and blue-collar voters who had traditionally supported Herman Talmadge. Wallace carried Georgia with 43 percent of the vote. Nixon came in second with 30 percent of the Georgia vote, and Humphrey ranked a poor third with only 27 percent.[5] Jimmy and Rosalynn voted for Humphrey and condemned those Georgia Democrats who did not remain loyal to the party.

As southern politicians who had grown up in the solidly Democratic South, the Carters, unlike their northern counterparts, understood the growing chasm between Georgia Democrats and the national party. With that understanding, they ran a well-organized centrist campaign. They identified their primary opponent, assembled a loyal team, raised money, and established goals for the state that would appeal to a wide spectrum of voters.

Jimmy and Rosalynn made their own decisions and ran the campaign as much as possible themselves. They contacted voters personally, solicited help from socially aware students, wrote mayors, welcomed volunteers, and asked for money. They selected campaign managers for every section of the state, hired researchers, and supervised the preparation of a manual entitled *Carter '70: The Difference Is You*. It explained to their volunteers the use of timetables, finances, the media, mail lists, telephones, signs, supplies, student assistants, home visits, and voter registration.[6] Both husband and wife kept copious notes about issues and individuals, devised plans to meet people, and practiced remembering names by sometimes quizzing each other.[7] They appealed to white working-class voters, sought help from Georgia's former governors, contacted their U.S. senators, gained the help of business and industry, and presented themselves as honest citizens who could be trusted. Hugh Carter, who had connections with Atlanta politicians and impeccable conservative credentials, chaired the campaign.

Jody Powell, another South Georgian, became a critical member of the team. Powell, twenty-six, had been dismissed from the Air Force Academy for cheating on a history exam but now was a graduate student in political science at Emory University. He went to see "Senator Carter" to ask the candidate permission to follow him around and glean information for a paper he was writing on George Wallace and southern populism. His interest in Wallace distinguished him from Jordan, whose respect for his Uncle Clarence may have brought a subtle, conservative strain into the campaign that neither he nor Carter realized. Carter immediately liked Powell and hired him as his driver and general assistant. Powell had grown up on a farm near Vienna, twenty-five miles east of Plains, where his father raised cotton and peanuts and his mother taught high school civics. Blonde, brash, and handsome, Powell joked about the Civil War and fundamentalist religion. Carter came to love him as a son, allowing him alone among his assistants to get close to him. Jody looked up to Carter with respect and filial piety, a bond that tightened after his own father's suicide in 1976.[8]

Like Jody, Hamilton Jordan, who managed the campaign, developed a close personal relationship with Carter and especially with Rosalynn, who shared his passion for political strategy. Since Jordan had last helped them in 1966, he had graduated from the University of Georgia and had served as a civilian in Vietnam with the International Volunteer Services. Ham, whose closest friend in

Vietnam had been a black man from Georgia, shared the Carters' ideals. In the Mekong Delta, he had worked with refugees and farmers and had learned that the natives had little use for the Americans there. Seriously ill with dengue fever that Christmas, he was lying in a military hospital when President Johnson visited "his boys" in the field. Towering over the sickbeds, Johnson looked ahead to Jordan and shouted, "Where you from, soldier?" Scarcely had Jordan proudly replied "Georgia" before a Marine who disliked sharing space with charitable civilians shouted, "He's not a soldier, Mr. President. He's a peacenik!" The president frowned, glared at Jordan, then moved away to speak to someone else, leaving Ham humiliated and deprived of his first chance to meet a president.[9]

After his Vietnam tenure, Ham found himself in complete agreement with Jimmy and Rosalynn. Jordan was stocky and had a self-effacing, country-boy demeanor that belied his brilliant mind for politics. His credentials included a degree in political science, an uncle, Hamilton McWhorter, who had served as president of the state senate, and an internship with the powerful senator Richard B. Russell. In mid-1968, Hamilton met with the campaign workers at the Pond House and created a grassroots organization in each of the state's 159 counties.[10] He wrote many of the memoranda that became the basis for the campaign and supervised the entire operation. He and Rosalynn agreed about how to conduct a campaign, which elevated both to an unusual level of power in the entire operation. When Hamilton and Nancy Konigsmark married, he used their wedding reception to introduce Carter to lawyers, bankers, a judge, a state senator, an assistant to the president of the University of Georgia, and a typical student.[11]

Ham frequently addressed Jimmy and Rosalynn by their first names, but he always referred to Charles Kirbo as "Mr. Kirbo." Old enough to be Carter's father, Kirbo, who had helped Carter in 1962 and 1966, believed that Carter could eventually win high political office. Only Kirbo, tight-lipped and loyal, could freely wander through the maze of Carter's public life offering unsolicited, but well-informed, advice and criticism. He recommended ideas for speeches and helped raise money.[12] Closer to the candidate than Mr. Earl would have been, or even Admiral Rickover, Kirbo appeared to many to be an avuncular country lawyer whose keen intelligence had carried him to the top of Atlanta legal circles.[13] He knew the politics of the state and sensed Carter's place in it.

More than a mentor, Kirbo became Carter's alter ego. Jimmy "and I just generally saw alike," he said. Their relationship was "based mainly on memoranda," because Carter wrote in the margins, then returned such communications to their senders. Kirbo found Carter to be ambitious, determined, and "absolutely free from corruption." Carter would not let anyone around him "cheat," nor would he use his political position "to try to profit," Kirbo said. Kirbo often did not like Carter's policy of "being open with everything," because it often served no good purpose. Conservative on fiscal matters, Carter wanted to help people in all areas of their lives. Kirbo shared the same goals and felt convinced that Carter would be good for the state.[14]

Another brainy attorney, this one Harvard-trained, brought limited political experience but considerable intellectual clout to the team. Twenty-seven-year-old Stuart Eizenstat, an Atlanta native who had worked in Humphrey's 1968 presidential campaign, discovered a philosophical soul mate in Carter. He had planned to work for Carl Sanders in 1970, but when a friend introduced him to Carter, he identified so closely with the so-called peanut farmer that he asked to join the team. He thought Carter might bridge the traditional rural-urban gap and unify the state. He researched issues, formulated questions and answers for the candidate, and gave suggestions to Gerald Rafshoon for the media campaign. Although he knew very little about South Georgia, the erudite Eizenstat, who was Jewish, brought common sense and a cosmopolitan outlook to the Carter camp.[15]

Peter Bourne added the perspective of an English-born psychiatrist who had been trained at Emory University. He stood in awe of Carter's stable personality, powers of concentration, willpower, and self-control. Bourne had served in Vietnam as a medical researcher, and he had marched in Atlanta's streets for civil rights. He had demonstrated outside the 1968 Democratic Convention in Chicago against the war in Vietnam and joined Vietnam Veterans for Eugene McCarthy. Impressed by Carter's ability to relate equally well to both whites and blacks, Bourne wanted to join the team. Bourne's wife, Mary King, also admired the Carters and intended to work for them. Bourne believed that Carter could win in 1970.[16]

No one, however, equaled Rosalynn in her husband's campaign. She was a strong-willed woman married to a strong-willed man. Sometimes they attempted to resolve their differences by kneeling side by side in prayer, each telling God his or her side of the issue.[17] Something worked for them, for, bound by the contractual ties of marriage and the mysterious vagaries of love, they shared responsibility for four children, a southern heritage, and similar ambitions. Rosalynn kept a "Special Subject Book" with biographical and financial information, some notes from Jimmy, some references to religion and scripture, and a guideline in Jimmy's handwriting on how to make index cards on voters and contributors.[18] She had her own issues and platform, political style, and dreams about how to use power. In a different time and place, she might have stayed at home to rear the children or floated free of her husband to achieve a distinguished career of her own. Instead, she made his career her own.

With the help of their closest advisers, the Carters developed an eight-page platform, which they published in late July. Avoiding controversial topics, they vowed to "serve all Georgians, not just a powerful or selfish few." To do so, they would strengthen Georgia's ties with neighboring states, enforce law and order under a strict system of justice at home, and expand and improve educational opportunities at all levels. They pledged to reduce property taxes, promote tourism, assist local governments, promote agriculture and industry, protect the environment, encourage "all young Georgians" to register to vote, and help people get off welfare. They promised improved facilities for both physically and mentally ill patients, a rapid transit system for Atlanta, and protection of Georgia's historic sites. They vowed to end the system of depositing the state's revenues in a few "pet banks" and to "make bank deposits in a fair, predictable and uniform manner throughout Georgia."[19]

The Carters added pollsters, attorneys, businessmen, relatives, and friends to their team. William Hamilton, a professional pollster in Washington, D.C., joined public relations specialist Gerald Rafshoon to determine what Georgians wanted and to create an image of Jimmy as precisely fitting the bill. Several Georgians who had helped Carter in previous years returned in 1970. Attorneys Robert Lipshutz and David Gambrell managed his campaign treasury. Realtor Philip Alston and his daughter Elke Cushman joined Cousin Hugh Carter and old friends Charles Kirbo, Bill Gunter, J. D. Deriso, Dot Padgett, and John Pope to help elect Carter. They represented a cross-section of Georgia society. As state senator, campaign chairman, and candidate's cousin, Hugh Carter reassured conservatives that his Cousin "Hot" could be trusted to preserve the status quo.

Other Carter friends, however, supported Sanders. State senator Brooks Pennington, Jr., the wealthy Madison farmer who ran Jimmy's 1966 campaign and was a close friend of Sanders, made a painful decision to back the former governor. Likewise, J. Frank Meyers, who had worked for Carter in 1966, switched to Sanders, whom he thought to be more liberal than Carter.[20]

Atlanta professionals who worked for Carter gave his campaign an organized, educated, and biracial focus, although those characteristics were not always obvious to the voting public. Frank Moore, who had worked with Carter earlier on the state planning commission, had experience dealing with local governments. Jerry Clotfelder, a political science professor at Emory, identified issues relevant to contemporary Georgia politics. Arkansan Jack Watson, a Harvard Law School graduate and a member of the King and Spaulding law firm, liked Carter's love of reading and his ability to focus and concentrate.

In 1969, Paul and Carol Muldawer invited Carter to a biracial fund-raiser at their Atlanta home. There he met local black attorney Vernon Jordan and the Reverend Andrew Young, a chief lieutenant of the late Martin Luther King, Jr., and soon to be a candidate for the U.S. House.[21] Those men thought they understood Carter and wanted him to win, but many of the speeches he gave in quest of the majority blue-collar voters tested their faith.

During the summer, the Carter family helped. Billy and Sybil Carter took charge of the warehouse in Plains, and Miss Lillian accompanied Rosalynn to ladies' teas, factory workers' shift changes, and poultry plants. Politics improved their relationship. Lillian at seventy-two was a relaxed speaker, and Rosalynn later joked about how she and her mother-in-law had given talks in every county of the state. Jeffrey, who planned to attend Georgia Southwestern in the fall, drove them around. Chip dropped out of Georgia Southwestern to solicit votes on college campuses. Amy rode in parades but mostly stayed at home with her Grandmother Smith. Gloria ran the headquarters in Plains with the help of Ruth's daughter Lynn. Other family members worked from the Atlanta headquarters in the Quality Inn on Tenth Street, an inexpensive motel in a poor neighborhood. Miss Lillian admitted that during the last days of the campaign, she and Rosalynn ate at the Varsity, a celebrated establishment adjacent to the Georgia Tech campus, "because it was the cheapest place we could find."[22] It was not a bad place for politicking either.

The man Carter would have to beat in 1970, Carl Sanders, had been a popular governor. A moderate on race relations, he had vowed to keep public schools open even if they became integrated. He did not favor social equality between whites and blacks, however, and had disapproved of the integration of the

University of Georgia.[23] Carter and Sanders shared many common friends from Carter's state senate career, and Carter admired the accomplishments of Sanders's governorship.

The demands of politics, however, dictated that Carter denigrate Sanders in every possible way to pry voters away from him. A reporter for the *Columbus Ledger-Enquirer* acquired a copy of a 1968 note that Carter scribbled on a legal pad for an aide: "Some images to be projected regarding Carl Sanders... more liberal... close connections with... Atlanta Establishment... pretty boy... ignored prison reform opportunities... nouveau riche... refused to assist local school boards in school financing... excluded George Wallace from state." Carter instructed his helpers, "You can see that some of these are conflicting, but right now we just need to collect all these rough ideas we can. Later we can start driving a wedge between me and him."[24] The note revealed a campaign style, namely driving a wedge between himself and his opponent, that would become typical of the way Carter sought public office.

Carter ruthlessly attacked Sanders verbally almost every day of the campaign. He accused his opponent of using the governor's office to "get rich," being too close to the national Democrats, ambitious for the ailing Richard Russell's Senate seat, and being in favor of integrating the races. Carter could not prove such allegations, and Sanders's administration had been scandal free. Carter nevertheless transformed Sanders into a monster who would, if elected, embrace social chaos and destroy the rights of common people. Carter contended that "Cuff Links Carl" was a "limousine liberal" who had robbed the people of Georgia and would do so again.[25]

For the next three months, Carter kept up the attack, accusing Sanders of teaming with businessman J. B. Fuqua to acquire five broadcasting stations, of favoring wealthy friends with state contracts, and of virtually accepting a bribe from Delta Airlines. Sanders and his friends denied all charges, and Carter never proved any of them.[26]

In the traditional battle of rural Georgia versus Atlanta, Carter found himself in a position to win votes from both the rural and metropolitan voters. He had attended college in Atlanta and served in the state senate. He and Rosalynn loved Atlanta, especially the shopping, cultural opportunities, and political ambience of the state capital, almost as much as they cherished their home in Plains. In May 1970, they decided to send their third son, Jeffrey, to Atlanta to attend the

elite Woodward Academy for his senior year. Carter delivered the commencement address at his son's graduation.[27]

Shortly thereafter, Jimmy and Rosalynn received *A Survey of Political Opinions in Georgia,* a report from their pollster, William R. Hamilton. The poll was
conducted May 18–26, during a season when a race riot in Augusta left six blacks
dead and seventy-five injured, the news of two black students killed by policemen in Jackson, Mississippi, made headlines in Georgia, and the Reverend Ralph
Abernathy announced that he would lead a one-hundred-mile march through
central Georgia to call attention to the growing repression of blacks throughout
the country. Hundreds of college and university campuses closed because students protested President Nixon's decision to expand the war in Vietnam into
Cambodia. At Kent State University in Ohio, national guardsmen killed four
students while trying to reestablish order. Elsewhere in the world, Israeli planes
conducted intensive sorties across the Suez Canal to make certain that Egypt,
which was receiving aid from the Soviet Union, did not establish missile sites
along the canal. In the United States, people feared that actions by the Soviet
Union might turn the Cold War into a hot one in an age when nuclear destruc-
tion of the planet was possible. Domestic turmoil and international danger
defined the world in which Georgians weighed their choices for governor.[28]

Hamilton reported that 45 percent of the voters liked the handsome, friendly
Sanders, but the 20 percent who did not like him often mentioned the fact that
he had become wealthy after becoming governor and that he was too close to
the country club set. Carter ran strongest among rural, blue-collar, and white
voters, whereas Sanders attracted sophisticated urban, highly educated, and
black voters. For Carter to succeed, the report continued, he must continue to
destroy Sanders's positive image, oppose busing to achieve racial integration,
take a moderately strong position in favor of law and order, take a hard-line stand
against student demonstrations, and favor education and the building of roads.
These themes were nearly identical with many of those George Wallace had campaigned on in 1968. The pollster advised Carter, however, to make daytime television appeals to female voters, target blue-collar voters in Atlanta who admired
Wallace, concentrate on small and medium cities, and deliver radio broadcasts in
which he promised roads for rural Georgia.[29]

Carter may have noted some intriguing data imbedded in the report, but he
did not comment on it. Only 29 percent of the surveyed voters saw racial prob-

lems as a major issue, and among them, 18 percent were problack or neutral, whereas the remaining 11 percent were antiblack. Georgia had changed, but a successful candidate still could not ignore the 29 percent who might decide how to vote on the basis of racial considerations.

Jimmy and Rosalynn followed the blueprint William Hamilton gave them. Rafshoon prepared two commercials, one showing a very relaxed Jimmy harvesting peanuts on his farm while a soothing voice assured viewers that Jimmy Carter knew what it was like to work for a living. The other, an attack on Sanders, showed an elegant door tightly closed, which a voice described as a country club where rich people drank cocktails, played cards, and raised money for Sanders. On June 10, Jimmy and Rosalynn paid the campaign entry fee and posed for photographers as Carter became the first of nine people to qualify as a candidate for the Democratic nomination for governor.[30]

The same day, Carter stepped up his attack on Sanders for having used the governor's office for personal gain, a charge Sanders vigorously denied. Carter challenged him to make a declaration of his personal wealth, but Sanders retorted that the money he had earned since leaving office was nobody's business. He did promise to account for his stewardship of public funds. Carter promised to disclose his own wealth later in the campaign, but in the meantime he planned to "kick around" charges that Sanders had abused the office of governor to make money and to dominate the state legislature. Georgia ought to have a "strong governor and a strong legislature," Carter said.[31]

Carter revealed his own worth at a very conservative $409,000, most of which represented his interest in the peanut warehouse and his lands in Sumter and Webster counties. He demanded that Sanders disclose the value of his holdings in real estate, banking, corporate stocks, and legal fees, which Sanders declined to do.[32] Mindful of the powerful lower-middle-class white vote, Jimmy entered a hog-calling contest in North Georgia and won. "I've been calling hogs all my life," the boastful champion said, as he accepted a handsome trophy.[33] Presenting himself as the people's candidate, Carter proclaimed that he would be a friend to the common Georgian. He promised to retain Governor Maddox's "Little People's Day" that allowed ordinary citizens to bring their problems to his office. Carter agreed with Maddox's opposition to legalized pari-mutuel betting, which pleased the state's conservative Christians. Often Carter simply smiled, touched, shook hands, and said, "I'm Jimmy Carter, and I'm running for Governor. I hope you will vote for me."[34]

Carter sometimes resorted to segregationist rhetoric and colorful antics to get the electorate's attention. "I am convinced that there is a permanent and important place in Georgia education for private schools," he said, to the delight of the segregationists, after he had been reported in opposition to private schools. He held a news conference on top of a viaduct over Interstate 75 during Atlanta's rush-hour traffic at which he vowed to build highways "on the basis of long-range need rather than political expediency." The following week, he stood barefoot in the sand next to a river spoiled with sewage and promised to fight environmental pollution in Georgia.[35] He could be a showman in the mold of "Ole Gene" Talmadge himself, a Georgia tradition certain to attract attention.

Whereas in 1966 Carter had projected a moderate image against Maddox and had won the more liberal voters, in a contest with the quasi-liberal Sanders, he took a different approach. He thought the presence in the race of black candidate C. B. King, an attorney from Albany who had been involved in the Southern Christian Leadership Conference's Albany Movement of 1962, would deny him black voters and that the better educated people in the state would support Sanders. He therefore put together a coalition of young people, conservatives, and anti-Sanders folk; he sought the voters who had supported Maddox in 1966 and Wallace in 1968.

Carter sometimes praised Maddox, took a hard line on law and order, and vilified Sanders for being cozy with the national Democrats and refusing to invite George Wallace to speak at the Georgia state Capitol. In the riot-torn late 1960s, Carter warmed the hearts of many Georgia conservatives when he promised to send "seasoned and trained troops" to quell riots in communities and on college campuses. He would accompany the troops personally, he said, as he urged young Georgians to be patriotic Americans.[36]

Likewise, Carter won points with rural conservatives by attacking the Atlanta newspapers for their "demagoguery" and "unfair" portrait of him as "profane" and "vengeful." He condemned the *Atlanta Constitution* for not reporting his positions and falsely portraying him as a racist. He promised home rule for Atlanta and other cities, reduced property taxes, and equitable allocation of highway funds. Carter himself, however, confused the public and the press about where he stood on the issues by including colorful and questionable attacks on Sanders in every speech.[37]

Campaigning separately from Jimmy, Rosalynn left the mudslinging to her husband. To a group of women in Savannah, she presented a succinct account of how her political family worked and what Jimmy would do for the state of Georgia. Although she had never dreamed of being married to a gubernatorial candidate, she said, "I've grown into politics." Because she worked almost full-time for his election, she gave up keeping the books at the warehouse, and she saw her husband on average once a week. She noted that the entire family, including her teenaged sons and her mother-in-law, campaigned for Jimmy. Even two-year-old Amy, she said, once told her, "I've just gone politicking." Rosalynn told her audience that women all over Georgia were working to get Jimmy Carter elected. He was for "good, clean, honest government," she said. His main goals would be to improve education, involve many citizens in the state's government, and promote conservation of natural resources.[38]

The issue of mental illness captured Rosalynn's attention that summer. Many voters seemed to have mentally ill or retarded relatives who needed help. One factory worker whom she met left her job at a cotton mill every day at 4:30 A.M. and rushed home to care for a mentally handicapped daughter. Later in the campaign, at Swainsboro, Rosalynn found herself in the unusual situation of being in the same town where Jimmy was holding a rally. She stepped into the receiving line to shake his hand, and then asked her shocked husband what he was going to do about mental health. He replied that Georgia would have the best mental health program in the country and that she would be in charge of it.[39]

Carter was well acquainted with the topic because he had two mentally ill, institutionalized first cousins. The Georgia Association for Mental Health addressed a letter to him as a candidate and attached a list of its goals for 1971–72, not the least of which was the development of community health centers and a bill of rights for the mentally ill.[40] At the time its president wrote the letter, the organization did not know that Carter would win, nor did it have any idea what a friend it would have in Rosalynn Carter.

A candidate might speak his mind safely about mental health, but race relations was another matter. Carter could not afford to alienate the white segregationist majority if he hoped to win, but he also wanted to appeal to black voters. Kirbo remembered that Carter, against the objections of some staffers, campaigned in black communities. He "went right to all the black beer joints ... shaking hands," Kirbo said, making appearances that the media used against him.[41] Claiming the support of some black clergymen, Carter told Vernon Jordan, "You won't like my campaign, but you will like my administration."[42]

Avoiding the media, Carter wrote letters to five presiding elders in the African Methodist Episcopal Church asking for their help.[43] Bishop William D. Johnson mailed an impassioned form letter explaining that "Jimmie Carter, My Neighbor, who grew up receiving from his father a sense of fair play," cared for blacks and whites, helped the poor, bridged the generation gap, and "understands the *old* and the *young* of both Races."[44]

Carter knew that there were not enough black voters in Georgia to elect the governor. He knew, too, that a candidate connected too closely with black voters risked his white support. He therefore used the issue of race to try to strip Sanders of both white and black votes. To take white votes from Sanders, the Carter campaign attempted to present Sanders as a "Negro lover." It printed and distributed thousands of leaflets showing Sanders, part owner of the Atlanta Hawks professional basketball team, receiving a "champagne shampoo" from Lou Hudson, a black player, after a victory. The photograph, which had originally been in the sports pages of the *Atlanta Journal,* showed up statewide in beauty parlors, barber shops, and mailboxes.[45]

To pry black votes from Sanders, Carter's campaign created the fictitious "Black Concern Committee" which peppered black pool halls, churches, and barbeques with pamphlets that accused Sanders of not keeping his promises to blacks and not having any empathy with them. His campaign secretly financed radio speeches for black candidate C. B. King to draw African-American voters away from Sanders.[46]

When citizens accused Carter of being a "nigger lover," he rushed to deny it. His campaign manager in North Georgia, a student at the University of Tennessee at Chattanooga, just across the border from Georgia, wrote him a secret letter saying that two prominent men in Walker County had heard a "ridiculous" rumor that Miss Lillian had participated in a civil rights march in Selma, Alabama, back in 1965 and were about to withdraw their support. Carter immediately wrote the men that the rumor was false and thanked the student for his good work.[47]

Carter also supported the segregationist university regent Roy Harris. Harris commented that "when the white people find out you have the Negroes, they get on the other side." Carter's press aide, who circulated Harris's comment to

Carter's staff, told a reporter, "When Mr. Roy talks, I listen." Carter promised that if elected, he would reappoint Harris to the Board of Regents.[48]

The Carter campaign's use of Sanders's "shampoo" photograph and acceptance of Harris's endorsement were nefarious tricks reminiscent of Lyndon Johnson's stealing the U.S. Senate race in 1948. Such antics contradicted Carter's image, but his campaigners were willing to sling mud and mislead the public. Morris Collins, a professor of political science and director of the Institute of Government at the University of Georgia, thought Carter himself was detached during the campaign and that it was Carter's workers who put out the scurrilous literature. Collins, a Sanders man, incurred the wrath of Hamilton Jordan for not supporting Carter, but he did not believe that Carter personally endorsed the dirty tricks against his opponent.[49] The truth remains unknown.

Carter understood that the power structure of the state rested in the hands of current U.S. senators and former governors, all of whom had taken conservative stands on the race issue. Furthermore, they all thought Sanders too liberal and did not want him to become governor again. Carter invoked their names and asked for their help in 1970. He visited former governor Marvin Griffin three times at his newspaper office in Bainbridge. He convinced Griffin that he was a simple peanut farmer, a "conservative in thought and deed." The thoroughly duped Griffin publicly endorsed Carter at the Atlanta Press Club meeting in the White House Motel in Atlanta shortly before the primary.[50]

Carter told a gathering of Democratic women in Marietta that he had Senator Richard Russell's backing. Russell's office in Washington denied it, saying that Russell had not changed his policy of refusing to endorse "any candidate seeking nomination to any office in a Georgia Democratic primary." Carter responded that the newspaper had not deliberately misquoted him, but it had misinterpreted him.[51] Russell had privately promised to help Carter, however, partly out of friendship but more likely because he wanted Sanders defeated. Russell had never forgiven Sanders for threatening to run against him four years earlier when he had been ill. The senator gave Carter his old lists of the names of his supporters, but they were too out-of-date to help.[52] Later, with characteristic hyperbole, Carter claimed that the senator "was an intimate personal friend of mine who encouraged me for four years against Sanders and who, in the general election, was a loyal Democrat."[53] Sanders maintained that Carter lied, because Russell did not know or have any relationship with him.[54] Senator Herman Talmadge avoided making a public statement, but he unofficially endorsed Carter to help him win traditional white Democratic votes.

Former governor Ernest Vandiver announced that he would support Carter. Because Vandiver's wife was Russell's niece, Vandiver's announcement was tantamount to a statement that the venerable senator, who refused to endorse anyone, favored Carter.[55] Since the elderly Russell was terminally ill, the new governor would appoint a temporary successor after Russell's death. Vandiver claimed that Carter promised Russell's seat to him, and Carter praised Vandiver for having kept the public schools open during the integration crisis.[56]

Knowing that he needed more than endorsements from political heavy-weights, Carter continued his personal campaign. From the mountains in northern Georgia to the sandy coastal plains of the south, he attended chicken dinners and barbecues, where the approving crowds seemed to get larger and larger. Laurens County banker Cecil Passmore, Jr., and William Wexler, international head of B'nai B'rith, went to hear him. One hundred young Democrats rallied in his behalf at Georgia Southwestern.[57]

Appealing to blue-collar workers, many of whom had supported Maddox, Carter condemned "Cuff Links" Carl Sanders again and again. A group of "Youth for Wallace" in southwestern Georgia declared their support for both Wallace *and* Carter.[58] In retaliation, the Sanders camp accused Carter of bargaining secretly for black votes. Carter denied it, but he stated categorically that the next governor would "need the help of qualified black leaders who don't have any selfish reasons to be in government service," and he visited black churches and schools seeking support.[59]

Trying to expose the alleged corruption of the Sanders administration, Carter made a dramatic, unannounced visit to State Highway Department director Jim Gillis. A chief lieutenant in the Sanders campaign, Gillis held one of the most powerful positions in state government. Carter pretended that he spoke to Gillis only about road-building projects, but he reminded Georgians that he had "laid open the Sanders record for all to see," implying that Sanders would conduct "moon-lighting business," thus enabling Gillis to favor certain road construction contractors.[60] The infuriated Sanders put out a handbill announcing that "Carter was born with a silver spoon in his mouth and inherited a 2,000 acre plantation in South Georgia where he makes his profits off the sweat of poor working people."[61] Carter had in fact been born into a more affluent family than Sanders, although Sanders had become wealthy by the time of the 1970 campaign.

By Election Day, September 9, most voters in Georgia had been convinced that Carter was not only a friend of working people but a working man himself, who would not embrace the radical policies of his national party. Reg Murphy, editor of the *Atlanta Constitution*, wrote bitterly that Carter's position allowed older segregationists to insist they were not racists.[62] Carter's description of himself as a conservative progressive was riddled with contradictions, but most working people, a few blacks, many friends and acquaintances, some business-men, and young people went to the polls to vote for him.

CHAPTER THIRTEEN

"A Trace of Demagoguery"

ON SEPTEMBER 9, 1970, Carter received 388,280 votes (48.65 percent) to Sanders's 301,179 (37.73 percent), leaving him just short of the 50 percent needed for the nomination. Carter was not distracted by the euphoria surrounding his large lead going into the runoff election. His Sumter County financial chairman bragged that Carter had defeated most of the business structure in the state, including powerful Jim Gillis of the highway department. The *Americus Times-Recorder* called the vote a "stunning upset" over the "press, power structure," and "politicos." Carter believed that his and his family's contact with more than half a million people had been the secret to his success, but he advised his staff not to become complacent.[1]

Carter knew what he had to do to win. Like most southern politicians of his day, he used cues for voters rather than outright statements; he thus avoided telling a lie, but he made it difficult for voters to know where he stood on the issues. He needed the votes of the Maddox and Wallace people, but he could not endorse their positions, especially on race relations. For example, in one speech he commented that Sanders had run strongly in Atlanta's black precincts, suggesting that Sanders was the candidate of African Americans, which was true. His crafty statement signaled to white segregationists to vote for Carter.[2]

No sooner had the runoff date been set for September 23 than both Carter and Sanders launched vicious campaigns. Sanders charged Carter with being "a liar," "a phony," and "a user of political snake oil."[3] Invading Carter country at Columbus, Sanders abandoned his natty image and tried to appear as one of the people. He removed his jacket, rolled up the sleeves of his sweat-stained shirt, loosened his necktie, and called Carter a "smiling hypocrite" who had tried to take God out of the state constitution and had promoted better housing while keeping his own tenants in shacks. "He turned his back on the people of Georgia," Sanders thundered. "He has toe-danced across Georgia, telling different people different things about issues. He has turned the truth of this state inside out." Carter replied airily that Sanders was "an embittered and desperate man" and that he, Carter, would win "because there are a lot more working people in Georgia than there are big shots."[4]

As the campaign progressed, the *Atlanta Constitution,* although no friend to Carter, began to question Sanders's integrity. While Carter staged "Hi Neighbor" days and "Old Time" rallies, Sanders and the *Atlanta Journal* sent teams into South Georgia to probe Carter's farm operation. After spending most of the day talking with tenants, they were unable to prove any of Sanders's accusations. Jimmy's brother "Bill," later famous as "Billy," jokingly asked, "You want to see the tenants we keep penned up, or the ones we let out to pick peanuts?"[5]

Sanders churned out handbills asking for the "real Jimmy Carter" to "please stand up." He sent letters to Carter friends, including Bill Gunter, asking for contributions. Gunter replied with a note: "Dear Carl: The extent of your ego and arrogance is indeed appalling." Lester Maddox endorsed Sanders but refused to say anything about Carter, whom he loathed. The Sanders people put out a handbill with pictures of tenant farmers' shacks allegedly on Carter's farm, implying that Carter did not care about poor people. A cartoonist for the *Gwinnett Daily News* captured Sanders's desperation perfectly. He drew a sketch of a neatly dressed Sanders, cufflinks gleaming, in "The New Image Clothing Store" asking the clerk for "A Pair of Overalls and a Bucket of Mud, Please."[6]

Meanwhile, Carter courted traditional white voters. Despite lieutenant governor–elect Lester Maddox's refusal to endorse him, he picked up most of Maddox's supporters. Carter visited the infamously corrupt Long County in southeastern Georgia, whose officials had received national attention when both the Sanders and Maddox administrations had attempted to rid the area of speed traps, rigged trials resulting in high traffic fines, and clandestine gambling operations. Carter intended his visit as a statement that he, too, would maintain law and order in Long County, but Sanders accused him of having "crawled in bed" with the gamblers there.[7]

Sanders and Carter each tried to portray the other as being cozy with African Americans, a sure way to cost the opponent white votes. Sanders declared that Carter had "sold out" the voters and met secretly with black leader Hosea Williams to "make a deal for votes." Black candidate C. B. King announced that he would not support Sanders or Carter, and the statewide Black Leadership Coalition split its support between the two.[8]

Both candidates wanted black votes, but neither dared risk alienating the white majority. Most black Georgians did not trust Carter. Robert F. Flanagan, Georgia field director of the NAACP, referred to him cynically as "Brother Carter" whose ambition took precedence over how much help he would give to African Americans. Flanagan remembered a meeting of the NAACP in Warner Robbins, Georgia, which Carter attended, supplying steaks for the small group. Carter wasted his money, however, for the blacks felt they could not trust anyone from South Georgia, and they voted for Sanders.[9]

Sanders challenged Carter to a debate, but Carter begged off with the excuse that Sanders would not reveal his wealth. Wherever Sanders spoke, he displayed an empty chair for Carter, a ploy that backfired on him when Carter drily commented, "Some folks say the chair was ahead." Five days before the election, Sanders finally listed his net worth at $685,624. Carter responded dubiously that his own "family never had been blessed with great wealth," but he refused to face Sanders in open debate. Denying that he was a "land baron or slaver," Carter stuck to his guns, insisting that he was only a poor farmer who struggled to pay his taxes, although his earlier admission that he was worth $409,000 scarcely put him in the poverty class.[10]

In separate interviews with an *Atlanta Constitution* reporter, both candidates answered questions about nineteen issues. Carter came across as more progressive than Sanders.[11] On most issues, there was no difference between them. Both favored improvement of education at the kindergarten and secondary levels, neighborhood schools, and vocational training. Neither made any promises about higher education. Carter specifically favored more programs and teachers for retarded and mentally handicapped students. Both promised tax relief for local districts, not to raise taxes, and to protect the environment from industrial pollution. Sanders now agreed with Carter that George Wallace should be allowed to speak in Georgia if the people wanted him. Both promised to hire and appoint women, youths, and blacks to state jobs and committees. Both promised to prevent and contain violence on and off college and university campuses.

The issues on which Carter and Sanders disagreed revealed that Carter had a major plan to reform and reorganize state government, eliminate entrenched corruption in the Highway Department, and concentrate on improving services for poor and sick people. Sanders wanted a new state constitution, whereas Carter preferred to amend the current one. Carter strongly favored switching from authority financing, which gave the governor and legislature absolute power in deciding which projects to fund, to general tax obligation bonds, to place more of the decisions in the hands of people who would vote for or against the bonds. The financially conservative Sanders feared such a change would lead to greater government spending. Carter planned to save the Georgia Bureau of Investigation in the Department of Public Safety, as opposed to Sanders's promise to place it under the attorney general.

Sanders thought his friend Jim Gillis had done a fine job as director of the Highway Department, but Carter had a plan for more equitable allocation of highway funds that would create "circumstances" under which "Mr. Jim Gillis would probably not wish to stay on as director." Carter would provide better staffing for mental hospitals and increased outpatient care, whereas Sanders favored a strong emphasis on community counseling. Sanders promised to make the lieutenant governor's office, a position everyone knew would soon be occupied by outgoing governor Lester Maddox, more meaningful. Sanders said he would take advantage of Maddox's executive experience to draw him into a close working relationship with the governor. Carter, who had vigorously courted Maddox's supporters, hedged on the question because the timing was not yet right for him to reveal how much he disliked Maddox. Carter thought the lieutenant governor should work with the senate and tend to ceremonial functions, but he declined to specify his duties.[12]

The voters ignored this boring newspaper article, the lone source of accurate public information revealing where each candidate stood. The day after the *Atlanta Constitution* published the interviews, Carter and Sanders renewed their battle. Carter ran a quarter-page advertisement in the *Americus Times-Recorder* proclaiming himself to be a wonderful neighbor, Christian, family man, businessman, public official, and civic leader.[13] Feeling confident of victory, he continued to decline to debate Sanders.

An angry Sanders responded with a handbill screaming *"HERE'S WHY! Jimmy Carter is Afraid to Debate Carl Sanders."* The facts, according to Sanders, were that Carter had lied about himself when he claimed to be a friend of the homeowner, a religious leader, a Wallace man, a poor farmer, a friend to the working man, and an advocate of private schools. In truth, Sanders continued, Carter had used his state senate office to oppose homestead exemptions for the elderly, had favored the words "freedom of conscience" rather than "right to worship God" for the state constitution, and would allow lotteries in the state. Furthermore, he claimed, Carter had paid Hosea Williams to travel the state to influence black voters, supported Lyndon Johnson and Hubert Humphrey, received $12,000 per year in federal farm subsidies, pushed for a sales tax increase that would harm workers, and had once blocked the building of a private school in Norman Park, Georgia.[14] Sanders twisted the details of Carter's senate career, doing unto Carter what Carter had done unto him.

On the day of the runoff, September 23, Carter won 63 percent of the vote. For the first time, he carried the urban counties; the black precincts in Atlanta gave him 6 percent of their votes, in Macon 10 percent, and in Savannah 52 percent.[15] The *New York Times,* which apparently did not know that Carter considered himself a "conservative progressive," dubbed him more accurately "a wealthy liberal whose tough campaigning won him some of his state's large Wallace vote." It noted that Carter's "conservative-sounding positions" appealed "to many of the followers of Governor Maddox" and that those positions did not alienate Carter's liberal and moderate support.[16]

Reg Murphy of the *Atlanta Constitution,* a clever observer, noted that Carter retained his voters from his primary victory, picked up many votes from the minor candidates, won votes among people who did not vote the first time, and had the support of Georgia's most powerful political factions. Former governors Ernest Vandiver and Marvin Griffin had endorsed him, and both senators Richard Russell and Herman Talmadge had quietly favored his victory. The majority of the black votes went to Sanders.[17] A very unhappy Sanders conceded and promised to support Carter in the general election.

The Carters attended a victory rally in Americus the next day. "This is where my heart is," Carter said, as he and Rosalynn waved and smiled to the cheering crowd of three thousand along their parade route.[18] After vacationing briefly on the Georgia coast, they prepared for the October 7 Democratic convention in Macon.

Carter hoped to win the state's business giants who had favored Sanders, especially Robert W. Woodruff of Coca-Cola. Earlier, Woodruff had given him the brush-off, but now that he was the Democratic nominee and would inevitably win the governorship in November, Woodruff might reconsider. Ovid Davis, an officer with Coca-Cola and a friend to both Sanders and Carter, urged Woodruff to meet with Carter. Davis informed his boss that Carter still had "his nose . . . just a little bit out of joint" but considered Woodruff the leading businessman of the state. Davis assured Woodruff that Carter would work with him after the election.[19] Woodruff, eighty and proud that he had encouraged the Republican Dwight D. Eisenhower to run for president in 1952, sent his Rolls Royce to bring Carter to his office to get acquainted.[20] Riding through the streets of Atlanta in a chauffeured Rolls Royce, Carter now had the endorsement of the state's largest business; where Woodruff went, others like him would soon follow.

At the Macon convention, Carter, by virtue of the nomination, rose to be leader of the party. He emphasized the strength that would come through Democratic unity, and he kept his campaign promise that should he become the part's candidate, he would transfer the gubernatorial candidate's power to choose the executive committee to the convention.[21] It was a major reform that would at least superficially grant more power to the people.

After the convention, Carter rewarded those who had supported him in the runoff and punished those who had not. He promised to "professionalize" the Georgia National Guard and the Georgia State Highway Patrol, many of whose members had backed Sanders. He appointed former governor Ernest Vandiver adjutant general of the National Guard. Carter demanded that veteran highway director, "Mr. Jim" Gillis, Sr., a Sanders man, resign, and he intended to remove Gillis's son Hugh from his position as president pro tem of the senate.

Carter snubbed Maddox by not inviting him to a Democratic caucus until the eleventh hour but made peace with him and later extolled him as the "essence of the party."[22] Before the election, Carter stuck to his political guns, promising that if he was elected governor he would "return control of our schools to Georgians."[23] No segregationist himself, Carter said what segregationists wanted to hear.

Carter faced a sudden crisis when Roy Harris, whom he had promised to reappoint to the state Board of Regents, unsuccessfully opposed the appointment of former U.S. Secretary of State Dean Rusk to the University of Georgia faculty. Rusk, a Georgian who had served presidents Kennedy and Johnson during the 1960s, was a well-known advocate of racial equality. When an Atlanta newspaper reported that Carter would not reappoint Harris, Carter denied the story.

Carter's promise to reappoint Harris had helped him win followers of Maddox and Wallace in the primary, and he needed their votes again in the general election. Hamilton Jordan drafted the letter Carter sent privately to one of Harris's defenders; he called "Mr. Roy" a "personal friend" whose "friendship and support" he appreciated.[24] Carter cagily avoided, on the eve of the election, saying whether he would or would not reappoint Harris, leaving the impression that he would. In fact, after he became governor, he did not.[25]

Race, money, government reform, taxes, and personal honesty issues dominated the general election. Republican Hal Suit had a charming personality and twenty years' experience in radio and television broadcasting, but he had not built a strong political base and stood little chance of defeating Carter. Nevertheless, Suit borrowed issues from Sanders's runoff campaign, charging that Carter had aligned himself with old Georgia politicians who did not favor progress, had met secretly with black leaders, and favored an increase in the sales tax. Carter was "a counterfeit conservative" who would change the state in ways the citizens did not want, Suit proclaimed, a bit prophetically. Suit joined Republican president Richard Nixon's daughter Tricia at a public appearance in Atlanta, hoping that Nixon's influence might help him.[26]

Carter ignored Nixon, denied Suit's charges, and posed as a more sophisticated, conservative politician who would take the high road in office. He promised that he would reform the government, restrict the governor's appointive powers, oppose legalized gambling, crack down on drug abuse, retain capital punishment, and provide better education for doctors. He agreed to debate Suit and refrain from using religion as a campaign issue against Suit, allegedly an atheist.[27]

The showdown between Carter and Suit on the race issue came before the Hungry Club in Atlanta. The mentor of Martin Luther King, Jr., Benjamin Mays, who chaired the Atlanta Board of Education and was a well-known black educator, accused Suit of being "paternalistic" and "condescending" with his statement that blacks should vote as individuals, not in a bloc. "The South has been bloc voting since the Civil War," Mays retorted, to hearty applause.

Carter at first received a warm welcome from the mostly black group when he said he would appoint qualified blacks to state boards, but he lost whatever gains he had made when he mentioned the name of staunch segregationist Roy Harris. Carter said that Harris had been a good regent but did not say whether he would reappoint him when his term expired. Carter then regained lost ground by pledging that in areas of pardons and parole, welfare, probation, and education, where blacks had particular needs, he would appoint "non–Uncle Toms." Carter's statement sounded paternalistic, but he was saved by the sudden appearance of uninvited black candidate Clennon B. King. Allotted two minutes to speak, King railed about not being invited and bitterly remarked that "no one treats niggers more like niggers than other niggers."[28]

Downplaying race, Jimmy and Rosalynn plotted his victory. Carter met Suit in a one-hour televised debate and promised to return control of the Democratic party in Georgia to Georgians. He and Rosalynn traveled the state separately, shaking hands, speaking, and asking their friends to remain loyal. On Saturday nights, when the family gathered in Plains, Rosalynn planned where they would campaign the next week. She had a map of the state, and different colored pins for herself, Jimmy, and Jeff. She placed the pins all over the state map as assignments for the week. After attending church services in Plains, they scattered to their posts.[29]

During the 1970 campaign, the Carters' oldest son Jack, now twenty-two realized that he had made a mistake in joining the Navy two years earlier, and he connived to get out. He told the authorities, after someone squealed on him, that he had smoked marijuana. Fearing that that confession might not be sufficient to get him discharged, he "threw in that I had had a couple of LSD tablets and some THC, just to make sure that... I got out." He not only got out, he also spent a month in San Francisco in an unlocked stockade marked "Barracks X." Laughing about it many years later, Jack said, "So they were busting me out of the Navy in a fairly mellow manner, about the time Dad was getting elected governor." The Navy gave him a general discharge in December 1970.[30]

A month earlier, on November 3, 1970, Carter became the first Sumter Countian to be elected governor of Georgia, receiving 62 percent of the vote. He retained his voters from the primary and added more blacks, with 42 percent of blacks in Atlanta and 85 percent of those in both Macon and Savannah. Woodruff helped him break into the business vote, and, despite growth of the Republican party in the South, Georgia had many "yellow dog" Democrats who would vote for their party no matter who the candidate was. Since Lester Maddox received 74 percent of the vote for lieutenant governor, Carter found himself clasping hands with Maddox as they raised their arms in victory for the photographers.[31]

Carter did, however, suffer a humiliating defeat at the hands of the Democratic senate caucus. Controlled by the friends of Maddox, Jim Gillis, and Carl

Sanders, it voted twenty-seven to seven against replacing Hugh Gillis with Carter's friend Robert Smalley as president pro tem of the senate.[32] In the midst of his victory celebration, Carter thus received a sharp reminder that as governor he would still have to contend with Maddox and other political enemies.

The debate over how and why Carter won in 1970 continued long after the election. The Sanders camp never relented from its accusations of improprieties, misleading statements, and outright lying, which made the campaign a lingering discredit to Carter in the minds of many. Sanders himself thought the campaign "rough and dirty" and used such words and expressions as "vicious," "sly innuendos," and "deceit" to describe it. He thought Carter's camp used "deceitful tactics" and Carter himself was "evasive, very deceitful."[33] Carter's enemies persistently maintained that the summer of 1970 was "a dark spot" in his career, whereas his friends exonerated him of all wrongdoing. Representative of Carter's friends, Bobby Rowan maintained that Jimmy did not mislead the people but used "rhetoric that…would make south Georgia white conservatives very comfortable."[34] Carter himself, when campaigning for the presidency in 1976, declared that he was "the same person before and after [he] became governor." He explained, "The ultraconservatives in Georgia…voted for me because of their animosity toward Carl Sanders."[35]

Both scholars and participants agreed that Carter had won not by race-baiting but by promising to invite George Wallace to speak in the Capitol and by opposing busing, both of which appealed to the Maddox voters. He also kept his young, liberal constituency from 1966, and he became the first gubernatorial candidate to win large numbers of votes in both Atlanta and rural areas.[36] The best analysis of the election comes from political scientist T. McNeill Simpson III, who concludes that Carter's 1970 victory revealed that "an intelligent, hardworking politician could, in those troubled years, exploit the factionalism characteristic of Georgia politics and, with merely a trace of demagoguery, win the governorship."[37]

For the moment, Jimmy and Rosalynn savored the victory. The next month, *Georgia Magazine* featured the new first family with handsome photographs of Jimmy, Rosalynn, their four children, and Miss Lillian and a brief biography that quoted Miss Julia Coleman saying, "Jimmy was an honor student all through school." Portrayed as a model family who loved their home, church, town, and hobbies, basking in their conquest of the state, the Carters seemed almost too perfect.[38]

GEORGIA

at the time of Jimmy Carter and
Rosalynn Smith Carter
1924–1974

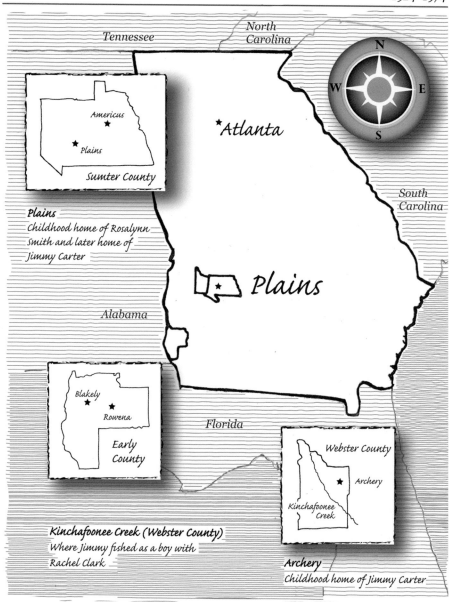

Tennessee

North
Carolina

N

W E

S

South
Carolina

Americus ★

★ Plains

Sumter County

*Atlanta

Plains
Childhood home of Rosalynn
Smith and later home of
Jimmy Carter

Plains

Alabama

Blakely ★ ★
Rowena

Early
County

Florida

Webster County

★ Archery

Kinchafoonee
Creek

Kinchafoonee Creek (Webster County)
Where Jimmy fished as a boy with
Rachel Clark

Archery
Childhood home of Jimmy Carter

Map of Georgia showing Archery and Plains, where Jimmy Carter and Rosalynn Smith grew up,
the creek where Jimmy fished, and Atlanta where they lived in the governor's mansion. Graphics
by Hal Mark Tribble

Plains in 1925. Courtesy of Jimmy Carter Library and Museum

Restored Carter boyhood home, Jimmy Carter National Historic Site, Archery, Georgia. Courtesy of Annette Wise

Home where Rosalynn Smith Carter lived with her parents and siblings from infancy in 1927 until her marriage to Jimmy Carter in 1946. This is a 2008 photograph of the home where she and the President sometimes visited at Christmas during their White House years. Courtesy of Library of Congress

Lillian Carter with her baby son Jimmy. Courtesy of Jimmy Carter Library and Museum

Above, left. Rosalynn Smith, a happy baby, propped up in her backyard on Bond Street, Plains. Courtesy of Jimmy Carter Library and Museum
Above, right. Jimmy Carter at age 2. Courtesy of Charles M. Rafshoon and Manuscript, Archives, and Rare Book Library, Robert W. Woodruff Library, Emory University

Right, Earl Carter at the door of his commissary with his three camera-shy children, Gloria (6), Ruth (3), and Jimmy (8). Courtesy of Jimmy Carter Library and Museum

Lillian Carter on the farm with her children Jimmy and Ruth during the Great Depression of the 1930s. Her husband had ordered the windmill from Sears, Roebuck, and Company, and Jack Clark rang the bell in front of the barn "an hour before daylight." Courtesy of Jimmy Carter Library and Museum

Above. Jack and Rachel Clark's reconstructed home, Jimmy Carter National Historic Site, Archery, Georgia. Courtesy of Annette Wise.
Right, Rachel Clark in her senior years, satisfied with her own life and that of the little white boy she helped rear. He called her a "queen." Courtesy of Jimmy Carter Library and Museum

Above, Mules on the restored Carter boyhood farm. The back and side of the restored home is to the right, the windmill to the left. Earl Carter operated a fifty mule farm, which was substantial for his day. Courtesy of Annette Wise.

Right, Young Jimmy on the farm with his pony Lady Lee. Courtesy of Jimmy Carter Library and Museum.

Above, left. Rosalynn Smith at age 8.
Courtesy of Jimmy Carter Library and
Museum.
Above, right. Jimmy Carter at age 10.
Courtesy of Jimmy Carter Library and
Museum.

Henry, Ruth, and Foriest Berry picking
cotton on the Carter farm in the 1950s.
Courtesy of Charlne B. Merritt.

Above, Plains Baptist Church. Photograph by Jeannie Godbold.

Miss Julia Coleman, English teacher and superintendent, and Mr. Young Thomas Sheffield, principal and coach, at Plains High School. Courtesy of Jimmy Carter Library and Museum.

Above, left. Jimmy Carter's inscribed photograph to his fiancee Rosalynn Smith, 1946. Courtesy of Jimmy Carter Library and Museum.
Right, Jimmy and Rosalynn Carter's wedding day at the Plains United Methodist church, July 7, 1946. Courtesy of Jimmy Carter Library and Museum.

Rosalynn Carter with baby Jack, 1947, when she was a teenaged mother and Navy wife. Courtesy of Jimmy Carter Library and Museum.

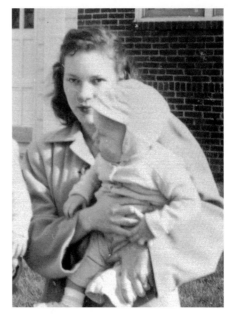

Jimmy Carter at Submarine School in 1948.Courtesy of Charles M. Rafshoon and Manuscript, Archives, and Rare Book Library, Robert W. woodruff Library, Emory University.

Jimmy Carter aboard the submarine USS Pomphret during his Navy years. Courtesy of Jimmy Carter Library and Museum.

Lillian and Earl Carter, 1950s. Courtesy of Charles M. Rafshoon and Manuscript, Archives, and Rare Book Library, Robert W. Woodruff Library, Emory University.

Rosalynn Carter and her son Jack at the Grand Canyon in the 1950s. Jimmy was stationed at San Diego in the Navy. Courtesy of Jimmy Carter Library and Museum.

Jimmy and Rosalynn Carter in the early 1950s at their modest apartment in a poor neighborhood of San Diego, a place Rosalynn did not like, 1950s. Courtesy of Jimmy Carter Library and Museum.

The government-subsidized apartment where the Carters lived when they returned to Plains in 1953. Photograph by Jeannie Godbold.

The "haunted" house near Plains that was the home of the Carter family, 1956- 1962. Courtesy of Annette Wise.

Senator Jimmy Carter in front of the Georgia State Capitol at the beginning of his political career in 1963. Courtesy of Jimmy Carter Library and Museum.

Above, Jimmy and Rosalynn Carter in front of their three- year-old home in Plains, 1965. He was a state senator, and she was housewife, attentive mother, and business woman. Courtesy of Jimmy Carter Library and Museum.

Below, Jimmy Carter (white shirt) working with West Georgia Area Planning and Development Commission, Sumter County, 1965. Courtesy of Georgia Archives, Vanishing Georgia Collection, sum083b.

Above, Jimmy Carter campaigning for governor in 1966. Courtesy of Charles M. Rafshoon and Manuscript, Archives, and Rare Book Library, Robert W. Woodruff Library, Emory University.

Below, The Carter family in Plains, December 1966. From left to right, Ruth, Jimmy, Miss Lillian, Billy, and Gloria. Courtesy of Jimmy Carter Library and Museum.

Carter examining a cotton plant on his farm in 1968. Courtesy of Charles M. Rafshoon and Manuscript, Archives, and Rare Book Library, Robert W. Woodruff Library, Emory University.

Jimmy, Rosalynn, and Amy Carter relaxing by the fire and reading, late 1960s. Courtesy of Charles M. Rafshoon and Manuscript, Archives, and Rare Book Library, Robert W. Woodruff Library, Emory University.

Jimmy and Rosalynn Carter celebrating his winning the governorship in 1970. Courtesy of Jimmy Carter Library and Museum.

Below, Jimmy Carter and his family at his inauguration as governor of Georgia on January 12, 1971. *From left to right,* Jimmy, Rosalynn, Amy, Miss Lillian, Jeff, Chip, Jack, and Miss Allie. Courtesy of Jimmy Carter Library and Museum.

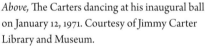
Above, The Carters dancing at his inaugural ball on January 12, 1971. Courtesy of Jimmy Carter Library and Museum.

Right, Governor Lester Maddox removes his name plate from the desk in the governor's office to make room for Governor-elect Jimmy Carter to assume the office, which was symbolic of a dramatic change in the state. January 12, 1971. Courtesy of AP Images

The Georgia Governor's Mansion at the time Jimmy, Rosalynn, and Amy lived there, 1971–1975. Courtesy of Georgia Archives, RG 1–16–118, Box 5.

Above, Rosalynn Carter, First Lady of Georgia, and unidentified gardener, working in flower beds at the mansion, 1971. Courtesy of Georgia Archives, RG 1–16–116, Box 15.

Rosalynn Carter, First Lady of Georgia, 1971. Courtesy of Georgia Archives, RG 4–10–71, Box 7.

Governor and Mrs. Carter at the Confederate cemetery and chapel near Americana, Brazil, April 1972. Rosalynn is on the left, Jimmy is standing in front of the monument containing the family names of the Confederates who moved there, and Press Secretary Jody Powell is on the far right holding the microphone. Courtesy of John V. Saunders.

Governor and Mrs. Jimmy Carter relaxing at home in Plains, December 23, 1972. Two months earlier they had decided secretly that he would announce for the presidency. One of his favorite hobbies was collecting Indian arrowheads. Courtesy of Jimmy Carter Library and Museum.

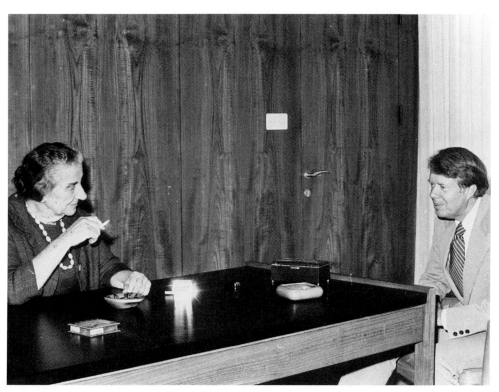

Governor Jimmy Carter visiting Prime Minister Golda Meir in her office at Jerusalem in May 1973. Courtesy of Jimmy Carter Library and Museum.

Governor Jimmy Carter dancing backstage with the Rockettes at Radio City Music Hall in New York. He was trying to entice the motion picture Industry to build a studio in Georgia. September 21, 1973. Courtesy of AP Images.

Betty Ford, First Lady of the United States, wearing a trainman's hat in Dalton, Georgia, when she cut the ribbon to start the Art Train to travel through the Southeast. First Lady of Georgia Rosalynn Carter welcomes Mrs. Ford and the train to her state. April 6, 1974. Courtesy of AP Images.

Coretta Scott King assisting Governor Jimmy Carter at the unveiling of the portrait of her late husband, Martin Luther King, Jr., at the Georgia state Capitol on February 18, 1974. Courtesy of AP Images.

Jimmy and Rosalynn Carter at home in 1975 planning their strategy. Courtesy of Charles M. Rafshoon and Manuscript, Archives, and Rare Book Library, Robert W. Woodruff Library, Emory University.

Jody Powell and Hamilton Jordan, 1976. Courtesy of Charles M. Rafshoon and Manuscript, Archives, and Rare Book Library, Robert W. Woodruff Library, Emory University.

Since there were no laws in 1970 that limited contributions to a gubernatorial candidate's campaign or demanded that he reveal the gifts, Carter kept secret those details for six years until the press and Gerald Ford's presidential campaign forced him to publish the list of his 1970 contributors. He spent $700,000 on the campaign, $200,000 of which he did not account for, probably because it was his own money. Some of the money came from small contributors to whom the Carters' populist platform had a major appeal. At least half of the remaining $500,000 came from "bankers, business executives, contractors and lawyers."[39]

Other contributions came from friends and individuals whom Carter later rewarded with state appointments. Campaign treasurer Robert Lipshutz, who advised Carter on political matters relative to Jewish citizens, gave $6,000; Bert Lance, who accepted the most controversial job in state government as head of the Highway Department, and his wife LaBelle gave $1,500. Gerald Rafshoon gave an unspecified amount in 1973 to complete repayment of the campaign debt. Carter later rewarded some of his other contributors. He appointed David Gambrell, whose family tendered $5,000, to Richard Russell's Senate seat after Russell's death. Individuals Philip Alston ($7,000), Joel Fryer ($1,175), Conley Ingraham ($770), and Bill Gunter ($600) later enjoyed appointments to the Board of Regents, the superior court, and the state supreme court, respectively.[40]

Large corporations, and even some segregationist organizations that thought Carter was on their side, also supported him. Three road construction companies gave $11,500, and the Georgia Package Stores Institute sent $1,000. Corporations that owned plantations in southwestern Georgia contributed. They included Olin-Mathison, Coca-Cola ($6,200), Gulf Oil, Delta Airlines ($4,995), and St. Joseph Paper Company. The Cox Broadcasting Company, which owned the *Atlanta Constitution and Journal*, gave $26,500, most of it after the fact to help Carter pay his campaign debt.[41]

As the largest single individual contributor to the campaign ($8,600), David Rabhan of Rabhan Associates in Savannah had his own agenda. Born of Iranian ancestry into a prominent Jewish family in Savannah, he was Carter's age and interested in art, agriculture, and business. The two men had much in common, except that Rabhan liked to wear blue jumpsuits and shave his head, and he questioned the hypocrisy of Southern Baptists who condoned racial segregation. After graduating from the University of Georgia, he became affluent by acquiring a chain of nursing homes. Concern for the elderly took him back to the University of Georgia to earn a master's degree in nutrition. It also piqued his interest in politics.

Rabhan had supported Ellis Arnall in 1966, but the day after both Arnall and Carter lost, Rabhan offered his services to Carter should he run again. He offered money, a luxury apartment in Atlanta, a private plane, himself as a skilled pilot, all things Carter needed, except the apartment, to run again in 1970. He became friendly with Miss Lillian after she returned from India, often staying at her house when he went to visit Jimmy and Rosalynn. Carter accepted Rabhan's offer and soon found himself flying long hours with him, sometimes under dangerous conditions, in Rabhan's twin-engine Cessna 310. Carter used other pilots, too, but Rabhan became his favorite.

The two men developed a rapport they kept from the public for the remainder of Carter's political career. In the airplane they clowned, sometimes with Carter at the controls, sometimes with Raban. They talked about art, agriculture, business, religion, and race. As a child, Rabhan had seen the body of a black man who had been killed by whites. As an adult, he treated blacks equally with whites and began to form friendships with Georgia's black leaders. He introduced Carter to Martin Luther King, Sr., popularly called "Daddy King." Carl Sanders had been correct when he accused Carter of secretly meeting with black leaders to win votes. Daddy King, Cameron Alexander, and Fred Bennett, all black ministers, worked for Carter but did not expect him to get many black votes. Rabhan brought the white candidate whom he knew to be liberal together with black clergymen in the shadows of political secrecy.

On the last day of the campaign, as Carter and Rabhan flew together, Carter asked Rabhan what he could do for him as governor. After hedging, Rabhan told him to use his inaugural address to promise to end racism in Georgia. Carter wrote on the back of a flight map, "I say to you quite frankly the time for racial discrimination is over." Rabhan cut the engines of the plane, letting it free fall through the sky. He asked Carter to sign it, and he did. Restarting the engines, the two men sailed smoothly to an easy landing, keeping the secret between themselves for many years.[42]

Carter liked to tell a good story, elaborate on it, and sometimes give others credit for what he had done. As he fell through the air with Rabhan, he did not suddenly decide at that moment to end segregation in Georgia. It had been one of his goals for nearly a decade, having evolved from his Navy experience, service on a local school board, religious convictions, and sympathy for his African-American neighbors.

Rabhan and Carter remained friends long after the Carter's presidency. During the 1970 campaign, however, Kirbo thought Rabhan a "loon" and feared that his large contributions might do Carter harm. Carter saw it differently; he clung to David as a joking buddy and even something of a mentor. Carter remembered the many hours with him in his airplane "when I was a lonely candidate with few friends." "He's an unbelievable pilot, artist, sculptor, businessman (& b-s. artist)," Carter later wrote in an affectionate and humorous vein.[43]

The victory won, Rosalynn fretted over the payment of their debts, but she found it "exciting to work hard" to achieve their dreams.[44] She had served the team well in business and the campaign, but her husband made appointments, planned programs, and took control of the state government. She and Jimmy kept private whatever role she had in his decision making. He replaced the deposed Jim Gillis with Bert Lance, the wealthy Methodist layman who said he wanted the Highway Department job not because it was "big politics" but because it was "big business" that affected all citizens.[45] Lance had a naturally jovial, gregarious, backslapping, hugging, deal-making, extroverted personality that Carter could only envy.

Carter signaled a new era in Georgia. He called for resignations from some of the state's most entrenched politicians, and he appointed people likely to share his vision as new heads of state agencies.[46] He opposed the legalization of marijuana but remained open to the idea of decriminalizing possession of small amounts of it. He promised not to raise the state sales tax and to support a 2-cents-per-gallon increase in the gasoline tax in order to build roads, a massive reform of the state's prison system, statewide public kindergartens, and additional special education teachers. He would raise the money, he said, by reforming the existing tax structure.[47]

Rosalynn panicked when she realized that Jimmy had won and that she would be expected to keep a high public profile. She attended a conference in North Carolina for governors-elect, many of whom had wives like her. Others reassured her from their experience that she could handle and even enjoy her new status as the state's first lady. When she visited Virginia Maddox at the governor's mansion in Atlanta, however, Mrs. Maddox was almost cruel, telling her that being first lady was a tough job and she must do all the cooking herself for everyone who visited the mansion.[48]

Three days before moving there, Rosalynn saw Georgia's new governor's mansion on West Paces Ferry Road for the first time and found it elegant and welcoming. An interior design major, she thought it "just beautiful" and so well furnished that she would have to bring nothing from Plains except her sewing machine. She and Jimmy would share the governor's bedroom, while three-year-old Amy enjoyed the adjacent first lady's bedroom. Sons Jeff, eighteen, a student at Georgia State University in Atlanta, and Jack, now twenty-three and a student at Georgia Tech, would also have upstairs bedrooms. Chip, twenty, also at Georgia State, had requested a more private room in the basement servants' quarters, where he could play loud music regardless of whether the servants minded.[49]

Carter worked in the governor's office at the Capitol, not at home. Most of his early appointments went to people who had helped him win the election or signaled a reform he intended to make. He appointed Thomas Jenkins, a black vice president of Georgia State University, to the three-member Board of Pardons and Paroles. He named Barney Ragsdale, a veteran Georgia Bureau of Investigation agent from Tifton, to head that agency, and Philip Alston of Atlanta to the Board of Regents. At a dinner meeting he discussed the banking needs of the state, promising a more equitable distribution of state funds among banks; many bankers, including some who had supported Sanders, now offered to help pay his campaign debt.[50]

Carter appointed Charles Kirbo chief of staff. Kirbo had convinced some of his partners in King and Spaulding that Carter would be better for the state than Sanders. Jack Watson, a member of the firm, shifted his allegiance. Other partners, not convinced, had signed an advertisement that said "One Thousand Georgia Lawyers Think Carl Sanders Ought to Be Governor Again." Carter kept a copy of it, and later when a lawyer came to his office seeking a favor, he checked to see if the supplicant's name was on it, and if so, sometimes laughed and granted the favor anyway.[51]

Groups that had been closely associated with Sanders, however, such as those working in higher education, quickly felt Carter's sting. When a concerned student at the University of Georgia asked if Carter would use armed National Guardsmen to quell riots on campus, the governor-elect reaffirmed that he would do so, an answer students did not like because Guardsmen's slaughter of students on the campus of Kent State remained fresh in their minds. Carter added that he would personally go to the scene of any disturbance and prevent a repeat of the Kent State disaster in Georgia.[52] More ominously, Carter sent a detailed, handwritten letter to George L. Simpson, Jr., chancellor of the University System of Georgia, mandating a detailed account of all programs and activities in the system, a 3 percent reduction in the budget, and an offer to meet with "Mr. Roy and his committee" to resolve any misunderstandings.[53] The letter made clear, as the campaign before it had done, that higher education would not be a major priority with the new governor.

Carl Sanders and many Georgia voters never forgave Carter for posturing as a segregationist to win, but the people who knew him well knew that he was no segregationist. Stuart Eizenstat could not imagine that Carter had participated in the "racial parts" of the campaign. Carter did run "a very conservative campaign" that would surprise some people who had voted for him, Eizenstat said, but he did not witness any racism on the candidate's part.[54] Atlanta's black senator, Leroy Johnson, predicted that Carter would "do more for blacks than any governor has ever done." Johnson and others were pleased that Carter was having his inaugural platform built in front of the Capitol in such a way as to obscure the statue of the fiery segregationist Tom Watson.[55]

In his own words many years later as a former president of the United States and a noted humanitarian, Carter justified the 1970 victory, saying, "We ran kind of a working man's campaign."[56] He saw no conflict between asking both blacks and the supporters of Lester Maddox to vote for him, he said, because both groups were "average working people."[57] In late 1970, he allegedly apologized to Sanders, prayed for the Lord's forgiveness, and told some of his friends that he "felt bad" about the campaign.[58] Nevertheless, he achieved peace with himself by rationalizing in the style of theologian Reinhold Niebuhr or that of Renaissance philosopher Niccolo Machiavelli that how he would govern now became more important than how he had won the right to govern.

In preparation for his inauguration, he wrote Admiral Hyman G. Rickover, inviting him to attend the ceremony on January 12, 1971. "I hope to serve...with the same pride and dedication that you have always demanded of yourself and all those who served with you," Carter informed the demanding admiral. Rickover did not remember Carter but replied that he was "very proud that one who was connected with the Naval Reactors program has been so outstandingly successful." He added that he regretted he would be "on sea trials" and thus unable to attend.[59]

CHAPTER FOURTEEN

"Enigma and Contradiction"

RIDING TO HER SON'S INAUGURATION, Lillian Carter turned to her sister and said, "Sissy, what are we doing here? We are not limousine people."[1] It was, as Carter said, a long way from Plains to Atlanta. Despite the family's claims of humility, Georgians had never before witnessed such pageantry at the installation of a new governor as they did on January 12, 1971. More than five thousand of them stood under a chilly, overcast sky to view a wooden platform, decorated in red, white, and blue, that had been built over the Capitol steps. Hanging directly above where the new governor would stand was a four-by-eight-foot portrait of Carter made from fresh camellia blossoms. Jimmy, Rosalynn, their children and other relatives, friends, and dignitaries mounted the festive platform just before noon. Two Baptist ministers offered prayers. The Naval Academy band played "Anchors Aweigh," and Morris Brown College's African-American choir sang "The Battle Hymn of the Republic."[2]

The bitterness of the campaign resonated from the stage, where three empty seats with large nametags for former governors Carl Sanders, Marvin Griffin, and M. E. Thompson were clearly visible. Thompson was unable to attend, but Sanders and Griffin boycotted the ceremony. Sanders remained bitter about the election, and Griffin became infuriated when he discovered that Carter had "duped" him into thinking he was a segregationist. Ellis Arnall was there, having supported his old rival in the general election and congratulated him on his victory.[3] As Jimmy—he insisted on being called Jimmy—began to speak, the sun broke through the clouds.

A few minutes into his speech, Carter declared: "I say to you quite frankly the time for racial discrimination is over." Some applauded, but more groaned. He did not sound like the man for whom they had voted. "No poor, rural, weak or black person should ever have to bear the additional burden of being deprived of the opportunity of an education, a job or simple justice," he continued. His audi-ence had not heard such remarks during the campaign. "I will not shirk [the] responsibility," he promised in an eight-minute speech, to bring efficient govern-ment, law and order, and a clean, safe environment to Georgia.[4] Dressed in an olive green suit, Jimmy placed his left hand on a Bible and raised his right hand to repeat the oath of office after Court of Appeals judge Robert H. Jordan, whose brother had founded Koinonia. Standing next to him, Lester Maddox took the oath as lieutenant governor. Rosalynn stood nearby holding Amy's hand. She smiled but appeared serious, and she looked stunningly beautiful in a seafoam-green dress with matching coat, a white hat, and navy blue accessories. Jimmy lifted three-year-old Amy high before the cheering crowd, church bells tolled, and a nineteen-gun salute shattered windows in a government building across the street.[5] Inside the Capitol's house chamber, Governor Carter administered the oath of office to Charles H. Kirbo as chief of staff, Tommy Irvin as agriculture commissioner, Arthur K. Bolton as attorney general, Ben Fortson as secretary of state, and others who, except for Kirbo, had been elected on November 3.[6]

From the Capitol, Jimmy and Rosalynn traveled to the mansion at 391 West Paces Ferry Road, where Rosalynn, now dressed in a gown of yellow wool crepe, took her place beside her husband and prepared to greet visitors. To the amaze-ment of Miss Lillian, who had never come to appreciate Rosalynn's social graces and intellect, her daughter-in-law knew how to dress and to act in her new role.[7] Conspicuously absent from the receiving line were Lester and Virginia Maddox. The Carters had not invited them, they said—in a thinly veiled insult—because their presence would impede the flow of the crowd. They had invited the people of Georgia, and an estimated twenty-five thousand of them lined West Paces Ferry Road. More than twelve thousand went through the receiving line, shaking hands with the governor and his wife. In the evening, the Carters made brief appearances at each of four inaugural balls.[8] On the dance floors with her husband, Rosalynn was resplendent in a flowing gown of starlight-blue chiffon with full sleeves of plain chiffon and a bodice interwoven with a sapphire and gold design.[9]

The parties over, the Carters retreated to one of the finest governor's residences in the country. Carter used the state's three-year-old, $2 million mansion as a political tool and a symbol of power. Built in the antebellum Greek Revival style, it stood on eighteen acres in Atlanta's wealthiest neighborhood. Thirty massive columns ringed the two-story brick twenty-four-thousand-square-foot rectangular building that served as the governor's home and the site of official dinners and other meetings. From the library and dining room on the first floor to the family's private living area on the second, it boasted many fine American and English antiques and wall hangings that documented highlights of American history.

The governor's bedroom was furnished with a four-post canopy bed (c. 1800), a fireplace, a needlework portrait of George Washington, and a gold leather wastebasket. Near the governor's bedroom, the Presidential Suite contained an antique Pennsylvania four-post bed, a desk, a wig stand, a dining area, and portraits of James Monroe and Thomas Jefferson. The halls of the second floor, lined with portraits of the presidents, connected the Carters' separate offices and eight more bedrooms. A family living room and dining room gave them more space than their large family needed.[10] Merely walking through the rooms and halls steeped the new residents in the history of England, America, and Georgia.

Ironically, as state senator, Carter had voted against the construction of the mansion, because he thought it a frivolous enterprise too costly for the taxpayers. J. B. Fuqua, a fellow senator and multimillionaire who supported Carl Sanders, had managed to get funding for the mansion by putting it under the State Building Authority without the legislature knowing it.[11]

From the West Paces Ferry Road entrance, the mansion loomed up like a plantation house from *Gone with the Wind*. It had white Doric columns, rose-tone brick walls, and a circular fountain in the front. The furniture was in the Federal style, handcrafted by cabinetmakers in New York, Pennsylvania, Maryland, and Georgia. Crystal chandeliers and marble mantels came from England; paintings by Benjamin West and other American artists adorned the walls; and Jean Antoine Houdon busts of George Washington and Benjamin Franklin dominated the statuary. Below the main floor, the State Facilities Room could seat three hundred.[12] a portrait of Alexander H. Stephens, vice president of the Confederacy, hung in a small library on the first floor that became Carter's favorite workplace. It contained books on the history of Georgia and the South, highlighted with first editions of Georgia writers Joel Chandler Harris, Erskine Caldwell, Flannery O'Connor, and Carson McCullers. Works on natural history, biography, folklore, travel, architecture, poetry, church history, politics, and education filled its shelves.[13]

Rosalynn learned to run the mansion and manage a staff of fourteen. She appreciated the state troopers who opened doors during the daytime and at night secured windows and flipped off the many light switches.[14] Rosalynn and her assistant Madeline McBean maintained an office on the second floor.[15] Madeline organized Rosalynn's staff and helped hire servants.

More than a servant, Mary Prince Fitzpatrick became three-year-old Amy's nanny. An African-American woman who had been convicted of manslaughter in the death of a male companion, she was a trusty from the state penitentiary. She may have been a victim of a penal system that discriminated against black women who defended themselves in domestic disputes; eventually she dropped the Fitzpatrick from her name to dissociate herself from her victim, whom she had never married. Like so many black servants in southern white homes, Mary had a close relationship with her employers, but the racial and servant/master divides were never truly crossed.[16]

Family life in the mansion became increasingly busy. The two older Carter sons married while living there. Jack wed Judy Langford, the daughter of state senator Beverly Langford, a close Carter family friend, and moved with her into the carriage house on the grounds. Chip, at his father's urging, married Caron Griffin, a lovely intern at the Capitol. Miss Lillian visited frequently to attend professional wrestling matches in Atlanta.[17] Rosalynn served pancakes and collard greens to Plains folks and to the German ambassador. She cooked for the family only if she wanted to, she did not buy designer clothes, and she selected Jimmy's suits from a department store in Americus. She opened the house on Tuesday, Thursday, and Sunday afternoons for walking tours guided by Miss Lillian, docents, or herself.[18]

Rosalynn took particular delight in the beautiful and well-tended grounds, where she sometimes worked clad in blue jeans. That work, and the row of peanuts Jimmy planted at the edge of the garden, made her feel at home, but she had embarked on a new life. Jimmy reminded her that she was now a public figure who must make appearances, and he coached her with her public speaking. Rosalynn rose to the professional demands of her position, overcame her shyness, and soon gave many speeches, some of which she wrote herself.[19]

Carter went to work the day of his inauguration defending his inaugural address. Journalist Reg Murphy wrote that the speech "strained credibility" because it denied everything Carter had said during the campaign.[20] Some writers for the Atlanta newspapers, the national press, and delighted black Georgians welcomed the change he promised, but many working-class whites to whom Carter had pitched his campaign were stunned.[21] One Georgia politician dryly commented that Jimmy had campaigned with "Maddox under one arm and Wallace under the other" but with his inaugural message had "kicked both of them out of the front door."[22] Senator Herman Talmadge said that Carter had been "elected as a segregationist," but the state Democratic party no longer embraced him after his inaugural address. Talmadge thought that Carter's national ambitions drove him to change "his stance overnight."[23]

A writer for the *New York Times* described the governor best: "Jimmy Carter, like the South itself, is…an enigma and contradiction." During the campaign, Carter "was accused of abandoning a political liberalism he had exhibited…in the state legislature," the writer continued, but his inaugural address indicated he "had put on his liberal hat again."[24] J. Paul Austin, president of Coca-Cola, persuaded *Time* to put Carter on the cover of its issue of May 31, 1971, giving him the national exposure he coveted.[25]

Privately, Carter explained to his outraged friend Tommy Irvin of Americus that what he had said was "a simple statement of fact." Georgians no longer believed in racial discrimination, Carter said, and his conservative friends would agree with his comment: "We Georgians are fully capable of making our *own* judgments and managing our *own* affairs."[26]

Dismissing criticism quickly, Carter worked on a rigid schedule, arriving at the Capitol by 7:15 A.M. His office was stark, with a dark blue carpet, a black leather couch and chairs, and a marble coffee table. Four pen-and-ink drawings of rural shacks by David Rabhan adorned the walls. Despite large windows, the room was dark, cold, austere, and uninviting to visitors who might want to tarry too long.[27] Bert Lance, confidant to the governor, stopped by every morning to talk about the day's activities.

Carter did not like to attend meetings, preferring instead to work in isolation or in consultation with individuals. Apart from Rosalynn, he saw as few people as possible. If he went to the mansion to attend a program or for lunch, he hurried back to work. Usually he ate lunch alone in his office, ordering the food from the cafeteria. On rare occasions he invited Jordan, Kirbo, Spinks, or Lance to dine with him, provided they paid for their own sandwiches. In the afternoons he studied serious academic books about politics and society;

he wrote notes by hand, held short appointments, or attended an Atlanta Braves game. When he traveled in Georgia, his personal bodyguard, Stock Coleman, drove for him.[28]

Ten days into his term, Carter received the first major test of his governance and veracity when Senator Richard Russell died. As chairman of the Senate Armed Forces Committee, Russell was one of the most powerful politicians in Washington. President Richard Nixon loaned Air Force One to transport the Senator's body to Atlanta, where it lay in state under the golden dome of the Capitol. Two days later Nixon arrived in Atlanta, affording the Carters their first experience of the pomp and circumstance and security surrounding a president. Nixon accompanied the entourage to the interment in Winder, a few miles east of Atlanta.[29]

On that rainy January 25, 1971, the nation's top political and military leaders came to Georgia. In addition to the president, the guests included Vice President Spiro Agnew, Secretary of State William Rogers, Secretary of Defense Melvin Laird, former Vice President Hubert Humphrey, and former Secretary of State Dean Rusk, as well as fifty-five U.S. senators and representatives. John Stennis of Mississippi, who succeeded Russell as chairman of the Senate Armed Forces Committee, gave the eulogy from Charleston, South Carolina, where bad weather stranded him.[30] At the graveside, Carter said: "He yet lives on in his country's strength...and in his duty to our state, which needed him and which he did not fail."[31] To white Georgians who opposed racial equality, Russell was a hero.

Speculation over who would be appointed to Russell's seat stretched back into the campaign. Carter had used that potential seat to gain the blessing of former governors, especially Vandiver, whom many expected would get the appointment, despite his closeness to Carl Sanders.[32] Carter, however, offered it to Charles Kirbo. Kirbo, who preferred to avoid the limelight, deadpanned that his wife, who was twelve years younger than he, "was too old to move to Washington" and recommended his former partner David Henry Gambrell.[33]

Carter named Gambrell to the Senate seat. A young, liberal attorney, Gambrell had served as state Democratic chairman and president of the Georgia Bar Association. He had a Harvard law degree, a wife, and four children and boasted a modest political following because he had worked in Richard Russell's 1952 presidential campaign.[34] Carter's friend Tommy Hooks lambasted the governor, reminding him that it was "the average fellow" in South Georgia who had voted for him, not "an Atlanta fellow." The talk in South Georgia was that Jimmy Carter had run a "poor man's—average man's—Lester Maddox type campaign" but "is now choking himself with a 'Carl Sanders' type man with David Gambrell." Hooks said that many who had voted for Carter would be appalled.[35]

Disgruntled by the appointment, Lieutenant Governor Lester Maddox lit on it as the catalyst to allow his long-simmering hatred of Carter to erupt into open verbal warfare. Maddox attacked Carter as "a bald faced liar," and used his committee appointees in the senate to try to block legislation Carter wanted. Maddox said Carter would undercut the independence of the legislature and defy the U.S. and the Georgia constitutions because his "lust for power" was like that of a dictator in a banana republic. Carter, Maddox contended, was an "honest, kind and gentle person before the public" but in private was "angry, mean, and cold," and acted "like an animal."[36] Carter retaliated by calling Maddox into his office and, according to Maddox, shaking his finger in his face and threatening to use the power of the governor's office to fight him. In public, however, Carter sustained a cordial demeanor and a sense of humor about his nemesis.[37]

Maddox would not give up. In November 1971, he sent Carter a five-page typed letter declaring his respect for the office but bemoaning the governor's "undercover attempts to ridicule and discredit me." Maddox did not object, he said, to Carter's "riding my coattail" into office, but deplored "your riding my back and trying to cut my throat all of this year." Furthermore, he found Carter to be "a liar, a coward, a hypocrite" and one who betrayed "the trust of the people." He would try to defeat Carter's beloved reorganization plan, he promised, if it would increase the power of the governor. Carter ignored the letter and later tendered kind words, offers of reconciliation, and public humor to defuse the feud.[38] The two men never reconciled.

Carter's trouble with Maddox exacerbated his difficulty with the General Assembly. According to Bert Lance, he made little effort to cultivate meaningful personal relationships with legislators. He thought he could use the power of his office to accomplish his goals. Always the engineer who wanted quick, logical solutions and the naval officer expecting obedience to his orders, Carter alienated legislators. Lawmakers complained of having to wait to see him, that his aides had the "tact of wild bulls," and that the inexperienced governor worked by railroading, ignoring, and apologizing. One stinging complaint came from Julian Bond, the African-American state senator, who thought Carter inept and devoid of the personality required to sway legislators.[39]

Carter learned from his early mistakes and made concessions. He did not hold grudges, he compromised to win votes, and he used patronage to reward friends and secure support. When one senator wanted to invite local citizens from his district to the governor's signing of a bill, Carter casually told him that it might be possible if the gasoline tax bill passed. The senator voted for it, it passed, and the man's friends witnessed the signing.[40]

Carter worked with the established Democratic leadership of both houses. He had a good working relationship with senate majority leader Al Holloway, whom he used to introduce the administration's legislation. That legislation had to be approved by seven of the ten members of the Senate Policy Committee, a compromise forced on him by Maddox and Hugh Gillis.[41] Carter's other friends in the senate included his cousin Hugh, Cy Chapman, Jack Henderson, Ford Spinks, Robert H. Smalley, Julian Webb, Paul Broun, Bill Fincher, and Lamar Plunkett. Plunkett, a Baptist friend since 1962 and the prosperous owner of a company that made suits Rosalynn liked to wear, chaired the powerful Senate Appropriations Committee. Like Carter, he was liberal on social issues, but conservative on fiscal ones.[42]

Carter counted on George L. Smith II, the speaker of the house, who believed the governor had good ideas.[43] The relationship between the two men was more political than cordial, but Smith helped Carter get health and consumer protection bills enacted.[44] Others in the house who supported Carter included Sidney Marcus, Peyton Hawes, Jr., Al Burruss, Sam Nunn, Carl Drury, Bob Farrar, and George Busbee. They shared his goals, but they also sought political favors. Carter used a small group within each house to help win a majority of votes.[45]

Carter's first order of business, after his appointment of Gambrell, was to get the assembly to approve House Bill 1. The bill gave the governor authority to reorganize and streamline the government, subject to veto by constitutional officers within fifteen days of convening. It passed the house easily by a vote of 163 to 8, but it faced a tough challenge in the senate. Maddox, Hugh Gillis of Soperton, Eugene R. Holley of Augusta, and Stanley Smith of Perry lined up against it. On February 10, 1971, Carter sat in his office in shirtsleeves, listened to the senate debate over a speaker system, and could scarcely contain his enthusiasm when he won, fifty-three to three. He signed the bill on February 15, 1971, fully understanding that it merely opened his path to many hurdles he would have to clear to accomplish his dream of reorganizing the state's government.[46]

During the short session that lasted from January to March 1971, Carter's friends got thirty-five of his forty-four proposed measures passed, with the other nine remaining in committees where they could be revived. The bills reflected his multitude of interests. Some provided for government reorganization, protection of the environment, a budget freeze, planning for Atlanta, and pay increases for state patrolmen and Georgia Bureau of Investigation agents. Others called for a 1-cent-per-gallon gasoline tax increase, bonds for urban highways, a 4-cents-per-pack cigarette tax, pardons for first offender narcotics cases, public drug education, pensions to encourage early retirement for judges, minimum salaries for sheriffs, and medical treatment for children under the care of the Georgia Division of Family and Children Services.[47] Carter's enemies, mostly Maddox people, grumbled that his victories were narrow and that his legislative program was far too complex and far-reaching.[48]

The gloating governor announced in April that the lieutenant governor's office was "too expensive" and should be abolished. An angry Maddox retorted that it was the governor who was the spendthrift and that he "oughta start being governor and quit trying to be God and king." Early in the summer, Maddox charged the governor with being liberal senator Edward M. Kennedy's voice in the South. Denying it, Carter said he had never met Kennedy.[49]

Carter and Maddox fought each other viciously for control of the senate throughout the summer. Maddox toppled Carter's ally senate majority leader Al Holloway of Albany by a vote of twenty-eight to twenty in favor of his crony Eugene Holley. Maddox's ally Culver Kidd of Milledgeville won reelection as Democratic whip, the senate's number two job. Carter accused Maddox of a power grab and said he hoped the senators would not be duped by the lieutenant governor.[50] He promised to work with the new senate leadership and invited Holley for an overnight stay at the mansion to talk politics. Holley went home the next day pleased about his relationship with the governor, but Carter hedged his bets by naming his cousin Hugh assistant floor leader in the senate.[51]

Putting aside his feud with Maddox, Carter yielded to a decade-old federal mandate and called a special session on September 25, 1971, to reapportion the state legislature. After the 1962 *Baker v. Carr* decision, the federal courts required reapportionment to equalize the population of districts. If a state did not comply, the national government would withhold federal funds and the federal courts would redistrict it. Former governor Vandiver had called a session that had redistricted the senate just in time to help Carter win in 1962, but the house had not yet conformed to the federal guidelines. Addressing the session, Carter urged the legislators to block the courts from making the decision for them. The assembly complied by reducing the house membership from 195 to 180 and holding the population of the districts to within the required 2 percent of each other.[52]

In the meantime, Carter manipulated the gears and levers of government to bring about economic, social, judicial, and political reforms. Calling his plan "Goals for Georgia," he placed Sam Nunn, a young attorney and Democrat in the house, in charge.[53] Carter, the engineer turned politician, had a passion to create a streamlined and efficient government just as surely as he had enjoyed building an atomic submarine and a peanut-shelling machine. Since 1931, the number of state agencies had mushroomed to three hundred, some with sub-agencies and all bloated with unnecessary costs and political favoritism. Since House Bill No. 1 allowed Carter to revamp the government, he devoted most of 1971 to fine-tuning and politicking for the massive changes he intended to present at the opening of the 1972 session of the General Assembly. He welcomed the offer of Morris Collins, director of the Institute of Government at the University of Georgia, to give briefings on state government to him and his staff.[54] He plotted a four-part approach to reshape the government. First, he would make a careful study of how it could be done, then he would sell his plan to the people, pressure the professional bureaucrats into submission, and finally pound it into law during the 1972 session of the General Assembly.

To conduct the study, Carter chose a dapper young man with military bearing, Tom M. Linder, Jr., who worked well with him.[55] Linder divided the government services into the areas of education, transportation, economic development, law enforcement, general government activities, natural resources, and human resources. He sorted a study team of about one hundred volunteers into groups assigned to each area. They sent recommendations to Linder, Carter, and an Executive Committee that consisted of the following members: Clifford Clarke, president of the Georgia Business and Industry Association; state senator Lamar Plunkett, chairman of the Senate Appropriations Committee; house majority leader George Busbee; state auditor Ernest Davis; and budget director Battle Hall.

Linder hired Arthur Andersen and Company, the management consulting firm; it in turn hired local accountant Richard Harden. Forty-eight major businesses in Atlanta, including Georgia Power, Coca-Cola, Delta Airlines, and Sears

Roebuck, contributed study committee volunteers from their top management for up to six months. When organized labor protested the exclusive use of business volunteers, Carter drew labor union officials into the discussions. State agencies, especially the universities, contributed support personnel. A total of 117 people worked full-time—forty-eight state employees, sixty-five volunteers from business and labor, and four consultants from Arthur Andersen. The governor funded the cost of $205,000, half of it from a federal grant, half from his emergency fund.[56]

Beginning in March, Carter met monthly with Linder, the Executive Committee, and other select bureaucrats. He gathered information about all aspects of state government, collected ideas for change and consolidation, and planned his "Goals for Georgia" program, which he envisioned as flowing naturally from government reordering.[57]

Carter's restructuring plan was simple in concept but had numerous complicated parts. Most of the government's work would be accomplished by three new umbrella agencies—Administrative Services, Natural Resources, and Human Resources. Five departments—the Attorney General, Defense, Veterans Service, Revenue, and the University System of Georgia—remained almost unchanged. The Department of Education surrendered vocational rehabilitation to the new Department of Human Resources. The comptroller general acquired both the Labor Department and the Board of Workman's Compensation; the secretary of state gained control of the state library; and securities regulation went to the Department of Financial Regulation. The Department of Agriculture retained its functions, but the Department of Human Resources became responsible for the inspection of eggs in restaurants and nursing homes. Sixty-five budgeted agencies were consolidated into twenty, and two hundred unbudgeted agencies were transferred to one of the twenty.[58]

When the press condemned the reorganization, Carter angrily accused a writer for the *Atlanta Constitution* of choosing such enemies as Roy Harris, Marvin Griffin, Carl Sanders, and Hal Suit to assess his progress. He asked the journalist to present a detached account of "reorganization, budgeting, goals, etc."[59] He and Rosalynn invited newspaper editors to the mansion to persuade them to support the plan, but the *Atlanta Constitution* remained an implacable opponent.[60]

Carter starred in a massive advertising campaign to sell reorganization to the public. Gerald Rafshoon produced an eight- to eleven-minute film showing

Georgians from a cross-section of society going about their business, implying how the state affected their lives. He followed with 145,000 brochures head-lined "Economize, Revitalize, Reorganize State Government." Rafshoon then distributed a twenty-page brochure explaining the proposed changes. Carter wrote the introduction, emphasizing that the plan to reduce three hundred departments to twenty would save $60 million per year. How many of the two hundred thousand copies actually got read is a matter of conjecture, but Georgians became aware that something was happening. When Linder informed Carter that he had distributed twenty-five hundred copies of a reorganization report, the frugal governor noted, "Don't print more." Carter gave speeches arguing the merits of reorganization and reassuring state employees that they would not lose their jobs.[61]

Bob Lipshutz headed the next stage of the campaign. He reassembled the old 1970 campaign committee into the Citizens' Committee for Reorganization, comprised of twenty-three members from the state's most populated areas. It mailed out thousands of newsletters that declared "JIMMY CARTER NEEDS YOUR HELP." Delta Airlines sent $5,000. Common Cause, the League of Women Voters, groups representing blacks and women, and public service organizations such as the Jaycees all sent money. Many small and medium-sized newspapers and television stations endorsed the project. Carter traveled the state, emphasizing the millions of dollars he claimed the plan would save the first year. He discussed specific topics at different locations in order to avoid attempting to explain the whole complicated plan in a single long speech. He denounced those who disagreed with him.[62] Using approaches that ranged from soft sell to explication to attack, Carter, Rafshoon, and Lipshutz convinced the public that Georgia's government needed to be reshaped.

Carter next took up the daunting challenge of selling his plan to bureaucrats who feared they would lose jobs or power. They fought back. "I'm not going to lie still like a catfish and be gutted," the much-loved secretary of state Ben Fortson informed the governor. Born in 1904, the colorful "Mr. Ben" had been confined to a wheelchair by an automobile accident when he was twenty-five; he used the handicap to get attention and power. Following service in the house and senate, in 1946 he became secretary of state. His office had jurisdiction over the state archives, but it also managed securities regulation, a function Carter intended to take away under reorganization.[63] The secretary wheeled into the governor's office, fuming, stomped the footrail of his wheelchair, and declared: "I've got on an old suit, but it's going to take some stripping to strip me." He lashed out in public at the governor's diabolical plan until Carter won his confidence with a promise to promote legislation to regulate securities.[64]

Other bureaucrats proved more difficult. Comptroller general Johnnie Caldwell balked when he saw that the issuing of fire permits for hotels and motels would be moved to the Department of Public Safety. Labor commissioner Sam Caldwell, a tough ex-marine and protégé of former governor Marvin Griffin and the deposed Jim Gillis, had close ties with Senator Herman Talmadge, the black community, and organized labor. Embittered because Carter had not appointed him to Russell's Senate seat, he called the governor "a liar" who wanted absolute power.[65] He accused Carter of meeting with Elliott Richardson, U.S. Secretary of Health, Education, and Welfare, the most hated cabinet position among conservative Georgians. Carter, he said, was trying to create a "Little HEW" in Georgia and establish "a dictatorship" to "seize control of all federal and state funds."[66]

Carter shocked agriculture commissioner Tommy Irvin with a plan to remove the agricultural laboratory from his jurisdiction. When Irvin, a close friend of Lester Maddox, protested, Carter wrote him that "agriculture ... is my life's work," but "the overriding consideration with you and me must ... be loyalty to the Georgians whom we represent."[67] Like Sam Caldwell, Irvin would not budge.

Others stood firm against the governor. State school superintendent Jack Nix expressed dismay when he learned that Carter intended to make changes in his department without first consulting him. Carter thought Nix gave too much authority to local school boards, making it easy for them to thwart racial integration. Nix miffed the governor by not supporting his plan for state kindergartens. State treasurer Bill Burson did not want to see his office abolished entirely; veterans did not want the Department of Veterans Service lumped with the Department of Human Resources; and the University System of Georgia's Board of Regents did not want a centralized budget.[68]

Carter stirred a hornet's nest with his intention to abolish what he saw as an ineffective Board of Health and replace it with thirty-three community health centers. Health care would be under the auspices of the mammoth Department of Human Resources, which would be governed by a board of both laypeople and professionals. The Medical Association of Georgia was horrified at the thought of laypeople supervising professionals and resolved to "oppose vigorously" Carter's plan. Carter, in a meeting of the State Board of Health, won support of other health care professionals, however, and got his way.[69]

Carter proceeded to appoint eight of the fifteen members of the governing board for the Department of Human Resources, letting the crippled Medical Association of Georgia choose the other seven. Carter appointed his mother, who was qualified for the job but whose appointment surely raised a few eyebrows. To assist her, the governor chose Bob Lipshutz, Hugh Gaston, Elgin Carmichael, Dean Fowler, Earl Zimmerman, and Robert P. Repass. He asked Jack Watson of King and Spaulding to serve as chairman. Watson later relinquished his position to twenty-eight-year-old Richard Harden. Carter continued to battle the doctors, accusing them of wielding too much power and not doing enough to halt drug abuse. He appointed a young psychiatrist, Peter Bourne, to head a drug treatment program and reduced the size of the board to nine, only three of whom came from the medical profession.[70]

Miss Lillian took her job seriously. Four months after her appointment, she wrote her son a letter asking specifically what she needed to do. "I have been trying to be successful in my Human Resources activities—but I *still* am not aware of my duties," she wrote. She had many calls from administrators and "gripes everywhere." She wanted to justify her membership on the board. "Please don't think I want to run your business—I *don't*—I'm *too humble*," she continued. "ILYTG, M." Jimmy answered his "Dear Ma" immediately, explaining, "The duties of Human Resources Board members are difficult to specify," a confession that he himself did not understand precisely how the massive department would work. He told her, "Specifically, your own involvement with nurses, family planning, hospital administrators and elderly citizens should be continued so that you can speak for them at the board meetings." He also suggested that "when convenient" she visit "state mental institutions, welfare offices, etc." to familiarize herself "with practical delivery of services to Georgia people." When she got questions she should forward them to him, he said, signing the letter with the personal family closing, "ILYTG, Jimmy."[71]

With a specific assignment, Lillian happily went to work, later writing her son: "Dear Governor, I have been all over this district, talking, getting feedback, and observing.... Sincerely yours, Lillian Carter."[72] Earlier, she reported that Webster County desperately needed food stamps and recommended that Jimmy, "if it is feasible," telephone the person at Preston who was holding them up. She also noted that she would be attending a meeting in Atlanta soon and would like to spend the night at the mansion; "I wanted to stay with Amy while R—is away, but Rosalynn assured me it is not necessary," she concluded. Jimmy ignored the references to Rosalynn and Amy but assured her, "Dear Ma, Webster County will have food stamps soon."[73]

While his mother worked for him, the governor continued to fine tune state government. He made small concessions, divided his opponents, and built support until he gained control of the bureaucracy. George Beattie, executive director of the Georgia Commission on the Arts, did not protest when Carter placed art projects directly under the governor.[74] Other bureaucrats yielded reluctantly; exercising their right to veto items related to their agencies, they cast forty-five vetoes. Of those, Johnnie Caldwell cast twenty-nine, and Irvin, Nix, Sam Caldwell, Fortson, and state treasurer Bill Burson cast the others. Carter disallowed all but six, accepting two from Johnnie Caldwell and one each from Nix, Fortson, Burson, and Sam Caldwell. Carter said the other vetoes were illegal or frivolous. Attorney general Arthur Bolton, a Carter ally, refused to override the governor's actions. Carter told a reporter that he looked on his dream as "almost a crusade," and he was "going to get it."[75]

With a tamed bureaucracy, Carter approached his final hurdle, the state legislature. He vowed to "dedicate all of my effort" to get the necessary legislation passed, but at the Democratic caucus in July 1971, he had not won the support he needed.[76] He turned for advice to his chief of staff Charles Kirbo and executive secretary Hamilton Jordan. Kirbo thought that failure in the caucus did not necessarily mean that the senate would kill reorganization and speculated about which senators from the opposition might be won over. By bringing in a few of them, Kirbo wrote to Carter, holding the ones they had, and adding some blacks and Republicans, they could win.[77]

Hamilton Jordan agreed with Kirbo but—passionately loyal to Carter—did so in a quite different, rebellious, youthful style. In a long handwritten memorandum, Ham vented his anger about being defeated in the caucus "by a group of selfish, petty bastards who used every means of threat and persuasion to get votes." He urged Carter to punish those who had voted against the reorganization plan and suggested that there were senators who were disgusted with Maddox and who might readily vote for Carter's programs, provided he did not irritate them by battling Hugh Gillis over secondary issues.[78]

Both Jordan and Kirbo complained that Carter took on too many projects instead of focusing on reorganization.[79] Kirbo advised Carter to explain that the governor would gain no power under the reorganization plan, for most of its functions were under the "Control of the constitutional officers" over whom the governor had "no direct control... except through persuasion." There would be no drastic reduction of personnel, and the real purpose of reorganization was to make the government "more responsive to the people and more efficiently meet their needs."[80]

Press secretary Jody Powell warned Carter that he could not count on public opinion to win the fight for reorganization. He recommended a "little show of temper" by letting key senators know he might veto any plan the senate had to gut his program. The public likes a fighting spirit, Jody said.[81]

Carter gave them the fight. He proposed a plan to save $55 million in his 1973 budget if reorganization won approval, but he threatened that if he did not get the savings there could be no salary increase for state employees. Sam Caldwell sneered in response, "The way the governor's been acting, it appears he might eliminate Santa Claus before Christmas arrives."[82] Former governor Marvin Griffin wryly commented, "A governor who goes to the General Assembly with a plan to reorganize state government and carries a companion appropriation bill along with him that is reduced by an amount of $50 million, will have little trouble getting it adopted."[83] Pinned to the wall by their governor, legislators had to either approve reorganization or come up with a similar cost-cutting plan. Most would take the easy route.

With the convening of the 1972 General Assembly still months away, Carter continued to lobby for reorganization. To the senators he thought would vote against him, he wrote friendly notes and "invited them to see me about it."[84] He appealed to conservative businessmen, many of them Republicans whose 1970 candidate Hal Suit, he reminded them, had campaigned for reorganization.[85] He advised Hamilton Jordan to distribute $10 million from the governor's emergency fund to the Apple Valley Center for Rehabilitation in such a way as to "maximize political benefit for legislators."[86] He met wealthy citizens in the Capital City Club's Gold Room, attended Governor's Club luncheons at various hotels, and explained to businessmen that the state and the Democratic party were themselves businesses. He joked about his problems with the legislature and convinced businessmen that his plan that would save money.[87]

Opposition in the legislature nevertheless remained strong. Led by powerful Stanley Eugene Smith, Jr., chairman of the senate Economy, Reorganization, and Efficiency in Government Committee, adversaries argued that Carter's plan would save nothing and might cost more. When holding committee hearings in December 1971, Smith called witnesses hostile to the governor.[88]

Ben Fortson, the inflamed secretary of state and brother of Carter's friend Warren Fortson, appeared before the committee and staged quite a show: "Don't pay any attention to that smile," he thundered from his wheelchair. "That man is made of steel, determination and stubbornness." He compared Carter to a "South Georgia turtle" that, when confronting a log, does not go around it but "just sticks his head in the middle and pushes and pushes until the log gives way."[89]

Carter, like the turtle, at the beginning of the new year made a major speech defending his program. Only one week before the legislature convened, he admonished it to decide whether "our government be controlled by the people or not." He invited the entire legislature to meet with him at the University of Georgia Continuing Education Center. Less than one hundred of the 251 members attended, but those who went found the governor well prepared. He answered numerous questions, the most persistent dealing with the Board of Health. Afterward, Carter's friends seemed pessimistic, but the governor and his staff hinted that the chief executive might retaliate against those who opposed him by working against their reelection.[90]

A few days before the General Assembly convened, Carter's enemies met at the Whitehall Salon of the Marriott Motor Hotel. Stanley Smith, Culver Kidd, and Eugene Holley invited Dr. Carl Pruett of the State Board of Health, state school superintendent Jack Nix, and lieutenant governor Maddox to join them. They contemplated bringing lawsuits to challenge the constitutionality of House Bill 1, substituting their own legislation for the governor's, or even delaying consideration of the 1973 budget until the reorganization issue could be settled. Culver Kidd, who had represented the Twenty-fifth District since 1963 and had won much pork-barrel legislation for Milledgeville, wanted appointive power to go to the legislature.[91] Despite Kidd's influence, he and the others, facing the governor, appeared to be desperate men pinned in their last ditch.

On the morning of January 10, 1972, Lieutenant Governor Maddox gaveled the General Assembly into session. Governor Carter gave a state-of-the-state address, making an impassioned plea for reorganization and begging the General

Assembly to help people of Georgia "take advantage of *a time for greatness.*"[92] The governor received a cool reception, but amendments and three lawsuits to gut his plan failed.

In a bizarre episode, Senator Kidd did an about-face and suddenly offered to sponsor an amendment that would assure Carter victory. His district included the Central Georgia Regional Hospital and six small loan companies he controlled. Kidd promised to support reorganization in return for advance notice of gambling raids by state agents in his district. Carter declined the offer, Kidd opposed every reorganization bill in 1972, and the two men remained implacable enemies. Kidd said that behind "the governor's desk," Carter was "a son of a bitch" who tried to bully the senate.[93]

Carter outmaneuvered his opponents. He used his $2 million annual emergency fund to finance reorganization and to reward friendly legislators. He made concessions, provided that they did not emasculate his bill.[94] Charles Kirbo, Bert Lance, and George L. Smith argued his case persuasively. Kirbo remembered that before a vote, "Bert and I ended up...fighting with a bunch of jerks."[95] In fact, Smith, a clever manipulator of people, thought the governor should have his way and did his best to see that he got it, knowing that Carter would reciprocate.[96]

Carter answered every query from Smith, defending the Department of Human Resources as one that would help all Georgians afflicted "with financial, social, mental and physical conditions."[97] The Georgia house debated Carter's volatile proposal to abolish the Board of Health and place its functions under the enormous Department of Human Resources. Despite the powerful medical lobby's opposition, the governor won, 130 to 55, which he called a *"beautiful"* vote.[98]

On paper, Carter's reorganization plan seemed clean and neat, but it remained to be seen whether it actually saved money and improved the lives of Georgians. It did prove that Carter was a hardworking, compulsive politician who refused to surrender until he had constructed the framework of the government that he wanted.

The administration's enemies, looking for a soft spot, went after Bert Lance, Carter's wealthy highway director, who with his wife LaBelle gave the Carters 1,250 shares of Calhoun First National Bank stock. The Carters were to use the gift for a project of their choice to aid the mentally ill, and Kirbo would hold the money until Rosalynn decided how to use it. The gift, in memory of LaBelle's father, A. B. David, exceeded the total salary Lance received from the state.[99] The Carters and the Lances managed to keep the gift secret, or the press would have surely gone after both with even more enthusiasm than it did.

One journalist attacked Lance for failing to get federal funds for a twenty-three-mile stretch of Interstate 75, for taking down "Jesus Saves" signs along Georgia's highways, and for using his department's airplane for private purposes. Complying with both state and federal law, Lance had ordered the removal of unapproved billboards. He had also appropriately ordered an ecological study of the area through which the disputed interstate would pass. After making a trip to Washington to ask Secretary of Transportation John A. Volpe for federal money, he was baffled by Volpe's negative response.[100] Lance wrote Carter that he had not used the airplane inappropriately and that he must be a sorry excuse for a highway director because of the other two offenses.[101] Carter reassured Lance and asked for his "continuing friendship and counsel."[102]

Realizing that his friend really needed help, Carter, who had had more experience with the hostile press and federal rejections, thought the episode ludicrous and joked about it. Carter answered Lance's gloomy letter: "I'm sure you are not superstitious about the JESUS SAVES signs.... The airplane inquiry and Volpe's decisions could not be connected with those signs." Still joking, Carter wrote a couple of days later, "I apologize for forgetting that you were a Methodist. No Baptist would have dared take down a JESUS SAVES sign."[103]

Fun aside, Carter scolded his enemies. He attacked Hugh Gillis, the senator who headed the independent Forestry Department and whom Carter had loathed since the day of his election. Hugh was the son of Jim Gillis, whom Carter had fired as head of the Highway Department. Hugh Gillis remained loyal to Maddox and opposed reorganization and shifting Forestry to Game and Fish. Carter summoned him to the mansion and in the presence of twenty-five others asked him what he intended to do with Forestry. When Gillis replied that he did not plan any changes, the governor lost his temper and vowed to campaign against him. In the fall of 1972, Carter kept his promise and supported Cecil Passmore, a banker from Laurens County, against Gillis, but Gillis kept his seat and his department.[104]

Another senator, Nathan Dean of Polk County, who voted against Carter, also received retribution. Dean had asked the governor for $36,000 to build a pavilion behind the Highway Patrol's office in Cedartown. When Carter found that the money had been approved, he told Dean that if he lost the senator's vote, the senator would lose his money. Dean later reported that Carter was a man of his word, because "I voted against him, and I lost my money."[105]

Carter gained support of the courts and the party. Arthur Bolton, the attorney general who had been appointed by Governor Carl Sanders in 1966, defended him. He forced out Democratic party chairwoman Marge Thurmond, a Sanders stalwart, and replaced her first with David Gambrell and later Charles Kirbo. Hamilton Jordan and Mike Jones, a college student who managed the campaign in North Georgia, helped the governor choose appointees who had contributed to the campaign.[106]

Concurrently with the battle for reorganization, Carter and Nunn proceeded with "Goals for Georgia." The program began on April 12, 1971. The committee consisted of Carter, Nunn, and twenty-four others. By involving citizens from every walk of life and Georgia's leaders and specialists, Carter hoped to produce specific guidelines for people in public and private life. Carter wanted the best education possible, economy in local government, a legal system to protect the public as well as the accused, essential social services, and a clean environment for Georgia. He held fifty-one meetings across the state, proclaiming that citizen involvement would improve quality of life and listening to what his audience had to say. Bobby Rowan said those meetings gave power "to the powerless" and a voice "to the voiceless."[107]

Carter turned to experts for help. He consulted ecologist Eugene Odum at the University of Georgia, who suggested that the state should plan waste management parks to attract and control industry. Beverly W. Forester, a physician who had married Carter's former girlfriend Marguerite Wise and had been his classmate at Georgia Southwestern, chaired the Board of Health, and supported his reorganization plan, and advised him on health matters; Rosalynn attended conferences related to health and reported to the governor. Lance advised him on matters related to transportation.[108] Using that information, Carter organized his "goals" into two groups, those related to business and economics, and those related to judicial and social reform.

From his massive, unproven reorganization plan and "Goals for Georgia" emerged a Jimmy Carter more like the man who delivered the inaugural address than the candidate for governor. "Destiny is not a matter of chance; it is a matter of choice," Robert Lipshutz wrote him, quoting William Jennings Bryan. "Destiny is not a thing to be waited for; it is a thing to be achieved."[109] Carter did not intend to wait, for he sought the national spotlight on television and in magazines while, as one journalist wrote, practicing "just enough Georgia-brand demagoguery to keep the natives from getting so restless that his program will be wrecked."[110] National journalists identified Carter as a "new voice in the South," a member of a group of governors who "may in the future have an equal chance to get to the White House."

CHAPTER FIFTEEN

Georgians at Home

"HOME" TO THE CARTERS MEANT GEORGIA. The governor had an ambitious agenda to improve his state. A reformer, he hoped to manage the state's economy more efficiently, improve education, reform the prison and judicial systems, and protect the environment. With a pragmatic temperament, Carter approached change cautiously, but when he decided to do something, he wanted it done quickly. He fought with the press, courted national politicians, and managed a large staff. He generated many ideas simultaneously, asked Rosalynn for advice, and frustrated his aids and the General Assembly with his drive to accomplish so much in a short amount of time. Sometimes he won his point, sometimes he did not. Rosalynn supported her husband with public appearances and an agenda of her own, but she left the task of governing to him.

Unwilling to separate his "born again" experience from his political opportunity, Carter believed that he had received "great blessings" from God and that as governor he should "share those blessings with others."[1] He spoke easily about his religion, taught a Sunday school class, and in political speeches often referred to his faith. He addressed Christian groups, advised the Baptist Brotherhood Commission in Memphis, and sometimes signed his letters "Yours in Christ."[2] At the Georgia Baptist Convention in Savannah on November 15, 1972, he emphasized his firm belief in the separation of church and state. Furthermore, he said he would "vigorously oppose" anyone's attempt "to force his religious beliefs" on him, nor would he impose "my beliefs upon others."[3]

At a Methodist church, Carter said theologians Paul Tillich and Reinhold Niebuhr had helped him understand that he had but one life to live, and that he must accept human imperfection and work for justice.[4] Before a Baptist audience, he explained that Paul Tillich was too liberal for "a Southern Baptist like me" but the theologian's writings stretched his mind. He thought Tillich's definition of religion as "a search for the truth about man's existence and his relationship with God" to be a point worth contemplating. He went to Detroit, Dallas, and back home to Georgia addressing large crowds with that message.[5] His sense of class conflict derived from his Christian faith, not Marxist theory.[6]

Carter told the World Mission Conference in Atlanta that he deplored "the absence of the essence of Christ's teaching in our international policies."[7] He bravely informed Baptist groups that he supported the Equal Rights Amendment for women and thought the state should legalize the sale of alcohol. Unbowed by the burdens of his office and his life, he put himself "in God's hands and let him worry."[8] He occasionally referred to Billy Graham, wrote one meditation for a Methodist devotional booklet, and confessed that he had "a tendency to exalt" himself. He corrected the latter fault by having his biography in *Who's Who in Georgia* for 1973 read simply: "Atlanta. Farmer."[9]

No farmer, Carter managed his state's government with as much of an iron fist and quick precision as an unruly assembly and intransigent bureaucracy would allow. He thought the government should run like a well organized business based on zero-base budgeting, an idea he borrowed from Peter Phyrr of Texas Instruments Corporation in Dallas. An unwieldy and controversial plan that required all departments to begin a new budget from zero each year, it may have saved money, but most bureaucrats disliked it.[10] Carter ignored his critics and believed that the method cut waste and promoted cooperation among business and professional groups and state government. The state's major chief executive officers had contributed to his campaign, and he in turn promoted their interests.[11]

Carter changed the way the state managed its money, because he wanted the state to earn more income from its investments and eliminate favoritism. He removed state funds from pet banks that paid little interest, created a depository board, and placed the money in a wider variety of banks at higher rates. For his four-year term in office, interest income increased by 244 percent, and the treasury accumulated a surplus of $200 million. He asked bankers, many of whom benefited from his new plan, not to oppose consumer bills and to contribute to the state's drug program. He mandated budget cuts and standardized state printing.[12]

While most agencies fumed about their tight budgets, the 1972 auditor's report showed Carter to be the highest spending chief executive for his own office in

Georgia's history. He dispensed almost $600,000 on salaries, communications, and travel.[13]

To increase revenue and provide more jobs for Georgians, Carter cast a wide net. He said the federal government's revenue-sharing was "a hoax and a mistake" because it increased the federal deficit, but he collected those monies for Georgia.[14] He tried to market peanuts and peanut products in Japan, promoted new airline intrastate and international flights, and invited the film industry to Georgia.[15]

Carter appointed a Motion Picture and Television Advisory Committee and then appealed to his old friend David Rabhan, whose businesses included Cinema Systems, Inc., of Los Angeles. In December 1972, following a schedule partly arranged by Rabhan, Carter visited nine cities from Miami to Los Angeles and San Francisco to recruit filmmakers and to develop a national reputation. By the spring of 1973, *Escape from Andersonville, Conrack,* and *Dead Gangsters Have No Friends* had all been produced in Georgia.[16] In September 1973, when searching for investments from the entertainment industry in New York City, Carter climbed on the stage with the famed Rockettes in Radio City Music Hall, fell in line with them and, dressed in business suit and leather shoes, kicked as high as they.[17]

By the spring of 1974, Carter had become a regular visitor to California. In May he met with former Democratic governor Edmund Brown, then returned home with a commitment for fifteen movies to be filmed in Georgia. They included *The Friday Job, First Blood,* the television series *Sounder, Blood, Sweat, and Doing Time, Poor Plain Jane, She Died Young, Bessie Smith.* He and Rosalynn attended the premier of *Cockfighter* in Roswell on July 30, 1974, because his Aunt Sissy Dolvin had landed a role in it as the "Colonel's mistress."[18] The movie titles and quality were not always a compliment to the state, but the revenue helped.

Carter planned to support education with the increased revenue and argued that advanced education would lead to economic growth, but the legislature would not cooperate. The assembly passed the Adequate Program for Education in Georgia and added special education teachers but denied the governor kindergartens and approved only one small pay increase for teachers during his term.[19] Carter's commencement and convocation speeches from Berry College in North Georgia to Valdosta State College in South Georgia yielded negligible results. The College Tuition Equalization Act became a setback for college students, because it raised the cost of attendance at the state's smaller four-year and junior colleges, which had had lower tuition and fees than the universities. Higher education lagged behind the national average and remained poorly funded. The chancellor of the University System of Georgia, George Simpson, and many of the faculty were frustrated with Carter. Simpson privately called Carter "a skunk."[20]

Carter's educational victories tended to be small and often personal. On June 7, 1973, Georgia Southwestern College named its new library in memory of Mr. Earl, and later the same year, Carter dedicated the Richard Russell Library at the University of Georgia.[21] When a home economics teacher at Plains High School wrote him that the school desperately needed equipment, he provided $5,000 from the governor's emergency fund to make the purchases. He persuaded the University System's Board of Regents to approve an art degree at Georgia Southwestern.[22] He documented the historical artifacts in the Capitol and commissioned a new history of Georgia.[23] Carter wrote the foreword to the book, which was edited by Kenneth Coleman and brought together the work of six historians. On reviewing the manuscript in 1974, he said he "liked the chapter" about himself but suggested that the contributors include a "consistent tie to national affairs" in Georgia's history; he got "lost in the parochialism," he complained, and forgot "where the world is."[24]

In a celebrated case, the governor joined Millard Fuller of Koinonia and forty-two private citizens in a lawsuit against four members of the Sumter County Board of Education. Since those four favored private schools, the litigants thought they did not support public education and should not serve on the board. Carter and his friends lost the case, and he lamented to a friend who advised him that his participation in the suit was bad politics but he could not "stand to see my own county have the worst school situation in Georgia."[25]

Despite limited success with improving education, Carter achieved other goals. The Lions Club gave him its International Presidential Award for outstanding leadership for his work with the blind.[26] He continued the Highway Patrol's work making continuous trips from the point of donation to the eye bank, despite the excessive "time requirement of hauling blood, eyes and other important cargoes."[27] He tried to improve health care in nursing homes, and he asked Peter Bourne to set up effective treatment centers to provide methadone to those addicted to narcotics, a program he hoped would reduce violent crimes.[28] He built a livestock arena in Douglas, subsidized low-income housing, purchased short-sleeved shirts for Georgia state troopers, financed a sweet potato research project, supported planned parenthood efforts, and operated a facility for treatment of crippling diseases in Warm Springs. He helped elementary schools and areas with dense black populations.[29]

Carter endorsed the legal sale of liquor to prevent "criminal activities" such as "drugs, prostitution, and the sale of pornographic literature" that often accompanied the illegal sale of alcohol. "It is important for the Baptists and others," he said, "to realize that just because a county is dry doesn't mean that liquor isn't being sold."[30] Hoping to win the help of clergymen, despite that comment, he sent them a form letter urging them to inform their congregations that the blind, aged, and disabled were eligible for millions of dollars each year through a new program called Supplemental Security Income administered by the Social Security Administration. Marijuana users should be punished lightly, he said, but he did not want the drug made legal. He gave impassioned speeches on world hunger, saying that it was as serious a problem as it had been during the Great Depression.[31]

Carter inherited a broken and prejudiced criminal justice system. He wanted to equalize justice for all, eliminate trial delays, and standardize sentences.[32] To these ends, his friends sponsored twenty-five successful bills in the legislature to reform the judiciary, including integrating Juvenile Court judges into the entire court system.[33] Voters elected judges, but the governor appointed a justice to fill an unexpired term, and that person usually got reelected. Carter appointed Robert Jordan, Bill Gunter, Conley Ingraham, and Robert H. Hall to the state supreme court, all of them in his circle of close political allies. He appointed H. Sol Clark as the first Jewish member of the Court of Appeals.[34]

In order to prevent attorneys from controlling judicial nominees, Carter created a fourteen-member Committee on Judicial Processes made up of judges, lawyers, and legislators to recommend men and women to serve as judges. By executive order, he established the Judicial Nominating Commission and appointed U.S. Senator Sam Nunn to serve on it. It publicized openings, held hearings on candidates, and submitted five names to the governor, from which he made the final selection.[35]

Rosalynn endorsed her husband's decisions, but she stayed in the background of his executive dealings. She made numerous public appearances and attended many social functions. She put most of her energy into her family and her own projects, which she and the governor would reveal as they saw fit.

One of Carter's toughest decisions involved the death penalty. When the state legislature reinstated the death penalty for murder, rape, armed robbery, kidnaping, airplane hijacking, and treason, Carter signed the bill. He hoped that a death sentence would not result in an execution but the "permanent incarceration of a person who is a proven threat to society."[36] Capital punishment might be employed for the murder of a prison guard, he said, but he was relieved that no prisoner was executed during his tenure in office. Because the Pardons and Parole Board alone decided on those matters, Carter did not have to make those tough decisions. He did, however, appoint the members of that board with a rotating chairmanship.[37]

Carter invested in prison personnel and programs rather than construction of new buildings. He chose Ellis MacDougall of Connecticut, a professional criminologist, to head the prison system. To experience the harshest prison life personally, he accepted MacDougall's invitation to spend a night at the Jackson Diagnostic and Classification Center, which housed the state's death row.[38] Mac-Dougall started prison educational programs, employed counselors for inmates, hired wardens with college degrees, and began early release programs. The number of parolees in Georgia increased from 111 per month in 1969–70 to 217 in 1973–74. Many parolees, especially if they were first-time offenders, regained their civil rights.[39]

An enlightened justice system required a better system of law enforcement. Carter reorganized and upgraded the Department of Investigation (DOI) and provided a vigorous training program for sheriffs and patrolmen. During the Jim Crow and civil rights eras many Georgia county sheriffs had a notoriously corrupt relationship with Georgia Bureau of Investigation (GBI) agents. Carter ended that opportunity, he said, by "establishing a highly professional, well qualified group of trained agents." He told a group of DOI agents in Atlanta that "If you feel the requirements are too tough ... or your ties to the local sheriff's office are too hard to break, we'll help you find other employment." He established "a blue ribbon police academy" that sheriffs-elect must attend, and he congratulated new sheriffs upon their election.[40]

An impassioned conservationist, Carter placed Joe Tanner in charge of the Department of Natural Resources, the most successful department in his reorganized state government. Atypically, he increased its annual budget from 55 to 70 million dollars. By executive order, he created the Georgia Heritage Trust

Commission in 1972; it identified more than 2,000 natural and historical sites, and acquired nineteen of them, including 142 acres of land along the Chatta-hoochee River, to preserve as natural areas. For purposes of building interstate highways in and around Atlanta, Carter made environmental concessions, but he asked the legislature for five million dollars to buy land elsewhere to preserve natural areas, restore historic sites, and provide recreational opportunities.[41]

The coast, especially the isolated and undeveloped islands, Carter jealously protected as his and Rosalynn's Shangri-la. "I love the Georgia coast," he wrote to a friend on Sapelo Island. He thought it beautiful whether viewed from outer space or standing in one of its marshes. He and Rosalynn frequently went there to fish, relax, and evade the public eye. "Rosalynn says your letters always make her cry & that she loves you," Jimmy went on to say to these friends who some-times gave them shelter away from the Atlanta crowds.[42]

Likewise, Carter resolved to keep the Flint River wild and free; it flowed through middle and southwest Georgia, with a tributary meandering through the land of his childhood. The Army Corps of Engineers wanted to build a dam at Spewrell Bluff that would enable development along Georgia's last totally wild river. Unwilling to accept anyone else's description of the river's natural beauty, Carter climbed into a canoe with Joe Tanner, put into the water at Thomaston, paddled downstream for most of a day, camped at Pasley Shoals, and enjoyed a supper of "steak and beer" before inspecting the dam site the next day. Back in Atlanta, arguing that the Army Corps of Engineers had outdated information about flood control and hydroelectric power, he ignored letters favoring the dam from businessmen who would profit from it. Carter canoed down the river a second time and twice viewed it from a helicopter. After he vetoed the bill that would have authorized the dam about fifty miles south of the capital city, he received two boxes full of thank-you notes. Thirty years later, he proudly wrote that if anyone wanted "to experience the way Georgia was when God made it," he could "go to the upper parts of the Flint River and see how beautiful it is."[43]

The Carters found beauty in art as well as in nature; they boosted the fine arts, including poetry, literature, music, and paintings. They hung paintings by local and famous artists in his office and in their home and encouraged schoolchildren to write poetry.[44] Carter appointed three consecutive poets laureate for the state, namely Conrad Aiken, James Dickey, and John Ranson Lewis, Jr. On one occa-sion, he declared "Flannery O'Connor Day" to memorialize the life and work of the Milledgeville author. During a special session of the legislature, he played recordings of Dylan Thomas reading his poetry.[45] The Carters enjoyed classical, popular, and folk music. They attended Atlanta Symphony performances, and after listening to the Allman Brothers and Bob Dylan on separate occasions, they invited them to the mansion.[46]

Rosalynn brought the Art Train to Georgia, and with it the opportunity to associate with national politicians. A project of the National Endowment for the Arts, the Art Train housed an exhibit intended for children that traveled from state to state. When it came to Atlanta, the Carters invited Nancy Hanks, chair of the National Endowment for the Arts, and vice president Gerald Ford's wife Betty to join them for the opening ceremony. Riding in a limousine, Rosalynn turned to Michael Straight, a member of the National Endowment for the Arts, engaged him in a long conversation about the arts, and told him that she and Jimmy would be going back to Plains when his term as governor ended.[47]

Carter grinned cordially at Betty Ford, who was drugged for pain, steadied her by holding her arm tightly at the bottom of the curved staircase in the mansion, and informed her, not too accurately, "Nixon is the first President in the two hundred years of the Republic to be personally dishonest." He predicted that Nixon would be impeached, thus elevating Ford to the presidency. He also noted that he himself was finished with politics and would be returning to the peanut farm when he left Atlanta.[48]

Carter's relationship with the press, however, was not that of a man who intended to retire from politics. He condemned or praised editors and newspapers as the occasion warranted. Hostile editors could expect a wrathful letter, but friendly newspapers benefited from his largesse with state printing contracts.[49] At midterm, journalists gave Carter mixed or cynical reports. Shelby McCash of the *Macon Telegraph* accused the governor of antagonizing the legislature, making his enemies look evil, and exaggerating the success of his government reorganization. Others, however, noted that Carter attempted to keep his promises. Irv Cuevas of WSB-TV in Atlanta reported that kindergarten and state aid to poor school districts had not been decided, but racial unrest had subsided and there had been no increase in taxes. Most journalists portrayed Carter as an attacking bulldog, but they also conceded that so far he had been a successful governor.[50]

The newspaper Carter disliked most, the *Atlanta Constitution,* and its editor, Reg Murphy, demanded his special attention when William A. Williams, who wanted to rid the United States of corrupt politicians and Jews, kidnaped Murphy from his home on February 20, 1974, and held him for $700,000 ransom. Carter grinned privately to an aide and said he guessed he ought to help him. Publicly he said he was shocked that "one of our most distinguished citizens" had met such a fate and that he would do anything to help him. Cox Enterprises, owners of the *Atlanta Constitution,* paid the ransom, and forty-nine hours after his capture, Murphy returned home. The kidnaper was brought to justice, and Murphy resumed work and his criticisms of the governor.[51]

Carter had the power to reward and punish politicians with highway projects and grants that he could personally dispense from the governor's $2 million emergency fund. The grants tended to be small, but they could influence an election. His staff kept a record of how the governor awarded grants in what they called a "Goody Book," a handy reference when Carter later called in favors. He gave money for beautification projects, traffic lights in small towns, elementary schools, gifted children, mentally challenged children, day care centers, alcohol treatment centers, coastal development, small airports, and new industries, showing favoritism toward Sumter County.[52]

Carter disliked stroking legislators to get them to vote his way, for he felt they should support bills on their merit. On one occasion, he invited the entire state legislature to the mansion and served them barbeque pork on paper plates. When told that the paper ware was an insult, he invited them back and served them a second time, using china and crystal.[53] The Carters sometimes invited small friendly groups to the mansion for Sunday supper, and they invited larger groups of legislators for breakfast. He wrote letters to other members of the assembly directly asking their help with bills he wanted passed.[54]

Like Maddox before him, he gave the people of Georgia access to him by opening his office between 1 and 3 P.M. on the second Wednesday of each month. Carter called it "Speak Up Day," whereas Maddox had labeled it the catchier and more condescending "Little People's Day."[55]

What he could not achieve by political maneuver Carter attempted to win through veto power. At the end of each legislative session, he gleefully announced that it was "veto time," and he analyzed each bill before deciding whether to sign or veto it. At the end of the 1973 session, he vetoed "pork barrel" legislation, poorly worded bills, and bills that were not in accord with his plans for the state, such as an exemption of the University System of Georgia Board of Regents from the Reorganization Act and comprehensive health insurance for teachers. In the spring of 1974, he vetoed 52 bills and signed 587 bills into law. Many of the vetoed bills gave too much power to a local official, changed his reorganization plan, or were detrimental to the environment or the social needs of the state.

Carter signed into law bills that required politicians to disclose contributions over $101, no-fault automobile insurance, and tax relief for the elderly. He reestablished the twenty-member World Congress Center Authority to supervise the construction of the $35 million convention and trade center that would make Atlanta competitive with New York City and Chicago in attracting conventions; he enhanced it with a rapid transit system. He got rid of the crime of public drunkenness in favor of medical help for alcoholics, and he endorsed many bills that protected the rights of citizens and provided them with vital medical and educational services.[56]

Carter endorsed Sam Nunn's 1972 candidacy for the U.S. Senate against David Gambrell. Nunn had supported Carter in 1966 and 1970 and had worked for the passage of most of the legislation he wanted as governor. Carter in the meantime had become disillusioned with Gambrell for opposing a proposed supersonic transport plane that would have been built by Lockheed in Marietta. Carter knew the plane was unnecessary, but he could not understand why Gambrell would vote against something that would mean jobs for Georgians, thus becoming guilty himself of favoring a little federal pork for his fellow Georgians. After Nunn's victory, Carter repaired his relationship with Gambrell by complimenting his "fine job in Washington."[57]

When dealing with his staff, Carter, like his father before him, was often distant, stern, and demanding, but he also joked with them and won their respect. Jordan later said that the governor was "a tough guy... [who] ... demanded high quality work" in unreasonably short time.[58] Susan B. Clough, a young divorcee with two small children, rose from an entry-level position in the news office to become the governor's personal secretary. Mary Beazley worked as appointments secretary, a position she had held under governors Vandiver and Maddox. Sarah Hurst Lee, a law school graduate who had retired from the Army and had worked for the U.S. State Department, became his confidential secretary.[59] Rosalynn developed a good rapport with both Mary and Sarah, sometimes using notes to them to send messages to her husband.

The male staff consisted of those who had served Carter faithfully since 1966. Charles Kirbo, Hamilton Jordan, and Jody Powell were joined in 1973 by Frank Moore. With a degree in finance from the University of Georgia, Moore had directed the Middle Flint Area Planning and Development Commission and generally understood the politics of the state.[60] He got straight to the point with brief, detailed memoranda that lacked Jody's humorous touch but impressed his boss.[61]

Jordan thought Jody Powell and Carter were like an older and a younger brother who often fussed at each other, especially if Jody arrived late to work. Jody sometimes got a bit cynical with a flippant sense of humor when speaking for the governor. Not always amused, an irate Carter once wrote him a cryptic note saying, "You don't need to comment publicly on every issue, & particularly if it involves me personally." Powell felt the sting of Carter's famous temper when he erroneously implied that Carter deliberately snubbed Senator Edward Kennedy and that he favored a park along the Chattahoochee River only because he sought publicity. Carter assured Jody that he had not slighted the Senator and that "I *am* interested in the Chattahoochee River & not just personal publicity";[62] Jody apologized for "being a smartass about it" but jokingly said the governor could have a worse press secretary; he could have Martha Mitchell, the flamboyant, loquacious wife of U.S. Attorney General John Mitchell, speaking for him.[63]

When Carter received an unsigned letter criticizing them, he had fun with it. The semiliterate writer said: "Your staff has the Big Head. They think theirselves above criticism. But many people think they are the least cordial staff a governor ever had." Jimmy sent them a note: "Notice: Any clumsey and inept members of my staff who think theirselves above criticism are hereby criticized."[64] Everyone who worked for Carter, however, knew he did not tolerate sloppily written memos or tardy paperwork, but they felt a strong commitment to him and knew they could count on his support.[65] Carter and his staff understood, too, that they needed each other to confront Georgia's problems, especially the thorny issue of race.

CHAPTER SIXTEEN

The Trail of Martin Luther King, Jr.

THE TOMB OF MARTIN LUTHER KING, JR., near downtown Atlanta was only two and a half years old when Carter took office. The martyred civil rights leader had won the Nobel Peace Prize and had become the most famous person in Georgia. Carter never met him, but he embraced King as a heroic Christian and public servant. He intended to use the office of governor to continue King's work and guarantee that the time for racial discrimination in Georgia had ended. Carter did not participate in the civil rights movement, but once elected in 1970 he supported equal rights for African Americans. In fact, when campaigning for president in 1976, Carter declared emphatically that one of the things he might have done differently was to have "spoken out more clearly and loudly on the civil rights issue."[1]

Cognizant of the fact that many Georgians did not agree with him, Carter created two units to deal with race-related disturbances. The first, which he thought would save the state money, consisted of only three officers in civilian dress. He called it "a biracial civil disorder unit" and it stayed in close contact with him and did most of the work mediating racial disputes.[2]

The other, the biracial Human Relations Council, existed largely as a public relations tool that had a high profile but accomplished very little. It was designed to investigate any form of discrimination, whether based on race, age, sex, or income. Kirbo warned Carter that "these types of councils or commissions have too many black people, Jews and way-out liberals to really be effective." He recommended "reasonable blacks, good businessmen, and maybe one or two lawyers," and at least one Republican and one woman.[3] Carter took Kirbo's advice and appointed a low-profile conservative group whose discussions had little impact.[4]

Carter disliked government-mandated quotas to bring about racial integration, but he would not stand in the way of them. Black state senator LeRoy Johnson from Atlanta argued that Carter was the best governor for blacks in the "history of the state." He thought the reorganization plan would give blacks increasing importance in the General Assembly. Privately, Johnson promised "personally [to] continue to support" Carter "on most issues" and urge other black legislators to do the same.[5] At least one black leader, however, who was the Georgia field secretary for the NAACP, had "mixed feelings about Brother Carter," arguing that he would give blacks just enough to win their votes, but not so much that he would lose too many white votes.[6]

Caught between blacks who wanted change and whites who did not, Carter attempted to keep his inaugural commitment and to enforce the federal legislation and judicial decisions on racial equality. He asked local school boards to take the lead in achieving peaceful integration because all children were "unique human beings," each "created by God in His image." He thought both public and private schools had useful purposes, and he developed personal and professional associations with African Americans. He appointed Bobbie S. Ware, a black woman, chief of Field Social Services in the Georgia Department of Family and Children Services, and he accepted an honorary doctor of laws degree from Morris Brown College, a traditionally black school in Atlanta. Hamilton Jordan introduced him to Andrew Young, a prosperous and well-educated minister who had been an aide to Martin Luther King, Jr., at the time of his death in 1968. Young, a candidate in 1972 for the U.S. House from Georgia's Fifth District, would soon become the first African American from Georgia to be elected to Congress since Reconstruction, and he was a close friend to the governor.[7]

One prominent black leader, however, doubted Governor Carter's sincerity. Hosea Williams, successor to Martin Luther King, Jr., in the Southern Christian Leadership Conference, accused Carter of being a racist for not stopping police brutality toward blacks. When a black delegation visited the governor without an appointment, Carter spoke to them very briefly and told them to come back with an appointment. He also warned the militant Black Panthers that they would not be welcome in Georgia.[8] No racist, Carter neither moved as forcefully as some prominent black civil rights leaders wished, nor did he tolerate violence by blacks. When organizations, white or black, emerged that threatened the tranquility of a community, Carter wrote privately that his approach to such organizations would be "cautious."[9]

Ronnie Thompson, the rabidly segregationist mayor of Macon, put Carter to his first major test. For the purpose of getting assault weapons out of irresponsible hands, Carter had offered to use state money to buy them with no questions asked. Thompson wrote the governor an open letter: "Since you are collecting machine guns, please be advised that I have 20,000 Thompson submachine guns that you may have at $1.00 each.... The proceeds will go to financing my reelection as mayor of Macon." When Carter condemned the mayor for his stand on race relations, many citizens defended Thompson, one writing, "Please criticize our Mayor again, we appreciate it."[10]

Carter sent Cloyd Hall, accompanied by a significant number of state highway patrolmen, to Macon. Hall talked with members of the black community as well as businessmen who did not want blacks to boycott their businesses. As Hall negotiated, the presence of the Georgia Highway Patrol became highly visible in the town. The black community had no outspoken leader, which made it easier for Hall to restore order after the mayor's "heated rhetoric" almost led to bloodshed.[11] The Macon episode remained in the realm of words, not bullets, thus averting a crisis on the magnitude of that which rocked nearby Sparta.

In the fall of 1971, blacks and whites almost went to war against each other in the small town of Sparta, in Hancock County. Located centrally in the state, the county was almost 70 percent black, but the town had a white majority, a fairly typical pattern in middle and southern Georgia. The energetic work of a black county administrator and the frightened response of a white funeral home owner who served as mayor nearly plunged the town and county into a blood bath. The administrator, John McGown, using a Ford Foundation grant and federal antipoverty legislation, promoted black businesses that were fronts for Black Power groups.

McGown had led voting drives, had led marches in favor of Black Power, and even had threatened to take over a white Baptist church, attracting extensive publicity. Sparta's mayor, T. M. "Buck" Patterson, pressured by angry and frightened segregationists, purchased ten submachine guns to arm the town's six white policemen. McGown threatened to organize a black boycott of white businesses in the Sparta area, because, he said, "it is self destructive to participate with merchants who will use profits earned from the black community to

purchase machine guns that will be used on black citizens and their children."
McGown responded in kind, ordering thirty submachine guns for the group he
dubbed the Hancock County Sporting Rangers. The chief of police took a thirty-
day leave of absence, tossing the crisis to the governor in Atlanta.[12]

Carter immediately wrote McGown, demanding "What are you trying to do?"
The governor had received a copy of a public notice from McGowan offering to
help "young men and women, ages 17 to 60," acquire "sporting rifles" through the
Hancock County Sporting Rangers by making payments to a local bank. "I consider your published notice concerning arming of citizens with rifles, shotguns,
and pistols to be dangerous and inflammatory," Carter continued in his note to
McGown. Exposing McGown to the legal, federal, and financial institutions
that would disapprove his actions, Carter sent copies of his note to the Federal
Bureau of Investigation, the Department of Health, Education, and Welfare, the
Office of Economic Opportunity, and the president of Citizens Trust Bank. The
governor wanted help dealing with McGown. He had several letters in his possession from a prominent Sparta physician contending that McGown used federal and private funds intended for the promotion of black businesses to build an
armed political empire for himself.[13]

McGown responded with a long letter written on Georgia Council on Human
Relations letterhead. He defended his actions, argued that his group's purchase
of weapons had been solely in response to action whites had taken to arm themselves and threats blacks had received from white law officers. He accused Carter
of not taking action earlier to bridge "the gap in communication in Hancock
County." McGown concluded politely that the governor could count on his
cooperation to make "Georgia a place where all of its citizens can enjoy peace
and prosperity and live in dignity." Seeking support for his viewpoint, he sent
copies to Georgia's U.S. congressman, the Ford Foundation, the Office of Economic Opportunity, the Department of Health, Education, and Welfare, and the
membership of the Georgia Council on Human Relations.[14]

With well-armed whites and blacks poised to kill each other, Carter rose to
the occasion with a troubleshooting style for which he would eventually become
famous. He sent a three-man unit led by Cloyd Hall to the county. Accompanied by black Justice Department agent Robert Insley and white Georgia patrolman Ray Stevens, Hall spent three weeks identifying people of goodwill and
reporting nightly to the governor. Carter told them to buy back any guns already

acquired with no questions asked. Finally, after seven hours of tense negotiations with the disputants, the mayor agreed to surrender the weapons he had stored at his funeral home, and the county administrator canceled his order for the submachine guns, a solution reached when Hall promised not to publicly humiliate the repentant mayor. Within a few years, McGown became discredited (he later died in a plane crash), and blacks more frequently were winning election to public office. In the fall of 1971, with the crisis defused, but ill will yet simmering, Carter proudly announced the resolution to the nation's newspapers without condemning the parties involved.[15]

Carter drew more and more blacks into state agencies. He created a drug squad staffed by blacks, met with black leaders to discuss how to recruit more blacks for the National Guard, and sought advice from both Andrew Young and Ralph David Abernathy, the successor to Hosea Williams. Carter urged a new relationship between young Atlanta businessmen and professors at Morehouse College. When Ray Pope's Department of Public Safety used its Civil Disorder Technical Assistance Unit to end a black boycott of the Wilkes County School System, Carter noted, "Good work!"[16]

Carter himself used the power of his office to improve the lives of Georgia blacks. He contributed $8,000 from the governor's emergency fund to establish the Sickle Cell Foundation in Atlanta.[17] He appointed a black woman, Rita Jackson Samuels, to advise him on African-American affairs, and he assured her and others that black-owned banks were "treated exactly the same as others." He invited members of the black media to the mansion, promised to study legislation relative to housing and other primarily black concerns, promoted trade with African nations, supported black businessmen, and placed two black men in the Division of Investigation for Sumter County.[18]

As the second year of his governorship ended, however, many blacks complained that Carter had not done enough. Rita Samuels reported that only twenty-two blacks were employed by state government above the janitorial level as of August 31, 1972. Reverend J. C. Hope, president of the state NAACP, threatened legal action to correct the matter but did not follow through. Hamilton Jordan arranged an appointment for Martin Luther King, Sr., with the governor, thus beginning an extensive correspondence between Carter and "Daddy King."[19]

At the beginning of 1973, Carter doggedly attempted to answer all black complaints, keep his inaugural promise, and curry favor with black voters. He met Vernon Jordan and Peter McCullough, CEO of Xerox and treasurer of the Democratic party, at a fund-raiser Carter chaired in Atlanta. He invited them to the mansion, which, Vernon Jordan recalled, had been built on the same property where Jordan had chauffeured the wealthy Robert F. Maddox twenty years earlier. When Carter told his guests that he would be the next president of the United States, Jordan said that it was not possible because no one knew who he was and because he was a southerner.[20] Carter had already privately made his decision to try for the presidency, and it was the first of many episodes in which he himself would be the source of news leaks. This one made little difference at the time, because, like Vernon Jordan, hardly anyone would believe that Carter had a chance to become president.

Undaunted by Jordan's negativism, Carter proceeded to support black causes and position himself to win black votes in 1976. He appointed a Spelman College administrator to the Georgia Heritage Trust Advisory Commission and proclaimed that the state of Georgia would observe the birthday of Martin Luther King, Jr., as a holiday.[21] Carter urged the mayor of Plains to pave "the loop street through an area of new Negro homes," instructed Bert Lance to pave a street in the black section of Americus, and asked his department heads in Atlanta to send him confidential memoranda about their plans to hire blacks and women for their agencies.[22]

Carter also prepared a detailed answer to five black ministers explaining what he had done. Although "we have a long way to go," he told them, the state had made progress in black employment, reform of the prison system, color-blind justice, and social programs. He asked God, he told the clergymen, "for the wisdom to know what is right and the courage to do it."[23]

Whether guided by God or political expediency, Carter confronted the race issue during the last two years of his governorship. Jesse Hill, Jr., a prominent black insurance executive in Atlanta, served him well as occasional adviser and member of the University System of Georgia Board of Regents. A black woman, Mamie B. Reese, of Albany served on the Board of Pardons and Paroles, an agency whose work frequently dealt with African Americans. Carter enticed two motion pictures, financed and produced by blacks, to be filmed in Georgia. *The House on Skull Mountain* and *Staggerlee* did not set box office records, but they were tangible evidence of the governor's support of black businesses.[24]

Carter sought approval from African-American ministers. He asked Andy Young to meet with him at a breakfast with other black ministers before a Billy Graham Crusade on June 18–24, 1973. The ministers thought Graham was anti-black and insensitive to their needs because he supported President Richard Nixon. Carter disagreed with Nixon on most points but attended Graham's Crusade when it convened in Atlanta. Carter used the occasion to convince Georgia's black clergymen that he did not always agree with the evangelist on matters related to race.[25]

Finally, Carter took the most dramatic and symbolic action of his gubernatorial career when he announced in October 1973 that he had appointed a committee to choose portraits of three successful black Georgians to hang in the state Capitol.[26] One of them would be of Martin Luther King, Jr., whose career before his death in Memphis in 1968 had ironically helped to bring about the changes in Georgia and the South that made it possible for Carter to win elections.

Elected president of the Southern Christian Leadership Conference in 1957, King had devoted most of his time to nonviolent protests. He received the Nobel Peace Prize in 1964 and the same year saw the fruits of his work in Congress's passage of the Civil Rights Act, which outlawed segregation in all public facilities. Relentlessly, he pressed on for the rights of blacks and poor people until his assassination. As a famous Georgian, his memory was revered by some and despised by others when Carter chose to honor him as no other black person had ever before been honored in the state.[27]

Portraits of two more black Georgians incited less fuss only because they were less well known. Lucy Craft Laney, an educator, had been born in Augusta in 1854, the daughter of free blacks during the age of slavery. A precocious child, she graduated in 1873 from Atlanta University's first normal school class and ten years later she founded the Haines Normal and Industrial Institution in Augusta. She organized the local chapter of the NAACP in 1918 and died in 1933.[28]

Henry McNeal Turner, a bishop in the AME Church, had been one of the few black agents in the Freedman's Bureau in Georgia and a member of the state legislature during Reconstruction. Born free in 1834, near Abbeville, South Carolina, Turner had white ancestors and a degree from Trinity College in Baltimore. After the Civil War and during the Progressive Era he lived in South Carolina and Georgia, where he condemned lynching and the convict leasing system. His support of the "Back to Africa" movement in the 1880s attracted so few Georgia blacks that he gave up in disgust and moved to Windsor, Canada, where he died in 1915.[29]

On Sunday afternoon, February 17, 1974, a small group of Ku Klux Klansmen gathered outside the Georgia Capitol, where the governor was unveiling the three portraits. The Capitol was packed with black and white spectators who listened to secretary of state Ben Fortson speak about King's accomplishments. Locking arms with Jimmy, Rosalynn, Coretta Scott King, and others present, Fortson then led them in singing the civil rights theme song, "We Shall Overcome." Other songs included "America the Beautiful," "In Christ There Is No East or West," and "The Battle Hymn of the Republic."[30]

Carter informed the audience that the corridors of the Capitol were hallowed halls containing portraits of Virginians George Washington, Thomas Jefferson, and Robert E. Lee. President Jefferson, "the great humanitarian...loved the common people," and Confederate General Lee "deserved the devotion and respect...and the admiration of those of us who have come to know his character." Likewise, he continued, black citizens of Georgia saw their hopes and dreams realized through Martin Luther King, Jr. All Georgians had been liberated, he continued, by King's work. Whites had been freed from "a millstone about our necks" and delivered from "an artificial distinction" between people. He repeated his inaugural declaration that the time for racial discrimination was over. He praised the work of Bishop Turner, and he quoted Laney's remark that "God didn't use any different dirt to make me than the first lady of the land."[31]

On leaving the ceremony, Carter directed the Georgia Highway Patrol to guard the portraits against theft. "[T]hat's some man you have for your Governor," one person later wrote in a note to Julian Bond.[32] A month later, Benjamin E. Mays wrote Carter that among all the governors he had known during forty-three years living in Georgia, or had read about in the state's history, "your name stands among those at the top in the leadership for justice and fair play for all of the citizens of Georgia."[33] King's widow, Coretta Scott King, who had participated in the ceremony, thanked Carter for it, suggesting that it "marked a significant step in the journey toward human dignity."[34]

For the balance of the year, Carter seized every chance to praise black Georgians. He addressed the National Association of Colored Women's clubs, Incorporated, the Clark College National Alumni Association, the forty-fifth birthday celebration of Martin Luther King, Jr., and the United Negro College Fund's

National Spring Conference on American Higher Education Atlanta.[35] He and Rosalynn attended the premier of the movie *Claudine,* featuring black actors James Earl Jones, Diahann Carroll, Curtis Mayfield, and Gladys Knight.[36]

Despite Carter's effort to bring racial tranquility to his state, racial hatred still erupted in some areas. He and Rosalynn were in Los Angeles for the Democratic party's telethon when he heard the news that Mrs. Martin Luther King, Sr., had been shot dead as she sat at the organ she played for the Ebenezer Baptist Church. He condemned the assassin for being "demented," and he praised "Daddy King" for having a heart free of hatred and setting an "example of Christian love" during a time of "personal grief."[37]

Hancock County, where Carter had worked so hard during the first year of his governorship to prevent a racial bloodbath, erupted anew. Carter announced that he would go there personally.[38] An angry woman in Sparta sent him a telegram informing him that the white people of Hancock County would never again vote for him.[39] Under heavy guard, Carter went to Sparta, spoke to private citizens, examined how money from the Ford Foundation grant was being spent, and recommended that its administrators make certain it be spent "in a way that is most helpful to the poor people of the area—both white and black." He found no magic solution to the hatred that had been seething there for years but expressed relief that at least the county was quiet now with state law enforcement on the scene.[40]

Despite racial setbacks in Georgia, Carter's image as an enlightened New South governor attracted national attention. The executive director of the Student National Medical Association in Washington thanked him for his kind words that welcomed them to Atlanta.[41] The executive director of the Southern Elections Fund, Incorporated, congratulated Carter on his handling of the Sparta situation and promised him support in the future. Carter invited him to the mansion, along with Julian Bond, chairman of the Fund's Board of trustees, as well as other liberals from Michigan, the Mississippi Freedom Democratic Party, the American Civil Liberties Union, Harvard University, Massachusetts Institute of Technology, Anne Wexler of the McGovern Commission that had been formed in 1968 to study party structure and delegate selection and first chaired by Senator George McGovern, and Congressman Andrew Young.[42]

Carter walked a tight wire between a national liberal audience and his critics in Georgia. He assured a citizen from Athens that the 1965 Voting Rights Act would not plunge Hancock County back into what his correspondent called "black Reconstruction."[43] He promised the people of Hancock that he would send observers there to make sure the elections were fair for both sides.[44] When another irate citizen criticized him for playing to the nation rather than to Georgia, he assured her that, with Rosalynn's help, he attempted to treat whites and blacks equally. Bishop Arthur J. Moore, a renowned white bishop in the Methodist Church in South Georgia, had died about the same time as Mrs. King. When their funerals where held on the same day, Rosalynn attended Bishop Moore's funeral while Carter joined the vice president's wife at Mrs. King's funeral. "Both [were] good and fine Georgians and personal friends of mine," he claimed.[45]

In November 1974, his assistant Rita J. Samuels claimed for him an impressive record improving race relations. From his inaugural address to the unveiling of the portraits, he had consistently taken strong and controversial stands for the rights of black Georgians. In four years, he had increased the number of black state employees from 4,850 to 6,684, with most of the additional appointments going to the Pardons and Paroles Board, Department of Family and Children Services, and Highway Patrol. Black security officers protected him and his family.[46]

A record that pleased blacks and liberal whites offended other Georgians who had supported Maddox and may well have remained a majority in the state. Since the state constitution forbade a governor from succeeding himself, Carter did not need to win reelection. Furthermore, he had a free hand to be a more aggressive advocate for black rights than other New South governors. He and Rosalynn understood the political advantage of taking a strong stand in favor of racial equality. From his observation of Georgia blacks, too, Carter got the idea that the world was divided between rich and poor and that many of the latter, regardless of race or nationality, needed an advocate for their human rights. Carter hoped to attain a position of power that would enable him and Rosalynn to keep alive the spirit of Martin Luther King, Jr., and to become that advocate.

CHAPTER SEVENTEEN

Rosalynn in Power

UNCERTAIN OF WHAT WAS EXPECTED OF HER, Rosalynn had to adapt to life in the mansion.[1] At first, her daily routine was much the same as in Plains. She cooked, planted flowers in the yard, decorated the house, and managed the family budget, although she quickly learned that, save for the budget, she did not have to do any of those things. With an office and secretaries she became a public servant, but she also maintained a home where the governor could relax and spend time with the family.[2] Realizing that the governor's wife did not have to solve everyone's problems, ultimately she found herself and her work, as she always did, through her inner strength, her ambition and intellectual curiosity, and a growing symbiotic relationship with Jimmy.

Rosalynn despised criticism of her husband and their lack of privacy as public figures. She missed cooking for her family so much that she went to weekly classes at Ursula's Cooking School near the residence to satisfy a need to prepare food. She felt trapped and lonely, separated from her friends and unable to visit stores without being recognized. She disliked not being able to leave the house without security. One day she slipped away and drove alone to Calhoun to visit her friend Edna Langford. Feeling guilty about the deception, she telephoned the mansion to report her whereabouts, only to learn that the Georgia Highway Patrol had had her under surveillance every moment.

Struggling to find her place as equal partner to a governor, Rosalynn became sensitive and angry about her society's treatment of females as second-class citizens. Once she walked out of a Bible class taught by a male evangelist who believed that wives should be subservient to their husbands. She and Jimmy believed that there should be mutual respect between husbands and wives. She supported and assisted her husband in whatever he did, but she had her own projects and hobbies.[3]

The painful stage of Rosalynn's adjustment to her new lifestyle quickly segued into her intense interest in what she might accomplish from her strange new bully pulpit. She borrowed original art works from Atlanta's High Museum of Art and hung them in the mansion's ballroom. The governor's social schedule became a full-time job, as Rosalynn planned dinners and receptions and scheduled artists and symphonies to entertain the guests. Sometimes she hosted 250 people two or three times a week, usually to win their support for a favorite cause. She discussed children, fashion, recipes, and interior design, but she was also knowledgeable about politics and world affairs. Nor did she buckle in the presence of powerful people. When the security detail for Secretary of State Henry Kissinger and his wife Nancy told Rosalynn that it would be necessary to drill twenty-three holes in the mansion floor to install the telephones the secretary would need, Rosalynn rerouted Henry and Nancy to a hotel. Before starting a Georgia Highway Wildflower Program, she flew to Austin, Texas, and visited the widowed Lady Bird Johnson at the LBJ Ranch to learn how to do it.[4]

Rosalynn tended the ceremonial aspects of her job, but she needed more involvement with people and the political process. From her position of power, she wanted to help the young, the elderly, the poor, blacks, females, the mentally challenged, and any groups or individuals who could not care for themselves. Repulsed by what she saw at the Fulton County prison from which she hired Amy's nurse Mary Prince Fitzpatrick, she joined the Women's Prison Committee of the Commission on the Status of Women. A Georgia spokesperson for the Equal Rights Amendment, she traveled widely in the state giving speeches at such diverse locations as Georgia Southwestern University and the Waycross Council on Alcoholism.[5] Just before her first Christmas in Atlanta, on December 13, 1971, she helped the governor light the huge Christmas tree on the mansion lawn. She listened with him and dozens more to the Wolf Boys Choir and watched the Santa Claus they had engaged to distribute gifts to the children assembled there.[6]

Whether Rosalynn was with Jimmy on a public occasion or not, he adored her, praised her, joked about her, and put her on a pedestal. In speaking to the League of Women Voters, he talked about his mother but he saved his more important comments for Rosalynn. Although they had been married twenty-five years, he said on that occasion and many others, he loved her more than he did at the time they married. To get a laugh, he conceded that his five-year-old daughter Amy now dominated his life. Returning quickly to Rosalynn, he talked about how she helped win the campaign in 1970 and how she "helped me as governor."[7]

In the summer of 1972, Rosalynn launched Operation Touch '72. Inspired by a recent project in Honduras in which doctors, dentists, and youths had offered medical and spiritual help to the poor, she pressed the Northside Drive Baptist Church into action. It organized a medical recreational center in Atlanta's Pittsburg neighborhood to offer poor children free dental and eye care and medical examinations. Rosalynn visited the clinic three times a week and held "rap sessions" about Jesus with the children. When asked about the name she had chosen for the endeavor, she replied, "You just have to touch people to let them know you care about them, and we do care."[8]

Hoping to improve mental health care in her state, Rosalynn was driven to learn more about the causes and cures of mental illness. Her vivid memories of Jimmy's cousins and nephew, the 1970 newspaper expose of the Central State Hospital in Milledgeville, and the people she met during the 1970 campaign whose relatives needed care would not go away. She visited twenty mental health facilities, then volunteered at the Atlanta regional mental hospital. She listened, learned, and gathered information that she hoped to translate into political action.[9]

For advice and help, the Carters consulted psychiatrist Peter G. Bourne, who served them as special adviser for Health Affairs and Resources. Founder and director of the Atlanta South Central Community Mental Health Center, Bourne had interests that ranged from the role of root doctors and faith healers among the urban black poor to the use of methadone substitutes for addictive drugs. His innovative approach to treatment for drug addiction attracted national attention, and in 1972 he moved to Washington to accept a position with President Nixon as adviser on drug abuse prevention. From the nation's capital, he maintained close communication with the Carters.[10]

Rosalynn did not distinguish mental illness from related problems such as drug addiction and retardation. She returned from a visit to Waycross to tell Jimmy how badly that town needed additional funds to deal with a drug problem. Hamilton Jordan immediately wrote the director of mental health services there and enclosed an application for help from the governor's emergency fund. The same day, Carter wrote Richard Harden, head of Human Resources, suggesting that testing areas be set up in Athens and Waycross. "We ought to *move* & get out of the debate state," he said with his typical enthusiasm to get things done.[11]

The next month, Rosalynn joined one hundred mayors taking Christmas gifts to Central State Hospital in Milledgeville to publicize the importance of mental health care. Every Christmas at the mansion, she gave a party for five hundred residents and staff of the Georgia Regional Hospital in Atlanta. On other occasions, she entertained hundreds of patients from eleven state mental hospitals, and several times during the year she and Carter hosted musical and theatrical performances for mentally handicapped children. The Atlanta Association for Retarded Citizens gave her the 1972 Bobby Dodd Award for service to the mentally retarded. The next year, when some Gainesville citizens protested the presence of a home for ten "slightly retarded women" in their neighborhood, Rosalynn visited "the girls" to reassure the community that such homes posed no threat.[12]

Rosalynn served on the Governor's Commission to Improve Services to Mentally and Emotionally Handicapped Georgians. Appointed to that position by her husband in 1971, she attended its meetings and became its liaison with the governor.[13] Finding herself in the company of top health care professionals from the Georgia Psychiatric Association, the Georgia Mental Retardation Association, the Georgia Alcoholism Advisory Council, and the Georgia Hospital Association, Rosalynn learned quickly. She visited state facilities to offer help and collect information. Shocked to discover that many mentally challenged people were happy, she suggested that the committee should recommend nonhospital, normal lifestyles for them. The Commission proposed hospitals easily accessible to patients' families and friends, community health programs, and community health centers in lieu of hospitals. So successful were they that the number of county mental health centers increased from 23 to 135.[14]

Supporting his wife's work, Carter approved a $3.5 million appropriation from the General Assembly for programs for mentally handicapped children. He invited Eunice Kennedy Shriver to hold the Special Olympics in Georgia. When she came to Atlanta with her husband Sargent Shriver, the Carters sat with them during the annual meeting of the American Association on Mental Deficiency. The political advantage of becoming associated with the Kennedys may have been as important to them as charitable concern for the mentally challenged.

As a result of that meeting, Carter thought Rosalynn had become close to the Kennedy family.[15]

For the next five years, Rosalynn chaired the Georgia "Special Olympics for Retarded Children" Committee. She worked to move physically and mentally handicapped children out of institutions into day care centers, where they got better attention and from which they went home at night to loving families. "Oh...to see retarded...or mentally handicapped children react to games and races just thrills me," she recalled. Winning a race "in a special Olympics gives them more confidence than anything possibly could."[16]

The Carters provided funds for summer camps for mentally handicapped children and helped the Warm Springs Foundation operate the Georgia Rehabilitation Center near President Franklin Roosevelt's Georgia White House.[17] By urging state and local governments to cooperate, they used regional hospitals to reduce by 80 percent the number of patients sent to Milledgeville, where state senator Culver Kidd resisted improvements and kept employees at the hospital beholden to his finance company. Nine grants from the National Institute of Mental Health helped to establish community outpatient services in each of Georgia's 159 counties. In addition, the creation of foster homes for children, drug and alcohol abuse programs, assistance for sickle-cell anemia victims, and mental health educational programs made Rosalynn virtually revered in professional health care circles.[18]

Equally important to her was the ratification of the Equal Rights Amendment to the Constitution (ERA). Since Rosalynn had demanded her own equality and got it, she wanted the same for all women. Unable to persuade Georgia to ratify the ERA, Rosalynn got into an amusing public debate with her husband. Thinking he understood what Rosalynn thought, he addressed an anti-ERA rally on the Capitol steps, where he said that he favored the ERA but Rosalynn opposed it. When Rosalynn saw the news story, she became livid, donned her pro-ERA button, collected two of her friends, went to Jimmy's office, and demanded that he take them to lunch. "Jimmy was just mistaken, that's all," Rosalynn later reported calmly to the press; "I am very much in favor of ERA." Jimmy confessed that in the car that day, he was "glad there wasn't a recorder...to hear what she said to me."[19]

Rosalynn, despite her firm rebuttal of her husband's remark, tried to cover for him. She thought she might have misled him with a sarcastic remark she had made about Gloria Steinem, and "he knows I get tired of that 'Ms.' stuff and the bra burning." Rosalynn described herself as a working woman who would not be made less feminine by having equal rights. "My first priority is being a home-maker and taking care of my husband and family," she said, but she also enjoyed work, and she wanted her rights. Carter recanted by telling the press, "I thought I knew what Rosalynn thought, but I was wrong." He answered the many letters he received on the subject by simply stating, "I am committed to ERA."[20]

Carter indulged in humorous correspondence about equal rights for women with "Vice President Charlenne," as he joked with the secretary of the Gerald M. Rafshoon Advertising Agency. She wrote him on January 28 asking him to sup-port the ERA and reminding him that a "WOMAN planned and bought all of the media for your 1970 election. And a MAN (GMR) took *all* the credit." Jimmy replied in a lighthearted vein: "I support ERA, I know who did all the *good* work on my campaign." He confessed that he also knew that his friend Rafshoon, with whom he liked to joke, had taken the credit for the work Charlenne had done. To appease her further, he added: "I know you're not a secretary & think that you should be President instead of GMR." He signed the note "Love," then thought better of it, struck through it, and concluded "Respectfully, Jimmy."[21]

On a more serious level, Rosalynn emerged as a model among governors' wives. Attracting attention because of the growing popularity of her husband, she impressed audiences and interviewers with discussions of the Carters' pro-grams in Georgia. Her soft, hesitant accent, petite stature, shy beauty, and south-ern ways seemed endlessly fascinating to those outside the region. At the June 1974 National Governors' Conference in Seattle, during the World's Fair, she gave an extensive interview. She thought that playing hostess to a state a major responsibility, but she preferred to talk about her work with the mentally handi-capped. Very few people were needed, she said, to bring about major changes, and a high profile politician's wife had a unique opportunity. She commented on the 132 community health centers in Georgia, the possibility for mentally handi-capped children to live with their families and go to learning centers during the day, and the use of drugs to return mentally challenged citizens to normal lives. "We shouldn't just say people are crazy and put them away," she concluded.[22]

Commenting on both her professional and personal lives in Atlanta, Rosalynn said that she and the governor sometimes entertained as many as 750 people a week for dinner at the mansion. By serving them in the ballroom, she could accommodate up to four hundred at a time, the maximum number for which she had china. Despite living in a mansion, Rosalynn avoided pretense and snobbery. Since it was so important for people to have personal contact with the governor and his family, she often traveled, sometimes with Jimmy, sometimes alone, to make speeches, visit institutions, and to get to know people and let them get to know her. When her husband's term ended, she opined, she intended to go home to Plains, put on her dungarees, and get back to work in the peanut warehouse.[23]

Rosalynn kept a busy schedule. She attended dinners and conferences with the governor. She participated with him in what they called "Operation Feedback." Usually during the summer months they traveled from one section of the state to the other giving speeches and attending town meetings. They discussed taxes, inflation, reorganization, and topics of local interest, but mostly they listened to what the people had to say. They attended Jewish dinners, conferences on preserving the coast, watermelon festivals, and fish fries. Rosalynn wrote thank-you notes to their hosts, and "Operation Feedback" helped keep them in touch with the people. Yet they could not expect to be universally loved in a state still split on issues of race and the war in Southeast Asia.[24] Carter thought his program of mixing with the people and listening to them made them happy,[25] but many Georgians never saw him in person or believed that he would resolve all their issues.

Rosalynn had her own activities. She spoke to such diverse groups as the Atlanta Club of Credit Women International, the National Council of Jewish Women, and the Happy Hour School for the Mentally Retarded in South Georgia. She entertained foreign dignitaries and lunched with Mrs. Hedley Donovan, whose husband edited *Time*. In interview after interview, she maintained that all she wanted was to go back to a peaceful life in Plains, but she had grown to love being first lady of Georgia.[26]

Mansion life, Rosalynn said, provided togetherness for her family. Amy, seven at the end of her father's term, had a full schedule of cultural and academic activities. Her parents scheduled the time they spent with her, especially on Saturdays. Amy could choose what she wanted to do and where she wanted to go, whether it was the library or the zoo. Rosalynn tried to be there when Amy awakened, when she left for school, and when she came home. She took Amy to birthday parties, choir rehearsals, dances with the Little General Cloggers, and performances for children at the Atlanta Memorial Arts Center. Amy grew very attached to her nurse, Mary Prince Fitzpatrick.[27] Rosalynn tried to give her daughter a normal child's life by letting her invite friends to the mansion and by sending her to the first grade in a nearby public school. Yet there was no way to disguise the special transportation and security detail that went with her. When Amy's dog Friskie escaped, Jimmy, like any father, made a public plea for Friskie's return and thanked the lady who found him "for reuniting us with Friskie who we consider to be a member of our family."[28]

The grown boys lived in the house with Amy and doted on her. Chip completed a master's degree at Georgia State University. He and his wife Caron lived at the mansion for a year, then moved to Plains, where he worked in the family business and she taught kindergarten. Jack, in his midtwenties, and his wife Judy lived with his parents before moving to Athens to attend the University of Georgia Law School. Jeff, a high school senior, hoped to attend the University of Georgia and avoid the shadow of his famous father. Jeff was particularly thrilled, however, when his parents allowed him and his brothers to entertain their favorite recording artist, Bob Dylan, at the mansion.[29] Rosalynn, remembering her own youth, encouraged the younger generation to save money and avoid addiction to an opulent lifestyle. They could do so, she thought, and still enjoy having the mansion as their home.[30]

The governor helped members of his and Rosalynn's families in various ways. They invited Miss Allie to visit them in Atlanta, rented her farmland, and sharecropped it.[31] He appointed his Aunt Sissy Dolvin to the Commission on the Status of Women, and he yielded to his sister Gloria's request that her friend Larry Cagle represent the motorcycling sport on an advisory committee to the department of Natural Resources. When Cousin "Beedie" Hugh injured his back and was hospitalized in Atlanta, Rosalynn invited his wife Ruth to stay at the mansion until he recovered. Their daughter Connie worked as an intern in Atlanta and often joined her Aunt Rosalynn and Uncle Jimmy for supper. When their Aunt Ethel Slappey died, Jimmy flew Hugh and Ruth down with him to attend the funeral at Lebanon Cemetery.[32]

Brother Billy and P. J. Wise bought the service station that Billy would later make famous as a public bar at which he dispensed "down home" philosophy and anecdotes about his family and the South.[33] More important, he and his wife Sybil took charge of the warehouse full-time in January 1971 and operated it for the next six years. Jimmy and Rosalynn retained majority ownership, but the younger Carters expanded the business and made a profit. Billy thought it was "the way Daddy had intended it to be" and bragged that during his tenure at the warehouse he had earned his keep. "The peanut business was my heart and soul," he said. "The service station was my bar." According to sister Ruth Stapleton, the warehouse grossed $2.5 million per year and the service station $100,000 while Jimmy was in Atlanta. Billy was a disciplined, hard worker, and he and his brother developed a mutual respect. A heavy drinker, Billy seemed then not to be impaired by it, and Jimmy had no idea of the magnitude of his brother's alcoholism.[34]

Miss Lillian remained incredulous that her son Jimmy could be governor and that Rosalynn could preside over the mansion with charm and efficiency. Lillian asked for favors, gave advice, served on committees, and became a beloved political asset. Promising that she did not "want *much,*" she asked Jimmy to have it arranged for her "to go to the [base]ball games (Dodgers especially)." She hoped he would have "someone reliable" tend to it "so there will be *no* slip up—or you know *me*—how sensitive I can be—you always say 'I want you to share with me'—but this is my greatest wish to go to Ball games—BB games because I am your *Mama.* . . . ILYTG M." Carter gave the job to Jordan, explaining that Miss Lillian could use the governor's lifetime pass to the Atlanta Braves game and take several friends with her. "This is *very* important," he said; and shortly Ham wrote Miss Lillian that all she had to do was call the press office for the number of tickets reserved in her name.[35]

Lillian gave speeches, peppered with jokes, homespun wisdom, and exhortations to live a Christian life. One of her fans declared that it was "obvious you're still basically a Methodist."[36] "Ma," as Jimmy called her, sometimes played the role of mansion and state hostess. When a group of Chinese editors visited the state, she attended a special breakfast at the Regency-Hyatt Hotel, then gave them a tour of the mansion, and attended a luncheon with them at Morehouse College. On another occasion she met with the Indian ambassador, who gushed that she "could serve as a model to people decades younger." Recalling her service in the Peace Corps and her love for the Indian people, he said that she was doing a fine job introducing Americans to Indian life.[37]

Yet it was Rosalynn, not Lillian, who truly enjoyed the power of being hostess at the mansion. Rosalynn had her distinctive style of campaigning and entertaining. Her style was gentle, warm, caring, informed, and sophisticated, very unlike the redneck image that so many held of the South. More important, she could give her husband candid advice and enjoy his reassurance of equality.

With friends, the governor could be as generous as he was with his and Rosalynn's families. He opened offices for the Georgia Bureau of Investigation in Americus, approved $315,919.10 worth of road resurfacing projects in Sumter County, gave additional funds of $42,691 to his Cousin Beedie, a.k.a. Senator Hugh Carter, to pave and expand the parking lot for the local hospital, and provided $10,000 in state funds for a swimming pool in Plains.[38]

On a micro scale, and without fanfare, Carter assisted numerous desperate individuals. He helped one elderly woman to receive Social Security disability benefits, and he signed a bill authorizing licensed embalmers to extract eyes from a deceased donor's body for transplant purposes.[39] When a distraught mother whose son was in prison condemned the governor and the prison system and made reference to Christian forgiveness, Carter answered with a handwritten letter. He reassured her that he cared about her feelings, attempted to protect both her son and the public, and was committed to training and rehabilitating prisoners. He promised to ask Ellis MacDougall to see what could be done to help her son. "I believe as you do that God will forgive us all our repented sins— both those in prison and those in the Governor's office," he concluded.[40]

The Carters visited or sent personal greetings to sick, old, or poor people with special needs. "You have my personal prayers in your time of sickness," he wrote to one dying man, and he instructed Richard Harden to find out how he could help an elderly couple in serious financial need.[41] The Carters sent their personal money to Millard English, their black neighbor in Plains, to help him pay for false teeth. The grateful man invited "Mr. Jimmy" and "Miss Rosalynn" to dine with him and his wife and said he wanted to buy the lot he rented from them. Carter later sold it to him.[42]

Life in the governor's mansion afforded the Carters opportunities to pursue their favorite forms of relaxation. Jimmy tied flies for them to use for fishing. They canoed, panned for gold, viewed some of the largest oaks in Georgia at the site of an old Cherokee gold mine, and square danced. Jimmy indulged his love for hunting, especially woodcocks and wild turkeys, sometimes accepting gifts of fine hunting clothes and often accompanying leading politicians and businessmen of the state.[43]

The Carters went together, or sometimes Jimmy went alone, to Georgia Tech football games and Atlanta Braves baseball games. They attended plays and musical performances, read poetry and philosophy, and discussed business management. They hunted for arrowheads left by Seminole Indian tribes and promoted the restoration of native fish to Georgia streams. They became renowned environmentalists.[44] Jimmy added to his soft-drink bottle collection and sometimes exchanged rare items with others.[45]

Jimmy's first love among sports was stock car racing, and Rosalynn learned to share it with him. While Carter was in the Navy, one of his submariners had got drunk regularly until he became fascinated with repairing an old car. He raced it in Connecticut and on Long Island, sometimes taking Carter with him. When Carter returned to Georgia, he discovered that stock car racing was a popular pastime in his native South as well as elsewhere. As governor, he promoted the Atlanta International Raceway, made personal appearances at races, and in 1971 held a reception at the mansion for stock car drivers and crews prior to the Atlanta 500. "I found them all to be a genteel lot," he said.[46] Before the race, he and a Baptist minister rode in the lead car at 160 miles per hour while their wives watched.[47]

At stock car events, the Carters mixed politics with fun. They attended the Talladega 500 in Alabama in the spring of 1972 and made plans to go to Indiana and Miami for other famous races.[48] In the summer of 1973, Carter welcomed the NASCAR Winston Cup Championship to the Atlanta Speedway. He told the drivers that he had "always been very envious of those with the courage and expertise to participate in this fast-paced sport." The cover of the souvenir program had a picture of Jimmy and Rosalynn mingling with the drivers amidst the cars.[49] In 1975 at the Atlanta International Raceway, they ate bologna sandwiches, yelled, waved their arms, and behaved "like plain folks."[50]

Like plain folks, Rosalynn and Jimmy also had to manage their personal budget, although the size of it would have been the envy of the masses. His governor's salary in 1971 was $42,500, plus a $50,000 allowance to operate the mansion. He declined a salary increase that year because it would have made him one of the highest paid chief executives in the nation. He thought, however, that the state should continue to pay for his and his family's security.[51]

Rosalynn was the family's primary bookkeeper, but Jimmy could not tolerate waste and once complained that the faucets leaked and the grounds keepers were wasting water on the mansion lawns.[52] "I'm not trying to be pure or holy or anything," he said, "but I don't want to monetarily benefit just because I was in the governor's office." His income from his share of the profits at the peanut warehouse in 1973 approached $80,000, and that did not include an undisclosed amount he and Rosalynn earned from Carter Farms, Incorporated.[53] Rosalynn and he did not need to profit from their public service, although it was inevitable that they would do so.

Two very private people, the Carters adjusted to a life of public scrutiny, much of it prejudiced or fabricated by observers who wished to portray them with a particular slant. Rosalynn found her place and her work in that new world. She was, as she said, a political partner with an equal voice in her marriage.

CHAPTER EIGHTEEN

Phoenix Rising

THREE MONTHS INTO HIS TERM, according to one journalist, the "Governor [was] bitten by [the] national bug." Carter thought that a southerner should get the 1972 Democratic nomination, but he claimed no interest in it himself, for he was just a working man, he said.[1] Nevertheless, like the phoenix rising from the South's discredited past, he created a national image for himself as a politician who had learned from Georgia's history how to lead the nation. Favoring a two-pronged approach, he took Kirbo's advice and attacked Nixon's foreign policy but not his domestic programs.[2] He and Rosalynn entertained prominent Democrats at the mansion, and he manipulated his state's Democratic party to guarantee he would be elected to the national convention. He missed no chance to brag that the South had left its sins behind and rejoined the Union at last.

A "New South" governor, Carter attracted the attention of pundits and politicians who used the term loosely to indicate the region's changes in race relations. When Henry Grady, editor of the *Atlanta Constitution,* coined the term in 1886, however, he applied it broadly to include economic progress and the South's desire to return to national politics after the Civil War.[3] Grady's definition suited Carter better, for he wanted economic progress and national redemption for his state as well as social justice. Hoping to be the first president elected from the Deep South since 1848, Carter moved into position to build on the progress made by his southern predecessors.

After the Civil War, the South had taken a long and torturous route back into the mainstream of American politics. Woodrow Wilson's 1912 election to the presidency had drawn his native South, as well as the Democratic party, back into the national fold. Most southern leaders, including Wilson, maintained the racially segregated status quo, prompting a massive migration of African Americans into northern cities; these leaders also supported military intervention to solve international problems.[4] Wilson failed to keep his country out of World War I, nor could he convince it to support an international peacekeeping institution. For his work at the Paris Peace Conference of 1919 that ended the war, however, he became the second president, following Teddy Roosevelt, to win the Nobel Peace Prize. Ill health ruined his ability to govern, and his own country rejected him as a peacemaker, replacing him with a Republican president.

After the rise of Woodrow Wilson in 1912, the White House increasingly looked southward. The Great Depression of the 1930s affected black and white, North and South, rich and poor, in enough similar ways to have an homogenizing impact on the country. Promising bold action to resolve the depression, Franklin D. Roosevelt of New York won the presidency. By setting up The "Little White House" in Warm Springs, Georgia, and by virtue of his marriage to the social activist Anna Eleanor Roosevelt, he became aware of economic and racial problems that plagued the South. His New Deal legislation, designed to lift the nation out of the depression, brought social awareness and progress to the South, but soon his administration became mired in World War II.

Roosevelt's successor, Harry Truman of Missouri, integrated the armed services racially by executive fiat. He appointed the Civil Rights Commission, which made recommendations for sweeping changes intended to grant equality to African Americans. Truman witnessed the advent of the atomic age, made the decision to drop atomic bombs on Japan, saw the beginning of the Cold War, and reluctantly embraced the nation's need for the most advanced military machine and extensive spying agencies in its history, all events that two generations later would have a major impact on the Carters' lives.

After Truman, the Republican general Dwight David Eisenhower enforced the Supreme Court's 1954 *Brown v. Board of Education* mandate to integrate public schools in Little Rock, Arkansas, in 1956. His youthful successor, John F. Kennedy of Massachusetts, and his brother Robert, whom he appointed Attorney General, used the weight of their offices to press for civil rights legislation and the total integration of the nation. They gave hope to African Americans and aroused southern discontent with the Democratic party, but they could not get congressional support to pass the legislation they desired.

When Kennedy died at the hands of an assassin in 1963 and his vice president Lyndon Johnson of Texas assumed the presidency, the task fell to the man from Texas, the "Big Daddy from the Perdenales River," of bringing dramatic social and economic reform to the South while at the same time fighting a major war in Southeast Asia. He exploited the militaristic nature of the South to pursue the increasingly unpopular war in Vietnam; he signed the massive civil rights legislation that made legal racial segregation a thing of the past, drove much of the South away from the Democratic party, and paved the way for a new kind of politician like Carter to emerge from Dixieland. Wilson, Roosevelt, Truman, and Johnson were all wartime presidents who needed the South to achieve international goals, but all suffered politically from their efforts to bring to the South domestic reform.[5]

The timing was better for Carter, for World War II, the civil rights movement, and the civil rights legislation of the 1960s gave him the chance to succeed where his southern predecessors had failed. The "inherent greatness of the South and Georgia must be developed," he said.[6] The South's great novelist, William Faulkner, he wrote, understood the "self-condemnation resulting from slavery, the humiliation following the War Between the States and the hope, sometimes expressed timidly, for redemption." Carter believed that those "former dark moods in the South" and "alienation from the rest of the nation" had been "alleviated" by the changes he had witnessed in his adulthood.[7] The South had moved into a position where it could "show the rest of the nation how to solve [racial] problems."[8] *Conservatism did not mean racism,* Carter emphasized; the South was ready to accept the challenge of national leadership.[9]

Lamenting that the nation did not consider southerners satisfactory "as presidential candidates,"[10] Carter became a leader among southern governors. He and Rosalynn hosted the annual meeting of southern governors in Atlanta in 1971, at which he eagerly accepted election to the Appalachian Regional Commission, the Coastal Plains Regional Action Planning Commission, the Growth Policies Board, and the chairmanship of the Southern Regional Education Board. His committees recommended long-term loans for students, more and better medical schools in the South, scholarly research that addressed social problems, and a "university without walls."[11]

The Carters attended national and Democratic governors' conferences, raising his profile. In September 1972, they journeyed to Hilton Head, South Carolina, an elegant venue, where they did not allow the opulence of the surroundings to blind them to their real business. They slipped away from the sumptuous banquets to visit the poor in Jasper and Beaufort counties.[12] Carter took a national view. He deplored federal action such as busing that seemed to punish the South more than other parts of the country, although it was implemented in Boston. He welcomed partnership programs to promote agriculture and to build safe nuclear power plants.[13] He asked Congress to treat southern cities equally to northern ones, and he requested federal money to build state parks. He wanted big businesses such as Georgia Pacific to help small farmers manage their forest lands not only in Georgia but throughout the nation.[14]

As Carter rose in stature as a southern governor, he had to fight comparisons between himself and the towering figure of George C. Wallace. Wallace's failed 1968 campaign for the presidency had won him a large following among southern segregationists and northern blue-collar workers, many of whom were also segregationists. Carter congratulated Wallace on his election as governor of Alabama but did not attend his inauguration in Montgomery.[15] In May, Carter invited Wallace to Atlanta, praised him for being the leader of the same kind of people in Alabama that lived in Georgia, and commended him for defying President Nixon on busing.[16] After Wallace announced his candidacy for the presidency, Carter repeated the invitation for him to address the Georgia General Assembly, an invitation he offered to every announced candidate for the presidency. Finally, on February 24, 1972, Wallace spoke in the Georgia Capitol and received a warm welcome. Since Carter hosted other national presidential candidates, he could include Wallace, keep his campaign promise to allow Wallace to speak in Georgia, and make no commitment to him that might jeopardize his own more liberal image.[17]

Two months later, a would-be assassin gunned down Wallace in a Maryland parking lot, leaving him permanently crippled. Carter offered prayers for both Wallace and the Democratic party. Sympathizing with Wallace, Carter accused Georgia's black state senator Julian Bond of being a racist for implying that white southerners did not support national Democratic candidates.[18]

But Wallace would not go away. Carter journeyed to Red Level, Alabama, on June 17, 1972, to speak at Wallace Appreciation Day. Jody Powell had advised him that it would not be racist to condemn tax breaks for the rich, to oppose busing of school children, or to favor a strong national defense. Carter carefully chose words to praise Wallace but not accept his racial views or endorse his candidacy for president.[19] Powell, who had recommended the tone of the speech, attempted to answer those who wanted Carter to support Wallace. "[T]wo men in politics," he wrote, "can often do more to help each other if they are not complete[ly] identified with each other."[20]

On June 21, 1972, Wallace sent "Dear Jimmie" a telegram assuring him that he was well enough to attend the national Democratic convention in Miami the next month. He asked for Carter's support, to which Carter responded that Wallace could expect support from within the Georgia delegation but that he personally would "remain uncommitted until we get to Miami."[21] The next month, Carter made a speech in Macon in which he said Wallace was "fighting," not "crying," but he refrained from endorsing the Alabamian.[22] Being friendly to Wallace without condoning his racial views helped Carter gain national attention and retain conservative, southern support.

The war in Vietnam meanwhile hung like a threatening cloud over Carter's attempt to build his national stature. He took the easy route, defending and supporting the troops but calling for an end to the conflict. When Lieutenant William Calley, a Georgian, was court-martialed in Atlanta for his role in the My Lai massacre that caused the deaths of innocent Vietnamese civilians, many citizens in Georgia and throughout the nation defended him. Carter thought Calley guilty and at a press conference on April 2, 1971, refused to declare William Calley Day in Georgia but declared American Fighting Men's Day instead. He defended servicemen, military colleges, and the right of eighteen-year-olds to vote. He wrote letters of condolence to families who lost sons in Vietnam and declared that he wanted "an early and honorable end" to the war.[23]

Despite his differences with President Nixon, Carter thought the chief executive was trying to end the war, save American prisoners of war, and protect the freedom of Vietnam. When Nixon escalated the war in May 1972, Carter recognized the "tremendous responsibility on his shoulders" and urged Americans not to criticize him. A few days later, when Nixon ordered the waters around Vietnam mined, Carter said that he was "deeply disturbed" because he thought it would risk war with Russia, China, and other nations but that Nixon still deserved the country's support.[24]

In 1976, when seeking national votes, Carter confessed to *Playboy* that he regretted not demanding that "our nation never get involved initially in the

Vietnam war." He thought that the American people had been "misled" by their presidents into believing that an early victory was possible. He noted that his son Jack had fought in the war but had decided it was "foolish" and "a waste of time." He had made his own decision without his father's prompting because "he felt it would have been grossly unfair for him not to go when other, poorer [and frequently black] kids had to."[25]

From their vantage point in the governor's mansion, the Carters comforted Americans who suffered in the war. He allocated $5,000 from the governor's emergency fund for a committee directed by Richard Harden to study the needs of Georgia's veterans. For a year and a half, Rosalynn wore a bracelet with the name of prisoner of war Lieutenant Colonel Quincy Collins on it; when Collins came home, she and Jimmy invited him to an appreciation ceremony for return- ing Georgia POWs. Veterans asked the governor what he thought of amnesty for draft evaders. Carter said categorically that he was against it until all POWs returned home, and he would "wait and see" on any future decision about it.[26] "Every war causes…changes," he wrote. Peace, he said, must be for all people, not just a few.[27]

Carter cultivated a cordial relationship with national Democratic politicians regardless of their views on the war. He told former vice president Hubert H. Humphrey that "a strong and united Democratic party" could "recapture the White House in 1972."[28] He and Rosalynn entertained Jane and Edmund Muskie, Hubert Humphrey, and Henry Jackson at the mansion, where he told them, as well as the press, that he expected to have a voice as a Georgia delegate in choos- ing the 1972 Democratic candidate.[29] All of them agreed with southern gover- nors' opposition to Nixon's impounding of funds.[30] Carter urged Democratic governors to ban from their convention any reference to the war in Vietnam, because opinions about it would divide regions of the country against each other. Furthermore, he pleaded, they should not endorse any presidential candi- date without first consulting each other.[31] Carter begged the national Democrats not to ignore the South. He wrote Larry O'Brien, chairman of the Democratic National Committee, that "it hurts us Democrats in the South to have our lead- ers insinuate that our nominee might be wasting his time to campaign down here." He reminded O'Brien that in 1960, Georgia had given John F. Kennedy his biggest percentage victory. He beseeched O'Brien to avoid statements that might leave "lasting adverse impressions."[32] Carter also wrote to the governor of Nebraska that he was trying to keep "7 or 8 states down here," including Alabama, in the Democratic party.[33]

A man with a mission, Carter traveled to national Democratic governors' conferences, meetings of the United Nations in New York City, and congressional hearings in the nation's capital. He served as a member of the secretary of state's Committee on the United Nations and attended a UN conference on the human environment. He and Peter Bourne testified before the House Select Committee on Crime, a trip that prompted the editor of the *Columbus (GA) Ledger-Enquirer* to wonder "if this trip to Washington...might be a harbinger of things to come." The next year Carter addressed a Senate subcommittee on economic development, arguing that regionalism would solve economic and social problems and suggesting that Georgia's system of planning commissions might be transferable to the nation.[34]

Carter went to New York City to meet David Rockefeller, CEO of Chase Bank, and thereby embarked on the road that led to the White House. Rockefeller invited Carter to lunch with New York businessmen who wished to invest in Georgia. After returning home, Carter wrote to "David" that he appreciated the opportunity to meet his guests; he and Rosalynn invited Rockefeller to visit them in Atlanta where they could introduce the New Yorker to "Georgia and perhaps Southern politics and attitudes." Carter hoped to be more student than teacher; he told the wealthy financier, "I want to learn more about the interrelationships between business and governments here and abroad." He added a personal touch by saying, "The trip was worthwhile just to see your bank's art collection." Rockefeller responded that "we see eye to eye on a good many subjects" and he would welcome the chance for a "leisurely conversation."[35]

Carter already knew about the interrelationship between business and government, but he wanted to know more and apply it on a national and international scale. As a successful small businessman, Carter's frugal nature and abhorrence of debt drove him to run the government like a business. David Rockefeller may well have been his hero and intended mentor, for the combination of great wealth and behind-the-scenes political power intrigued him.

Despite gallons of ink spilled to quench the public's curiosity about Carter's "born again" Baptist religion, Carter in truth had less interest in religion and politics than in business and politics.

Step by fast step, Carter worked toward grasping power in the Democratic Party. He planned to deliver a major speech at the 1972 Democratic National

Convention at Miami Beach. With a "fervent desire" to select a nominee who could defeat Nixon, Carter pushed through a reform that would allow Georgia to elect its delegates to the convention. Under the new plan, forty of Georgia's delegates would be elected at ten congressional district conventions and the remaining thirteen at-large delegates would be chosen by the forty at a statewide convention in Macon. Previously, delegates had all been handpicked by the governor. Carter wanted an uncommitted delegation with himself at its head, and he got it.[36]

Carter's election as a delegate from the Third District on March 11, 1972, did not come easy. Carter loyalists in South Georgia faced a major challenge when powerful insurance executive John Amos hired buses to bring black college students to vote for two black candidates. Angry because Carter had not appointed him to an elite Democratic committee, Amos, who was president of the American Family Life Assurance Company in nearby Columbus, tried to defeat Carter. Miss Lillian and Gloria joined others in the campaign to get out and vote, thus giving the governor the victory by fifteen votes. Although he claimed not to be committed to any candidate, Carter secretly supported Scoop Jackson.

Urban and black voters in Atlanta, Americus, and Albany wanted delegates pledged to the liberal South Dakota senator George McGovern or his African-American rival, Congresswoman Shirley Chisholm of New York. Their candidates swept the metropolitan and suburban congressional districts that encompassed Atlanta. The lone exception among the winners, black legislator Julian Bond, claimed to be uncommitted but actually favored McGovern. A majority of the fifty-three delegates, however, were uncommitted and loyal to Carter. Some of the others supported George Wallace or Edmund Muskie. The McGovern delegates included women and African Americans and thus gave the Georgia group an attention-getting liberal aura.

Carter played the same game he had in 1970; he put up a conservative smoke screen to divert attention from his progressive ideas. Hamilton Jordan extinguished some politically dangerous fires by reassuring voters that the delegation would include white conservatives and not just women, blacks, and "hippies." The national Democrats took note when Senator Kennedy of Massachusetts praised Carter and other governors of the New South for the common concerns they shared with many northern big-city mayors.[37] Carter thus began to surmount the challenge of heading a delegation that could remain in favor with both Georgia and national Democrats.

The internal workings of Democratic politics in the once solid South remained incomprehensible to those outside the region. Typically, the national media understood little about Georgia politics; the *New York Times* reported erroneously that Carter controlled all fifty-three delegates, save one (Julian Bond), apparently losing track of the McGovern supporters. Carter, however, had mastered his state's politics and had acquired the skills to rise in national Democratic circles.[38]

A man on fire with ambition, Carter raced through the months before the convention making a name for himself and strengthening his hand in the party. He needed to stop the most liberal and the most conservative candidates for the nomination. The convention would belong to George McGovern, and Carter had little chance of changing that; he could be evasive with George Wallace, who also sought the nomination. By taking the middle of the road, Carter hoped to maintain his Georgia base and win respect in the nation.

Carter projected himself in the national media as the leader of a "stop McGovern movement." He urged southern governors to stick together to choose a candidate other than McGovern, whom he thought unfriendly to the South and unable to defeat Nixon. At a mock Democratic National Convention at the College of William and Mary, Carter amused himself and his listeners by arguing that Nixon should follow Lyndon Johnson's example and step down because of the way he had mishandled the war in Vietnam.[39] Kirbo advised Carter not "to risk your political base" by making concessions to McGovern but to "remain moderate and progressive," in order to be "attractive" to "anyone who is...interested in you on a national ticket."[40]

Late in May, Carter issued a press statement contending that McGovern "alone among all the candidates refuses to promise equal treatment under the federal law for the southern states."[41] He and Hamilton Jordan worked on a strategy to derail McGovern. Carter noted that McGovern was riding a wave of "anti-establishment, anti-political" feeling in California, and that only George or Cornelia Wallace might effectively go to California and expose McGovern as not being the friend of working people. Carter listed seven reasons why delegates should vote against McGovern: (1) he had refused to support Truman in 1948, (2) he had supported Henry Wallace, (3) he spoke under the Viet Cong flag, (4), he favored withdrawing from South Vietnam and abandoning the prisoners of war, (5) he would slash defense spending by $30 billion per year, (6) he favored abortion and legalization of marijuana, and (7) he had signed a "release Angela

Davis" petition for a notorious Communist sympathizer. Jordan condemned McGovern's plan of amnesty for draft dodgers while Carter attempted unsuccessfully to turn Joseph P. Kennedy II against him. He wrote southern senators asking them not to support McGovern.[42]

In public Carter treated McGovern the same way he did all presidential candidates; he invited him to visit Georgia and stay at the mansion. McGovern and his wife accepted the invitation in a gesture of friendship toward the South. At a rally on the steps of the Georgia Capitol, McGovern declared he intended "to put an end to the notion that I am writing off the South." Carter treated him cordially but did not change his opinion, nor did many other southern politicians.[43]

Carter, Jody Powell, and Hamilton Jordan discussed among themselves what relationship Carter should have to Wallace. Widely admired for his fighting spirit since his near death at the hands of a would-be assassin, Wallace remained popular in Georgia. Carter sent Wallace a brief note expressing thankfulness for his improved health but declaring his intention to remain uncommitted before the convention.[44] Carter had to distance himself from national Democrats in 1970 to win the governorship, but in 1972 he tried to bring southern and national Democrats together by remaining aloof from both McGovern and Wallace.

Carter thought Wallace would remain in the party even if he did not get the nomination. For the sake of party unity, he said, Scoop Jackson was the man. He claimed that Wallace had known for weeks that he would not second the Alabamian's nomination.[45] On July 8, Carter, his four children, his brother Billy, Rosalynn, and his closest advisers boarded the plane from Atlanta to Miami. Carter sat with Ham and Jody to discuss their strategy. None in this group had ever attended a national convention. Rosalynn, excited by the looming campaign, offered her analysis of the political celebrities who had visited them in the mansion. None were any better than Jimmy, she thought.[46]

Both Jody and Ham speculated that if Carter nominated Wallace, it would attract attention and give him more visibility at the podium than he would get otherwise. Carter would have nothing to do with it. He shot back at Jody, "If you think George Wallace is fit to lead the American people, you tell them. Not Me." Rosalynn agreed with Jimmy that if he delivered a prime time nominating speech for someone other than Wallace, it would give him the favorable national visibility they sought.[47]

Immediately after the plane landed, Carter met with other governors. Soon thereafter, Julian Bond, egged on by the McGovern delegates, accused Carter of racial discrimination because the Georgia delegation did not include enough black members, and he threatened to lead a fight to block its being seated. Carter avoided the damaging struggle by allowing some blacks and whites, including Peter Bourne, to join the delegation, giving its members partial votes. The next day, after church, Senator Henry "Scoop" Jackson telephoned Carter to request that the Georgia governor nominate him.[48]

The Georgians entered the hall on Monday, awestruck by the red, white, and blue balloons, the waving banners, and the loud music. McGovern controlled the convention with a clear majority of the 3,194 delegates being female, young, or black. They loudly protested the war in Vietnam, the very issue Carter had attempted to avoid because he knew it would divide southerners among themselves as well as against other parts of the country. The young McGovernites focused on Jackson as the enemy, for Jackson had supported the United States' involvement in Vietnam through the Kennedy, Johnson, and Nixon administrations. Anyone who spoke in favor of Jackson invited scorn from those enthusiastic McGovern fans.[49]

Already committed to nominate Jackson, Carter realized that he might discredit himself in national politics by supporting the cold warrior. Peter Bourne attempted to rescue him by suggesting a speech that would deal mostly with his own accomplishments and barely mention Jackson, but Jackson insisted that his name and record dominate Carter's remarks. The resulting compromise, an address crafted mostly by Carter himself, evoked the name of John F. Kennedy and concentrated on social issues, frugal government, and the advancement of peace.[50]

No candidate or even the president could have predicted the impact of a generally unnoticed news story the previous month. On June 18, 1972, some wiretappers had broken into the Democratic National Headquarters at the Watergate hotel and condominium complex in Washington, D.C. At first dismissed as a simple burglary, the break-in would mushroom over the following two years into one of the greatest scandals in American history and have a larger impact on the lives of those at the Miami convention than anything they said in their speeches. Innocent of any knowledge about Watergate, the delegates continued with their business.

On Wednesday night, July 12, Carter gave his speech, but the hour was late, and much of the television audience had gone to bed. Only those delegates on the floor who had a personal interest in Carter, Georgia, or Jackson seemed to be attentive. The McGovern delegates milled about making noise, sometimes drowning out the speaker, whom they mostly wanted to get out of the way to make room for their candidate. The *Atlanta Journal* later reported that Carter's speech went "unnoticed."[51] The next morning the convention ratified McGovern's nomination, with the Georgia delegation voting 14.5 for McGovern, 14.5 for Jackson, 12 for Chisholm, and 11 for Wallace.[52]

Jimmy and Rosalynn remained in their suite the whole day, naively hoping McGovern might call and offer the vice presidential position to Carter. They were listening to their friends, in defiance of the reality that McGovern would not choose a politician who had not supported him. When Andrew Young, running for the Atlanta Fifth District congressional seat, had arrived at the convention, Carter had asked him to suggest his name to McGovern as a possible vice president. Carter's men showed Pat Caddell, McGovern's young pollster, data suggesting that McGovern would have a better chance for victory if he placed a southerner on the ticket. After the Carters learned that McGovern had chosen Senator Thomas Eagleton of Missouri, Ham Jordan learned that pressure from George Meany, president of the AFL-CIO, and the tradition of choosing senators as vice presidential candidates led to McGovern's decision.[53] Carter did receive twenty-seven votes for the vice presidency, all from the Georgia delegation.[54] He later learned that McGovern had responded with "vile language" rejecting the man who had run a "stop McGovern" campaign.[55]

Undeterred by the defeat of Jackson and not particularly disappointed by Carter's failure to win the vice presidential nomination, Jordan wrote his boss a long letter containing his thoughts "regarding your own future."[56] The convention over, Carter supported his party's nominee but did not get involved in the campaign. He advised Bebe Smith, a Georgian who had led the McGovern delegates, that McGovern's "natural demeanor and prairie background" might help him "erase" the "radical image" he had in the South, but he doubted it.[57]

Not one to make concessions, Carter defended his nomination of Jackson on the grounds that Senator Russell before his death had advised Carter to support him, that Jackson's wife had family connections in Georgia, and "because I deeply felt he was the best man to be President."[58] Hedging his own bets, Carter wrote that Jackson deplored "forced bussing of school children for racial balance," favored "a strong national defense," and held "positions on many issues" that coincided "with those of Governor Wallace and myself." Furthermore, he had seen Jackson "as the only hope of preventing the nomination" of McGovern.[59]

As the campaign progressed, Carter became increasingly intransigent about McGovern. He wrote that McGovern had "shown an abysmal ineptitude in handling the campaign ever since his nomination & therefore greatly weakened an already weak position." Carter said he would have difficulty keeping his promise to vote for him. "Maybe he'll improve. I hope so."[60] McGovern stirred a hornet's nest when he dropped Eagleton, who had a history of treatment for depression, and replaced him with the Kennedy family's popular Sargent Shriver.

McGovern attempted to appease the South and Carter. He attended the annual meeting of the southern governors on Hilton Head Island, South Carolina, to try to mend fences. Afterward he wrote to "Dear Jimmy" that he had enjoyed his visit, and "Sarge Shriver and I are going to do everything in our power to win this election, and we need and welcome your counsel and support."[61]

Carter announced in the *Atlanta Constitution* that he would vote the straight Democratic ticket, but he expected Nixon to win by a landslide. He hoped Georgians who favored Nixon knew how to vote a split ticket, he continued, in order to help Democrats Sam Nunn and Andrew Young win their congressional seats. On November 5, he and Rosalynn watched McGovern go down to defeat, but they were pleased with the victories of Nunn and Young.[62] Fearing a massive southern exodus from the Democratic party, Carter asked Jackson to appoint Georgians to committee and military assignments over which he had control and suggested: "If we can get people like Herman [Talmadge] & Sam [Nunn] to 'rejoin' the national party, we'll have a chance in 1976."[63]

Carter attended Nixon's inaugural ceremony on the steps of the Capitol on January 20, 1973,[64] but he deplored the "almost impenetrable screen" around Nixon that would not allow him access to the president. To Nixon himself, Carter confessed in a personal letter: "our Governor in Georgia has been, in the past and is now, extremely critical of you." Nevertheless, he told the president that 75.8 percent of Georgians had voted for him, and he asked that members of Nixon's cabinet be accessible to all the governors.[65] To curb inflation and reduce federal expenses, Nixon impounded $65 million that Congress had appropriated for the states, an action that irritated most governors. Carter's agents filed papers with the U.S. Supreme Court seeking "judicial relief for the people of Georgia" from damages that the impoundment caused them.[66]

As a courtesy, Carter attached his name to invitations various groups sent to Nixon to visit Georgia. In April 1973, when Nixon declined to attend the Atlanta 500 stock car race, a favorite of Carter's, he commented wryly, "Gee, this is heartbreaking"—in answer to which Jody Powell penned a note: "If we keep joining in all the invites to Nixon to visit Georgia we may be able to keep the S.O.B. out of the state for the next two years."[67]

Carter continued his effort to reintegrate the South into the national Democratic party. At every opportunity, he urged southerners to remain loyal Democrats, a message he thought essential in the wake of the McGovern defeat. At the Democratic governors' conference in St. Louis, he helped oust Jean Westwood, a McGovernite, and replace her with Robert Strauss of Dallas as the national Democratic Party chairman.[68] Strauss, a long time Texas pro with extensive political contacts, might give wise advise to a candidate and a president.[69] After complimenting Strauss, Carter grabbed the spotlight briefly with a speech about the importance of the 1974 elections.[70]

The Carters liked to party at the governors' conferences. In 1973 they went to White Sulphur Springs, West Virginia. While there, Carter picked up one bill for liquor that he served to his guests and another for Rosalynn's use of the swimming pool. At Austin, Texas, in 1974, he and Rosalynn shared a beautiful condominium and joined the others to enjoy impersonator Rich Little and country singer Johnny Cash. Mrs. Lyndon Johnson, widow of the former president, treated the wives to a Texas-style party at the LBJ Presidential Library.[71]

Carter enjoyed fun, but he also tended to business. Making a pitch for state rights, federal aid, he said, must not destroy state integrity, especially since the South had shed its problems related to race.[72] In October 1973, Carter urged the governors at a national conference to help shape the nation's foreign policy. Not only would it improve their state's economies, he said, but also it would promote friendship, concern, and understanding among nations. He cited Georgia's example of sending two hundred of its citizens to live with the Brazilian people and Japan's plan to establish thirty-five new companies in Georgia.[73]

Carter understood that cooperation among the states and friendship with other countries was becoming urgent early in 1973 as Georgia and the nation confronted a major energy crisis. The Organization of Petroleum Exporting Countries reduced exports of petroleum to the United States, and oil and natural gas companies thus raised their prices. Masked by the furor of Watergate—the collective events stemming from the 1972 election that would lead to Nixon's 1974 impeachment—the energy crisis slipped into the country almost unnoticed. In March 1973, Carter asked his aides to compose a notebook for him on "Energy—Consumer vs. Oil interest," as well as such other topics as Watergate, balance of trade, and the environment.[74]

Carter built his energy speeches carefully, relating them to national politics, the world economy, and the environment. He asked University of Georgia ecologist Eugene Odum for a copy of his speech entitled "Harmony between Man and Nature: An Ecological View," which Odum had delivered at Yale University the previous year.[75] The following month, Carter added President Nixon's address to Congress proposing an energy policy to his own notebook. Nixon outlined a program that Carter thought might work in Georgia and later for the nation. Nixon urged conservation of energy sources, ending quantitative controls on oil imports, and establishing a "National Energy Office." Nixon also called for the acceleration of leasing oil lands on the Outer Continental Shelf; building a huge pipeline across Alaska to move fuel from that oil-rich state to the coast, from which it could be shipped to the lower forty-eight states; the development of deepwater ports to enhance importation; and the encouragement of both the coal and natural gas industries. He recommended use of solar and nuclear energy sources, conservation projects, and new research.[76]

Despite Nixon's good ideas, the nation did nothing, prompting Carter to prod the government to act. To create his own policy, Carter borrowed Nixon's ideas and other similar ones from a speech on the oil crisis that an Iranian diplomat had delivered in the nation's capital.[77] He wrote his science advisory counsel Ted Mock a letter, copying it to Dean Rusk, in which he suggested "that we need to establish immediately an organization such as the Manhattan Project or NASA with full funding to do research and development work on all possible sources of energy for the future." Carter recommended investigating "the gasification of coal, the economic exploitation of oil shales, the utilization of winds, solar energy, tides and ocean currents, thermal water, the heat in the crust of the earth four or five miles beneath the surface, [and] thermonuclear fusion."[78] Nixon ignored him, and when Chancellor Helmut Schmidt of Germany asked him about his country's energy policy, Carter replied with disgust that it had none.[79]

Carter defiantly prepared an energy conservation plan for Georgia.[80] He confronted the powerful Georgia Power Company, arguing that it wasted energy, inflated prices, and mismanaged its finances. Georgia Power responded: "there is no energy crisis today."[81] Carter pressed the issue, meeting with business leaders and the agricultural community to collect more information. He ordered the strict enforcement of the new national fifty-five-miles-per-hour speed limit to conserve gasoline, and he instructed his staff to drive small, energy-efficient automobiles, a rule that was particularly obnoxious to the portly Bert Lance.[82]

On August 21, 1973, Carter delivered a major policy speech to a Seminar on Energy that he had organized in Atlanta for Georgia Business and Agricultural leaders. "There is an energy crisis or shortage," he declared, introducing an unexciting topic that had attracted little press coverage or public interest. He blamed the federal government for not doing enough, noted that except for hydroelectricity, most of Georgia's energy came from outside the state, and lamented that farmers already had trouble getting adequate fuel supplies. Since air conditioning units consumed more energy than anything else, he recommended turning up thermostats. He thought nuclear power plants safe and pushed for more of them. The only solution, he thought, would come from more efficient use of fuel, self-discipline, and a "comprehensive long-range national energy policy." Predicting that the energy crisis would take a heavy economic toll on Georgia, he gloomily speculated that the worst lay ahead for the next five to eight years.[83]

In a major address on Educational Television, "Great Decisions '74—The Energy Crisis," Carter reiterated his earlier comments. He excoriated the federal government for lack of long-range planning and expressed fear for the future of the environment. He called for recycling, denial of tax breaks to oil companies, new explorations, and more research. He warned against dependency on foreign oil, especially that from the Soviet Union. Later in the summer, when his chairman of the State Energy Board suggested the crisis had ended but "a *certain amount* of retrenchment is in order," Carter fired back at him, "Give me a plan for *substantial* retrenchment."[84]

Provoked with the national government, and secretly ambitious to win control of it himself, Carter delivered a speech at Harvard University on December 2, 1972, in which he faulted the government for not delivering services to its citizens. Only the states, he said, in an oration that sounded like that of the "state rights" advocates of the Old South, utilizing methods like his "Goals for Georgia" program, could fill the gap. From Massachusetts he and Rosalynn went to California, where they tried to get the chairman of the board of the Security

Pacific National Bank to do business in Georgia but also urged the Democrats of that state to help Strauss plan strategy to put a Democrat in the White House in 1976.[85] Carter later wrote his "friend" Scoop Jackson: "In my opinion, Bob Strauss is doing an excellent job."[86]

Former president Lyndon Johnson, in retirement at his Texas ranch, delivered a speech to a December 1972 symposium at the University of Texas in Austin that aroused Carter's ire. Johnson said that Nixon secretly supported the liberal social programs of his Great Society. Carter responded that he had "long admired" Johnson personally and appreciated his "tremendous and unprecedented achievement as President," but he did not share Johnson's "optimistic assessment of Mr. Nixon's secret attitude about social programs."[87] Carter may have been too severe, or possibly uninformed, on Nixon's social programs, but he understood that Johnson remained a political hot potato; it seemed equally dangerous for a rising Democratic candidate to embrace or reject him.

When former president Harry Truman died later the same month, Carter praised him profusely. "President Truman was one of the greatest Presidents and leaders of all time," he said, noting the Marshall Plan, the establishment of Israel, and Admiral Rickover's creation of the nuclear navy. Truman, Carter said, had great sensitivity to the feelings of average Americans.[88]

Carter's comments on the sitting Republican president and the previous Democratic ones helped him create his own image. "*Politically,* of course, *the image is the reality,*" Carter wrote to an admirer who compared him to John F. Kennedy. Kennedy "still occupies a position representing youth, idealism, vigor... which he may or may not actually deserve," Carter said.[89]

Throughout 1973, particularly after the Watergate scandal implicated Nixon in illegal activities and abuses of power, Carter made numerous national appearances condemning the discredited president, exalting the Democratic party, and creating an image for himself. Scenting the opportunity for a Democratic victory in the South for the first time since Lyndon Johnson had written off the region with his signature on the Civil Rights Act of 1964, Carter resorted to his characteristic hyperbole and long speeches.

On February 9, 1973, Carter addressed the Press Club in Washington, condemning the Nixon administration and revealing his vision of a government of "benevolent conservatism." Andrew Young read the entire speech into the *Congressional Record,* declaring the governor of Georgia to be "an exponent of vigorous and compassionate government."[90] The next month Carter appeared, rather nervously, on William F. Buckley, Jr's television show *Firing Line*. Afterward, Carter wrote he had enjoyed the occasion but hoped for a "more contentious session on politics" in the future.[91]

Appearing before Tennessee Democrats in Memphis on April 21, Carter condemned Nixon as "sick" and the Watergate scandal as a denial of "truth." He talked about inflation, the balance of international trade, the rise of the Democrats, and the need for good candidates. Like a modern Paul Revere, he excitedly proclaimed, "The Democrats are back. The Democrats are back."[92]

Afterward, Jody Powell gently criticized the speech. He suggested that in the future Carter should speak for only about fifteen or twenty minutes and concentrate on brief statements of major themes. "Even your worst speeches are generally pretty good," Jody said; "but since we are moving into the big leagues now...it is my responsibility...to make sure that you always leave the best possible impression." Although he was one of the few people close to Carter to criticize him, Jody played it safe when he added: "Certainly, you do not need to be reassured of the great respect, admiration and affection that I and all of us who work for you have for you—as an individual and as a governor."[93]

Unfazed by Jody's advice, Carter went to Princeton University in May 1973 to participate in a forum entitled "The New Federalism" at the Woodrow Wilson School of Public and International Affairs. The speakers included New York governor Nelson A. Rockefeller and New Orleans mayor "Moon" Landrieu. Again, Carter condemned Nixon for freezing money that should be used for housing. "Being from the South," he said, "I feel an acute responsibility for the willingness of myself and my predecessors to permit black people to be deprived of the right to vote." Only the responsibility and power of the states, he said, could save the progress that had been made in racial relations from the secrecy and hypocrisy of the sitting president.[94]

In August 1973 he gave an address to the American Bar Association entitled "The Role and Responsibility of the Political Candidate," calling for candidates with high standards of integrity. He implied that the Watergate scandal not only revealed the weaknesses of the embattled Nixon but also undermined the very strength of the nation itself. "If the trumpet give an uncertain sound," he said quoting the Bible, "then who shall prepare himself for the battle?" Clearly, Nixon had shirked his responsibility, he said, but he did not say who he thought the new trumpeter should be.[95]

Late in 1973, Carter made a frivolous appearance on the popular television program *What's My Line?* He stumped a panel of actors who attempted to guess his occupation. None of them knew that Jimmy Carter, sitting there grinning at them, was the governor of Georgia.[96]

As Watergate continued to undermine the Nixon presidency, Carter moved into the vacuum. Nixon had taped his conversations in the Oval Office, and his prosecutors now demanded the tapes as evidence. Nixon fought to keep them, but he seemed doomed. In March 1974 Carter attended the National Governors Conference in Washington, where he was the most sought-after chief executive. He granted interviews to journalists, appeared on national television, and attended many receptions. On March 15, 1974, he declared that Nixon should resign. "If he is innocent, why doesn't he go ahead and give...the tapes and let his innocence be proven."[97]

In April, at the national Democratic governors' conference in Chicago, Carter shared the stage with Robert Strauss and Senator Hubert H. Humphrey.[98] Although many in the party, in the country, and even in Georgia might have thought it incredible, Jimmy Carter finally stood behind the podium as one of the top Democrats in the nation, where he flashed his trademark grin.

In June, Carter appeared on *Meet the Press* with five other governors who were attending a conference in Seattle. His message was no different from what he had been saying, but more national Democrats began to take notice. "Congratulations on your fine performance on *Meet the Press* on Sunday," Senator William Proxmire wrote him. "You did a great job and made me proud to be a Democrat!"[99]

At regional and national conferences, Carter carried his fight for an energy program and southern prosperity to higher levels. In January 1974, as chair of the southern governors' Commission on the Future of the South, he published a pamphlet entitled *Southern Growth and Promise*. It announced their intent to bring together academicians, businessmen, creative artists, and government representatives to make studies and recommendations for future southern progress.[100] Six months later, Carter predicted a new era of southern prestige in both national parties. Lest anyone misunderstand, he concluded, coyly: "I'm not running for any office, as you know. I'm going out of office."[101]

Carter did not act like a man abandoning politics. On August 16–18, 1974, he staged a retreat for the Commission on the Future of the South and invited members of the Southern Regional Council, an organization concerned about poor and black people. The retreat was held at a remote mountain retreat, Unicoi Station, in Helen, Georgia; "Unicoi," a Cherokee word, means "The New Way." Carter billed the retreat as a time for relaxation and family fun. There would be time for canoeing, fishing, mountain music, and appreciation of mountain art and culture at an elegantly rustic facility surrounded by the natural beauty of the Blue Ridge Mountains.[102] Rosalynn, Amy and her nurse, Jack and Judy, Rosalynn's assistant, and two security men traveled there by helicopter from Atlanta. Carter shunned the recreational activities, but he welcomed the Commission's report that help for poor and black people in the South was equal in importance to land use, health care, and energy conservation, finding in it ideas he could use in a future political campaign.[103]

As the nation prepared to celebrate its bicentennial in 1976, Carter emphasized Georgia's national rather than regional history. Carter joined historians and archaeologists aboard a DC-3 flight to New York to search for the bones of William Few, Jr., one of Georgia's signers of the U.S. Constitution.[104] Few served the state as a U.S. Senator, a state representative, and a federal judge before departing for New York City in 1799. Vowing never to return, he became president of City Bank in New York and died there in 1828. Almost a century and a half later, however, the weight of history overpowered Few's personal wishes, for the governor of Georgia and his team used scientific methods to identify his bones, exhume them, and take them back to Georgia. With military honors and patriotic fanfare, Few was buried in the churchyard of St. Paul's Episcopal Church in Augusta. The publicity surrounding that event, Carter hoped, served as a reminder that Georgia had helped form the Union and remained an integral part of the United States of America.

Trying to prove that he was a patriotic Democrat, Carter worked to develop a political and personal relationship with Israelis and Jewish Americans. Some were friends in South Georgia, such as Charles Harris, whom he appointed to the Board of Regents.[105] Robert Lipshutz and Stuart Eizenstat, both Atlanta attorneys, had connections that led to Carter's invitations to address Jewish groups ranging from B'nai B'rith (at Callaway Gardens) to the National Jewish Community Relations Advisory Council (meeting in Atlanta). Israel's consul general invited Carter to meet with Yitzhak Rabin, the Israeli ambassador to the United States. Carter did so in a meeting more formal than substantive, then issued a proclamation on Israeli Independence Day declaring friendship between the people of Israel and the people of Georgia.[106]

Many Jewish citizens outside the South did not like Carter, but he attempted to reach them through Jewish friends in Georgia. He declared before the National Jewish Community Relations Advisory Council on June 21, 1971, that Georgia had been enriched by its Jewish citizens, "most of all in the fields of human relations, education, and social justice." They were, he said, the people of the Old Testament, which teaches that nations must pursue social justice.[107] He signed a national proclamation relating to "Solidarity Day for Soviet Jewry." He addressed the Temple, a Reformed Jewish Congregation, on Peachtree Street in downtown Atlanta, at which time he touched on such topics as religious freedom, Reinhold Niebuhr, race relations, moral principles, prominent Jewish Americans, Paul Tillich, and the pursuit of righteousness.[108]

Not limiting his focus to Georgia, Carter tendered sympathy to Israel and to the families of the Israeli athletes who were kidnaped and murdered at the 1972 Olympic games in Munich. When President Nixon announced the impending visit of Premier Leonid Brezhnev of the Soviet Union, the president of B'nai B'rith asked Carter to write to both the Soviet and American leaders. Carter did so, informing Brezhnev that "there is great concern in my state that Jewish citizens of the Soviet Union are still subjected to discrimination of various kinds in their attempts to exercise the right of emigration." Carter sent a copy of his letter to Nixon with the additional note: "the Georgia General Assembly adopted a resolution expressing its concern over the Soviet Union's refusal to honor the basic right of all people to leave their country." An assistant to the president thanked him for the letter and noted that the rate of Jewish emigration from the Soviet Union had increased but still was not high enough.[109]

Carter's comments on international affairs, especially those involving Israel, the Arabs, and the Soviet Union, gave him a national image rare for southern governors. Nationally viewed as a politician in the mold of John F. Kennedy, Carter had been in the forefront of the ideas that had caused Atlanta and Georgia to flower for the past few years. The age of Lester Maddox had been replaced with the age of Eugene Odom's introduction of "ecology" and architect John Portman's changing of the face of cities with his distinctive high-rise architecture.[110] Addressing the Policies Board on Southern Growth at Atlanta's Colony Square Fairmont Hotel on November 14, 1974, Carter declared that Georgia, like the rest of the nation, stood to be directly affected by what happened in the world.[111]

CHAPTER NINETEEN

Georgians Abroad

FROM THEIR NAVY YEARS, both Carters held a fondness for foreign travel and an interest in international affairs. Carter's fascination with international business and politics brought the world to Georgia and afforded him and Rosalynn the opportunity to travel in ten different countries. He relied on publications of the U.S. State Department for information and collected a complete set of the State Department country reports. He sought foreign investments for his state, encouraged the establishment of consulates in Atlanta, and opened state trade offices in Bonn, Brussels, Sao Paulo, Tokyo, and Toronto.[1] The International Trade Division within the Department of Industry and Trade served Georgia businessmen, who in turn served their communities, but it also afforded the governor and his wife opportunities to pursue personal interests as well.[2]

Carter, along with several of his fellow southwestern Georgia entrepreneurs, envisioned Japan as the land of opportunity. It became a good market for Georgia's textiles and poultry, and the American Family Life Assurance Company of Columbus set up an international operation there. Japanese shippers agreed to serve the port of Savannah and to establish offices in Atlanta. Japan also located its first multimillion-dollar industry in the United States, the YKK Zipper Company, in Macon. On December 7, 1972, the thirty-first anniversary of the Japanese attack on Pearl Harbor, Carter proudly announced the arrival of that plant and goodwill with Japan. The next year, he and Rosalynn hosted the Japanese ambassador in Atlanta.[3]

In 1974, Carter gave the keynote speech at the ground-breaking ceremony for the Georgia World Congress Center. Financed with state and private funds, it had been planned by Atlanta business leaders who had supported Carl Sanders in 1970. Carter embraced the project after his inauguration, relented on his effort to give it to a developer who had supported him, and finally welcomed the massive structure that would transform Atlanta into one of the nation's premier convention centers.[4]

With the help of former Secretary of State Dean Rusk, Charles Kirbo, and Cloyd Hall, Carter transformed Atlanta into an international city.[5] At various times, he entertained the South Korean ambassador, the assistant secretary of state for Near Eastern and South Asian affairs, and Shimon Peres, Israel's minister of transportation and communications. The ambassador of the Republic of China, after meeting the Georgia governor, chose Atlanta as the site for the first Chinese consulate in the southeastern United States. After several groups of Israelis visited his farm to learn about seed peanuts, a major Georgia seed company planned to open an office in Nazareth. The Japanese ambassador and his "sweet wife," according to Carter, promised a consulate in Atlanta.[6]

A student of international affairs, Carter, with the approval of U.S. Secretary of State William P. Rogers, hosted the 1974 meeting of the Organization of American States in Atlanta.[7] On other occasions, he met with the Soviet Environmental Delegation to plan exchange programs and thanked Dean Rusk for all he meant "to our state." The governor shared with the former secretary his ideas about sending trade representatives from Georgia to Brussels and Tokyo and having Brazilian agents represent Georgia in San Paulo and Recife. He took particular note of a speech Kissinger delivered in Panama on February 7, 1974, on the occasion of signing a joint statement of principles to negotiate a new Panama Canal treaty. The ambassador from Ghana visited his office and later sent Rosalynn a copy of *The Art of West African Cooking*. Carter wrote the Egyptian ambassador and through him invited President Anwar El-Sadat to visit Georgia the next time he was in the United States.[8]

Rosalynn relived her dream of foreign travel, no longer as a Navy wife but as the privileged companion to an internationally active governor. When they prepared to make their first official visit to Central and South America, Dean Rusk advised Carter that as governor he would rank just below the president and vice president. Since so few governors took such trips, Rusk said, Carter would be enthusiastically received by heads of state and ambassadors. He recommended that they travel on diplomatic passports, visit the State Department for briefings, and take a State Department representative with them. They should be patient if formal dinners did not start on time. He also warned them that they should be prepared to answer questions about Nixon's lack of success concerning the "Alliance for Progress" and offer to meet personally with Nixon after they returned.[9]

Carter took most of Rusk's advice, but instead of going to Washington for a briefing, he acquired background notes from the State Department on the countries he and Rosalynn planned to visit.[10] He wrote the president of Brazil that he planned to visit on the invitation of Deputado Pereira Lopez, president of the Chamber of Deputies, for the purpose of strengthening "relations between Georgia and all Latin America." He hoped also to learn how South and North America "can be more united in our efforts to build a Western Hemisphere of opportunity and prosperity for all."[11] The Carters studied Spanish together in preparation for their two-week trade mission to Mexico, Costa Rica, Colombia, Brazil, and Argentina. Carter announced that their purpose was to promote the sale of Georgia products, reduce the dollar drain from the United States, and build goodwill between the United States and Latin America.[12]

On April 4, 1972, the governor, Rosalynn, Louis Truman of the Georgia Department of Trade and Transportation, Jody Powell, a highway patrolman, and an interpreter boarded a Georgia-made Lockheed jet for the trip to South America. Robert P. Roche, a vice president of Lockheed, supplied the jet free of charge and boarded with them, hoping to sell his company's aircraft in Latin America.[13] On their arrival in Brazil, Carter spoke at the Presidential Prayer Luncheon, where a local politician informed him that they "should know each other as brothers in Christ." Carter welcomed "an opportunity to cement personal relationships on the basis of God" and later told a church group in Atlanta that his primary function in Brazil had been to be a Christian witness.[14]

The next day the Carters visited Americana, Brazil, a town founded after the Civil War by Confederate exiles, one of whom was an ancestor of Rosalynn. The first southern governor to visit the site, Carter found a Protestant cemetery, a plain Confederate memorial, and a small chapel there. Before a group of about two hundred Confederate descendants, he gave an impromptu speech, preached, prayed, and cried. Overcome with emotion, Carter discovered in that remote spot a monument to the peculiar history of his South. He grieved over the poor judgment of his ancestors who had refused to accept the new, postslavery order in their own country and had left their children and grandchildren to fend in a strange land where they still retained much of their southern and American identity. He and Rosalynn buried a time capsule beside the cornerstone of the church.[15]

When Carter told the story of their visit to Americana, he described it as a village "established by refugees from the Yankee invaders after the War Between the States." The fine people there spoke English and might have been from Waycross, Georgia, he said. "Some of them were college professors," and the church had a Confederate flag flying in front of it and on the altar inside. What had held them together for a hundred years, he said, was that "their ancestors' God was their God." He found people "everywhere in the world hungering for Christ," he concluded, transforming the event into a religious experience instead of a melancholy historical footnote.[16]

At the conclusion of their trip on April 23, Carter declared Latin America to be a large untapped market, and he left it to Rosalynn to recount their adventures.[17] When the mayor of Bogotá gave Carter a key to the city, he turned to give it to Rosalynn, and the photographer got only Rosalynn in the picture. The headline of the Colombia newspaper referred to her as "Governor Jane Carter." She noted that the countries of Latin America were "eager for better relations with the United States." She seemed pleased that much of Latin America, like a growing faction of the American Northeast, "thought Jimmy looked like President Kennedy and he is loved in those countries." She particularly enjoyed a tour of the presidential home that the president of Colombia conducted, the home that former first lady Jackie Kennedy had called "the most beautiful well-preserved palace in the world." Rosalynn marveled at the "gold-inlaid ballroom" and noted that the bedroom remained "just as it was when Simon Bolivar slept there."[18]

After they returned home, Carter followed Dean Rusk's advice and briefed the State Department about his trip, but Nixon ignored him.[19] Both he and Rosalynn wrote thank-you notes to the people who had befriended them, Carter often referring to the "spiritual tie" that bound him with his South American friends.[20] Expanding his ties beyond Latin America and the spiritual realm, Carter served on a United Nations subcommittee on the environment, and in early June he joined businessmen, industrialists, and Ambassador George H. W. Bush to attend a UN conference in Stockholm.[21]

From May 13 through 30, 1973, the Carters traveled in Europe and Israel, their most politically significant foreign travel. Billing their journey as a trade trip to establish outlets for Georgia products in London, Brussels, West Germany, and Israel, Carter had a hidden agenda. He intended to educate himself in foreign policy, meet high government officers and heads of state, and return home to speak knowledgeably about the role of the United States in world affairs. On May 14 they toured the Lloyd's of London insurance company and attended a reception and dinner with British government and business officials. The next day they inspected the underground transit system, met with U.S. Ambassador Walter H. Annenberg, visited the House of Commons, and attended a reception and dinner with British politicians.[22]

Arriving in Cologne, West Germany, they were greeted by Ambassador Martin J. Hillenbrand, Chancellor Willy Brandt, and Finance Minister Helmut Schmidt. Carter asked Schmidt about building a Volkswagen plant in Georgia, but Schmidt wanted to talk about Watergate. Carter evaded discussion of President Nixon's problems and grabbed a suitcase to join his hosts to tour a Volkswagen plant. He left Rosalynn behind with another suitcase and plans for them to reunite in Berlin. When Rosalynn went to change her clothes, she discovered that Jimmy had taken her suitcase, leaving her only with a pair of his trousers. She fixed herself up quite attractively in a blouse and a topcoat that she had and passed the day in the public eye politely declining to remove her coat. When she met Jimmy in Berlin, according to him, she was "hysterical with laughter."[23]

Fun aside, the Carters moved on to the ancient city of Heidelberg, where they met with the commander of American forces in Europe. After a stop in Frankfurt they went to Berlin, where they attended the opera, toured East and West Berlin, and attended the Allied Armed Forces Day ceremonies. On Sunday, May 20, they attended church in Berlin, then traveled to Brussels. United States ambassador Robert Strausz-Hupe greeted them and assisted them in establishing a Georgia trade office there. For three days in France they became typical American tourists, but they also met with business executives to discuss French investment in Georgia—investments that never came about.[24]

For Jimmy and Rosalynn personally and professionally, the last five days of their trip, which took them to Israel, became the most moving and important. Like most devout American Christians, they found the Holy Land to have a breathtaking appeal. Students of the Bible since childhood, they wanted to see the land where the stories of the Jews and of the Christ took place. Carter also wanted to learn about the people, the politics, the plight of the Palestinians, the Arabs, the energy crisis, and the relationship of Israel to the United States. Carter's love for the Holy Land that he had not yet seen also fired within him a lifelong passion for peace in the Middle East. General Yitzhak Rabin, a hero of the 1967 Six Day War, had invited the Carters to Israel when he had visited them two years earlier. Officially the guests of Prime Minister Golda Meir, Jimmy and Rosalynn had plenty of free time to follow their own itinerary. The prime minister provided them with an old Mercedes station wagon with a driver and guide, Giora Avidar, who could answer their questions.[25] They went to Haifa, Acre, Safed, the Golan Heights, and Tel Aviv. The Holocaust memorial reminded them of the six million Jews who were slaughtered.[26]

Driving from their lodging in the King David Hotel in Jerusalem, they visited holy sites in Galilee, Nazareth, and the old city of Jerusalem. During three days in Jerusalem, they tried to envision what it was like in ancient times before it became a commercial tourist attraction. A banquet featuring both Muslim and Christian hosts, huge quantities of food, and bottles of Johnny Walker Red Label Scotch whiskey did not particularly recall the life of Christ. In contrast to the contemporary city of Jerusalem, they thought the Sea of Galilee, the Mount of Olives, the Garden Tomb of Jesus, and the Jordan River might have been as they were in biblical times. The Jordan River was not the mighty torrent they had envisioned but more like one of the small streams on the Carter farm. Carter slipped past his guard and took a quick dip near the site where he speculated John the Baptist had baptized Jesus.[27]

The balance of their trip became more political and economic than religious. In Nazareth they met the mayor, who promoted tourism, and they conversed with a few Jewish Soviet immigrants, whose arrival the old settlers resented. At the Golan Heights, which Israel had wrested from Syria in 1967, they found young families who showed them hillside gun emplacements once used by the Syrians. Those families were now determined to control those guns forever. Carter was not disturbed by the plight of the displaced Palestinians. He naively believed that they could be compensated or safely relocate in East Jerusalem, the West Bank, or Gaza.[28]

Since he was a public official, Carter received privileged information about the contemporary military and political life of his host country. He handed out Hebrew Bibles, which they called "Swords of the Spirit," at a military graduation ceremony and learned that Israel was intimately involved in the diamond trade in South Africa and that his host, General Rabin, expected to get a cabinet post with the Labor Party. Foreign Minister Abba Eban impressed on him the incompatibility and danger of having Arabs living side by side with Jews in occupied territories, complicated by the fact that Israel was one very small country surrounded by thirty-nine hostile Arab states. The top military and intelligence officers conceded that their country's superior might and invulnerability depended on continuously receiving military materiel and permission to replicate it from America. Carter, then a novice on U.S.-Israeli relations, thought he heard therein a message he was to take back home.[29]

Near the end of their stay, the Carters observed a session of the Knesset and enjoyed an informative lunch with Eppi Evron, Israel's deputy director general of the Ministry for Foreign Affairs. When they asked why Israel did not turn to the United Nations to help solve her problems, they quickly learned that the tiny nation feared the large number of Arab nations there who could always outvote it. Since they could not count on the UN for help, they needed the unqualified support of the United States.

Prime Minister Golda Meir, the housewife from Milwaukee who emigrated to Israel and became the fledgling nation's head of state, hosted their visit to the Knesset. A chain smoker, she ignored the "No Smoking" signs as conveniently as she ignored the fundamentalist Jews in the Knesset. She and several of her cabinet members were noted for not being devout Jews. During biblical times, Carter shyly told her, the Israelites had always prospered when they were close to Yahweh. She laughed and told him that there were plenty of "orthodox" Jews in the Knesset. The prime minister talked about Israel's pride, confidence, military might, and prosperity. She invited the Carters to participate with her in opening the Third Israeli Economic Conference. They did so, attended a departing tea in their honor, and returned to Atlanta on May 30.[30]

"My recent trip to Israel," Carter wrote two weeks after he got home, "had a profound impact on my own life. It gave me a greater insight into and appreciation for the Jewish faith and the long and heroic struggle of the Jewish people for basic human rights and freedom."[31]

Carter noted comments he had most frequently heard in Israel. Many people there thought that the United States was their most important friend, that the Soviet Union wanted peace in the Middle East, that Arabs were incompatible with them and that they must outnumber them with Jewish immigration, and that the "Arab oil weapon" was not a threat because the Arabs needed dollars more than the world needed its oil. The Arabs had been easily defeated in military conflicts, and soon they would want a permanent peace, many believed. Only four months later, however, in October 1973, Egypt and Syria, well equipped with Soviet weapons, launched surprise attacks on the Sinai and Golan Heights. A rapid infusion of weapons allowed the Israelis to turn the tide, but not before the Soviet Union and the United States went on high military alert. After twenty-five days of fighting, the two superpowers forced a cease fire.[32]

In Georgia, Governor Carter witnessed the resulting energy crisis that threatened the existence of Israel and fostered new forms of anti-Semitism in the United States. He and Robert Strauss attended an Atlanta-Israel Dinner of State, arranged by Bob Lipshutz, for a thousand guests. At the annual dinner of the State of Israel Bond Organization in Atlanta, Carter mentioned the politics and economy of the modern state of Israel and praised the Israeli people's commitment to "tame the savageness of man and make gentle the life of this world." The group awarded him the Eleanor Roosevelt–Israel Humanities Award, and afterward he received many fan letters from Jews in Georgia.[33]

The next year, Carter addressed the Atlanta chapter of B'nai B'rith. He told his audience that secretary of state Henry Kissinger would be going to Israel and Syria the next week and that "he knows of my intense interest in Israel."[34] He applauded Kissinger's negotiation of permanent disengagement agreements between Israel and Egypt.[35]

Carter's interest in international politics and business earned him an invitation in April 1973 to join the Trilateral Commission, a small group of the most powerful political and financial thinkers in the free world.[36] Organized by David Rockefeller, the Commission had members from Japan, North America, and western Europe. Its purpose was to discuss common economic, environmental, and political problems that those areas of the free world had in common. Politicians, academicians, scientists, diplomats, business executives, representatives of the media, labor, and agriculture, and two governors—Daniel Evans of Washington and Carter—made up the fifty members of the august group. Rockefeller and Dean Rusk recommended him for membership. Carter let it be known to Peter White, executive director of the Southern Council on International and Public Affairs, that he would be pleased to serve.

The executive director of the Commission, Zbigniew Brzezinski, a foreign relations scholar at Columbia University, hoped the Commission might influence the U.S. government. Its meetings dealt with political principles, monetary problems, trade, the politics of energy, east-west relations, and internal violence. On October 16, 1973, Carter attended his first meeting, at which he found himself in the company of several men who would later become his top cabinet officials.[37]

The reports, articles, memoranda, and meetings of the Trilateral Commission provided Carter with an advanced education in world economics and politics. Eager to learn, he took advantage of the opportunity. Shortly after one of his first meetings, Carter sent Brzezinski a handwritten note: "We should...[explore] the long range development of other energy sources in concert with Japan & the European countries." Brzezinski answered in agreement with Carter's idea, marking the beginning of a deep mutual respect.[38]

Quite likely, Carter read Brzezinski's article "A Plan for Peace in the Middle East," in which Brzezinski recommended decoupling security from possession of land and that the United States gain leverage by supplying arms to Israel. He suggested that Israel ought to seek a peace treaty because Arab nations would eventually modernize enough to defeat her.[39]

The members of the Trilateral Commission, the guest speakers, and the position papers they studied provided Carter with accurate information and brainstorming about the modern world. For example, at the May 1974 meeting in Washington, D.C., he listened to banker Paul Volcker express his ideas about dealing with inflation and the world's economy.[40] As a member of the Trilateral Commission, Carter became involved with people and issues far removed from the routine of a southern governor and found himself privy to elite discussions of major world events. Rosalynn shared his enthusiasm for international diplomacy. The experience they had had in the Navy and their foreign travel as representatives of Georgia began to pay rich dividends.

CHAPTER TWENTY

Jimmy, God, and Fortune

ON OCTOBER 17, 1972, the Carters reached their decision that he would run for president, but they kept it secret from everyone except a small group of friends and advisers. After serving as governor, Carter had no future in state politics. He and Rosalynn, and their advisers, assessed the opposition in both parties, pushed to win name recognition beyond their home state, and planned to gain control of the Democratic party's machinery. Carter had already made his fortune and did not have to return to work when he left the Capitol. For the more than two years remaining in the governor's office, Carter could use his domestic and international trips, his goals for Georgia, and his advocacy of everything from government reorganization to hanging the portrait of Martin Luther King, Jr., in the state Capitol to appeal to a national audience. His governorship took on the aura of a blueprint for the presidency. He strove to make a record in Georgia that would not only improve his state but serve as a platform for him to campaign for president of the United States.

Charles Kirbo had suggested the run for the presidency in 1966 after Carter lost his first bid for the governorship. Kirbo wanted a southerner to become president, and he thought "Carter was a great man" who could win the office. Kirbo's slow-talking, slow-walking, country boy demeanor masked his knowledge of the law and American politics.[1] In July 1972, immediately after the Democratic convention in Miami, Peter Bourne, who knew Carter well, thought he should use his "personal charm" and take the risk to run for president. "What is critical is the psychological and emotional decision," Bourne said with the precision of a doctor who understood his patient, "to run for the Presidency to win, whatever the eventual outcome might be."[2] Bourne knew that Carter would intend to win, would stay focused, and would not accept defeat as final.

Three months after the Miami convention, on October 17 at seven A.M., the Carters met with Bourne, Ham Jordan, Jody Powell, Gerald Rafshoon, and Atlanta businessman and conservationist Landon Butler at the mansion. Carter told them that he and Rosalynn had decided he would run. As they left the meeting, Rafshoon turned to Jordan and said, "The son of a bitch, he wants it."[3] In November, after Nixon won reelection, Kirbo, Jordan, Philip Alston, and Bert Lance agreed to assist the governor. Carter directed Jordan to prepare a four-year plan to win the Democratic nomination.[4]

Jordan advised Carter to share plans only with his family and closest friends until he could achieve a position of leadership in the national Democratic party. Carter agreed, drawing into his circle Jack Watson, Greg Schneider, John Pope, William Gunter, David Gambrell, and Robert Lipshutz. At Christmas, Jimmy and Rosalynn told both their families, who were shocked but excited to hear the news.[5]

On November 4, 1972, Jordan completed a seventy-page memorandum "to set forth in a logical fashion some specific thoughts and recommendations on your national effort." Ham thought that McGovern and Shriver would lose in 1972 and fade from power. Ted Kennedy and Wallace would be his major opponents, but neither they nor anyone else appeared to be strong candidates. Carter's personal weaknesses seemed minor. He did not speak well on television and had insufficient knowledge of foreign affairs and economics, but they were faults that could be addressed. Entering all the Democratic caucuses and primaries would give him personal contacts that would overcome a weak oratorical style.

Jordan recommended that Carter read national newspapers, study foreign policy, and learn about defense, economics, and the details of previous elections. He should create task forces to inform him, befriend the northeastern Democratic establishment, "cultivate the Kennedy smile," and run as an outsider against Washington. A strict budget, a competent staff, and a plan for raising money would be essential. He must create a national campaign based on his inaugural address as governor.[6] Many years later, Carter thought Jordan's plan "a timeless user's guide for anyone with political aspirations."[7]

Aware that George Wallace remained an icon in much of the South as well as the industrial, blue-collar Midwest, Jordan cautioned Carter not to ignore him. "It is my guess that George Wallace resents you...as we used him...beneficially in our campaign [for governor in 1970] but refused to nominate him at the [1972] Democratic Convention." Jordan advised Carter to "court Wallace" to win his support.[8]

Rosalynn, whose role Ham took for granted, had reservations about herself, not about Jimmy. Certain that Jimmy was capable of running for, winning, and doing the job of the presidency, she could not imagine herself in the White House. Her anxiety about moving into the governor's mansion had vanished once she got there, but the White House with its awesome responsibilities intimidated her. Typically, she asked how they would "raise the money" for the campaign, who would deal with "practical things," and whether she could "measure up" to the demands of the campaign and the responsibilities of the job. She did, however, find the possibility of being first lady exciting and believed it would give her the chance to help people.[9]

Carter began an ambitious reading program. James Barber's *Presidential Character: Predicting Performance in the White House,* an analysis of the personality types of the men who had become president, inspired him to enhance his "positive/active" traits. He wrote Barber: "What the presidency needs now is an element of greatness, & there is a yearning in our nation for this to occur."[10] Carter envisioned himself in 1976 as that "element of greatness."

When Chancellor George Simpson of the University System of Georgia gave him a copy of Catherine Drinker Bowen's *Miracle at Philadelphia,* a classic scholarly and semipopular account of the Constitutional Convention of 1787, Carter graciously accepted it. Simpson, who was no friend of the governor, may have been meanly suggesting that Carter needed to know and respect the Constitution.[11] Carter, who was neither attorney, political scientist, nor scholar, nevertheless put the book to good use and soon sprinkled his speeches with correct references to the Constitution.

Carter devoured contemporary analyses of the environment, industrial societies, and the changing needs of families and the Earth's peoples. Much of his reading was typical of the literature of the late sixties and early seventies that predicted change and called for reforms to accommodate it. Carter particularly liked *Habit and Habitat* by Robert Theobald, describing the relationship between human life and the environment in a modern industrial society. Theobald argued that the expansion of wealth hurt the environment, and that the middle and upper classes needed to adjust their standard of living to protect the Earth.

Alvin Toffler's *Future Shock,* predicting that physical and psychic trauma caused by a changing industrial society would destroy family tradition and must be controlled by government regulation, captured Jimmy's attention.

Influenced in part by his reading, Carter thought that big business needed to be more sensitive to the needs of the people. He advised Harold McKenzie, a vice president of the Georgia Power Company, that "a profound change" had taken place that caused the people to distrust those in positions of authority. "Georgia Power has become an adversary against the people, me, [and] the P[ublic] S[ervice] C[ommission]," he said. He urged McKenzie to read *The Greening of America, Habit and Habitat,* and *Future Shock. The Greening of America,* by Yale professor Charles Reich, published in 1972, reflected the ideas of the free thinkers and counterculture advocates of the 1960s who thought that industrial capitalism impeded social reforms.[12]

For information about national defense, Carter turned to his former boss Admiral Rickover and to Senator Sam Nunn. Rickover shared the governor's work ethic, religious principles, and patriotism. Carter congratulated the admiral and asked for "information on defense & national affairs" that he might use in his speeches.[13] Carter asked Nunn for copies of the part of the Senate Defense Appropriation Subcommittee 1974 hearings that included Rickover's testimony. Carter received practical advice on national defense from other career military men whom he trusted and whose advice he kept secret. His Annapolis classmate, Stansfield Turner, then a vice admiral commanding the Second Fleet, helped answer Carter's questions about the Navy.[14]

To learn how to run a presidential campaign, Carter read Gary Hart's book *Right from the Start: A Chronicle of the McGovern Campaign.* A senator who might have gotten the nomination himself in 1972 had he not been involved in a personal scandal, Hart wrote a detailed analysis of McGovern's 1972 failed campaign. Peter Bourne sent the book to Carter, explaining that "apart from the fact that he spelt your name wrong" ("Jimmie"), it would be a useful handbook for the campaign. The key to McGovern winning the nomination was his early declaration, appeal to idealistic young people, ability to handle people with giant egos, and firm belief that he could win. McGovern's staff had been responsible for organizational failures because they did not plan as well for the general election as for the nomination. Carter studied the book intensely, finding there good ideas for his own campaign.[15]

On the Constitution, Carter sounded much like the old southern politicians who placed state rights and individual integrity above all else. He thought "the separation of powers with its system of checks and balances" and "states' rights" were among the "most sacred" characteristics of the Constitution." The "spirit of the Constitution," he said, guaranteed "individuals and states their rights."[16]

As for politicians, they were born, not made, because "no one can train to be a politician," Carter said. A politician was merely "a concerned and enlightened citizen" who studied government, banking, history, and every field in which he could have an impact. Politicians should be "open and honest" and not "deceive" people. "Our country needs not only capable, intelligent leadership, but also compassionate, honest and sincere leadership," he concluded.[17] He implied that the country needed a type of politician it did not have in President Nixon and his chief advisers.

"There are truths and standards which never change," Jody Powell wrote in a letter that Carter signed to a Georgia state senator. Jody, who devilishly enjoyed this aspect of his job, continued that such truths "arise from a restudy of the tortuous historical development of our nation...and from a restudy of the Bible." He thought the American people "are simply hungry for something finer than they have." He quoted Tillich's comment: "Religion is the *search* for the truth about man's existence, and his relationship with God." No doubt referring to Carter's, as well as the nation's, political future, he concluded, "Maybe our search will be fruitful."[18]

The Bible and Tillich aside, Carter was a pragmatic politician who agreed with Hamilton Jordan that he needed to get a position of leadership in the Democratic party. Carter therefore wrote the party's chairman, Robert Strauss, to volunteer to help with the 1974 elections. Strauss had already hired Terry Sanford of North Carolina, but he agreed to make Carter cochairman of the Committee to Elect Democrats in 1974. While Sanford was bogged down with the almost impossible task of writing a new charter for a splintered party, Carter welcomed the job of advising Democrats how to win reelection. Carter used that workhorse committee to put together his own team, incur major political obligations from the lowly and the mighty in his own party, and place himself among the top Democratic presidential candidates in 1976.[19]

Stuart Eizenstat congratulated Carter on his appointment as chairman of that campaign committee and offered his assistance.[20] After Carter delivered a speech to the International Press Club the next year excoriating Nixon for slash-ing domestic funding, Eizenstat praised him for condemning the Nixon admin-istration. "It continues to be a source of hope for the future," Eizenstat wrote, "that leaders such as yourself are concerned with openness and compassion in government."[21]

Bob Strauss asked Eizenstat to prepare position papers that could be sent to Democratic congressional candidates. The papers would delineate important issues, make suggestions, and criticize Nixon. For six to eight months, Eizen-stat worked on the papers and collected the names of others who might help, including Henry Owen of the Brookings Institute and Brzezinski. Eizenstat innocently suggested to Carter in 1974 that he should run for president because Ted Kennedy could not possibly win. Carter "laughed," Stu wrote, "and invited me at that point to join people who had long since been planning the effort."[22]

Carter took control of his committee. In early May 1973, he sent Strauss a handwritten note saying, "Hamilton will be in Washington early next week"— to talk about their plans for a "nationwide election concept." Carter planned to attend some of the delegate selection meetings with Strauss, discuss campaign strategy with many of the Democratic candidates, and personally get involved in the dozens of looming campaigns. Carter, as Strauss requested, included in the same post an autographed picture of himself to be hung in the Democratic national headquarters in the Watergate complex.[23]

Strauss announced that Hamilton Jordan would be the executive director of the Democratic National Committee's 1974 Campaign Committee, which was chaired by Governor Jimmy Carter.[24] Jordan had the intellect, the drive, the tal-ent, and the loyalty to Carter to do the job. Carter sent him a list of seventeen thousand associations and organizations of national scope, divided into seven-teen categories. Those divisions included trade, agriculture, government, edu-cation, society, religion, veterans, labor, sports, and Greek letter societies. The Carters divided the country into regions and groups, including ethnic groups, whose particular interests they intended to address.[25]

Carter and his team created a "Campaign Summary Book" in which they docu-mented every Democratic race for the House, the Senate, and the governorships. Carter pored over the information, making notes on many of the candidates. For example, he thought Senator Mike Gravel of Alaska "in trouble" for reelection and that Mike Dukakis of Massachusetts would defeat incumbent governor

Francis W. Sargent. Carter sent the gubernatorial candidates an account of what he had done as governor and how well he thought it had worked.[26]

Carter crisscrossed the country, meeting candidates, giving speeches for them, and often inviting them to the mansion in Atlanta. He endeared himself to almost every prominent member of his party; toward that end, Rosalynn frequently accompanied him.[27] Carter sometimes chastised such leading Democratic senators as Ted Kennedy, Walter Mondale, and Edmund Muskie for not working harder to help other Democrats get elected. He did not want them to use the 1974 elections to begin their own campaigns for the presidency in 1976, nor did he want them to know that he planned to run for the office himself in 1976.

In a more relaxed atmosphere, Carter addressed the Naval War College in Rhode Island on June 26, 1973. Its president, Stansfield Turner, had been Carter's Naval Academy classmate, but they had not been close friends. Turner described Carter's political philosophy as an "enlightened conservatism addressing self-reliance, personal responsibility, and individual participation in government." He bragged that Carter was a forward-looking Navy man. Carter responded that it was a great honor for a "lieutenant to speak at the Naval War College." As governor he commanded the national guard, consisting of twelve thousand troops, eighty-five to ninety tanks, one hundred airplanes, and twenty-five to thirty helicopters. He talked about his trip to the Middle East, the responsibility of the military and of civilians to protect the freedom of the individual, and how politicians sometimes had to decide between military and social concerns.[28]

From the "old home" day at the War College, Carter turned his attention back to the campaign. It irritated him to hear speeches or read articles by prominent Democrats who commented on the party's chances for success in 1976. He urged them to concentrate on the 1974 elections. Senator Walter Mondale, with a mind of his own, published a piece in the *Christian Science Monitor* arguing that the Democrats could win in 1976. Annoyed with Mondale for jumping ahead to 1976, Carter wrote him that he had met Democratic leaders in thirty-nine states, and they wanted "the leaders of our party like you, Kennedy, Jackson, etc." to concentrate on 1974, and "forego to the maximum extent possible any preoccupation with 1976 until November of next year."[29]

Carter reminded Mondale of all the work they had to do in 1974, raising money, recruiting candidates, creating harmony, and training campaign organizations. "I've only met you in passing—during testimony before Sen. Muskie's committee," Carter continued, "but would welcome sometime a chance to talk with you."[30] Carter knew more about Mondale than Mondale knew about him. He knew Mondale worked for social justice, counted Hubert Humphrey as a close friend, and favored dialogues to normalize relations with both the Soviet Union and China.

Carter continued to march across the United States singing praise for Robert Strauss, bragging about his programs in Georgia, avoiding preoccupation with Watergate, and insisting that presidential politics not be discussed until after the 1974 elections. He spoke to the United Auto Workers and to the AFL-CIO in late August. Before the latter group, he commented that "In our country... there is a certain *malaise*" because men and women in public office had underestimated the people, imposed an unfair tax structure, failed to provide health care, and governed in secret.[31] In Florida, Carter pounded on his theme that stability, vision, self-reliance, and administering the people's affairs "as a business" were southern examples that the nation might well imitate.[32]

Carter invited influential leaders and Democratic contributors to Atlanta to enjoy the culture and sports of the city and to discuss the party. He visited the offices of freshmen House incumbents who faced stiff opposition. After Senator Lloyd Bentsen of Texas, a potential presidential candidate, met Carter at a Southern Governors' Conference in Point Clear, Alabama, he wrote the Georgian, "I know of the tremendous effort you are making on behalf of the party and I assure you that it is much appreciated by those of us who are concerned with both 1974 and 1976."[33]

In Asheville, North Carolina, and elsewhere, Carter followed Ham's advice to kill "them with kindness" and "demonstrate that you do not intend to be petty and envious as the others have been." This approach was especially important, Ham said, because Barney Gottstein of Alaska would be there, and "he will be worth knowing because he has money and is willing to help." Jordan also suggested that they "accommodate Strauss with a few first selections" of campaign committee members; "then we can do anything we wish with others." Carter took the suggestions, praised Strauss and Bentsen in his speech, modestly noted that he was only one of fifty on the committee, and talked at length about strategy for victory.[34]

Carter's enthusiasm for his committee's work knew no limits. He addressed the Jefferson-Jackson Day dinner in Atlanta on February 18, 1974, gave speeches in Georgia and New Hampshire, and addressed the American Bar Association in the nation's capital. At the National Democratic Governors' Conference in Chicago, he predicted that in 1974 the party would win enough congressional seats to make it veto proof, a necessity to deal with the devious president Nixon. Carter declared that Nixon was a "millstone around the Republican Party's neck." The Democrats nevertheless had a vested interest in keeping the vilified president in office. "If Nixon were replaced" by his appointed vice president Gerald Ford before the November elections, Carter speculated, "that would put things back where they should be" but would result in fewer Democratic victories in the fall.[35]

From New York to Georgia to Nebraska and Michigan, he spread his message and, not quite coincidentally, introduced himself to new audiences. Adamant that 1976 should not be discussed until after the 1974 elections, Carter quipped to one hometown journalist, "I've had some run-ins with Mondale. I might strive for a place on the '76 ticket myself."[36]

Carter achieved his finest hour at a Law Day celebration on May 4 at the University of Georgia. Events included a moot court using real Georgia judges and the unveiling of a portrait of Dean Rusk, a Georgia native who had served as secretary of state under both presidents Kennedy and Johnson. Senator Edward "Ted" Kennedy, the brother of the late president, had been invited to give the keynote address, after which the governor of Georgia would deliver a speech. The Carters hosted Kennedy at the mansion and thus got to know him before the ceremony began, but Kennedy later remembered that Carter vacillated between being friendly and callous on that occasion.[37] In his speech, Kennedy attempted to draw historical connections between Massachusetts and Georgia. He noted that Harvard was the first private university in the country, the University of Georgia the first public one. *Old Ironsides,* then in Boston and dating back to the American Revolution, had been built of Georgia wood, he noted. In a more serious vein, Kennedy waxed eloquent about the history of wars from the Civil War to Vietnam, with criticisms of Watergate and Nixon and the misuse of the CIA. In deeply moving tones, he spoke of the "ancient virtues" of "courage and hope, work and duty, faith and sacrifice," and the "worth of the common citizen" that alone made the Constitution viable.[38]

Since Kennedy had used many of his ideas, Carter had to rewrite his own speech to emphasize the sacrifice and value of ordinary people. Carter attacked lawyers with a passion, for they often favored their own interests above those of the citizens. As a scientist, Carter said, he probed his life every day for change and improvement, and as a farmer, he had the same motivations, but lawyers were reluctant to change. He had been a part of change in Georgia, especially those changes related to justice for African Americans, but he admitted there was still "a long way to go." Lawyers had opposed an ethics bill he wanted to get passed. "Senator Kennedy," he said, had described very well "the *malaise* that exists in this nation, and it does."[39] Carter let the leaders of the Georgia bar know he believed that they could do much more to advance social justice in the state.

Carter's purpose, however, was more personal than political, more private than public. His son Jack, a third-year law student, sat in the audience. Carter feared that law school might narrow his son's horizons and used his public address to exhort his son to see a law career in terms of public service.[40] Jack remembered the speech well. Although "Dad really isn't an orator," he said, he could speak with convincing intensity. The core of the speech told the story of an old black woman on the coast of Georgia whose husband had died. The sheriff and the county assessor tricked her into signing papers that gave up her land. She hired a lawyer who missed a filing date, and thus she lost her property. Carter attacked the very life of the legal system in Georgia. "I get chill bumps thinking about it," Jack said. "I mean, [it was an] incredible speech."[41]

Carter's speech flowed with such passion that one could hardly believe he was a politician, much less one well known for mediocre oratory. Not a lawyer himself, he said, he had learned about "criminal justice and the system of equity" by reading Reinhold Niebuhr and Bob Dylan. Dylan had said it well in such songs as "The Lonesome Death of Hattie Carroll," "Like a Rolling Stone," "The Times, They Are A-Changin,'" and "I Ain't Gonna Work on Maggie's Farm No More." Niebuhr had said that the sad duty of politics to establish justice could not be done without constantly revising laws. Laws, according to Niebuhr, should be based on Christian ethics.

After more references to his own career than his audience might have wanted to hear, Carter concluded with a reference to Tolstoy's *War and Peace*. "The point of the book," he said, is that Tolstoy wrote "about the students and the housewives and the barbers and the farmers and the privates in the Army." "Even the greatest historical events," he continued, "are controlled by the combined wisdom and courage and commitment and discernment and unselfishness and compassion and love and idealism of the common ordinary people."

In America, Carter said, "the Constitution charges us with a direct responsibility for determining what our government is and ought to be." The Watergate scandal, and especially the lying of U.S. attorney general John Mitchell, who was supposed to be the nation's chief law enforcement officer, denigrated the Constitution. "I can't imagine somebody like Thomas Jefferson tiptoeing through a minefield on the technicalities of the law, and then bragging about being clean afterwards," he concluded.[42]

One man in the crowd who had come to hear Kennedy, counterculture journalist Hunter S. Thompson, was electrified by Carter's words. Thompson, still skeptical of the southerner, wrote a glowing article for *Rolling Stone,* which placed a grinning Carter draped in toga and the Confederate flag on its cover and gave him unexpected major national attention.[43]

After the event ended, Kennedy wrote Carter: "The people of Georgia are fortunate to have the Carters as their first family, and it was a delight for me to feel so welcome in your home." When the Carters had invited Kennedy to stay with them at the mansion, they had said it would be "just a personal visit," but in reality Carter was sizing up the man who might be his most formidable rival in 1976.[44]

Carter wasted not a day in the remainder of the 1974 campaign season. He drew closer to his colleagues on the Trilateral Commission, including Cyrus Vance, Warren Christopher, Lloyd Cutler, Paul Warnke, Anthony Solomon, and Henry Owen. Brzezinski began to pay him special attention and helped him compose a major foreign policy speech. Carter went to Omaha to address the National Federation of Democratic Women, to Seattle to a national governors' conference, and to New York City to attend a meeting of the Trilateral Commission. Everywhere he condemned Nixon and Watergate, collected information to disseminate to Democratic candidates, and received accolades for his work to reelect Democrats. In Seattle, he said categorically for the first time: "I personally think the President is guilty and I think the release of evidence will prove it." In June, he appeared on *Meet the Press,* a major forum.[45]

By July, the *New York Times* listed Carter as a potential Democratic presidential nominee. In "Democrats at the Gates," William Shannon mentioned nine possible candidates. He noted that George Wallace could not win, then named Edward Kennedy, Hubert Humphrey, Edmund Muskie, Henry Jackson, Birch Bayh, Terry Sanford, Fred Harris, Sargent Shriver, and Jimmy Carter. Of Carter, he said that the Georgian was "almost unknown, but he impresses small audiences with his charm and his skill in defining issues." The Democratic party, he continued, "having once been the home of the 'solid South' and then having lost most of its support there in national elections, is now politically and psychologically prepared to nominate a Southerner."[46]

Carter declined to make predictions about 1976, standing firm in his determination to focus on the 1974 elections. He was more interested in building personal political relationships than creating publicity or formulating political philosophy, and he succeeded in ingratiating himself with the most prominent people in the party. "Using Carter's role with the DNC [Democratic National Committee] as cover," Ham and his wife Nancy and Peter Bourne and his wife Mary King went to New Hampshire on March 14, 1974, to assess Carter's possibilities for victory there in the crucial first presidential primary of 1975. They also established contacts for a future visit by Jimmy and Rosalynn.[47]

Events in Washington in the late summer drew the nation's attention from bland midterm elections to the shocking resignation of Nixon on August 9, 1974. As the House prepared to vote on his impeachment, Nixon handed over tapes of his telephone conversations that would have surely led to his conviction. His appointed vice president, Gerald R. Ford, assumed the presidency, and on September 8, 1974, issued Nixon a blanket pardon for any crimes he might have committed. Never before had a president resigned or an unelected person assumed that office. Nixon's resignation and Ford's pardon, which some mistakenly thought resulted from a deal he had made with Nixon, left the Republican party in disarray and a vacuum in the presidency itself.

On October 1, 1974, in the midst of the midterm campaigns and the wake of Watergate, Carter celebrated his fiftieth birthday. Bert and LaBelle Lance sent him roses, but his eldest son Jack and his wife Judy sent him a hammock. "I'm still sitting here enjoying the beautiful roses," he wrote Bert and LaBelle. "Jack and Judy gave me a handmade hammock for my 'sunset years.' Roses are more encouraging."[48]

More in a sunrise than a sunset mood, Carter enjoyed a spectacular victory on Election Day, November 5, 1974. The Democrats gained four seats in the Senate, increased their number from 248 to 291 in the House, and won thirty-six statehouses. In Georgia, Lester Maddox lost the governorship to George Busbee, a defeat that would assist Carter's national ambition. Kennedy, who won reelection in Massachusetts, wrote to Carter congratulating him and expressing his thanks for "those victories which you helped to make possible." Soon after the votes were counted in 1974, Carter opened a tiny presidential headquarters for himself in a back room of Robert Lipshutz's law office at 64 North Pryor Street in Atlanta.[49]

Charles Kirbo laughingly said, "Bob Strauss was an innocent victim." Carter had asked Strauss for a job nobody wanted and had performed it so well that he created a national reputation and placed the nation's leading Democrats in his debt. "About two-thirds of the way, Strauss and the Senate leadership and the House leadership realized what had happened, but it was too late," Kirbo said;[50] Carter had become a major force in the Democratic party. On September 23, 1974, Kennedy announced that he would not be a candidate for president. He cited his son's cancer, his wife's alcoholism, his responsibility to care for his two slain brothers' children, and his own automobile accident at Chappaquiddick, Massachusetts, in which a young woman had died. Two days later, Carter sent him a handwritten letter expressing regret for "the personal & family tragedies which have made it necessary for you to withdraw from consideration for the Presidency in 1976." He praised Kennedy's principles and continued "that as one who has considered becoming a candidate myself, I've always viewed you as a formidable opponent." Still, he claimed, he took "no pleasure from your withdrawal," wished Kennedy a bright future, and invited him to visit often in Georgia.[51]

By December, Carter's secret was pretty much known among Democrats. He began openly to solicit African-American votes for 1976. He sought help from Coretta Scott King, Daddy King, state senator–elect Julian Bond, and Representative Andrew Young. With Kennedy and Mondale out of the race, blacks had no place else to go. Young announced that he would "work in any way I can to help Jimmy Carter get a fair hearing by the American people."[52]

Carter and Jordan attended a conference on Democratic Party organization and policy in Kansas City, Missouri, in December. In preparation for their trip, Gerald Rafshoon printed a glossy, eight-page brochure with photographs of Carter trying to look like John F. Kennedy and accounts of his accomplishments in Georgia and mailed copies to the Kansas City delegates prior to their arrival at the conference. Ham marketed Carter as a moderate, while Carter himself worked tirelessly to win support from the left wing of the party. Carter won over Pat Derian, who had led the Freedom Democrats in Mississippi, Anne Wexler of the McGovern campaign, and Marjorie Craig Benton, a wealthy McGovern contributor from Chicago.[53]

Despite public charades, Carter disliked Ted Kennedy and feared competition from him. When Kennedy addressed a small group in Kansas City, one Georgia delegate claimed he heard Carter say, "I'm glad I don't have to kiss his ass to be president."[54]

Carter made his own decisions, but he turned to Jordan for advice. In August 1974, as the midterm November elections approached and with less than six months remaining in the governor's term, Jordan sent Carter a 110-page memorandum telling him how to pursue his drive for the presidency after November. He recommended that Carter be a good governor for the balance of his term, keep his staff members and advisers, and especially retain Kirbo as state party chairman. Ham warned that they should not be overwhelmed by "the enormity of a Presidential campaign." Carter should take credit for the defeat of Maddox and be positive and serious in his comments. Since Carter was a southerner and an outsider, Jordan thought it mandatory that he declare his loyalty to the national Democratic Party and discuss his plans with Strauss after the 1974 elections.[55] Peter Bourne also sent Carter a memorandum urging him to avoid the image of a regional candidate, get the endorsement of national figures, and "move significantly to the left."[56]

Carter created an informal brain trust with Brzezinski as his adviser on foreign policy and Stuart Eizenstat on domestic policy. "Somehow or other we complemented each other," Brzezinski later said, "Somehow or other I had the feeling that I understood [Carter]."[57]

Long before the primaries in either party, Jordan sensed that the most powerful rising political star in the country was the governor of California. He and Carter began to analyze Carter's record as governor and compare it to that of Governor Ronald Reagan. Carter declared that "I'll stack up Georgia's business-like government budgeting, organization, planning, management, reduction in welfare rolls, etc., against Reagan's in California." He contended, "You can't find an able bodied man on welfare in Georgia—unless he's breaking the law."[58] He told another correspondent that a Reagan tax proposal for California had merit, but Georgia was not in such bad shape because the personal income tax in Georgia, at 5.8 percent, fell below the 8.75 percent in California. When Reagan sent Carter a copy of his tax proposal, Carter replied airily that he would look at it.[59]

Carter exaggerated his record as governor, but according to political scientist T. McNeill Simpson III at the University of Tennessee, who studied it in great detail, it would have been good without the exaggeration. Carter's reorganization plan had increased the power of the governor, but he had not raised taxes, had provided additional relief for the poor, and had saved the state money through zero-based budgeting and improved investment of its revenues. The debate over the effectiveness of Carter's reorganization has never been totally resolved. On paper, the reduction of more than three hundred agencies to twenty-two seems quite an accomplishment, although some of the old ones were never funded and some of the new ones were umbrellas that encompassed others. The state auditor argued that no money was actually saved, but there is little doubt that Carter did produce a more streamlined government that made the work of his successors more productive and prosperous.[60]

Education, Carter's pet project, did advance for the very young and the handicapped, and there were small increases in teachers' salaries. Higher education remained a different matter, for most people who worked in it had supported Sanders, a political crime for which Carter, and more especially Jordan, never forgave them. The chancellor of the University System of Georgia did not get along with Carter, and Carter insisted on referring to the disorganized and poorly paid professors as a "lobby." The sheer weight and size of the major institutions in Athens and Atlanta kept them intact, with good personnel and notable progress in research and teaching, but the rest of the system, except for the Carters' alma mater in Americus, felt the sting of the governor's penury.

At the middle and lower levels of society, Carter had greater successes. He reformed the judicial structure by creating a nominating process to choose judges, and he provided rehabilitation programs and early release for Georgia's prisoners. He preserved many natural areas in the state. Care for the mentally ill and the drug addicted improved dramatically under his and Rosalynn's leadership.[61]

The most obvious changes under Carter's leadership were in race relations. He appointed the first black judge, increased the number of blacks on state boards and commissions from three to fifty-three, boosted black enrollment in statewide intern programs to 20 percent, hung the portraits of three historically important black Georgians in the state Capitol, and appointed the first black governor's staff member. Andrew Young told a Democratic convention in Kansas

City, Missouri, that Carter represented the "authentic voice" of the New South for both poor whites and blacks. Under Carter's leadership, progress for blacks outstripped that under other New South governors.

Many whites, however, condemned Carter, and there was no chance that he could have been reelected governor had it been constitutionally possible for him to succeed himself. White males and others quietly feared for their jobs in an "equal opportunity" society. They quietly and massively turned away from the Democratic governor to explore what better chances they might have under a Republican regime.[62] Roy Harris, the segregationist member of the University of Georgia's Board of Regents whom Carter had replaced with black Jesse Hill, said Carter was a "hypocrite" who campaigned on a platform like those of Wallace and Maddox but turned out to be "the most liberal governor in the South." Despite Harris's complaint, the state still had plenty of Maddox and Wallace voters, and many citizens who liked Carter's reforms did not trust him. Although African Americans and their white sympathizers applauded their progress, they thought it not enough and still remembered Carter's segregationist 1970 campaign. The gleaming skyscrapers of Atlanta, the influx of industry into the state, and the state's elevated image were tempered by an energy shortage, gasoline lines, and the reality that the promise of prosperity and justice had not yet been fully delivered.

Furthermore, some of the state's media and many of its politicians, including Democrats, had no use for Carter. Reg Murphy, editor of the *Atlanta Constitution*, remained a major antagonist. Kirbo thought Murphy's hatred of Carter personal because Carter had once called him "a kept bastard."[63] Politicians whom he had fought and public servants whose jobs were jeopardized by his reorganization were pleased to see Carter leave office. Carl Sanders had never forgiven him for winning in 1970. He and others portrayed Carter as a disaster and a phony, a wastrel, and the creator of a bureaucratic nightmare.[64] State representative James H. "Sloppy" Floyd, chairman of the house appropriations committee, rebuked Carter's reorganization for bogging down services and wasting money. He admitted that Carter was knowledgeable and hardworking but thought him too "bullheaded" to accomplish much. Lester Maddox vowed to campaign against him.[65]

Keeping a wary eye on California, Carter rose above the discontent in his own state. He had put together a coalition of diverse individuals and groups in Georgia, establishing a pattern he intended to use for the nation. He had won

African-American votes, appealed to organized labor, rural and urban whites, women, young liberals, businessmen, and bankers.[66] Carter's career, personality, and promises cemented factions that were not natural allies, enabling him to win elections but making it impossible to please them all once in office. The coalition that elected him disintegrated once he assumed power.

Carter enjoyed being governor. "I like the challenges," he said. "I like the diversity of responsibility, the constantly changing aspects of my life, the difficult problems that arise that I have to deal with." He liked "the debate" and the "opportunity to meet a lot of interesting people in various aspects of life."[67] On another occasion, he said, "I like to manage government.... I like detailed management of government." In spite of the Watergate scandal and the petroleum crisis, he said, shifting his attention to the nation, his outlook "for the future is one of hope"—for a country whose leaders cared about "those who look to us for leadership."[68]

For months before the end of his term, the newspapers were filled with rumors that he would run for the presidency. Carter had been a poor keeper of his secret. He had drawn more advisers into his inner circle, and his public addresses after late 1972 sounded like campaign speeches. On November 25, he, Rosalynn, and Miss Lillian hosted about 250 relatives and friends at the mansion. Almost enough people to elect him, as one journalist joked, they declared their loyalty and willingness to help.[69]

"The main difficulty I had to overcome," Carter said a few days before his appointed hour, "was embarrassment, telling folks I was running for—you know, for President."[70]

Carter labored over his announcement speech for several days. He produced a handwritten draft, then got comments from Stuart Eizenstat, Charles Kirbo, Jody Powell, Gerry Rafshoon, Peter Bourne, and Hamilton Jordan. Eizenstat advised him to get rid of the "hokey" references about "why not the best" and Rickover and to quit harping on the "I am a Christian" theme. Bourne advised him to overcome the prejudice against a southerner at the top of a national ticket by avoiding the image of a regional candidate and making as few references to Georgia as possible. Kirbo urged him to avoid political stereotypes. Carter paid no attention to any of them.[71]

At one P.M. on December 12, 1974, with Rosalynn sitting on the stage behind him, Jimmy stepped to the podium at the National Press Club in Washington, D.C.

In a speech entitled "Why Not the Best?" he said that Americans were a great and diverse people with dreams and a shared belief in "the greatness of our country." They had seen their trust betrayed when a recent administration had dropped a veil of secrecy over government proceedings and isolated itself from the people. He called for sunshine laws, limits on gifts to public officials, control of lobbyists, the selection of judges and diplomats on merit alone, and fair treatment of all Americans. He wanted a government "that is honest and competent," one with an energy policy and a plan to protect the environment. He mentioned the building of interstate highways, equitable tax policies, decent health care, control of nuclear weapons, and "adequate military preparedness" to guarantee the nation's security. He recalled that he had recently attended a governors' conference at Carpenter's Hall in Philadelphia where he felt mysteriously connected with the Founding Fathers. He told again the story of his first meeting with Admiral Rickover, and ignoring his political advisers, declared: "For our nation—for all of us—that question is 'Why not the best?'"

"I am a candidate for president of the United States in 1976," he concluded. "Although I shall make a total personal commitment to this campaign, I will not compromise my own integrity or any of the high principles of this nation in order to be elected."[72] The next day the *New York Times* declared him to be "a Southern Kennedy."[73]

Carter returned home on December 12 to tell his friends at an evening reception in Atlanta that he would enter all Democratic caucuses and primaries. His governorship, he said, had been scandal free; he had helped seventy-four national Democrats win reelection; and he would run an honest campaign and operate a just government. In lofty, if not too elegant, language, he promised: "Being President is not the most important thing in the world to me," and he continued that there "are a lot of things I would not do for an office or honor in this world." A chagrined friend who did not get his invitation to the reception in time to attend wrote Carter the next day: "may God and fortune attend your efforts."[74]

What the Georgia crowd remembered best, however, was not the body of the speech but how he began it. He walked into the Atlanta Civic Center to the cheers of three thousand people, and he said: "Hello! My name is Jimmy Carter, and I am running for President."[75]

NOTES

THE FOLLOWING NAMES are abbreviated in the notes: Jimmy Carter (JC), Rosalynn Smith Carter (RSC), Jimmy Carter Presidential Library and Museum (JCL), National Archives and Records Administration (NARA), National Park Service (NPS), Georgia Department of Archives and History (GDAH), Record Group (RG), Georgia State University Library (GSUL), Georgia Government Documentation Project (GGDP).

INTRODUCTION

1. Author interview with John Van Dyke Saunders and Julia Vissotto Saunders, Starkville, Mississippi, March 24, 2009; Harter, *Lost Colony of the Confederacy*, ix–x, 95, 125.

2. Author interview with Saunders and Saunders; *The Last Confederates* (PBS television documentary), produced by Edwin Cohen, Mississippi Public Broadcasting, 1984.

3. Quoted in Harter and Dawsey, "Reflections of a Confederado," in *Confederados*, 210.

4. Press Releases, April 7, 1972, RG 1-10-43, JC, box 3, GDAH; Phil Garner, "Jimmy Carter in Latin America," *Atlanta Journal and Constitution Magazine*, June 11, 1972; Dawsey and Dawsey, *Confederados*, 209–10; Harter, *Lost Colony*, xii–xiii, 94–95, 125.

5. Philip Alston, Sr., quoted in William V. Shannon, "The Other Carter in the Running," *New York Times*, September 15, 1976, sec. L, p. 45.

6. Cobb et al., "Jimmy Carter's Roots," 47, 48. The research for this article was done by distinguished genealogists and historians Noel Currer-Briggs in England, William Price in North Carolina, Kenneth H. Thomas, Jr., in Georgia, and others. See also Collins, *Search for Jimmy Carter*, 20–25; Shannon, "President in the Family," 8–9, 19–23; Brinkley, "Time for Reckoning," 1–16; Thomas, "Georgia Family Lines"; Thomas, *Rock House*, 2, 44–46, 49, 61–67; William Bailey Williford to JC, August 16, 1973, and JC to Bill Williford, August 21, 1973, Carter Family Papers, box 2, JCL: Warren Co. Tax Digest, 1849, 22–21, GDAH; and Hardin, *Wiley Carter Story*, 2.

7. 1860 Census (Schley and Sumter counties, Ga.), Slave Schedule, 22, 28, Agriculture Schedule, 13, notes, Kenneth H. Thomas, Jr., Private Collection, Atlanta.

8. Callaway, *Bloody Links*, 96–98, copy in Civil War Miscellany, microfilm 283, box 20, GDAH; *Americus Sumter Republican*, June 17, 1864. See also Williford, *Americus*, 76–88, Shannon, "President in the Family," 20, and JC, *Hour before Daylight*, 234.

9. Wiley Carter's Will, Sumter County Court of Ordinary, October 12, December 6, 1864, microfilm reels 135–37, GDAH.

10. *Weekly Sumter Republican*, November 21, 28, December 5, 1873; Sumter Co. Superior Court, Grand Jury Minutes, 1872–76, microfilm reels 134–148, GDAH; Sumter County

1872 Tax Digest, GDAH; Cobb, "Carter's Roots," 48; Shannon, "President in the Family," 21; Carter, *Beedie and Hot*, 167–68.

11. *History of Plains*, 4–5; *Americus Times-Recorder*, May 15, 1985, 5, 20; Cox, *History of Sumter County*, 24–25.

12. Author interview with Mary Grist Whitehead, Blakely, Georgia, October 17, 1994; *Early County in 1976*, 18: JC, *Hour before Daylight*, 237–38.

13. JC to Eunice Branyon, October 12, 1974, JC to J. Oscar Hunter, August 1974, JC to Uncle Buddy, October 25, 1974, all in Carter Family Papers, box 2, JCL; NARA interview with Betty Jennings Carter and Jeannette Carter Lowery, November 11, 1978, 1–3, 31–32, JCL; Bourne, *Jimmy Carter*, 10–11; *Greenwood (SC) Index Journal*, February 17, 2002; *Inside Erskine* (Erskine Alumni Association), spring 2002, 1, 4; and *Arlington (GA) Courier*, n.d., quoted in *Cuthbert (GA) Liberal-Enterprise*, September 11, 1903. For a family account that exonerates Billy from all guilt, see JC, *Hour before Daylight*, 239.

14. *State v. Will Taliaferro*, case no. 1187, Criminal Docket, October Term 1903, Early County Superior Court, 12, and Minutes of Early County Superior Court, 1903 and 1904, 140 and 211, both in Early County Courthouse, Blakely, Ga.; *Americus Times-Recorder*, September 4, 5, 11, 1903; *Early County (Blakely) News*, September 3, 10, October 15, 22, 1903; *Cuthbert (GA) Liberal-Enterprise*, September 11, 1903.

15. *Early County News*, October 29, November 12, 1903; Goolsby et al., *Randolph County*, 132, copy in Thomas Private Collection; Price, "Family Stories," 21, 26; Cobb, "Carter's Roots," 48; author interview with Howard Jones, July 22, 1996, Plains; NARA interview with Lowery and Carter, 35–36, JCL; NARA interview with Hugh A. Carter, Sr., October 21, 1978, JCL; *Americus Times-Recorder*, April 17, 1978; Bourne, *Carter*, 12. The house, known as the Slappey House, now belongs to the Methodist church.

16. Thomas, "Georgia Family Lines," 38–39.

17. Marion County Ordinary Court, Homestead Book A, 1866–1924, 350–52, microfilm drawer 141, box 78, GDAH; Bourne, *Carter*, 58.

18. Karl, *William Faulkner*, 816.

CHAPTER 1

1. JC Baby Book, VF, Carter, Jimmy, biog., JCL.

2. Charles Cobb, "Carter's Roots," 48.

3. Dennis McCafferty, "The Boys of Discipline," *Atlanta Constitution*, November 21, 1993.

4. James K. Mooney to JC, October 22, 23, 1973, JC to Mooney, October 19, 25, 1973, RG 1-1-5, box 28, JC, GDAH. Except for the 1910–11 yearbook, Riverside's records were destroyed in fires in 1917 and 1918.

5. Author interview with JC, October 12, 1994; NARA interview with Lillian Carter, September 26, 1978, JCL; Betty Glad, *Jimmy Carter in Search of the Great White House* (New York, 1980), 24.

6. Registration Card, June 5, 1917, and Discharge Papers, August 6, 1918, of J. E. Carter, both in VF, James E. Carter, Sr., JCL; NARA interview with Jeannette Carter Lowery and

Betty Jennings, November 11, 1978, 45, JCL; Official Service Records, Army, Navy, Marine Corps, 1917–19, Carter, James E.-1,342,448, copy in Special Collections, Lake Blackshear Regional Library, Americus, Georgia.

7. Shannon, "President," 21; Glad, *Carter*, 25; Cobb, "Carter's Roots," 49; Cox, *Sumter County*, 24–30; NARA interview with Oliver C. Smith, November 10, 1978, 8–9, 19, JCL; NARA interview with Lillian Carter, September 26, 1978, JCL.

8. NPS interview with Gloria Carter Spann, December 7, 1988, 78–79, JCL; Henry Allen, "Just Plains Folk," *Washington Post/Potomac,* August 15, 1976, 28; Glad, *Carter,* 25; Lillian Carter as told to Beth Tartan and Rudy Hayes, *Miss Lillian and Friends: The Plains, Georgia, Family Philosophy and Recipe Book* (New York, 1977), 23–24; James Neyland, "The Carter Family Scrapbook," *Good Housekeeping,* July 1977, 100; Orde Coombs, "The Hand That Rocked Carter's Cradle," *New York Magazine,* June 14, 1976, 42. See also JC, *Hour before Daylight,* 241–42.

9. Allen, "Just Plains Folk," 28; JC, *Why Not the Best?* (Nashville, 1975), 85–86; Tartan and Hayes, *Miss Lillian,* 23–24.

10. NARA interview with Lillian Carter, September 26, 1978, JCL; NARA interview with Emily Gordon Dolvin, June 28, 1979, 5–8, JCL; Bruce Mazlish and Edwin Diamond, *Jimmy Carter: An Interpretive Biography* (New York, 1979), 43; Woodward, *Tom Watson,* 245–46, 303–5, 357–58, 398–99; and JC, *Hour before Daylight,* 244–47.

11. NARA interview with Lillian Carter, September 26, 1978, JCL; NARA interview with Mary Elizabeth Braunstein, November 14, 1979, 3, JCL; JC, *Hour before Daylight,* 241–42.

12. William Lusk Crawford, Sr., *Ancestors and Friends: (A History and Genealogy)* (Dallas, 1978), 342–46; Thomas, "Georgia Family Lines," 41, 46; Hugh Carter, *Beedie and Hot,* 197; Glad, *Carter,* 26–27; JC, *Best,* 77; J. J. Gordy to Tom Watson, n.d., *Watson's Magazine* 4, no. 2 (April 1906): 269; *Columbus (GA) Ledger-Enquirer,* January 17, 1948, 2; Allen, "Just Plains Folk," 28.

13. NARA interview with Lillian Carter, September 26, 1978, JCL; NARA interview with Donnell Carter, November 3, 1979, 16, 17, JCL; NPS interview with Jimmy and Rosalynn Carter, May 12, 1988, 340–42, JCL; Bourne, *Carter,* 21; JC, *Hour before Daylight,* 119; JC, *Remarkable Mother,* 21–23.

14. NARA interview with Lillian Carter, September 26, 1978, JCL; Paul H. Elowitz, "Three Days in Plains," *Journal of Psychohistory* 5 (fall 1977), 196; Simmons, *Rosalynn Carter,* 23; NPS interview with Gloria Carter Spann, December 8, 1988, 85–86, JCL.

15. NARA interview with Lillian Carter, September 26, 1978, 21, JCL; "Sister Ruth," *Newsweek,* July 17, 1978, 61–62; Ruth Carter Stapleton, *The Gift of Inner Healing* (Waco, TX, 1976), 15–17; JC, *Remarkable Mother,* 29.

16. NPS interview with JC, May 11, 1988, 200, JCL.

17. NPS interview with Gloria Spann, December 8, 1988, 29, JCL; NPS interview with Ruth Jackson, December 20, 1985, 10, JCL.

18. Lillian Carter, "The Measles Christmas," *Plains Echoes* 4, no. 4 (December 1996): 1–2.

19. Angelo, *First Mothers,* 263, 270.

20. NARA interview with Lillian Carter, September 26, 1978, JCL; *Ideal Magazine,* November 1976, 18–19; John Osborne, "Carter Talk," *New Republic,* September 25, 1976, 17; Eleanor Randolph, "The Carter Complex," *Esquire,* November 1977, 166–67; Elowitz, "Three Days," 176–77, 185–86, 189, 198; Hugh Carter, *Beedie and Hot,* 27, 195–208; Mazlish and Diamond, *Carter* (New York, 1979), 41–56; Carter, *Best,* 17–18; Glad, *Carter,* 32–33; Allen, "Just Plains Folk," 13.

21. NPS interview with JC, May 11, 1988, 207, JCL.

22. NPS interview with JC and RSC, December 10, 1988, JCL; JC, *Best,* 13; JC, *Hour before Daylight,* 33, 119.

23. NPS interview with Gloria Spann, December 7, 1988, 5–11, JCL; JC, *Hour before Daylight,* 29–31.

24. Carter, *First Lady,* 26; Glad, *Carter,* 34; Elowitz, "Three Days," 177, 185. JC, "Video," Plains Depot, July 22, 1996; NARA interview with Don Carter, November 3, 1979, 25, JCL.

25. Mazlish and Diamond, *Carter,* 27–30; Collins, *Search for Jimmy Carter,* 38; Lisa Battle, "Carter's Sister Remembers Their Father," *Columbus (GA) Ledger-Enquirer,* January 24, 1977.

26. Author interview with JC, October 12, 1994; Hugh Carter, *Beedie and Hot,* 44; Beth Tartan and Rudy Hayes, *Miss Lillian and Friends* (New York, 1977), 18.

27. NPS interview with JC, May 11, 1988, 195–96, JCL.

28. Ibid., 203.

29. JC, *Sharing Good Times* (New York, 2004), 3, *An Outdoor Journal: Adventures and Reflections* (New York, 1988), 19–20, 43, and *An Hour Before Daylight: Memories of a Rural Boyhood* (New York, 2001), 122.

30. JC, *Best,* 14–15; Glad, *Carter,* 31; Elowitz, "Three Days," 192; Mazlish and Diamond, *Carter,* 33–40; NARA interview with Donnell E. Carter, November 3, 1979, 25; JC, *Hour before Daylight,* 122, 224–25.

31. JC, *Remarkable Mother,* 23, 25–26.

32. *Americus Times-Recorder,* April 25, 1933; Glad, *Carter,* 30; Mazlish and Diamond, *Carter,* 30–33; Anderson, *Wild Man;* JC, *Hour before Daylight,* 67–68.

33. Glad, *Carter,* 86, 57.

34. NARA interview with Lillian Carter, September 26, 1978, JCL; Mazlish and Diamond, *Carter,* 27–40, 79–81, 89; Glad, *Carter,* 30; JC, *Best,* 22, 27; NARA interview with Donnell E. Carter, November 3, 1979, 9, 14, 15, 23, JCL; NARA interview with Carter and Lowery, November 11, 1978, 27, JCL; NARA interview with Hugh Carter, Sr., October 21, 1978, 8, 18–19, JCL.

35. NARA interview with Lillian Carter, September 26, 1978, 20, JCL; "My Son, the President," *US News and World Report,* March 7, 1977, 53.

36. JC, "I Wanted to Share My Father's World," *Reckoning,* 100.

37. Author interview with JC, October 12, 1994. See also Program for Jimmy Carter Boyhood Farm, Grand Opening Ceremony, Jimmy Carter National Historic Site, Friday, November 17, 2000, and *Atlanta Journal-Constitution,* November 12, 2000, sec. M.

38. JC, *Hour before Daylight,* 35–42, 51, 183–88.

39. David Dawson, "Comparisons of *An Hour before Daylight* by Carter and *Revolt Among the Sharecroppers* by [Howard] Kester, typescript, April 25, 2005, private collection.

40. NPS interview with JC, May 11, 1988, 3–5, 166–69, 175, 224, JCL.

41. Ibid., 3–6, 166, 172, 187, 216, 231. See also *An Hour before Daylight,* and "The Jimmy Carter Boyhood Farm," special section of the *Americus Times-Recorder,* November 17, 2000.

42. William Patrick O'Brien, *Special History Study: Jimmy Carter National Historic Site and Preservation District, Georgia* (N. p., 1991), 10.

43. JC, *An Outdoor Journal* (New York, 1988), 43–44, and *Hour before Daylight,* 101–3.

44. JC, *Reckoning,* 93–94; Hugh Carter, *Beedie and Hot,* 28; Simmons, *Rosalynn Carter,* 23; NPS interview with JC, May 11, 1988, 212, JCL; NPS interview with Gloria Carter Spann, December 7, 1988, 10, 32, 85, JCL.

45. NARA interview with Lillian Carter, September 26, 1978, 30, JCL.

46. Elovitz, "Three Days," 189–90, 194–95; NPS interview with Gloria Carter Spann, December 8, 1988, 21, JCL.

47. *Atlanta Constitution,* July 17, 1976.

48. NARA interview with Rachel Clark, November 9, 1978, 1, 2, 4–7, 19–3, 25, JCL.

49. JC, *Reckoning,* vii, 3–7; and *Hour before Daylight,* 39–41.

50. NARA interview with Lillian Carter, September 26, 1978, 30–31, JCL.

51. Mark Rockwell, "Archery Community Rich in History," in *The Jimmy Carter Boyhood Farm,* special dedication sec., *Americus Times-Recorder,* November 17, 2000. See also *Atlanta Constitution,* June 12, 1971, and JC, *Hour before Daylight,* 21.

52. JC, *Best,* 33–35; NARA interview with Lillian Carter, September 26, 1978, 8, JCL; NARA interview with Rachel Clark, November 9, 1978, 13–16, JCL.

53. JC, *Best,* 14, 34; Elovitz, "Three Days," 193–94; NARA interview with Rachel Clark, November 9, 1978, 16–17, JCL; JC, *Hour before Daylight,* 74, 91, 95; Hutchinson, *People of Plains,* 90–93.

54. JC, *Best,* 36–37; NARA interview with Lillian Carter, September 26, 1978, 31–32, JCL; JC, *Hour before Daylight,* 32–33.

55. Joyce Carol Oates, "The Avenger," review of David Margolick, *Beyond Glory: Joe Louis vs. Max Schmeling, and a World on the Brink* (New York, 2005), *New York Times Book Review,* October 2, 2005, 10–11.

56. JC, *Outdoor Journal,* 22–23.

57. Ibid.

58. JC, *Outdoor Journal,* 30–35.

59. JC, *Outdoor Journal,* 38–43.

60. JC, *Best,* 34; Glad, *Carter,* 28; Hugh Carter, *Beedie and Hot,* 40.

61. JC, *Best,* 24–25; Hugh Carter, *Beedie and Hot,* 35–37; Glad, *Carter,* 37; Haugabook, *Remembering Plains,* 22–27.

62. Author interview with JC, October 12, 1994; NARA interview with Donnell E. Carter, November 3, 1979, 30–41, JCL; NARA interview with Hugh Carter, Sr., October 21, 1978, 23, 24, 27, JCL.

63. Author interview with JC, October 12, 1994; JC, *Hour before Daylight,* 143, 245, 251.

64. Tom to "Jimmy and All," July 20, 1932, Tom Gordy File, JCL; see also JC, *Hour before Daylight,* 189, and *Best,* 41.

65. Tom to "Jimmie," February 5, 1933, Tom Gordy File, JCL.

66. Tom to Jimmy, March 13, 1933, Tom Gordy File, JCL.

67. Tom to "Jimmie," May 20, 1933, Tom Gordy File, JCL.

68. JC, *Remarkable Mother,* 31–35.

69. JC, *Hour before Daylight,* 152; for a slightly different account, see JC, *Best,* 25.

70. JC, *Best,* 35; NARA interview with Rachel Clark, November 9, 1978, 16, JCL.

71. JC, *Best,* 15–16. See also *Americus Times-Recorder,* special ed., November 17, 2000.

72. NPS interview with Gloria Carter Spann, January 7, 1988, 58, JCL; NPS interview with JC, May 11, 1988, 172, 207, JCL.

73. NPS interview with JC, May 11, 1988, 208–9, JCL.

74. JC, handwritten essay, "Cleanliness," VF, JC, biog., JCL.

75. NARA interview with Rachel Clark, November 9, 1978, 26, JCL.

CHAPTER 2

1. NARA interview with Allie Smith, November 10, 1978, 10–17, 23–25, 41, 47, 49, 50, JCL.

2. Wilburn Edgar Smith Registration Card, VF, Carter, Jimmy, Addresses, Governor (2), JCL; author interview with "Miss Allie" Smith, October 12, 1994, Plains.

3. Thomas, "Georgia Family Lines," 38, 40; *Americus Times-Recorder,* October 22, 1940; Kandy Stroud, "Growing Up with Rosalynn," *Good Housekeeping,* January 1977, 174; NARA interview with Oliver C. Smith, November 10, 1978, 4–5, JCL; NARA interview with Elder Fulford Smith, December 22, 1978, 2–4, JCL.

4. RSC Application for Membership in Daughters of the American Revolution, November 7, 1972, copy in Thomas private collection.

5. JC to Author, March 30, 1995.

6. Eighth U.S. Census, 1860, Sumter County, Georgia, Slave and Population Schedules, copies in Thomas Private Collection; Thomas, "Georgia Family Lines," 38; NARA interview with Oliver C. Smith, November 10, 1978, 1–2, JCL.

7. *Americus Times-Recorder,* August 24, 1927 (name misspelled "Rosalind"); author interview with Rosalynn Carter, October 12, 1994.

8. NARA interview with Oliver C. Smith, November 10, 1978, 4–5, JCL; NARA interview with Elder F. Smith, December 22, 1978, 4, 12, 15, 30, JCL.

9. NARA interview with Elder F. Smith, December 22, 1978, 42; RSC, *First Lady,* 13.

10. NARA interview with Oliver C. Smith, November 10, 1978, 11, JCL.

11. NARA interview with Elder F. Smith, December 22, 1978, 7–9, JCL; NPS interview with RSC, May 11, 1988, 145, JCL.

12. NARA interview with Oliver C. Smith, November 10, 1978, 5–7, JCL; NARA interview with Elder F. Smith, December 22, 1978, 10–11, JCL.

13. NARA interview with Oliver C. Smith, November 10, 1978, 5, 9, JCL; NARA interview with Elder F. Smith, December 22, 1977, 3, JCL; RSC, *First Lady*, 11, 14.

14. NARA interview with Allie Smith, November 10, 1978, 42, 48, 49, JCL; December 19, 1979, 1, JCL; NARA interview with Murray Lee Smith, October 21, 1978, 6, JCL; NARA interview with Jerrold Smith, June 23, 1979, 21, JCL.

15. RSC, *First Lady*, 12–14; Bourne, *Carter,* 57–58.

16. NARA interview with W. Jerrold Smith, June 23, 1979, 17, 56, JCL; NARA interview with Murray Lee Smith, October 21, 1978, 13, JCL; RSC, *First Lady*, 13–14. See also Scott Kaufman, *Rosalynn Carter,* 2–3.

17. RSC, *First Lady,* 11–12; NARA interview with Allie Smith, November 10, 1978, 24, 34–35, 40–41, JCL; NPS interview with RSC, May 11, 1988, 154, JCL.

18. Author interview with RSC and JC, October 12, 1994.

19. NARA interview with Jerrold Smith, June 23, 1979, 35, JCL; NARA interview with Allethea Smith Wall, October 21, 1978, 4–5, JCL.

20. NPS interview with RSC, May 11, 1988, 11–12; NARA interview with Allie Smith, November 10, 1978, 51–54, JCL; Miss Allie and Jerry quotations in Eric Brown and Joe West, "The Childhood of Rosalynn Carter," *National Enquirer,* January 11, 1977, 10.

21. RSC, *First Lady,* 12; NARA interview with Allie Smith, November 10, 1978, 51–54, JCL; December 19, 1979, 1–2, JCL.

22. RSC, *First Lady,* 9–10; Bourne, *Carter,* 56–57; Charlotte Curtis, "What Kind of First Lady Will She Be?" *McCall's,* January 1977, 26; author interview with RSC, October 12, 1994.

23. NARA interview with Allie Smith, November 10, 1978, 43, 46; NARA interview with Jerrold Smith, June 23, 1979, 2–5, JCL; Bourne, *Carter,* 58.

24. NARA interview with Allethea Smith Wall, October 21, 1978, 6–7, JCL.

25. NPS interview with RSC, May 11, 1988, 116–17, JCL; NARA interview with Murray A. Smith, October 21, 1978, 2–3; JCL.

26. RSC, *First Lady,* 10–11; Bourne, *Carter,* 57; NARA interview with Allie Smith, December 19, 1979, 7–8, JCL; NARA interview with Murray Smith, October 21, 1978, 13–15, JCL; author interview with RSC and JC, October 12, 1994.

27. NPS interview with RSC, May 11, 1988, 16, 120–21, JCL; RSC, *First Lady,* 10.

28. RSC, with Susan K. Golant, *Helping Yourself Help Others,* 15–18; RSC, *First Lady,* 16–18. See also NPS interview with RSC, May 11, 1988, 14, 154; NARA interview with Allie Smith, December 19, 1979, 12; both in JCL.

29. NPS interview with RSC, May 11, 1988, 14–15, JCL.

30. RSC, *First Lady,* 18; NARA interview with Murray Smith, October 21, 1978, 2–3, JCL; NARA interview with Jerrold Smith, June 23, 1979, 23–25, JCL; NARA interview with Allie Smith, December 19, 1979, 21–24, JCL; NARA interview with Elder Smith, December 22, 1978, 11–2, JCL; Howard Norton, *Rosalynn,* 15–27.

CHAPTER 3

1. Carolyn Sherwin Bailey, *What to Do for Uncle Sam: A First Book of Citizenship* (Chicago, 1918), 204, copy in Plains High School Museum, Plains; see also Bourne, *Carter,* 33.

2. Millard Simmons, "Mr. Y. T. Stood Tall," *Plains Echoes* 4, no. 2 (1996), 1; JC to Monica Rush, September 20, 1974, RG 1-1-5, JC, box 2, GDAH; NPS interview with JC, May 11, 1988, 28, 58, JCL; author interview with Annette Wise, August 8, 2005.

3. NPS interview with RSC and JC, May 11, 1988, 55, JCL.

4. Haugabook, *Remembering Plains,* 6–37.

5. Bourne, *Carter,* 33–34.

6. Hugh Carter, *Beedie and Hot,* 48–51; Bourne, *Carter,* 33.

7. NPS interview with Eleanor Forrest, December 18, 1985, 8–9, 18–19, JCL; Hugh Carter, *Beedie and Hot,* 51.

8. Glad, *Carter,* 45.

9. NPS interview with JC, May 11, 1988, 70–77, JCL; Hugh Carter, *Beedie and Hot,* 51; "Report of Jimmy Carter, 1935–36," VF, JC, biog., JCL; Bourne, *Carter,* 34; JC, *Hour before Daylight,* 213–14.

10. Bourne, *Carter,* 34–37.

11. Plains Historical Preservation Trust, Inc., comp., *History of Plains, Georgia* (Fernandina Beach, Fl., 2003), 95, 345–54; NPS interview with Beth Walters, December 17, 1985, 3, JCL.

12. NPS interview with RSC and JC, May 11, 1988, 17–19, JCL; JC, *Best,* 30–32; Bourne, *Carter,* 39–41; JC, address at Plains High School, October 1, 1996, Grand Opening of Plains High School as the Jimmy Carter Welcome Center. See also JC, *Hour before Daylight,* 98, 208–9, and *Plains Echoes* 8, no. 4 (2000): 1, and 9, no. 1 (2001): 1.

13. NPS interview with JC, May 11, 1988, 20, 93; JCL.

14. Glad, *Carter,* 45–46.

15. Cindy Williams, "Life on the Farm near Plains," *Plains Echoes* 6, no. 2 (1998): 1; Morris, *Jimmy Carter,* 29.

16. Bourne, *Carter,* 43; Hugh Carter, *Beedie and Hot,* 60–62; Glad, *Carter,* 45.

17. JC, *Hour before Daylight,* 217.

18. NPS interview with JC, May 11, 1988, 28–30, JCL; Glad, *Carter,* 46; Bourne, *Carter,* 43.

19. NPS interview with Eleanor Forrest, December 18, 1985, 17–18, JCL; NPS interview with RSC, May 11, 1988, 74, JCL; Simmons, *Rosalynn Carter,* 24–25.

20. *Plains Echoes* 4, no. 4 (1996): 4.

21. NPS interview with RSC, May 11, 1988, 17–20, 88, JCL.

22. S. Kaufman, *Rosalynn Carter,* 3–4.

23. "Rosalynn Smith Carter, 1927–1940," quoting Allie Smith, VF, Carter, Jimmy, Addresses, Governor (2), JCL; NPS interview with Lauren Blanton, December 21, 1985, 6, JCL.

24. NARA interview with Murray Smith, October 21, 1978, 9; NARA interview with Jerrold Smith, June 23, 1979, 16, 38; NPS interview with RSC, May 11, 1988, 23, all in JCL.

25. NPS interview with RSC, May 11, 1988, 13, 81, 94–99, JCL; Haugabook, *Remembering Plains*, 20, 32–39; RSC, *First Lady*, 21; *Americus Times-Recorder*, December 9, 1942, April 10, 1944.

26. Rosalynn Smith, notes for valedictory address, Plains High School, 1944, Carter Family Papers, JCL.

27. NPS interview with RSC, May 11, 1988, 23, JCL. Rosalynn Smith, notes for valedictory address, JCL.

28. JC, *Best*, 41–42; Bourne, *Carter*, 44, 47; *Americus Times-Recorder*, February 4, 5, July 7, 1942.

29. Mary Bishop Gray, *Through the Years*, 23, 24, 26; Georgia Southwestern Transcript, VF, Carter, J., Educational Records, JCL; Bourne, *Carter*, 46.

30. JC, *Best*, 42; Glad, *Carter*, 46–48; *Americus Times-Recorder*, April 1, 1942; Hugh Carter, *Beedie and Hot*, 53, 60, 65; Bourne, *Carter*, 46, 52.

31. *Americus Times-Recorder*, May 25, 1942; Tom Gordy Diary, 1941–45, Emily Gordon Dolvin File, box 1, JCL; JC, *Best*, 41–42; Bourne, *Carter*, 46–47; JC to Tommy Irvin, July 11, 1971, Carter Family Papers, box 2, JCL.

CHAPTER 4

1. *Americus Times-Recorder*, July 7, 1942; JC, *Best*, 42; Bourne, *Carter*, 47; JC, Hour *before Daylight*, 256.

2. *Americus Times-Recorder*, November 4, 6, 30, December 23, 1942 February 17, 1979; *Georgia Tech Whistle* 5, no. 6, February 20, 1979, 2–3.

3. Georgia Tech Transcript, VF, Carter, J., Educational Records, JCL; Bourne, *Carter*, 47; author interview with O. M. Harrelson, September 12, 1994.

4. Consent and Declaration of Parent, [September 1942], Naval Records, VF, Carter, J., Navy, JCL; NARA interview with Lillian Carter, September 26, 1978, 32–33, JCL.

5. JC, Annapolis Diary, 26, 27, 28–30, 1943, VF, Carter, J., Naval Career, JCL; Mazlish and Diamond, *Carter*, 96.

6. WPA Writers' Program, *Guide to the United States Naval Academy*, 29–30, 112; *Americus Times-Recorder*, June 28, 30, 1943.

7. JC to "Dear Folks, Thursday Night" [n.d.], VF, Carter, J., Naval Career, JCL; Mazlish and Diamond, *Carter*, 99.

8. JC, Diary, June 28–30, July 1–7, 31, 1943, JCL; author interview with Stansfield Turner, April 6, 1992.

9. JC, Diary, August 13, 21, 25, September 20, November 8, 15–30, November 30–December 30, 1943, JCL; *Americus Times-Recorder*, November 22, 1943.

10. JC, Diary, July 7–24, September 1, 1943, May 25, 1944, JCL.

11. JC, Diary, May 18, 25, 1944, JCL; *Guide to the United States Naval Academy*, 153; Mazlish and Diamond, *Carter*, 96–99.

12. JC, Diary, August 15, September 11, October 9, 16, 31, 1943, JCL.

13. JC, Diary, August 22, October 31, 1943, JCL.

14. JC, Diary, July 7–24, 26, 29, August 1, 4, 10, 26, September 13, October 22, 1943, May 23, 1944, JCL; Medical History, February 6, 1944, and March 5, 1945, VF, Carter, J., Navy Career, JCL.

15. NPS interview with JC, May 11, 1988, 32, JCL; JC, Diary, July 7–24, August 25, 1943; author interview with Rear Admiral James R. Stark, U.S. Navy (ret.), March 31, 2008.

16. Author interview with Stansfield Turner, April 6, 1992.

17. JC, Diary, September 27, October 22, 1943, January 2, February 6, April 17, May 3, 1944, JCL; Carter, *Best,* 42–43; Bourne, *Carter,* 49–51: Morris, *Carter,* 95.

18. JC, Diary, October 1, 1943, May 3, 1944, JCL.

19. JC to Joe Marzluff, August 13, 1976, Susan Clough File, box 15, JCL; author interview with JC, October 12, 1994; JC, *Best,* 45, 49.

20. Preston, *Battleships,* 244.

21. JC, *Best,* 45–47; Bourne, *Carter,* 51.

22. *Guide to the United States Naval Academy,* 31, 38, 41, 43.

23. *Americus Times-Recorder,* February 13, 26, 1945, January 23, 1946.

24. Sissy Dolvin, unpublished memoir, January 1, 1992, typescript, 192, Emily Gordon Dolvin File, box 1, JCL.

25. Bourne, *Carter,* 51; see also Albert H. Rusher to JC, January 31, April 15, 1975, JC to Sidney McKnight, February 17, 1975, all in Clough File, box 26, JCL.

26. For a good account of Brown's life at Annapolis, see Gelfand, *Sea Change,* 52–55.

27. Wesley Brown to JC, October 19, 1976, Clough File, box 4, JCL; Col. Palmer Hamilton to JC, October 11, 1976, JC to Palmer Hamilton, October 19, 1976, Clough File, box 10, JCL.

28. *All Things Considered,* NPR, June 25, 2005, transcript, 4; Schneller, Jr., *Breaking the Color Barrier,* ix, 217–20.

29. Carter, *Best,* 44; Glad, *Carter,* 50–53.

30. Bourne, *Carter,* 49–50.

31. Mazlish and Diamond, *Carter,* 100.

32. JC, *Best,* 47; JC, Letter to the Opening of the Carter Library's World War II Exhibit, January 20, 1994, VF, Carter, J., Navy Career, JCL; *Americus Times-Recorder,* April 13, 20, 1945; *Atlanta Journal/Constitution,* January 27, 1994.

33. Author interview with RSC, October 12, 1994; NARA interview with Jerrold Smith, June 23, 1979, 39, JCL; RSC, *First Lady,* 22.

CHAPTER 5

1. JC, "Georgia Lions Club Speech," June 8, 1971, RG 1-1-45, JC, box 11, p. 2, GDAH; Mrs. Allie Smith, "Rosalynn Smith Carter," VF, RSC, JCL; NPS interview with JC and RSC, December 10, 1988, 304, JCL.

2. Sheehy, "Ladies and Gentlemen," 54.

3. Author interview with JC and RSC, October 12, 1994; JC, *Best,* 62; Mazlish and Diamond, *Carter,* 104–5; RSC, *First Lady,* 22–24; NPS interview with Allie Smith, December 19, 1985, 8–9, JCL.

4. Author interview with JC, October 12, 1994.

5. RSC, *First Lady,* 25. Five letters of JC to a Jacquelyn Reid, fall 1945, privately owned by a manuscript dealer, are known to exist but have not been viewed by the author.

6. RSC, *First Lady,* 25; NARA interview with Jerrold W. Smith, June 23, 1979, 39, JCL.

7. RSC, *First Lady,* 25–26; JC, *Best,* 62.

8. Anne Briscoe Pye and Nancy Shea, *The Navy Wife,* rev. ed. (New York, 1945), 3, 4, 10, 16, 21, 24, 26, 27, 77, 131, 133, 143, 134, 147, 85; copy with JC annotations in VF, Carter, J., Navy Career, JCL.

9. NARA interview with Jerrold W. Smith, June 23, 1979, 39, JCL.

10. RSC, *First Lady,* 26; Mazlish and Diamond, *Carter,* 107; NARA interview with Jerrold Smith, June 23, 1979, 39–41, JCL; *Americus Times-Recorder,* September 16, 1946; Angelo, *First Mothers,* 271.

11. Commander of United States Navy to Ensign James E. Carter, Jr., June 5, 1946; Greetings, Harry S. Truman, President of the United States of America, to All Who Shall See These Presents, June 5, 1946; Acceptance and Oath of Office by James Earl Carter, Jr., Ensign, June 5, 1946, all in VF, Carter, J., Navy Records, JCL.

12. Glad, *Carter,* 53–54; author interview with Statefield Turner, April 6, 1992.

13. *Americus Times-Recorder,* July 8, 1946; RSC speech to Carter Museum Docents, May 8, 1996.

14. Bourne, *Carter,* 55; *Americus Times-Recorder,* July 16, 1946; RSC, *First Lady,* 27; Charlotte Curtis, "What Kind of First Lady Will She Be?" *McCall's,* January 1977, 26.

15. *New York Daily News,* March 17, 2001, 21.

16. Memorandum, Chief of Naval Personnel to James Earl Carter, Jr., et al., May 13, 1946, VF, Carter, J., Navy Records, JCL; *Americus Times-Recorder,* June 15, July 12, 1946.

17. Gibbons, *Battleships,* 190–91; NPS interview with JC, May 11, 1988, 33, JCL; Officer Form, James E. Carter, ENS, to Officer in Charge, August 31, 1946, VF, Carter, J., Navy Records, JCL.

18. Author interview with RSC, October 12, 1994; RSC, *First Lady,* 28–29.

19. NARA interview with Allie Smith, December 19, 1979, 29–30, JCL.

20. NPS interview with JC, May 11, 1988, 33–34, JCL. Memorandum, Ensign James E. Carter, Jr., to Chief of Naval Personnel, June 3, 1947; Memorandum, Chief of Naval Personnel to ENS James E. Carter, Jr., June 10, 1947, both in VF, Carter, J., Navy Records, JCL.

21. Morris, *Carter,* 95, 103; Glad, *Carter,* 58–59; Bourne, *Carter,* 64; Mazlish and Diamond, *Carter,* 102.

22. Preston, *Battleships,* 250.

23. Memorandum, Chief of Naval Personnel to JC, April 28, 1948, VF, Carter, J., Navy Career, JCL; author interview with JC, October 12, 1994; RSC, *First Lady,* 29; JC, *Best,* 49, 63.

24. NPS interview with JC, May 11, 1988, 144; RSC, *First Lady,* 29–30; Bourne, *Carter,* 65.

25. RSC, *First Lady,* 30; author interview with JC and RSC, October 12, 1994; Stapleton, *Billy,* 93.

26. Report on Fitness of Officers, December 16, 1948, and Memorandum, Chief of Naval Personnel to ENS James E. Carter, December 1, 1948, both in VF, Carter, J., Navy Records, JCL.

27. *Americus Times-Recorder,* December 20, 1948; RSC, *First Lady,* 30.

28. *Americus Times-Recorder,* January 19, 1949; RSC, *First Lady,* 30–31; JC, *Best,* 49–51.

29. Memorandum, Chief of Naval Personnel to Navy Central Disbursing Office, May 10, 1949; Memorandum, Commander of Submarine Force, U.S. Pacific Fleet to Chief of Naval Personnel, April 19, 1949, all in VF, Carter, J., Navy Career, JCL.

30. RSC, *First Lady,* 31; Glad, *Carter,* 61.

31. Report of Commanding Officer R. C. Smallwood, Jr., February 1, 1951, VF, Carter, J., Navy Records, JCL.

32. Memorandum, Commanding Officer to Ensign James E. Carter, Jr., May 19, 1949; Greetings, The President of the United States of America to All Who Shall See these Presents, June 5, 1949; and Memo, James Earl Carter, Jr., Lieutenant (jg) to Secretary of the Navy, June 5, 1949; all in VF, Carter, J., Navy Records, JCL.

33. Reports of Commanding Officer J. B. Williams, Jr., March 1 and July 10, 1950, VF, Carter, J., Navy Records, JCL.

34. Goldman, "Sizing Up Carter" (quotations), and Bourne, *Carter,* 67.

35. RSC, *First Lady,* 33; Glad, *Carter,* 61; NARA interview with Lillian Carter, September 26, 1978, 25, JCL.

36. JC, *Reckoning,* 29–31; see also Bourne, *Carter,* 88.

37. Report of Commanding Officer R. C. Smallwood, Jr., February 1, 1951, VF, Carter, J., Navy Records, JCL; JC, *Best,* 52.

38. RSC, *First Lady,* 33–34.

39. Program, Commissioning Ceremonies U.S.S. *K-1,* November 10, 1951, and Joan Poro, "Four Former Crewmen on *K-1* Recall Carter—They Liked Him," unidentified newspaper clipping, September 3, 1976, both in VF, Carter, J., Navy Records, JCL. See also Goldman, "Sizing Up Carter."

40. JC, *Best,* 52–53; Bourne, *Carter,* 70; Mazlish and Diamond, *Carter,* 112–15; Goldman, "Sizing Up Carter."

41. Report on the Fitness of Officers, March 1, 1952; Greetings, The President of the United States to All Who Shall See These Presents, April 9, 1958; Memorandum, Commanding Officer F. A. Andrews to Chief of Naval Personnel, August 16, 1952; Report on the Fitness of Officers, by Commander F. A. Andrews, September 1, and October 16, 1952, all in VF, Carter, J., Navy Records, JCL.

42. Transcript of JC interview, "The Dawn's Early Light, 1988," 1, Ralph McGill Papers, box 109, Manusript, Archives, and Rare Book Library (MARBL), in Robert W. Woodruff Library, Emory University, Atlanta; see also Bourne, *Carter,* 71; JC, *Best,* 37; Morris, *Carter,* 73–74.

43. JC, *Best,* 55.

44. Polmar and Allen, *Rickover,* 269.

45. Author interview with Dan Edwards, April 13, 1992.

46. JC, *Best,* 59; see also Rockwell, *Rickover,* 265.

47. Polmar and Allen, *Rickover,* 10–11; Rockwell, *Rickover,* 350; see also Glad, *Carter,* 63–65, Morris, *Carter,* 110–11, and Bourne, *Carter,* 72–74.

48. Polmar and Allen, *Rickover,* 11, 23, 27–40, 50–60, 187–205; "The Man in Tempo 3," *Time,* January 11, 1954, 36–39.

49. Voucher for Reimbursement for Expenses Incident to Dependents Travel, December 9, 1952, VF, Carter, J., Navy Records, JCL; JC, *Best,* 55; RSC, *First Lady,* 35.

50. JC, *Best,* 55–56.

51. JC, *Best,* 56; Paul Harvey, "The Rest of the Story: Meltdown," typescript, VF, Carter, J., Navy Career, JCL; Rockwell, *Rickover,* 350.

52. H. G. Rickover, Report on the Fitness of Officers, April 24, 1953, VF, Carter, J., Navy Records, JCL.

53. NPS interview with JC, May 11, 1988, 34–37, JCL. According to official Navy records, Rickover was born in 1900 and retired in 1982, but his biographers prove that he was born in 1898.

54. Glad, *Carter,* 65–66; Morris, *Carter,* 113; Bourne, *Carter,* 75.

CHAPTER 6

1. *Americus Times-Recorder,* June 21, January 19, 1946, February 12, 1949; Stapleton, *Billy,* 50–51; Bourne, *Carter,* 78; Morris, *Carter,* 29.

2. JC, "Dawn's Early Light," 2, Ralph McGill Papers, MARBL, Robert W. Woodruff Library, Emory University, Atlanta.

3. Glad, *Carter,* 30, 77; Bourne, *Carter,* 35–36, 78; Morris, *Carter,* 30–32; *Columbus (GA) Ledger-Enquirer,* January 24, 1977; Stapleton, *Billy,* 54–55: JC, *Best,* 60.

4. *Americus Times-Recorder,* March 8, 1948.

5. Morris, *Carter,* 32–33.

6. Biographical Questionnaire, BQ3, Sumter County, Statistical Register, Carter, James Earl, Sr., with attached brochure marking dedication of James Earl Carter Library, Georgia Southwestern College, 1972, GDAH; Cox, *Sumter County,* 29–30.

7. Morris, *Carter,* 33–35; Anderson, *Talmadge,* 62–81, 187–92, 197, 226, 236–38; Coleman, *Georgia,* 311–15, 378–79, 389–90; JC, *Turning Point,* 7–9.

8. Coleman, *Georgia,* 389–93; Bourne, *Carter,* 103–4; Arnall, *Shore,* 43–61.

9. Coleman, *Georgia,* 295, 389.

10. James Frank Meyers, Jr., Biographical Questionnaire, GDAH.

11. Stapleton, *Billy,* 51; Bourne, *Carter,* 85, 105; Glad, *Carter,* 87; Morris, *Carter,* 35; Talmadge, *Talmadge,* 310; *Americus Times-Recorder,* July 22, 1953.

12. *Americus Times-Recorder,* February 28, 1953.

13. NARA interview with Lillian Carter, September 26, 1978, 36, JCL; see also Bourne, *Carter,* 86–87.

14. *Americus Times-Recorder,* November 21, 1952; Stapleton, *Billy,* 53–54; Stapleton, *Inner Healing,* 9–22.

15. Mazlish and Diamond, *Carter,* 123; Bourne, *Carter,* 77.

286 | Notes to Pages 74–79

16. Mazlish and Diamond, *Carter,* 12–21.

17. Wooten, *Dasher,* 201–4.

18. Mazlish and Diamond, *Carter,* 122; JC, *Best,* 60; JC, *Reckoning,* 103–4.

19. *Americus Times-Recorder,* July 22, 1953; *Starkville (MS) Daily News,* August 28, 1994. Because of a succession of marriages, Annie Mae's last name changed and was not Clark in 1953.

20. Stapleton, *Billy,* 54–56.

21. *Americus Times-Recorder,* July 22, 24, 1953; JCL interview with Jack Carter, June 25, 2003, 3, JCL.

22. Stapleton, *Billy,* 56; Bourne, *Carter,* 86–88.

23. Will of James Earl Carter, Sr., and Oath of Executor, July 25, 1953, both in Sumter County Courthouse, Americus, Georgia, Will Book C, p. 354, and loose papers; Hugh Carter, *Beedie and Hot,* 91; *Wall Street Journal,* September 24, 1976.

24. Memorandum, James E. Carter, Jr., to Secretary of the Navy, August 17, 1973, VF, Carter, J., Naval Records, JCL.

25. Memorandum, W. B. York, Jr. to James Earl Carter, Jr., August 6, 1953; Memorandum, J. D. Anderson to Director, Division of Reactor Development, U.S. Atomic Energy Commission, Washington, D.C., August 17, 1953 (contains quotation); Memorandum, H. G. Rickover to Secretary of the Navy, August 31, 1953, all in VF, Carter, J., Naval Records, JCL.

26. Russell, August 31, George, August 28, and Forrester, August 18, all 1953, to Chief of Naval Personnel, all in VF, Carter, J., Naval Records, JCL.

27. Vice Admiral J. L. Holloway, Jr., to Russell, October 6, 1953; Holloway to JC, September 21, 1953; JC, Acceptance and Oath of Office, October 10, 1953, all in VF, Carter, J., Naval Records, JCL.

CHAPTER 7

1. Bourne, *Carter,* 81.

2. JC, *Best,* 65; RSC, *First Lady,* 36; Morris, *Carter,* 114; Bourne, *Carter,* 81–82.

3. Mazlish and Diamond, *Carter,* 124; Bourne, *Carter,* 83; Morris, *Carter,* 115; Simmons, *Rosalynn Carter,* 39–40.

4. JC, *Best,* 64; RSC, *First Lady,* 37–39; Bourne, *Carter,* 83.

5. Author interview with JC and RSC, October 12, 1994. See also Bourne, *Carter,* 100–101.

6. *Americus Times-Recorder,* October 2, 1954, September 8, 1956; author interview with JC and RSC, October 12, 1994; Nancy Roberts, *Southern Ghosts* (Garden City, NY, 1979), 5–8; Cliff Linedecker, "Rosalynn Carter's Haunted House," *Examiner,* May 3, 1983; RSC, *First Lady,* 40–41.

7. Author interview with JC and RSC, October 12, 1994.

8. Harvey Shapiro, "A Conversation with Jimmy Carter," *New York Times Book Review,* June 17, 1977, 1.

9. Godbold, "Dusty Corners of the Mind," 110–11; Thomas, *Collected Poems,* 201; Bourne, *Carter,* 82.

10. Bourne, *Carter*, 32, 209.

11. Shapiro, "Conversation," 35.

12. RSC statement in letter of Madeline Edwards to Jeannie and Stanly Godbold, October 15, 1998, in possession of recipients; see also Simmons, *Rosalynn Carter*, 42; Shapiro, "Conversation," 35.

13. Author interview with JC, October 12, 1994; Bourne, *Carter*, 91–92.

14. Cindy Williams, "Life on the Farm near Plains," *Plains Echoes* 6, no. 2 (1998): 1.

15. Author interview with JC, October 12, 1994; RSC, *First Lady*, 37–38.

16. Author interview with JC and RSC, October 12, 1994; Hugh Carter, *Beedie and Hot*, 92; Glad, *Carter*, 70.

17. JC, Annual Qualifications Questionnaire, 1954–61, VF, Carter, J., Naval Records, JCL.

18. JC to Uncle Buddy, October 25, 1971, Carter Family Papers, box 2, JCL.

19. JC, *Best*, 65–66; Bourne, *Carter*, 84.

20. *Atlanta Constitution*, August 14, 1992.

21. NPS interview with Maxine Reese, December 17, 1985, 15, JCL.

22. Misc. Interview with RSC, December 21, 1974, JCL.

23. Author interview with JC and RSC, October 12, 1994; Sheehy, "Ladies and Gentlemen," 51; JC, *Best*, 65–66; RSC, *First Lady*, 39; Glad, *Carter*, 70; Stroud, *How Jimmy Won*, 107–8.

24. Bill Thomas, "Dogman Digs His July Gig," *Memphis (TN) Commercial Appeal*, June 28, 1998.

25. *Georgia Crop Improvement News*, 1959–66, copies in Pre-Presidential File, 1962–74, JCL; Sumter County Tax Digest, 26th Militia District, 1960, p. 1, GDAH; Bourne, *Carter*, 90; Mazlish and Diamond, *Carter*, 124–25; Morris, *Carter*, 115–16.

26. Author interview with JC, October 12, 1994; Bourne, *Carter*, 90–91; JC, *Best*, 79; Mazlish and Diamond, *Carter*, 124–25; RSC, *First Lady*, 46; and "The Carter Brothers *Speed* Fertilizing," *Cotton*, January 1969, 14–15.

27. RSC, *First Lady*, 39; interview with Allie Smith excerpted in "Rosalynn Smith Carter," VF, Carter, Jimmy, Addresses, Governor (2), JCL; Misc. Interview with RSC, December 21, 1974, JCL.

28. Stapleton, *Billy*, 92–94; JC comments at dedication of Boyhood Farm, Archery, November 17, 2000.

29. Spann, "Other Carter," 49–54; "President Carter's Nephew Dying of AIDS," *Boston Globe*, August 18, 1992, 5; Rick Hampson, "The Desperate Life of a Bad Peanut," *Atlanta Constitution*, March 16, 1997. William Carter Spann's memoir is a vitriolic attack on the entire Carter family that he wrote for pay after Jimmy became president; at the time that he sold the article to *Hustler*, Spann was incarcerated in the California Correctional Training Facility in Soledad, serving a sentence of five years to life.

30. *Americus Times-Recorder*, June 4, August 23, November 9, 1955; author interview with JC, October 12, 1994; *Americus Times-Recorder*, August 10, 1956; Stapleton, *Billy*, 57–66; Billy and Sybil Carter, *Billy*, 57–61; Glad, *Carter*, 70–71.

31. "My Son, The President," *U.S. News and World Report*, March 7, 1977, 53.

32. Eleanor Randolph, "The Carter Complex," *Esquire*, November 1977, 168.

33. *Atlanta Constitution*, April 30, 1995.

34. Biography of Lillian G. Carter, Richard Harden File, box 7, JCL; Sheehy, "Ladies and Gentlemen," 55; *Americus Times-Recorder*, November 23, 1955; Bourne, *Carter*, 88; JC, *Best*, 72; RSC, *First Lady*, 41; Glad, *Carter*, 71.

35. Alcee F. Maxfield, State Secretary, Lions of Georgia to Cody De Vore, January 5, 1971, RG 1-1-5, JC, box 2, GDAH; JC, "Georgia Lions Club Speech," June 8, 1971, RG 1-1-45, box 11, GDAH; GGDP interview with JC, February 17, 1987, 10, 20, GSU.

36. *Americus Times-Recorder*, May 21, July 28, August 1, September 30, 1955, January 16, March 7, 22, 1956; Collins, *Search for Jimmy Carter*, 52–53; Mazlish and Diamond, *Carter*, 124–25; JC, *Best*, 79; RSC, *First Lady*, 42–43.

37. *Americus Times-Recorder*, November 10, 1956, March 15, May 3, June 11, October 4, 1957, February 13, June 6, August 12, 1958, September 16, 1960.

38. *Americus Times-Recorder*, November 25, 1955; RSC, *First Lady*, 43–44; Bourne, *Carter*, 91–92; Mazlish and Diamond, *Carter*, 126; Glad, *Carter*, 73; Morris, *Carter*, 116–17; Collins, *Search for Jimmy Carter*, 53.

39. Goldman, "Sizing Up Carter."

40. Ibid.

41. JC, *Best*, 66; *Americus Times-Recorder*, December 22, 1978; NPS interview with JC, May 11, 1988, 38–39, JCL; Mazlish and Diamond, *Carter*, 128–31; Glad, *Carter*, 78; Morris, *Carter*, 118–20.

42. Michael, *Carter*, 17–18.

43. Simpson, "Carter and Transformation," 63–65, 74; Minutes of the Sumter County School Board, 1954–62, Pre-Presidential File, 1954, box 22, JCL.

44. Course of Study, Plains High School, 1961–62, Pre-Presidential box 22, JCL.

45. JC, *Best*, 66–67; RSC, *First Lady*, 44–45

46. Chancey, "'Demonstration Plot," 321–53; Bourne, *Carter*, 93–98; Lee, *Cotton Patch Evidence*; Scheer, "Jimmy, We Hardly Know Y'all," 186; Simpson, "Carter and Transformation," 65; Tracy Elaine K'Meyer, *Interracialism and Christian Community in the Postwar South: The Story of Koinonia Farm* (Charlottesville, VA, 1997), 11–24, 81–98.

47. Bourne, *Carter*, 98, 100–101; Mazlish and Diamond, *Carter*, 135–38; Scheer, "Jimmy, We Hardly Know Y'All," 186–87; NPS interview with RSC, May 11, 1988, 47, 318, JCL; Glad, *Carter*, 84–85.

48. Mazlish and Diamond, *Carter*, 136.

49. Bourne, *Carter*, 98–100; interview with Singletary cited in Mazlish and Diamond, *Carter*, 136–37; Scheer, "Jimmy, We Hardly Know Y'all," 188–89.

50. NPS interview with RSC and JC, May 12, 1988, 274–84, and December 8, 1988, 1–5, JCL; Bourne, *Carter*, 102; Morris, *Carter*, 116.

51. Hugh Carter, *Beedie and Hot*, 77–79; Glad, *Carter*, 72; "Sister Ruth," *Newsweek*, July 17, 1978, 59; JC to Author, March 30, 1995; Shapiro, "Conversation," 34–35; Safran, "Women," 92; JC, *Living Faith*, 78–81; JCL interview with Jack Carter, June 25, 2003, 5, 10, 11, 13, JCL.

52. Michael, *Carter*, 27–31; RSC, *First Lady*, 47–49; JC, *Best*, 79; JC, *Turning Point*, 58–60.

CHAPTER 8

1. Randolph, "Carter Complex," 178; Glad, *Carter,* 87.

2. Hefley, *Church,* 198–99; JC, *Best,* 79–80.

3. Hefley, *Church,* 197.

4. JC, *Turning Point,* 50.

5. Bartley, *New South,* 324–28.

6. JC, *Turning Point,* 9–10; Simpson, "Carter and Transformation," 66.

7. *Greenwood (SC) Index-Journal,* August 27, 2005; Mel Steely, "Elbert Parr Tuttle (1897–1996), *New Georgia Encyclopedia,* www.georgiaencyclopedia.org.

8. JC, *Turning Point,* 34–48.

9. Glad, *Carter,* 88; JC, *Turning Point,* 9–12, 28–48; Bourne, *Carter,* 110–12.

10. Simpson, "Carter and Transformation," 67.

11. Bourne, *Carter,* 114–16; RSC, *First Lady,* 49–50.

12. Bourne, *Carter,* 114–15; JC, *Turning Point,* 66–73.

13. JC, *Turning Point,* 61.

14. JC, *Turning Point,* 76–84.

15. Quoted in Louis Elson, "Jimmy Carter's 1962 State Senate Campaign," 6, typescript, White House Central File, box PP-1, JCL.

16. *Americus Times-Recorder,* October 1, 6, 17, 22, 1962; JC, *Turning Point,* 81, 84–89, 93–95, 99, 129–30; JC speech at Griffin Kiwanis Club, September 17, 1973, RG 1-1-45, box 1, GDAH.

17. *Americus Times-Recorder,* October 22, 23, 1962; Bourne, *Carter,* 121–22.

18. *Americus Times-Recorder,* October 17, 30, 1962; JC, *Turning Point,* 101–9; JC, *Best,* 80–83.

19. Louis Elson, "Jimmy Carter's 1962 State Senate Campaign"; Kirbo quoted in Wooten, *Dasher,* 237; GGDP interview with George Busbee, March 29, 1987, 18–20, GSU; Miller Center interview with Griffin Bell, March 23, 1988, 2, 3, JCL.

20. Miller Center interview with Kirbo, January 5, 1983, 1, 2, JCL.

21. Ibid.

22. *Atlanta Journal,* October 22, 23, November 1, 1962; *Atlanta Constitution,* October 27, 30, 1962; *Americus Times-Recorder,* November 2, 1962.

23. *Americus Times-Recorder,* November 2, 1962; Walton, *Native Son,* 40–43, 51–52; JC, *Turning Point,* 112–56.

24. Wooten, *Dasher,* 237–39; *Americus Times-Recorder,* November 3, 1962; Tom Waller, "How the President Hunkered Down with Old Joe Hurst," *Atlanta Magazine,* May 1979, 166; JC, *Best,* 84–85; Hugh Carter, *Beedie and Hot,* 114.

25. Bourne, *Carter,* 128; JC, *Turning Point,* 158–60; JC to J. B. Fuqua, January 14, 1975, RG 1-1-5, JC, box 18, GDAH.

26. Quoted in Louis Elson, "Jimmy Carter's 1962 State Senate Campaign," 21, JCL.

27. *Americus Times-Recorder,* November 6, 8, 1962; John Pennington, *Atlanta Journal,* November 4, 5, 6, 7, 1962; Glad, *Carter,* 128–29; JC, *Turning Point,* 160–69; Louis Elson, "Jimmy Carter's 1962 State Senate Campaign," 13; Wells, *The First Hundred Years,* 237–44.

28. *Americus Times-Recorder,* November 10, 1962.

29. *Americus Times-Recorder,* November 29, 1962.

30. JC, *Turning Point,* 174–82; Bourne, *Carter,* 130–31.

CHAPTER 9

1. Rowan, *Georgia's Modern Day Legislature,* 50.

2. GGDP interview with JC, February 17, 1987, 19, GSU; Goldman, "Sizing Up Carter."

3. GGDP interview with Bobby Rowan, October 6, 1992, 17–18, GSU.

4. Bourne, *Carter,* 133–34; Glad, *Carter,* 93; *Journal of the Senate of the State of Georgia,* 1963 (Hapeville, Ga., 1963), 187, 202, 244, 392, 393, 549, 561, 563, 565, 567, 642.

5. *Atlanta Constitution,* February 11, 1963.

6. *Journal of the Senate* (1963), 586, 641; Bourne, *Carter,* 134.

7. *Journal of the Senate* (1963), 195, 255–56, 847.

8. Michael, *Carter,* 39–40.

9. GGDP interview with George T. Smith, August 19, 1992, 75, GSU.

10. RSC, *First Lady,* 52–53; Bourne, *Carter,* 133.

11. Hefley, *Church,* 165–72; Bourne, *Carter,* 134–37; Williford, *Americus,* 354–58.

12. Bourne, *Carter,* 138–39.

13. Bourne, *Carter,* 139–40; Williford, *Americus,* 358–60.

14. *Americus Times-Recorder,* October 18, November 29, 1963.

15. *Americus Times-Recorder,* October 30, November 29, 1963.

16. Bourne, *Carter,* 143; Glad, *Carter,* 98; Simpson, "Carter and Transformation," 69.

17. Glad, *Carter,* 83–94; Williford, *Americus,* 360.

18. JC, *Turning Point,* 183–84.

19. Bourne, *Carter,* 140, 143; *Journal of the Senate* (1963), 83, 114; JC, *Turning Point,* 185–86; JC to Leroy Johnson, March 22, 1965, Johnson to JC, March 10, 1966, both in Pre-Presidential File, box 8, JCL.

20. Bourne, *Carter,* 140–41.

21. *Atlanta Constitution,* January 16, 20, 1964; *Journal of the Senate of the State of Georgia at the Regular Session,* January 13 through February 21, 1964 (Hapeville, Ga., 1964), 23, 40, 105, 155, 186, 210, 295, 330, 340, 348–49, 626, 695, 727; A Bill to be Entitled an Act to Amend the Minimum Foundation Program and Senate Resolution 64, both in Pre-Presidential File, box 12, JCL; Glad, *Carter,* 95.

22. *Atlanta Journal,* March 2, 5, 1964; *Americus Times-Recorder,* March 4, 1964; *Columbus (GA) Ledger-Enquirer,* September 14, 1963, Glad, *Carter,* 93; JC, *Best,* 85; JC, *Turning Point,* 201–2.

23. NPS interview with JC and RSC, May 11, 1988, 52–53, JCL.

24. *Americus Times-Recorder,* April 8, 1964.

25. Michael, *Carter,* 43–44.

26. Georgia Southwestern College Scholarship-Loan Fund Advisory Committee, April 1, 1964, Alexander A. Palamiotis to JC, January 26, 1965, JC to Palamiotis, February 4, 1965,

Nancy A. Joiner to JC, February 22, 1965, all in Pre-Presidential File, box 9, JCL; Acting Chancellor S. Walter Martin to JC, February 2, 1965, JC, handwritten speech, n.d., and JC, handwritten notes on meeting of University Sub-committee of the Senate Educational Matters Committee, January 29, 1965, all in Pre-Presidential File, box 12, JCL.

27. Speech quoted in Collins, *Search for Jimmy Carter*, 63, and transcript of interview with JC, "Dawn's Early Light," 1988, 5, Ralph McGill Papers, box 109, MARBL, Woodruff Library, Emory University; GGDP interview with JC, February 17, 1987, 13, GSU; Bourne, *Carter*, 144; Glad, *Carter*, 98; Michael, *Carter*, 45; *Journal of the Senate of the State of Georgia at the Extraordinary Session, May 4–June 25, 1964* (Hapeville, Ga., 1964), 300.

28. *Journal of the Senate Extraordinary* (1964), 309–10, 315, 514–15.

29. Glad, *Carter*, 96; Bourne, *Carter*, 144; JC, *Best*, 89.

30. Quoted in Glad, *Carter*, 99; see also Mazlish and Diamond, *Carter*, 144–45.

31. Bourne, *Carter*, 141–42; Williford, *Americus*, 359–60. Wooten, *Dasher*, 244–45; JC, *Best*, 95–96.

32. Lillian Carter, *Miss Lillian*, 89; RSC, *First Lady*, 54–55; Bourne, *Carter*, 142; and JC, *Remarkable Mother*, 81.

33. *Americus Times-Recorder*, October 5, 7, 9, 14, 1964; Atlanta Journal, October 10, 1964; see also Bourne, *Carter*, 142, 144, 148; Glad, *Carter*, 97; and JC, *Best*, 95–96.

34. "Dawn's Early Light," 7, McGill Papers, MARBL, Woodruff Library.

35. *Americus Times-Recorder*, August 7, 14, 1964; *Atlanta Journal*, October 8, 1964; Bourne, *Carter*, 145.

36. *Journal of the Senate of the State of Georgia at the Regular Session, January 11–March 12, 1965* (Atlanta, 1965), 29–31; *Americus Times-Recorder*, January 14, 1965.

37. JC, handwritten notes for a speech, addressed to "Jim Cheny," Pre-Presidential File, box 12 (1965), JCL.

38. *Americus Times-Recorder*, January 28, February 5, 6, 11, 13, 20, 25, 1965; *Atlanta Journal*, January 10, 12, 24, 1965; *Journal of the Senate* (1965), 260–71, 459, 506, 806, 1259–76; Cook, *Sanders*, 224.

39. JC to "Mr. Wade," September 15, 1965, and JC to William B. King, September 15, 1965, both in Pre-Presidential File, box 8, JCL; *Americus Times-Recorder*, March 4, 6, 9, 1965; Goldman, "Sizing Up Carter."

40. "Carl" to "Jimmy," March 25, 1965, Pre-Presidential File, box 8, JCL.

41. Quoted in Lovelace Hair and Jane Hiers, "From Submarines to the Senate," *Columbus (GA) Sunday Ledger-Enquirer Magazine*, November 28, 1965, 15.

42. *Americus Times-Recorder*, July 19, 24, August 28, 1965; *Atlanta Journal*, August 1, 28, December 30, 1965; Simpson, "Carter and Transformation," 70.

43. Hair and Hiers, "From Submarines," 15; *Americus Times-Recorder*, May 21, 1965; JC to Hair, November 24, 1965; JC to William Rowe, November 24, 1965, both in Pre-Presidential File, box 8, JCL.

44. [Jane Hiers] to JC, October 1, 1965, Pre-Presidential File, box 4, JCL.

45. JC, *Best*, 68; JC, "Dawn's Early Light," 6, McGill Papers, MARBL, Woodruff Library; RSC, *First Lady*, 55–56; Simmons, *Rosalynn Carter*, 47; Bourne, *Carter*, 146–47.

46. Williford, *Americus*, 363–71; Bourne, *Carter*, 147.

47. RSC's List of Improvements since August 15, 1962; JC to Mr. S. R. Hunter, President, Citizens Bank of Americus, John P. Latimer to S. R. Hunter, August 4, 1965, all in Pre-Presidential File, box 2, JCL.

48. JC to Partners, December 20, 1965, M. B. Adams (National Bank Examiner) to JC, December 22, 1965, Comptroller of the Currency Application for a National Bank, n.d., *Americus Times-Recorder*, January 29, 1966; William B. Camp to JC, June 27, 1966, and Thomas G. DeShazo (Deputy Comptroller of the Currency) to J. Frank Myers, July 11, 1966, all in Pre-Presidential File, box 2, JCL.

49. *Americus Times-Recorder*, January 21, 1966; Glad, *Carter*, 98–99.

50. *Atlanta Journal*, December 28, 1965, January 21, 22, 1966. *Journal of the Senate of the State of Georgia at the Regular Session, January 10–February 18, 1966* (Atlanta, 1966), 1635, 546; see also 290–91, 293, 545, 1087, 1092, 1306, 1464, 1544, 1551, 1634–35, and 1657.

51. JC to Charles Cox [1966], Pre-Presidential File, box 10, JCL.

52. Misc. Interview with RSC, December 21, 1974, JCL.

53. Morris, *Carter*, 141–43; see also JC, *Best*, 87–93; Cook, *Sanders*, 262.

CHAPTER 10

1. Black and Black, *Rise of Southern Republicans*, 143–52; Coleman, *Georgia*, 397.

2. NPS interview with JC, May 11, 1988, 149, JCL.

3. Hefley, *Church*, 72, 193–94; Ribuffo, "God and Jimmy Carter," in Ribuffo, *Right Center Left*, 222–23.

4. Quoted in Mazlish and Diamond, *Carter*, 146.

5. *Atlanta Constitution*, June 7, 12, 1966; *Americus Times-Recorder*, June 8, 10, 11, 1966; JC, *Best*, 97; Bourne, *Carter*, 150; Glad, *Carter*, 99–100; Morris, *Carter*, 144–45; Wooten, *Dasher*, 250.

6. Author interview with Morris W. H. Collins, Starkville, Mississippi, September 14, 1994.

7. JC to Flynt, March 26, 1966, JC to Mackay, March 28, 1966, JC to Weltner, March 28, 1966, JC to Landrum, March 28, 1966, all in Pre-Presidential File, box 8, JCL.

8. JC to Herman Talmadge, March 28, 1966, Pre-Presidential File, box 8, JCL.

9. Russell to JC, September 8, 1965, Pre-Presidential File, box 8, JCL.

10. *Americus Times-Recorder*, May 4, 6, 7, 14, 17, 18, 1966.

11. *Atlanta Constitution*, April 18, 1966; see also Bourne, *Carter*, 149–50.

12. GGDP interview with Arnall, March 25, 1986, 92, GSU; Short, *Maddox*, 69.

13. Miller Center interview with Griffin Bell, March 23, 1988, 66, JCL; Wells, *First Hundred Years*, 244.

14. Misc. Interview with RSC, December 21, 1974, JCL.

15. Glad, *Carter*, 99, 515.

16. *New York Times*, August 21, 1966; *Americus Times-Recorder*, June 1, 1966; Glad, *Carter*, 100.

17. Bradley R. Rice, "Lester G. Maddox," in Henderson and Roberts, *Georgia Governors* 193–229; Morris, *Carter*, 146–48.

18. Bourne, *Carter*, 152.

19. Gulliver, *Friendly Tongue*, 106.

20. Bourne, *Carter*, 152–53.

21. Miller Center interview with Rafshoon, April 8, 1983, 1–1, JCL; *Atlanta Constitution*, May 24, 1966; *Americus Times-Recorder*, June 13, 14, 1966; NARA interview with Rafshoon, September 12, 1979, 1, JCL; Jody Powell File, Cabinet and Staff Biographies, JCL; Mazlish and Diamond, *Carter*, 101–2.

22. *Atlanta Constitution*, June 14, 18, 24, 1966; Glad, *Carter*, 101–2.

23. RSC biog., Staff Secretary File, box 260, JCL; *Atlanta Constitution*, September 15, 1966; *Americus Times-Recorder*, July 19, 1966; RSC, *First Lady*, 59–60; RSC, *Helping Yourself Help Others*, 21; Billy and Sybil Carter, *Billy*, 63; Bourne, *Carter*, 156.

24. Memoranda from Gloria Spann, June 15, 17, 1966, Pre-Presidential File, box 4, JCL.

25. *Atlanta Constitution*, July 1, 2, 5, 13, 1966; JC, *Best*, 98; author interview with JC, October 12, 1994; Cook, *Sanders*, 275–76; Bourne, *Carter*, 102.

26. Kirbo to Mr. And Mrs. Tucker, July 12, 1966, Robert M. Heard to Kirbo, September 20, 1966, Kirbo to James W. Smith, September 21, 1966, and David Gambrell to JC, December 6, 1966, all in Pre-Presidential File, box 4, JCL; Sissy Dolvin, unpublished memoir, January 1, 1992, typescript, 2, Emily Gordon Dolvin File, box 1, JCL; Mazlish and Diamond, *Carter*, 148–49; Glad, *Carter*, 102.

27. Miller Center interview with Charles Kirbo, January 5, 1983, 3, 11, 12, JCL.

28. Lance, *Truth*, 15–16, 29; Lance biog., Jody Powell File, Cabinet and Staff biographies, JCL; Miller Center interview with Bert Lance, May 12, 1982, 2, JCL.

29. Jordan, *Crisis*, 23; Bourne, *Carter*, 156–61; Glad, *Carter*, 102; NPS interview with JC, December 8, 1988, 6–7, JCL.

30. Jordan, *No Such Thing*, 140–41.

31. Bourne, *Carter*, 159–62; Glad, *Carter*, 103.

32. *Atlanta Constitution*, September 10, 1966.

33. *Americus Times-Recorder*, August 30, 1966.

34. *Atlanta Constitution*, July, 1, 6, 24, September 10, 1966; *Americus Times-Recorder*, July 23, 28, August 15, 1966; *Waynesboro (GA) True Citizen*, July 28, 1966; *Atlanta Journal of Labor*, July 29, 1966; *Savannah (GA) Evening Press*, August 15, 1966; Glad, *Carter*, 103–5.

35. *Americus Times-Recorder*, August 24, 1966.

36. Allen, *Atlanta Rising*, 148–49; *Atlanta Constitution*, September 10, 1966.

37. *Augusta (GA) Chronicle*, August 20, 1966; *Americus Times-Recorder*, August 19, 1966.

38. *Atlanta Constitution*, July 1, 12, 13, 27, 1966; *Americus Times-Recorder*, August 11, 17, 1966; Glad, *Carter*, 105.

39. *New York Times,* September 16, 1966, October 1, 1966; Sissy Dolvin, unpublished memoir, January 1, 1992, typescript, 4, Emily Gordon Dolvin File, box 1, JCL; Walton, *Native Son,* 54–60.

40. *Americus Times-Recorder,* October 13, 15, 19, 28, 1966.

41. GGDP interview with Ellis Arnall, March 25, 1986, 94–95, GSU.

42. Glad, *Carter,* 106; Allen, *Atlanta Rising,* 152; Short, *Maddox,* xi.

43. *Americus Times-Recorder,* November 4, 7, 9, 1966; Carter, *Best,* 98; Mazlish and Diamond, *Carter,* 149; Morris, *Carter,* 150; Jordan, *Crisis,* 24; Bourne, *Carter,* 164–65; Hugh Carter, *Beedie and Hot,* 117.

44. Robert M. Heard to Kirbo, September 20, 1966, Kirbo to James W. Smith, September 21, 1966, both in Pre-Presidential File, box 4, JCL.

45. McGill to Kennedy, November 17, 1966, McGill Papers, ser. II, MARBL, Woodruff Library, Emory University.

46. *Atlanta Constitution,* November 5, 1966; David Gambrell to JC, December 6, 1966, Pre-Presidential File, box 4, JCL; Glad, *Carter,* 123.

47. Jordan, *Crisis,* 24.

48. *Americus Times-Recorder,* January 31, 1967.

49. List, JC for Governor Campaign Workers for 1966, with RSC note "all written," Pre-Presidential File, 1962–76, box 24, JCL; Miller Center interview with Kirbo, January 5, 1983, 2, JCL.

50. JC, *Best,* 112–13; Stroud, *How Jimmy Won,* 181.

CHAPTER 11

1. "Sister Ruth," *Newsweek,* July 17, 1978, 59; Bourne, *Carter,* 167–68; Glad, *Carter,* 108; Mazlish and Diamond, *Carter,* 153–55; Stroud, *How Jimmy Won,* 51–52; Leo P. Ribuffo, "God and Jimmy Carter," in Ribuffo, *Right Center Left,* 223–24; Pippert, *Spiritual Journey of Jimmy Carter,* 8–9.

2. Hefley, *Church,* 195–97, 249; Bourne, *Carter,* 169–70.

3. JC, *Living Faith,* 20–21.

4. Sheehy, "Ladies and Gentlemen," 56; see also RSC, *First Lady,* 65–66.

5. JC interview with Jack Anderson, September 16, 1977, Jody Powell File, box 63, JCL; JC, *Best,* 99; Mazlish and Diamond, *Carter,* 153–54; Garry Wills, "The Plains Truth: An Inquiry into the Shaping of Jimmy Carter," 51, 53–54, VF, JC, biog., JCL.

6. Fowler, *Stages of Faith,* 174–75, 285–86, 290.

7. JC, *Living Faith,* 24–32; see also Mazlish and Diamond, *Carter,* 163–64, Holifield, "Three Strands," 15–17, and Ribuffo, "God and Jimmy Carter," 141–57.

8. Frank A. Ruechel, "Politics and Morality Revisited: Jimmy Carter and Reinhold Niebuhr," *Atlanta History* 37, no. 4 (winter 1994): 19–31; Arthur Schlesinger, Jr., "Forgetting Reinhold Niebuhr," *New York Times Book Review,* September 18, 2005, 12–13; Bourne, *Carter,* 171; Mazlish and Diamond, *Carter,* 167–68.

9. Peter Beinart, "The Rehabilitation of the Cold-war Liberal," *New York Times Magazine,* April 30, 2006, 41–45.

10. McLellan, *Unto Caesar,* 37–41, 45, 49.

11. Brown, *Niebuhr*, 56, 115, 142, 147, 246–47.

12. Mazlish and Diamond, *Carter*, 162–68; Bourne, *Carter*, 171–72; Fox, *Niebuhr*; Burns F. Stanfield, "Faith and Politics," 13–25; Clark, *Serenity, Courage, Wisdom*.

13. Henry Allen, "Just Plains Folks," *Washington Post*, August 15, 1976, 37–38.

14. *Americus Times-Recorder*, December 16, 1966; Angelo, *First Mothers*, 281.

15. Lillian Carter and Spann, *Away from Home*, 154; *Atlanta Constitution*, December 12, 1966; biography of Lillian G. Carter, Richard Harden File, box 7, JCL. See also JC, *Remarkable Mother*, 87–124.

16. *Americus Times-Recorder*, October 19, 1967; RSC, *First Lady*, 63–64; Bourne, *Carter*, 173–74.

17. Stroud, *How Jimmy Won*, 107–8; RSC, *First Lady*, 64.

18. JC, *Living Faith*, 80–81; JC interview with Jack Anderson, September 16, 1977, Jody Powell File, box 63, JCL.

19. RSC, *First Lady*, 64–65; Bourne, *Carter*, 174.

20. *Atlanta Journal-Constitution*, June 30, 1978, September 18, 1991; JC interview with Jack Anderson, September 16, 1977.

21. John Pennington, "Visit with Jimmy Carter," November 1968, newspaper clipping, Carter Clippings, RG 1-1-111, box 1, GDAH.

22. "The Carter Brothers *Speed* Fertilizing," *Cotton*, January 1969, 14–15.

23. *Americus Times-Recorder*, March 10, December 11, 1967, January, 3, 4, March 22, May 20, 29, June 20, 28, July 31, August 21, September 27, October 9, 1968; see also Carter, *Best*, 99–100.

24. JC, handwritten notes, January 28, 1968, Pre-Presidential File, box 2, JCL.

25. *Americus Times-Recorder*, May 22, 24, 1968; Bourne, *Carter*, 178; Glad, *Carter*, 109–11; Miller, *Yankee*, 176–77.

26. JC to Ed [Meredith], July 27, 1968, September 28, 1976, Meredith to JC, September 7, 1976, all in Susan Clough File, box 16, JCL.

27. JC, *Living Faith*, 217; *Atlanta Constitution*, March 6, 1995; Glad, *Carter*, 111–12.

28. Coombs, "Hand," 42; see also Glad, *Carter*, 114–18.

29. *Americus Times-Recorder*, September 16, October 8, 11, December 14, 1968; *Atlanta Journal and Constitution Magazine*, January 19, 1969, 9, 20; Sheppard, "Man from Plains," 19.

30. *Atlanta Constitution*, 24 March, 14 April, 16, 18 October, 13, November 21, 1969; *Americus Times-Recorder*, November 6, 1968, October 17, 1969.

31. *Americus Times-Recorder*, February 22, March 26, June 12, 16, July 23, 1969.

32. *Americus Times-Recorder*, October 27, November 11, 12, 1969, January 10, February 9, 1970.

33. *Atlanta Journal-Constitution*, November 5, 1997; *Humanist*, July–August 1977, 46; *Mt. Pleasant (TX) Daily Tribune*, February 2, 1978; *Atlanta Constitution*, September 14, 1973; JC comments, Historical Press Conference, Jimmy Carter Presidential Center, Atlanta, February 20, 1997, author's notes.

34. JC to Woodruff, January 8, 1969; Woodruff to JC, January 13, 1969, both in Woodruff Papers, box 15, MARBL, Woodruff Library, Emory University. See also Frederick Allen, *Secret Formula*, 363–64; author interview with Frederick L. Allen, May 16, 1994.

35. *Columbus (GA) Ledger-Enquirer,* February 27, 1970; JC, handwritten notes for speech, n.d., Pre-Presidential File, box 2, JCL.

36. Rafshoon to JC, March 4, 1970, Staff Secretary File, box 3, JCL.

37. Charles Pou, "Georgia Politics," *Atlanta Constitution,* March 22, 1970.

38. *Americus Times-Recorder,* March 26, 1970.

39. *Atlanta Constitution,* April 4, 1970.

40. Hugh Carter, *Beedie and Hot,* 119; *Americus Times-Recorder,* April 1, 3, 6, 26, 1970.

CHAPTER 12

1. Morris, *Carter,* 158–71; Witcover, *Year the Dream Died,* 467–507.

2. *Americus Times-Recorder,* February 27, 1970.

3. Carter, *Addresses,* 98; Anderson, *Electing Jimmy Carter,* 172–73.

4. Glad, *Carter,* 124.

5. Coleman, *Georgia,* 399; Walton, *Native Son,* 65.

6. Copy of manual in White House Central File, box PP-79, folder PP 12, 1/20/77, 1/20/81, JCL; see also JC to Howard Atherton, January 14, 1969, JC to Clay Long, August 20, 1969, RSC to Fred Long, November 19, 1969, Richard M. Harden to JC, October 1, 1969, Bob Hurley to Hamilton Jordan, October 1, 1969, all in Pre-Presidential File, 1962–76, boxes 27 and 28, JCL.

7. JC, handwritten notes, Pre-Presidential File, box 23, JCL.

8. Bourne, *Carter,* 186; Glad, *Carter,* 124–25; RSC, *First Lady,* 67; author interview with JC, October 12, 1994.

9. Jordan, *No Such Thing,* 46–54.

10. Hugh Carter, *Beedie and Hot,* 119–20; Glad, *Carter,* 124; Bourne, *Carter,* 185; RSC, *First Lady,* 67: Mazlish and Diamond, *Carter,* 186.

11. "Jimmy Carter Campaign for Governor—1970," typescript, [January 7, 1970]; Hamilton to JC, January 21, 1970, both in Pre-Presidential File, 1962–76, box 33, JCL.

12. Kirbo to JC, April 6, 8, 1970, both in Pre-Presidential File, 1962–76, box 24, JCL.

13. Author interview with Edmund S. Muskie, Washington, D.C., April 3, 1992.

14. Miller Center interview with Kirbo, January 5, 1983, 3–6, JCL.

15. Miller Center interview with Eizenstat, January 29–30, 1982, 2, JCL; NARA interview with Eizenstat, January 10, 1981, JCL; Gerald M. Rafshoon to JC, January 16, 1970, Pre-Presidential File, 1962–76, box 33, JCL; Bourne, *Carter,* 187; RSC, *First Lady,* 67; Mazlish and Diamond, *Carter,* 185.

16. Mazlish and Diamond, *Carter,* 185.

17. Goldman, "Sizing Up Carter."

18. Pre-Presidential File, box 23, JCL.

19. "Platform: Jimmy Carter for Governor, 1970," typescript, RG 1-1-45, JC, box 12, GDAH, copy also in Pre-Presidential File, box 23, JCL; *Gainesville (GA) Daily Times,* August 30, 1970, *Columbus (GA) Ledger-Enquirer,* August 30, 1970, both in RG 1-1-111, box 1, Carter Clippings, GDAH. *Atlanta Journal,* July 29, 30, 1970.

20. Glad, *Carter,* 125–26; *Americus Times-Recorder,* August 4, 1970, 2; Morris, *Carter,* 172–75.

21. Bourne, *Carter,* 187–88; RSC, *First Lady,* 67.

22. "'Miss Lillian' Reminisces," *Georgia Tech Whistle* 5, no. 6 (February 20, 1979), 3; RSC, *First Lady,* 66–67, 71–72; Bourne, *Carter,* 195; Hugh Carter, *Beedie and Hot,* 120–21; Sheppard, "Man from Plains," 18.

23. Sanders, "Sad Duty," 616; Bourne, *Carter,* 183.

24. Cited in Glad, *Carter,* 127; see also *Atlanta Constitution,* November 8, 1970, clipping in President Ford Committee for Reelection File, box H27, Gerald R. Ford Presidential Library, Ann Arbor, Michigan.

25. Bourne, *Carter,* 190–92; Sanders, "Sad Duty," 619, 625; *Atlanta Journal,* April 6, May 8, June 25, 28, 1970.

26. *Americus Times-Recorder,* August 26, 27, 28, 31, 1970.

27. *Americus Times-Recorder,* May 29, 1970.

28. William R. Hamilton and Staff, *A Survey of Political Opinions in Georgia,* prepared for JC, June 1970, RG 1-1-111, box 1, Carter Clippings, 1–3, GDAH.

29. Hamilton and Staff, *Survey,* 15, 21–26. See also Black and Black, *Vital South,* 161–69; Dan T. Carter, *Politics of Rage,* 345–47, 363–70.

30. Bourne, *Carter,* 189; *Americus Times-Recorder,* June 8, 10, 1970; *Augusta Chronicle,* June 11, 1970. The other candidates included Jan Cox, a bearded former carpenter in touch with his "inner self"; Linda Jenness, a young socialist; McKee Hargrett, a Democrat for Republican Candidate Barry Goldwater; Clennon B. King, the first African American to run for governor of Georgia; white supremacist J. B. Stoner; and unknowns Thomas J. Irwin, Charles F. Swint, and Adam B. Matthews. None of them posed a challenge to Carter or Sanders. See Cook, *Sanders,* 320.

31. *Americus Times-Recorder,* June 10, 16, 18, 1970; *Augusta (GA) Chronicle,* June 11, 1970.

32. *Americus Times-Recorder,* June 19, 1970. The equivalent of $400,000 in 1970 was $2.1 million in 2007.

33. *Americus Times-Recorder,* June 22, 1970.

34. *Americus Time-Recorder,* June 4, 1970; *Atlanta Journal,* April 7, July 28, 1970; *New York Times,* August 30, 1970; Sanders, "Sad Duty," 620; Glad, *Carter,* 126, 128.

35. *Americus Times-Recorder,* July 30, 31, 1970; *Atlanta Journal,* July 27, August 5, 1970.

36. *Americus Times-Recorder,* July 11, 1970.

37. *Americus Times-Recorder,* July 7, August 18, 1970; *Atlanta Journal,* August 17, 25, 26, 27, 1970; Brill, "Jimmy Carter's Pathetic Lies," 79–80.

38. *Savannah (GA) Evening Press,* July 28, 1970, clipping in RG 1-1-111, Carter Clippings, box 1, GDAH.

39. Misc. interview with RSC, December 21, 1974, 13, JCL; RSC, *First Lady,* 73; RSC, *Helping Yourself Help Others,* 23–25.

40. Misc. interview with RSC, December 21, 1974, 13, JCL; I. W. Gregory, Jr. to JC, July 28, 1970, with attachment, Pre-Presidential File, 1962–1976, box 38, JCL.

41. Miller Center interview with Kirbo, January 5, 1983, 3, JCL.

42. Quoted in Sanders, "Sad Duty," 628; see also "Case Study: The 1970 Campaign," in *Citizen's Guide* (n.p., n.d.), 19–24, copy in Charles McCall File, box 66, Gerald R. Ford Presidential Library; and Hugh Carter, *Beedie and Hot,* 124–25.

43. Myldred P. Hill to JC, January 7, 1970, JC to A. J. Harris, March 24, 1970, both in Carter Family Papers, box 2, JCL.

44. W. D. Johnson to "Dear Fellow Georgian," n.d. [1970], Pre-Presidential File, 1962–76, box 28, JCL.

45. Sanders, "Sad Duty," 627, Glad, *Carter,* 134, Cook, *Sanders,* 330, Collins, *Search for Jimmy Carter,* 78; Mazlish and Diamond, *Carter,* 179.

46. Bourne, *Carter,* 193; Glad, *Carter,* 135; Cook, *Sanders,* 326–31; "Case Study: The 1970 Campaign," in *Citizen's Guide* (n.p., n.d.), 19–24; Collins, *Search for Jimmy Carter,* 80.

47. Mike Jones to JC, n.d., JC to Mike Jones, September 19, 1969, Pre-Presidential File, 1962–76, box 27, JCL.

48. *Atlanta Constitution,* November 9, 1970, *Chicago Sun-Times,* May 19, 1976, both clippings in President Ford Committee for Reelection File, box H27, Gerald R. Ford Presidential Library; see also "Case Study."

49. Author interview with Collins, September 14, 1994.

50. Marvin Griffin, "A Georgian's Views: 'Carter Will Not Fool Me Twice,'" *Manchester (NH) Union-Leader,* September 10, 1976, Charles McCall File, box 67, Gerald R. Ford Presidential Library.

51. *Americus Times-Recorder,* July 9, 1970; *Atlanta Journal,* August 7, 1970.

52. Author interview with JC, October 12, 1994; see also Bill Shipp, "Carter Career Owes Everything to Russell," *Atlanta Constitution,* January 23, 1971.

53. JC to Bernice McCullar, January 27, 1972, RG 1-1-5, JC, box 22, GDAH.

54. GGDP interview with Carl Sanders, March 28, 1989, 9–10, GSU.

55. *Atlanta Journal,* August 16, 1970; *Americus Times-Recorder,* August 18, 1970.

56. *Chicago Sun-Times,* May 19, 1976, clipping in President Ford Committee for Reelection File, box H27, Gerald R. Ford Presidential Library; *Americus Times-Recorder,* August 18, 1970; GGDP interview with Vandiver, March 28, 1986, 69–71, GSU.

57. *Americus Times-Recorder,* August 11, 18, 1970.

58. *Americus Times-Recorder,* August 26, 1970; John Simpkins to George C. Wallace, June 16, 1970, Pre-Presidential File, 1962–76, box 24, JCL.

59. *Americus Times-Recorder,* September 3, 1970; Hugh Carter, *Beedie and Hot,* 123; *Atlanta Journal,* August 30, September 1, 3, 1970.

60. *Columbus (GA) Ledger-Enquirer,* September 3, 1970, clipping in RG 1-1-111, box 1, Carter Clippings, GDAH.

61. Copy in Rafshoon Donated Materials, box 7, JCL.

62. *Atlanta Constitution,* 4, 5, September 10, 1970.

CHAPTER 13

1. *Americus Times-Recorder,* 9, 10, 11, 12, September 15, 1970; *Atlanta Journal,* September 10, 11, 15, 1970, *New York Times* September 10, 11, 1970.

2. R. W. Apple, Jr., "New Figures in South's Politics," *New York Times,* September 11, 1970; Walton, *Native Son,* 60–63.

3. *Americus Times-Recorder,* September 11, 12, 1970.

4. *Columbus (GA) Ledger-Enquirer,* September 12, 1970, clipping in RG 1-1-111, box 1, Carter Clippings, GDAH.

5. *Valdosta (GA) Daily Times,* September 17, 1970; *Americus Times-Recorder,* September 15, 17, 21, 1970; *Atlanta Constitution,* September 14, 1970.

6. John J. Harte Associates, Inc., to JC State Headquarters, September 15, 1970, with attachments; Sanders to Gunter, September 11, 1970, with Gunter's note; *Atlanta Constitution,* September 19, 1970; assorted handbills; *Gwinnett Daily News,* September 14, 1970, all in Pre-Presidential File, 1962–76, box 38, JCL.

7. *Atlanta Constitution,* September 18, 22, 1970; *Atlanta Journal,* September 18, 19, 20, 1970.

8. *Americus Times-Recorder,* September 16, 19, 21, 22, 1970, *Atlanta Constitution,* September 16, 1970; "Look Who's Meeting Who," handbill, Rafshoon Donated Materials, box 7, JCL; Cook, *Sanders,* 337–38.

9. GGDP interview with Robert F. Flanagan, January 9, 1986, 75, GSU.

10. *Atlanta Constitution,* September 15, 18 (quotation), 20, 1970.

11. Sanders, "Sad Duty," 619.

12. *Atlanta Constitution,* September 20, 1970.

13. *Americus Times-Recorder,* September 21, 1970.

14. September 23, 1970, author's private collection.

15. Walton, *Native Son,* 64.

16. *New York Times,* September 24, 1970.

17. *Atlanta Constitution,* September 24, 1970.

18. *Americus Times-Recorder,* September 23, 24, 1970.

19. Memorandum, Davis to Woodruff, October 5, 1970, copy to J. Paul Austin, Woodruff Collection, box 15, MARBL, Woodruff Library, Emory University.

20. Bourne, *Carter,* 198.

21. *Atlanta Constitution,* October 8, 1970; *Americus Times-Recorder,* October 8, 1970.

22. *Atlanta Constitution,* 15, October 27, 1970; *Americus Times-Recorder,* October 18, 1970.

23. JC to Mrs. W. R. Spillers, October 6, 1970, RG 1-1-5, JC, box 40, GDAH.

24. JC to Judge Randall Evans, Jr., October 20, 1970; Hamilton Jordan, handwritten draft, Evans to JC, October 19, 1970, all in RG 1-1-5, JC, box 18, GDAH; see also *Atlanta Constitution,* October 18, 1970.

25. Sanders, "Sad Duty," 631–32.

26. *Atlanta Constitution,* September 29, October 1, 1970; *Americus Times-Recorder,* October 2, 20, 1970.

27. *Americus Times-Recorder,* October 10, 14, 1970; *Atlanta Constitution,* October 8, 12, 16, 20, 21, 22, 27, November 1, 1970; see also Sanders, "Sad Duty," 633–35.

28. *Atlanta Journal,* October 22, 1970.

29. Gerald Rafshoon, "Jimmy Carter vs. Hal Suit," typescript, n.d., Staff Secretary File, box 3, JCL; *Atlanta Constitution,* October 3, 1970; *Americus Times-Recorder,* October 1, 1970; Misc. Interview with RSC, December 21, 1974, JCL.

30. JCL interview with Jack Carter, June 25, 2003, 22, 25–27, JCL; *Reno (NV) Gazette-Journal,* October 14, 2005.

31. Walton, *Native Son,* 65–71; *Americus Times-Recorder,* November 4, 1970; *Atlanta Constitution,* November 4, 5, 1970; *New York Times,* November 4, 1970.

32. *Atlanta Constitution,* November 6, 11, 1970.

33. GGDP interview with Sanders, August 5, 12, 1986, 28, 65, 67, 68, GSU.

34. GGDP interview with Bobby Rowan, October 6, 1982, 20, GSU. For the "dark spot," see Allen, *Atlanta Rising,* 170, and for the Sanders camp viewpoint, see Cook, *Sanders,* 323–43, and Sanders, *Mighty Peculiar Elections,* 146–69.

35. Scheer, "Jimmy, We Hardly Know Y'all," 75.

36. Lamis, *Two-party South,* 97–98; Gulliver, *Friendly Tongue,* 102–9; Bass and Devries, *Transformation of Southern Politics,* 144–46.

37. Simpson, "Carter and Transformation," 73.

38. Sheppard, "Man from Plains," 16–19.

39. *New York Times,* October 22, 1976.

40. William Safire, "What Did Donors Get From Carter?" *Charlotte (N.C.) Observer,* October 23, 1976.

41. Interview with Robert Lipshutz, February 15, 1978, 2, Oral History Research Office Collection, Columbia University Library; Miller Center interview with Lance, May 12, 1982, 3, JCL; JC to Gerald Rafshoon, July 9, 1973, Carter Family Papers, box 4, JCL; statement for Mary Louise Smith, A. J. Reichley File, box 5, Gerald R. Ford Presidential Library; Memorandum, Ralph Stanley to Bill Greener, September 26, 1976.

42. Rabhan's story is told most completely in Bourne, *Carter,* 180–82, 199; it is based on Bourne's interviews with Rabhan and with Carter. See also RSC, *First Lady,* 72; JC, *Best,* 103; *St Louis Post-Dispatch,* October 24, 1976, clipping in President Ford Committee for Reelection File, box H27, Gerald R. Ford Presidential Library; and Douglas Brinkley, "What It Takes," *New Yorker,* October 21, 1996, 78.

43. JC to Lee J. Cobb, October 17, 1972, RG 1-1-5, JC, box 47, GDAH.

44. Misc. Interview with RSC, December 21, 1974, JCL.

45. *Calhoun (GA) Times,* December 2, 1970, clipping in RG 1-1-5, JC, box 26, GDAH; *Atlanta Constitution,* November 20, 27, 1970; Fink, *Prelude,* 114; JC to Bert Lance, August 9, 1971, Lance to JC, August 11, 1971, both in Carter Family Papers, box 3, JCL.

46. *Atlanta Constitution,* November 24, 27, December 2, 8, 15, 16, 18, 30, 1970; Press Releases, January 6, 1971, RG 1-10-43, GDAH.

47. Speeches, RG 1-1-45, box 12, GDAH; Henry S. Bishop to JC, January 5, 1971, RG 1-1-5, JC, box 1, GDAH; *Atlanta Constitution,* January 1, 5, 6, 1971.

48. Misc. Interview with RSC, December 21, 1974, JCL.

49. *Atlanta Constitution,* January 10, 1971; Misc. Interview with RSC, December 21, 1974, JCL.

50. *Americus Times-Recorder,* December 14, 17, 1970; Sherman Drawdy to JC, December 15, 1970, JC to Drawdy, December 22, 1970, Memorandum, Yvonne Redding to Governor Carter, December 17, 1970, all in RG 1-1-5, JC, box 37, GDAH.

51. Wells, *First Hundred Years,* 244–46.

52. JC to David Hall, December 4, 1970, RG 1-1-5, JC, box 7, GDAH.

53. JC to George, confidential, December 10, 1970, George L. Simpson, Jr., to J. Battle Hall, State Budget Officer, December 15, 1970, both in RG 1-1-5, JC, box 65, GDAH.

54. Miller Center interview with Stuart Eizenstat (1982), 29, 30 24, JCL.

55. *Atlanta Constitution,* January 7, 1971.

56. Author interview with JC, October 12, 1994.

57. Quoted in Morris, *Carter,* 184.

58. Sanders, "Sad Duty," 637; Norton and Schlosser, *Miracle,* 48; Wooten, *Dasher,* 284–85.

59. JC to Admiral Hyman G. Rickover, November 30, 1970; H. G. Rickover to Governor Carter, December 24, 1970, both in RG 1-1-5, JC, box 54, GDAH.

CHAPTER 14

1. Margaret Shannon, "A President in the Family," *Atlanta Journal and Constitution Magazine,* January 16, 1977, 23; Sissy Dolvin, unpublished memoir, January 1, 1992, typescript, 13, Emily Gordon Dolvin File, box 1, JCL.

2. *Atlanta Constitution,* January 13, 1971; Bourne, *Carter,* 200–201.

3. *Atlanta Constitution,* January 13, 1972; GGDP interview with Arnall, May 25, 1986, 107, GSU.

4. Executive Minutes, RG 1-1-3, JC, box 23, GDAH; JC, *Government Good as People,* 13–16. For full text of speech, see Carter, *Addresses,* 79–81.

5. *Atlanta Constitution,* January 13, 1971; Bourne, *Carter,* 201; *Americus Times-Recorder,* January 22, 1971; inauguration video, JCL.

6. Oath of Public Officers, January 13, 1971, RG 1-1-5, JC, box 79, GDAH; *Atlanta Constitution,* January 13, 1971.

7. Misc. Interview with RSC, December 21, 1974, JCL; *Atlanta Constitution.* January 13, 1971; Sissy Dolvin, unpublished memoir, January 1, 1992, typescript, 9–12, Emily Gordon Dolvin File, box 1, JCL.

8. *Atlanta Journal-Constitution,* January 3, 1971; *Atlanta Constitution,* January 11, 13, 1971; Sissy Dolvin, unpublished memoir, January 1, 1992, typescript, 9–12, Emily Gordon Dolvin File, box 1, JCL.

9. *Americus Times-Recorder,* January 22, 1971; RSC, *First Lady,* 80. She wore the same gown to inaugural balls when Jimmy became president, and it is now permanently preserved in the Smithsonian Institution.

10. RG 1-16-118, boxes 4, 5, and RG 61-16-120, box 1, GDAH; *Atlanta Journal-Constitution,* September 29, 1991.

11. Kenneth W. Dunwoody to JC, November 21, 1972 RG 1-1-5, JC, box 2, GDAH; J. B. Fuqua to JC, January 9, 1975, JC to J. B. Fuqua, January 14, 1975, both in RG 1-1-5, JC, box 18, GDAH.

12. "Georgia Governor's Mansion," *Architectural Digest,* March–April 1974, 32–37.

13. *Atlanta Journal-Constitution*, July 9, 1996; Lisby, "Trying," 92–95; *A Tour Through the Governor's Mansion*, pamphlet in RG 1-16-120, box 1, GDAH.

14. Misc. Interview with RSC, December 21, 1974, JCL; Simmons, *Rosalynn Carter*, 54; Bourne, *Carter*, 208.

15. Sissy Dolvin, unpublished memoir, January 1, 1992, typescript, 15–16, Emily Gordon Dolvin File, box 1, JCL; Sheehy, "Ladies and Gentlemen," 57; RSC, *First Lady*, 83–84.

16. Glad, *Carter*, 142; Simmons, *Rosalynn Carter*, 54; First Lady Press File, box 42, JCL.

17. Glad, *Carter*, 143; Bourne, *Carter*, 208.

18. Misc. Interview with Rosalynn Carter, December 21, 1974, JCL; Sheehy, "Ladies and Gentlemen," 57; Sissy Dolvin, unpublished memoir, January 1, 1992, typescript, 15–16, Emily Gordon Dolvin File, box 1, JCL; Simmons, *Rosalynn Carter*, 55–59; RSC, *First Lady*, 82.

19. RSC, *First Lady*, 86; "The Governor's Mansion," brochure, RG 1-16-120, box 1, GDAH; Sheehy, "Ladies and Gentlemen," 57.

20. Morris, *Carter*, 190; *Atlanta Constitution*, January 13, 1971.

21. Richard Walter Roper to JC, January 13, 1971, RG 1-1-5, JC, box 50, GDAH; *New York Times*, 13, January 14, 1971; Morris Abram to JC, January 14, 1971, Morris B. Abram Papers, MARBL, Robert W. Woodruff Library, Emory University.

22. GGDP interview with George T. Smith, August 19, 20, 1992, 12, GSU.

23. Herman Talmadge, interview by Jeff Broadwater, July 24, 1991, 18, 25, John C. Stennis Oral History Collection, Mississippi State University.

24. Jon Hardheimer, "Yes, That Was a Georgia Governor Speaking," *New York Times*, January 17, 1971.

25. Bourne, *Carter*, 201.

26. JC to Tommy Irvin, January 14, 1971, Carter Family Papers, box 2, JCL.

27. Bourne, *Carter*, 206.

28. Bourne, *Carter*, 209–10; Mary Bowers Wilson Beasley, Biographical Questionnaires, GDAH; Glad, *Carter*, 146–49.

29. *Atlanta Constitution*, January 22, 24, 1971; RSC, *First Lady*, 84.

30. Gilbert C. Fite, *Richard Russell, Jr.: Senator from Georgia* (Chapel Hill, N.C., 1991), 493.

31. *Atlanta Journal-Constitution*, January 25, 1971, January 22, 1972.

32. *New York Times*, January 22–23, 1971; Bourne, *Carter*, 201.

33. Wells, *First Hundred Years*, 246, 247.

34. Letter of Appointment, February 1, 1972, RG 1-1-3, JC, box 23, GDAH; *New York Times*, February 2, 3, 1971.

35. Hooks to JC, February 8, 1971, Carter Family Papers, box 2, JCL.

36. GGDP interview with Lester Maddox, November 22, 1988, 169–70, 203, GSU.

37. Fink, *Prelude*, 32–33; Morris, *Carter*, 189; "Beforehand," *Atlanta*, April 1988, 16, copy in VF, Maddox, L., JCL.

38. Maddox to JC, November 17, 1971, RG 1-1-5, JC, box 61, GDAH; JC to Maddox, March 19, 1974, RG 1-1-5, JC, box 61, GDAH; Short, *Maddox*, 134, 137, 149.

39. Bowen, "Gubernatorial Administration," 31, 37, 38, 41, 48, 61; *Atlanta Constitution*, February 26, 28, 1971; Glad, *Carter*, 188–90; Mazlish and Diamond, *Carter*, 206.

40. Glad, *Carter,* 190; *Atlanta Constitution,* March 3, 13, 1971.

41. Fink, *Prelude,* 33–35.

42. Glad, *Carter,* 190; Fink, *Prelude,* xxv; *Mercerian,* March 1971, 4–8, copy in RG 1-1-5, JC, box 2, GDAH; *Atlanta Constitution,* January 15, 17, 18, 1971.

43. Fink, *Prelude,* 33, 35, 37–38; author interview with Morris Collins, September 14, 1994, 1994.

44. JC to Smith, January 10, February 27, 1973, RG 1-1-5, JC, box 11, GDAH; JC to Smith, April 18, 1973, RG 1-1-5, JC, box 15, GDAH.

45. After George Smith's death on December 9, 1973, Thomas Murphy won election to the speakership. Murphy had supported Sanders in 1970, and although initially he attempted to get along with Carter, the two soon drifted apart. An old-fashioned politician who liked face-to-face banter, the new speaker angrily wadded up the governor's memoranda and tossed them in the wastebasket. Carter failed in his plan to get Murphy out of the speakership. Glad, *Carter,* 190; Hyatt, *Mr. Speaker,* 72–77, 198; Fink, *Prelude,* 188; JC to Tom Murphy, January 4, 5, 1974, RG 1-1-5, JC, box 29, GDAH; Margaret Shannon, "The Unexpected Speaker," *Atlanta Journal-Constitution,* February 3, 1974.

46. Mazlish and Diamond, *Carter,* 198; Fink, *Prelude,* 42–43; *Americus Times-Recorder,* January 14, 1971; *Atlanta Constitution,* February 11, 13, 1971.

47. *Atlanta Constitution,* March 14, 1971.

48. *Americus Times-Recorder,* March 8, 1971.

49. *Americus Times-Recorder,* April 4, 1971; *Americus Times-Recorder,* June 10, 1971.

50. *Atlanta Constitution,* August 24, 25, 1971; *Americus Times-Recorder,* August 8, 1971.

51. Holly to JC, September 13, 1971, RG 1-1-5, JC, box 37, GDAH; H. Carter to JC, September 21, 1971, RG 1-1-5, JC, box 39, GDAH.

52. *Carter, Addresses,* 38–39. *Atlanta Constitution,* September 25, 1971; JC, Handwritten Notice to the Georgia Senate, September 28, 1971, Carter Family Papers, box 6, JCL; Press Releases, RG 1-10-43, box 3, GDAH.

53. Robert H. Zieger, "The Quest for National Goals, 1957–81," in Fink and Davis Graham, *Carter Presidency,* 43.

54. Author interview with Collins, September 14, 1994.

55. Fink, *Prelude,* 45; Bourne, *Carter,* 207.

56. Fink, *Prelude,* 47–50; Glad, *Carter,* 162–63.

57. Minutes of these meetings in "Manual," Executive Committee Progress, March 31–July 28, 1971, RG 1-15-68, GDAH.

58. Fink, *Prelude,* 57–62.

59. JC to Harry Murphy, August 30, 1971, Carter Family Papers, box 2, JCL; see also *Atlanta Constitution,* June 19, 1971.

60. W. H. Champion to JC, box 31; JC to George L. Smith II, June 20, 1971, box 15; Michael Trotter to Jackson W. Taver, July 21, 1971, box 24; all in RG 1-1-5, JC, GDAH.

61. Fink, *Prelude,* 75–81; Glad, *Carter,* 163; *Atlanta Constitution,* January 20, 28, February 1, March 1, 1971; Speeches, RG 1-1-45, JC, box 13, GDAH; Memorandum, Tom Linder, Jr., to JC, December 6, 1971, RG 1-15-64, box 1, GDAH. *State of Georgia Reorganization and*

Management Improvement Study (November 1971), booklet, copy in RG 1-1-5, JC, box 73, GDAH. The twenty departments were as follows: (1) Governor's Office (legal, news, liaison with state and federal governments, staff for speeches and correspondence); (2) Office of Attorney General; (3) Department of Agriculture; (4) Office of Comptroller General; (5) Department of Labor; (6) Public Service Commission; (7) Office of Secretary of State; (8) Office of Planning and Budget; (9) Department of Administrative Services (included cash management); (10) Department of Revenue; (11) Department of Community Development; (12) University System of Georgia; (13) Department of Education; (14) Department of Natural Resources; (15) Department of Human Resources; (16) Department of Veterans Services; (17) Department of Defense; (18) Department of Public Safety; (19) Department of Financial Regulation; and (20) Department of Transportation.

62. Fink, *Prelude,* 81–91; Glad, *Carter,* 164; Citizens' Committee letters, RG 1-15-66, box 1, GDAH.

63. Fink, *Prelude,* 93, 95–96.

64. Fink, *Prelude,* 95–96.

65. *Americus Times-Recorder,* November 10, 1971; *Atlanta Constitution,* November 17, 1971; *News of Gwinnett-Buford (GA),* November 21, 1971; Fink, *Prelude,* 97–100.

66. *Griffin (GA) Daily News,* December 8, 1971; *Columbus (GA) Ledger-Enquirer,* December 8, 1971; *Columbus (GA) Ledger-Enquirer,* December 2, 1971; Press Releases, RG 1-10-43, box 3, GDAH.

67. JC to Irvin, December 30, 1971; Irvin to JC, December 28, 29, 1971, all in RG 1-1-5, JC, box 55, GDAH. See also *Columbus (GA) Ledger-Enquirer,* December 19, 1971.

68. JC to Jack Nix, May 4, 1971, January 25, 1972, both in Carter Family Papers, box 3, JCL; Battle Hall to JC, January 24, 1972, Carter Family Papers, box 6, JCL; JC to George Busbee, January 27, 1972, Carter Family Papers, box 5, JCL; (GA)House Appropriations Committee Hearings, January 27, 1971, January 25, 1972, copy in Carter Family Papers, box 6, JCL; Fink, *Prelude,* 98, 100–101; *Atlanta Journal,* December 27, 1971.

69. Minutes, Meeting of the State Board of Health, November 18, 1971, Carter Family Papers, box 5, JCL; Fink, *Prelude,* 101–2.

70. Notes for Remarks by Governor Jimmy Carter, Southern Governors' Conference, November 8, 1971, Carter Family Papers, box 7, JCL; JC to Dr. John. H. Robinson, III, December 8, 1971, RG 1-1-5, JC, box 40, GDAH.

71. Lillian Carter to JC., n.d., Pond House, JC to Lillian Carter, August 4, 1972, both in Carter Family Papers, box 2, JCL; *Atlanta Constitution,* April 7, 1972.

72. Lillian Carter to JC, December 6, 1971, RG 1-1-5, JC, box 60, GDAH; *Atlanta Constitution,* November 22, 1971.

73. Lillian Carter to JC, n.d., JC to Lillian Carter, August 21, 1972, both in Carter Family Papers, box 2, JCL.

74. Fink, *Prelude,* 103.

75. Fink, *Prelude,* 101–4; Glad, *Carter,* 164; *LaGrange (GA) Daily News,* December 10, 1971; *Macon (GA) News,* December 10, 1971; *Augusta (GA) Chronicle,* December 23, 1971; *Atlanta Constitution,* December 15, 28, 1971.

76. Memorandum, JC to Legislative Control Team, February 8, 1972, RG 1-1-5, JC, box 73, GDAH.

77. Memorandum, Kirbo to JC, July 12, 1971, Carter Family Papers, box 3, JCL.

78. Two confidential memoranda, n.d. [c. summer 1971], Carter Family Papers, box 3, JCL.

79. Memorandum, Jordan to JC, [1973], Carter Family Papers, box 3, JCL.

80. Memorandum, Jordan to JC, November 16, 1971, Carter Family papers, box 3, JCL.

81. Memorandum, Jody to JC, n.d., Carter Family Papers, box 2, JCL.

82. *Savannah (GA) Morning News,* December 18, 1971; Fink, *Prelude,* 114.

83. Quoted in Fink, *Prelude,* 114–15. See also Memorandum, Hamilton Jordan to JC, December 12, 1971, RG 1-1-5, JC, box 27, GDAH.

84. JC to Lamar Plunkett, March 2, 1972, JC to Sen. Harry Jackson, February 29, 1972, JC to Carl Drury, February 1, 1972, JC to Mr. Speaker, February 15, 1972, all in Carter Family Papers, box 6, JCL.

85. Fink, *Prelude,* 115–16; Bourne, *Carter,* 202.

86. JC, note on letter of John S. Prickett, Jr., to JC, October 7, 1971, Carter Family Papers, box 3, JCL; *Atlanta Constitution,* August 27, 1971.

87. Memoranda, Kirbo to JC, July 27, August 31, 1971, Zell Miller to JC, August 30, 1971, all in Carter Family Papers, box 3, JCL; see also James Clotfelter, "Populism in Office or, Whatever Happened to Huey Long?" *New South* 28, no. 2 (spring 1973): 57, copy in VF, Carter, Jimmy, Governor (2), JCL.

88. Fink, *Prelude,* 116–17.

89. Fink, *Prelude,* 117.

90. Speeches, RG 1-1-95, JC, box 12, GDAH. Fink, *Prelude,* 118–20.

91. Fink, *Prelude,* 127; *Atlanta Constitution,* December 5, 1995; *Atlanta Journal,* November 20, 1971.

92. JC, *Addresses,* 119–27.

93. Fink, *Prelude,* 129–38; *Atlanta Constitution,* December 5, 1995. GGDP interview with Kidd, October 20, 1988, 10, GSU.

94. Memorandum, Tom Linder, Jr., to JC, January 4, 1972, RG 1-15-64, box 1, GDAH; Glad, *Carter,* 168.

95. Miller Center interview with Kirbo, January 5, 1983, 6, JCL; Miller Center interview with Bert Lance, May 12, 1982, 6–7, JCL; GGDP interview with George Busbee, March 24, 1987, 33, GSU.

96. GGDP interview with Bobby Rowan, October 6, 1992, 24, GSU.

97. *Atlanta Constitution,* January 19, 27, 1972.

98. JC to Richardson, January 19, 1972, JC to Hal Suit, January 26, 1972, both in RG 1-1-5, JC, box 22; JC to Celestine Sibley, January 19, 1971, RG 1-1-5, JC, box 23, GDAH; JC to George L. Smith II, February 23, 1972, RG 1-1-5, JC, box 11, GDAH; *Atlanta Constitution,* February 23, March 2, 11, 1972.

99. Lance to JC, March 9, 1972, Lance to JC, April 4, 1973, JC to Lance, April 8, 1973, Carter Family Papers, box 3, JCL.

100. News releases, May 21, 1971, Carter Family Papers, box 4, JCL.

101. Lance to JC, July 29, 1971, Carter Family Papers, box 3, JCL; Lance to JC, January 25, 1972, Carter Family Papers, box 2, JCL.

102. JC to Lance, May 17, JC to Lance, June 8, JC to Lance, July 1, 1971, Lance to JC, June 30, 1971, all in Carter Family Papers, box 3, JCL.

103. JC to Lance, January 26, 1972, JC to Lance, January 28, 1972, both in Carter Family Papers, box 2, JCL.

104. GGDP interview with Hugh Gillis, March 25, 1988, 49, GSU; *Americus Times-Recorder,* January 21, March 2, 1972; JC to Cecil Passmore, August 30, 1971, RG 1-1-5, JC, box 31, GDAH.

105. GGDP interview with Nathan Dean, October 2, 1989, 42, GSU.

106. *Atlanta Constitution,* March 3, May 13, 1971; Hamilton Jordan to Joe T. Andrews, May 6, 1971, Mike Jones to JC, May 8, 1971, both in RG 1-1-5, JC, box 1, GDAH; JC to Wilbur H. Homer, May 7, 1971, RG 1-1-5, JC, box 11, GDAH.

107. Rowan, *Georgia's Modern Day Legislature,* 116; "A State in Action, 1971–1975," pamphlet, RG 1-1-5, JC, box 73, GDAH; Fink, *Prelude,* 12; Bowden, "Gubernatorial Administration," 16; JC, *Government Good as People,* 19.

108. JC to Charles W. Coss, Executive Director of Coastal Plains Regional Development, June 15, 1971, RG 1-1-5, JC, box 52, GDAH; Tom Wicker, "New Mood in the South," *New York Times,* April 25, 1971; *Atlanta Constitution,* June 5, 6, 1971. Gene Odum to JC, August 28, 1971, Odum to Hamilton Jordan, July 28, 1971, both in RG 1-1-5, JC, box 2, GDAH; JC to Thomas F. Sellers, October 8, 1971, RG 1-1-5, JC, box 23, GDAH; notebook, December 1971, RG 1-1-5, JC, box 75, GDAH; Bourne, *Carter,* 52, 214.

109. Lipshutz to JC, March 19, 1971, RG 1-1-5, JC, box 20, GDAH.

110. Bill Shipp, "Carter Encountering an 'Image' Problem," *Atlanta Constitution,* April 16, 1971.

CHAPTER 15

1. JC, *Government Good as People,* 17; JC to David B. Collins, April 24, 1972, RG 1-1-5, JC, box 17, JC to John T. Simmons, May 31, 1972, RG 1-1-5, JC, box 40, GDAH.

2. Julian T. Pipkin to JC, June 22, 1972, RG 1-1-5, JC, box 22; Governor's General Subject File, August 3, 1972, RG 1-10-125; JC to Glendon McCullough, September 8, 1972, RG 1-1-5, JC, box 51, all in GDAH.

3. *Savannah (GA) Morning News,* November 15, 1972; JC to Ronnie Thompson, November 20, 1972, RG 1-1-5, JC, box 2, GDAH.

4. JC, handwritten notes, January 14, 1973, RG 1-1-45, Speeches; Max Cleland to JC, January 29, 1973, RG 1-1-5, JC, box 12, both in GDAH.

5. JC, handwritten notes, April 3, 1974, RG 1-1-45, Speeches, box 13, GDAH; *Americus Times-Recorder,* June 15, 1974.

6. Fink, *Prelude,* 17; Jack U. Harwell, "Georgia's Governor Carter," News Services of the Baptist Church, October 7, 1974, Southern Baptist History Collection, Southern Baptist Historical Library and Archives, Nashville, TN.

7. JC notes for speech, March 3, 1973, Speeches, RG 1-1-45, GDAH.

8. JC to Baraca Class Members, June 11, 1973, RG 1-1-5, JC, box 39; Speeches, March 2–4, RG 1-1-45, JC to Bishop Ramond W. Lessard, April 1973, RG 1-1-5, JC, box 2, GDAH; Memorandum, Jack Partain to JC, March 7, 1972, Carter Family Papers, box 7, JCL.

9. JC, World Mission Conference Speech, March 4, 1973, RG 1-1-5, JC, box 18, GDAH: January–February issue of *Upper Room* mentioned in *Americus Times-Recorder,* January 11, 1974; *Who's Who in Georgia, 1973* (Atlanta, 1973), 70.

10. Bourne, *Carter,* 207; Glad, *Carter,* 179–80; Morris, *Carter,* 197.

11. JC, *Best,* 111–14; Eleanor McGovern to JC, January 30, 1973, JC to Eleanor McGovern, February 23, 1973, both in RG 1-1-5, JC, box 53, GDAH; Glad, *Carter,* 154–59.

12. JC to Dave Padget, January 16, 1973, RG 1-1-5, JC, box 22; Russell A. Blanchard, to JC, April 19, 1971, JC to Mills Lane, August 1, 1971, Lane to JC, August 23, 1971, both in RG 1-1-5, JC, box 20; series of letters thanking bankers for their contributions to the drug program, December 15, 1971, RG 1-1-5, JC, box 58; JC to T. Hogan, May 22, 1972, RG 1-1-5, JC, box 55; JC to Philip Alston, May 21, 1974, RG 1-1-5, JC, box 17; Press Releases, August 25, November 19, 1971, RG 1-10-43, JC, box 1, all in GDAH; JC, *Best,* 115.

13. Mazlish and Diamond, *Carter,* 197, 199; *Macon (GA) Telegraph and News,* July 30, 1972; Minutes of House Appropriations FY73, March 1, 1972, Carter Family Papers, box 6, JCL.

14. JC to Mrs. E. O. Porter, January 19, 1973, RG 1-1-5, JC, box 5, GDAH.

15. D. W. Sands to JC, February 15, March 3, 1973, JC to Ambassador Ushiba, March 3, 1973, all in RG 1-1-5, JC, box 23, GDAH; JC to Ernie O'Neal, October 2, 1973, RG 1-1-5, JC, box 55, JC to Fred Cannon, April 22, 1974, RG 1-1-5, JC, box 17, JC to Edwin C. Eckles, June 15, 1971, RG 1-1-5, JC, box 4, Louis W. Truman to JC, November 27, 1972, RG 1-1-5, JC, box 56, all in GDAH.

16. Press Releases, July 5, 1972, RG 1-10-43, JC, box 2; David Rabhan to JC, October 10, 1972, RG 1-1-5, JC, box 47. Duane Riner to JC, March 1, 1973, RG 1-1-5, JC, box 56, all in GDAH; *Atlanta Constitution,* December 9, 1972.

17. McMorrow, *Jimmy,* 27 (photographs).

18. Press Releases, May 21, 1974, RG 1-10-43, JC, box 4; Jack Rigg to JC, July 12, 1974, with JC note to Mary Beazley, RG 1-1-5, JC, box 22, both in GDAH.

19. JC to "Mr. Speaker, February 29, 1972, box 5, JC to Jack Partain, June 9, 1972, box 7, both in Carter Family Papers. JCL; Bourne, *Carter,* 260; Fink, *Prelude,* 10; *Atlanta Constitution,* February 17, September 3, 9, 16, March 17, 1971, 1972; JC to Edmund Muskie, September 17, 1971, RG 1-1-5, JC, box 53; "Regional Action," *Southern Regional Board* 23 (January 1972): 3–4, copy in RG 1-1-5, JC, box 66; JC to Larry R. Gess, April 21, 1972, RG 1-1-5, JC, box 58, all in GDAH; see also Michael, *Carter,* 54, 65, 71, 78, 83–84.

20. *Georgia Southern College Alumni Record,* vol. 3, no. 2 (March 1972): 8–9, copy in RG 1-1-5, JC, box 4; Louis C. Alderman, Jr., to JC, September 29, 1972, RG 1-1-5, JC, box 3, JC to Jack W. Powers, October 6, 1972, RG 1-1-5, JC, box 22, speech at Middle Georgia College, November 2, 1972, RG 1-1-45, JC, box 11, M. S. McDonald to JC, November 19, 1972, RG 1-1-5, JC, box 3, JC to S. Walter Martin, September 26, 1972, RG 1-1-5, JC, box 32, JC notes for speech at Valdosta State, RG 1-1-45, JC, box 11, all in GDAH; JC to George Simpson, with attached

notes, August 3, 1971, Carter Family Papers, box 7, JCL; Bryant, *Plunkett,* 71. Information about Simpson in author interview with Morris Collins, September 14, 1994.

21. JC to William B. King, June 7, 1973, RG 1-1-5, JC, box 39; Rick Cobb et al. to JC, with JC's notes, July 27, 1973, RG 1-1-5, JC, box 64; JC to Herman Talmadge, June 22, 1974, RG 1-1-5, JC, box 54, all in GDAH.

22. JC to Angela McDonald, March 12, 1973, RG 1-1-5, JC, box 39, Hugh Carter to JC, with attached list from Angela McDonald, April 13, 1973, RG 1-1-5, JC, box 70; JC to George Simpson, March 8, 1971, RG 1-1-5, JC, box 69, all in GDAH.

23. JC to George Beattie, April 13, 1973, RG 1-1-5, JC, box 55, GDAH.

24. JC to F. N. Boney, June 18, 1974, RG 1-1-5, JC, box 7, GDAH. Published by the University of Georgia Press in 1977, the book became a standard text.

25. JC to Tommy Hooks, April 24, 1972, Carter Family Papers, box 2, JCL; *Atlanta Constitution,* 7, 12, 1972; Millard Fuller to JC, April 14, 1972, RG 1-1-5, JC, box 39, JC to Kathryn G. Hardwick, April 27, 1972, RG 1-1-5, JC, box 37, both in GDAH; *Americus Times-Recorder,* May 20, 1974.

26. Press Releases, September 27, 1971, RG 1-10-43; Eugene Sanders to JC, May 23, 1973, with JC notes, RG 1-1-5, JC, box 23, all in GDAH.

27. JC to Charles Chapman, January 29, 1973, RG 1-1-5, JC, box 36, GDAH; see also Don W. Schmidt to JC, May 29, 1972, RG 1-1-5, JC, box 98, GDAH.

28. R. D. Fowler to JC, May 26, 1971, Lena Grace Cornelious to JC, July 3, 1974, both in RG 1-1-5, JC, box 32, GDAH; JC to John Crown, April 5, 1972, RG 1-1-5, JC, box 17, JC to Congressman Don Edwards, April 7, 1973, RG 1-1-5, JC, box 2, GDAH; Speech to Lions Club in Savannah, June 12, 1972, RG 1-10-125, box 3, GDAH; Peter Bourne to JC, June 28, 1971, Carter Family Papers, box 5, JCL; Peter Bourne to H. C. Freidman, December 8, 1971, with attachment, Georgia Narcotics Treatment Program Progress Report, November 1971, RG 1-1-5, JC, box 26, GDAH.

29. Governor's Emergency Fund Transfers F. Y. 1973, RG 1-1-5, JC, box 70, GDAH; Press Releases, May 10, 1973, RG 1-10-43, JC, box 4, GDAH; Memorandum, Frank Moore to JC, February 28, 1974, RG 1-1-5, JC, box 70, GDAH.

30. Carter quoted in Gulliver, *Friendly Tongue,* 6–17.

31. JC to "Dear Pastor," January 1974, RG 1-1-5, JC, box 60; JC to Brian Baker, April 25, 1974, Martin M. McLaughlin, to JC, July 23, 1974, RG 1-1-5, JC, box 17; JC speech, August 1, 1974, RG 1-1-45, JC, box 11, all in GDAH; Mazlish and Diamond, *Carter,* 204–5.

32. JC to Robert Chambers, *Athens (GA) Banner Herald,* June 14, 1971, RG 1-1-5, JC, box 7, GDAH.

33. JC to Senator Julian Webb, March 3, 1972, RG 1-1-5, JC, box 38, GDAH.

34. Morris, *Carter,* 198; Arthur Bolton to JC, December 10, 1971, Harold N. Hill, Jr., to JC, December 23, 1971, both in RG 1-1-5, JC, box 61, Press Releases, RG 1-10-43, JC, box 3, all in GDAH.

35. Simpson, "Restyling Georgia Courts," 282, 284–87; JC, *Best,* 108; Glad, *Carter,* 183–84; Bourne, *Carter,* 212; *Atlanta Constitution,* October 15, 1995; Executive Order, June 4, 1973, RG 1-19-100, GDAH. Bowden, "Gubernatorial Administration," 22.

36. Bourne, *Carter,* 212; *New York Times,* February 23, March 29, 1973; D. M. Stafford to JC, March 8, 1973, RG 1-1-5, JC, box 6, GDAH; JC quotation in his letter to Mrs. D. W. Johnson, May 2, 1973, RG 1-1-5, JC, box 50, GDAH: Bryant, *Plunkett,* 292–93.

37. JC to the Rev. James E. Bowden, October 25, 1974, RG 1-1-5, JC, box 7, GDAH; JC to Judge Jack Partain, December 30, 1971, RG 1-1-5, JC, box 22, GDAH; JC note on Judge Robert H. Hall to JC, August 30, 1971, RG 1-1-5, JC, box 19, GDAH. See also Bourne, *Carter,* 202–3; JC to Jack Partain, June 9, 1972, Carter Family Papers, box 7, 1972, JCL.

38. Glad, *Carter,* 182; *Atlanta Constitution,* December 15, 1972; JC quotation in letter to James A. "Sloppy" Floyd, December 14, 1972, attached to Memorandum, Floyd to Ellis G. MacDougall, December 12, 1972, RG 1-1-5, JC, box 2, GDAH.

39. JC, *Best,* 108; *Americus Times-Recorder,* January 5, 1971; Press Releases, RG 1-10-43, August 2, December 13, 1971, GDAH; Griffin Bell to JC, January 24, 1972, JC to Bell, December 1, 1971, RG 1-1-5, JC, box 17, GDAH; JC to Joe Andrews, October 25, 1972, RG 1-1-5, JC, box 1, GDAH; Cecil C. McCall to JC, Status Report, July 1972–October 1974, RG 1-1-5, JC, box 63, GDAH; Fink, *Prelude,* 7; JC to Ellis McDougall, January 7, 15, 28, 1972, Carter Family Papers, box 7, JCL.

40. *Americus Times-Recorder,* October 3, 1973; JC to Ray Pope, November 20, 1972, form letter, Frank Moore to JC, December 15, 1972, both in RG 1-1-5, JC, box 64, GDAH.

41. Glad, *Carter,* 180–81; Fink, *Prelude,* 8; JC, *Best,* 118; Press Releases, May 8, 1971, RG 1-10-43, Governors General Subject File, July 29, 1972, RG 1-10-125, box 3, GDAH; *Americus Times-Recorder,* June 28, 1972; *Atlanta Journal-Constitution,* May 6, 1995.

42. JC to Fred [Marland], January 2, 1972, RG 1-1-5, JC, box 33, GDAH.

43. Joe Tanner to JC, September 15, 1972, Jack Crockford to JC, September 28, 1972, both in RG 1-1-5, JC, box 63, GDAH; Tanner to JC, January 19, 1973, Carter Family Papers, box 6, JCL; Spewrell Bluff Dam Debate, September 27, 1973, RG 1-1-5, JC, box 71, GDAH; *Americus Times-Recorder,* October 1, 1973; *National Wildlife Federation News,* November 1, 1973, 5; Press Releases, RG 1-10-43, JC, box 4, GDAH; JC quotation in preface to Fred Brown, *The Flint River* (guidebook), quoted in *Atlanta Journal-Constitution,* April 29, 2001; JC to Dear Sirs, n.d., Carter Family Papers, box 7, JCL; Eugene T. Methvin, "The Fight to Save the Flint," *Reader's Digest,* August 1974, 17–26. See also Eugene P. Odum, "Harmony between Man and Nature: An Ecological View," Fall 1972, unpublished paper, copy in Carter Family Papers, box 5, JCL.

44. Beattie Statement, June 9, 1972, JC to Beattie, June 12, September 26, 1972, JC to Mrs. Gerald E. Anderson, April 29, 1974, all in RG 1-1-5, JC, box 17, GDAH.

45. JC to Cook Barwick, April 6, 1973, RG 1-1-5, JC, box 17, Beattie to JC, November 20, 1973, RG 1-1-5, JC, box 5, Press Releases, RG 1-10-43, JC, box 4, all in GDAH; Hamilton Jordan to JC with JC note, January 31, 1973, RG 1-1-5, JC, box 21, GDAH; *Americus Times-Recorder,* January 12, 1972; JC to Holcombe T. Green, March 14, 1973, RG 1-1-5, JC, box 18, GDAH. Mazlish and Diamond, *Carter,* 170.

46. James M. Burt to JC, October 6, 1973, RG 1-1-5, JC, box 41, GDAH; *Record World* clipping in RG 1-1-5, JC, box 2, GDAH, *Atlanta Journal-Constitution,* January 19, 1992, January 12, 1995; *Time,* August 6, 1998.

47. Nancy Hanks to JC, April 18, 1973, RG 1-1-5, JC, box 41, GDAH; interview with Michael Straight, November 8, 1981, 800–803, Oral History Research Office Collection, Columbia University Library.

48. Quoted in *People,* April 22, 1974, 39.

49. JC to "Quimby," August 2, 1972, RG 1-1-5, JC, box 38, JC to Georgia Senate, March 16, 1973, RG 1-1-45, JC, box 12, both in GDAH; JC to James Beverly Langford, August 18, 1972, RG 1-1-5, JC, box 26, GDAH.

50. "Jimmy Carter: A Midterm Report," *Georgia* 16, no. 7 (winter 1973): 23–25, 60.

51. *Atlanta Journal-Constitution,* 22, February 23, 1974; *Atlanta Constitution,* August 3, 1974.

52. Goody Book, Pre-Presidential File, box 14, JCL; Fink, *Prelude,* 178; JC to Tommy Hooks, September 20, 1972, RG 1-1-5, box 39; Duane Riner to JC July 26, 1972, RG 1-1-5, JC, box 2, Jordan to Lamar R. Plunkett, August 16, 1972, RG 1-1-5, JC, box 2; Jordan to JC, September 12, 26, 1972, RG 1-1-5, JC, box 70; James I. Parker to Frank Moore, May 8, 1973, with attached memoranda from JC and Jordan, RG 1-1-5, JC, boxes 70 and 2; Clark D. Hill, Sr. to JC, June 12, 1973, RG 1-1-5, JC, box 38; Frank Moore to JC, August 8, 1973, RG 1-1-5, JC, box 70; JC to Mayors and County Commissioners, June 12, 1974, RG 1-1-5, JC, box 61; unidentified news clipping, May 16, 1974, saying Carter gave $16,800 to projects in Plains area, RG 1-1-5, JC, box 69; all in GDAH.

53. Bourne, *Carter,* 278.

54. JC to Turner Scott, August 16, 1971, RG 1-1-5, JC, box 43; JC to Robert Smalley, January 11, 1973, RG 1-1-5, JC, box 62, JC to Gene Holley, March 13, 1973, RG 1-1-5, JC, box 37, JC to "Sloppy" Floyd, March 14, 15, 1973. RG 1-1-5, JC, box 7, all in GDAH.

55. Press Releases, June 14, 1972, RG 1-10-125, JC, box 3, GDAH.

56. Executive Minutes, April 24, 1973, RG 1-1-3, JC, box 3, JC to Thomas B. Murphy, April 5, 1974, and JC to Maddox, April 5, 1974, RG 1-10-43, JC, box 4, all in GDAH; *Americus Times-Recorder,* September 21, 1973; *Atlanta Constitution,* April 4, 1974; Allen, *Atlanta Rising,* 70–72; Martin, *Good Man,* 47–48.

57. JC to Gambrell, February 7, 1972, Carter Family Papers, box 4, JCL; Bourne, *Carter,* 221; *New York Times,* August 30, 1972. See also Robert M. Gamble to JC, June 14, 1971, JC to Tommy Hooks, August 24, 1972, and Gambrell to Alan Otten, September 15, 1972, all in Carter Family Papers, boxes 3 and 4, respectively, JCL; JC to Mrs. Gambrell, July 18, 1974, Carter Family Papers, box 4, JCL.

58. Jordan to JC, n.d. [c. 1973], Carter Family Papers, box 3, JCL.

59. VF, Clough, Susan, JCL; Glad, *Carter,* 143.

60. VF, Moore, Frank, JCL; Glad, *Carter,* 143–44.

61. Press Releases, March 12, 1973, RG 1-10-43, JC, box 4, Moore to Penny Brasington, April 24, 1973, RG 1-1-5, JC, box 17, Lance to Moore, RG 1-1-5, JC, box 26, all in GDAH; *Americus Times-Recorder,* April 4, 1973.

62. Miller Center interview with Jordan, November 6, 1981, 73–74, JC to Jody, October 5, [no year], Carter Family Papers, box 4, both in JCL.

63. Memorandum, Jody to JC, n.d., Carter Family Papers, box 2, JCL.

64. July 7, 1973, RG 1-1-5, JC, box 62, GDAH.

65. "Notice," JC to Mary, Frank, Jody, Bill, J. Burris, Jim McIntyre, and others, June 27, 1974, RG 1-1-5, JC, box 62, GDAH; Jordan to JC, n.d. [c. 1973], Carter Family Papers, box 3, JCL.

CHAPTER 16

1. Scheer, "Jimmy, We Hardly Know Y'all," 70.

2. JC, *Best*, 107.

3. Memorandum, Charles Kirbo to JC, September 12, 1971, Carter Family Papers, box 3, JCL; see also Memorandum, Rita Jackson to JC, n.d., Carter Family Papers, box 2, JCL.

4. JC, *Addresses*, xxxiii, 45.

5. Handwritten notes, "Jimmy" to "Leroy," Johnson to JC, January 20, 1972, Carter Family Papers, box 2, JCL. See also *Atlanta Constitution*, March 4, 1971; Fink, *Prelude*, 13, 15.

6. GGDP interview with Robert F. Flanagan, January 9, 1989, GSU.

7. *Atlanta Constitution*, March 22, June 12, 1971; News Release, May 3, 1971, RG 1-1-5, JC, box 60, GDAH; Jordan to Young, August 23, 1971, RG 1-1-5, JC, box 24, GDAH.

8. *Atlanta Constitution*, June 5, 1971; JC to Hugh A. Inglis, September 21, 1971, RG 1-1-5, JC, box 7, GDAH.

9. JC to George F. Green, May 10, 1971, Carter Family Papers, box 2, JCL.

10. Thompson to JC, October 1, 1971, a citizen to JC, November 4, 1971, both in RG 1-1-5, JC, box 3, GDAH.

11. Hall to JC, July 6, 1971, Carter Family Papers, box 6, JCL.

12. John L. McGown to "Whom It May Concern," n.d., Carter Family Papers, box 2, JCL; Bourne, *Carter*, 211; Tuck, *Beyond Atlanta*, 221.

13. Handwritten note, JC to McCown, September 18, 1971; George F. Green to JC, September 14, 1971, with attached "NOTICE"; JC to Green, May 10, 1971, Green to JC, April 26, 1971, all in Carter Family Papers, box 2, JCL.

14. McGown to JC, September 27, 1971, Carter Family Papers, box 2, JCL.

15. Bourne, *Carter*, 211; *New York Times*, October 2, 1971; Grant, *Way It Was*, 434–35.

16. JC to Ray Pope, November 30, 1971, RG 1-1-5, JC, box 65; Press Releases, RG 1-10-43, JC; Hughes Spalding to JC, February 18, 1972, RG 1-1-5, JC, box 23; Memorandum by Ray Pope, March 17, 1972, RG 1-1-5, JC, box 65, all in GDAH.

17. JC to David Rabhan, May 18, 1972, RG 1-1-5, JC, box 22; Executive Minutes, RG 1-10-43, box 4, Press Releases, both in GDAH.

18. Rita Samuels Report to JC, August 21, 1972, JC to Samuels, November 30, 1972, JC notes on Memorandum, Herschel Saucier to JC, December 7, 1972, RG 1-1-5, JC, box 62; John B. Smith to JC, August 30, 1972, RG 1-1-5, JC, box 23, JC note on memorandum, Jordon to JC, September 18, 1972, RG 1-1-5, JC, box 56, all in GDAH.

19. Samuels, Minorities and Females Preliminary Report, August 31, 1972, RG 1-1-5, JC, box 62, GDAH; *Atlanta Constitution*, October 9, 1972; Jordan to King, Sr., October 19, 1972, and Jondell Johnson to JC, December 2, 1972, both in RG 1-1-5, JC, box 20, GDAH.

20. Jordan, *Vernon Can Read*, 271.

21. Julius S. Scott, Jr., to JC, January 19, 1973, RG 1-1-5, JC, box 23, GDAH; JC note on letter of J. Frank Myers to Rep. Janet Merrit, January 20, 1971, RG 1-1-5, JC, box 39, GDAH.

22. JC to Billy Ferguson, February 7, 1973, JC to Heads of Departments, February 16, 1973, both in RG 1-1-5, JC, box 62, GDAH.

23. JC to Ministers, February 20, 1973, RG 1-1-5, JC, box 23, GDAH.

24. Mrs. Harry A. Pfifner to JC, May 4, 1973, RG 1-1-5, JC, box 22; Mamie B. Reese to JC, May 22, 1973, RG 1-1-5, JC, box 14; Press Releases, April 5, 1973, RG 1-10-45, all in GDAH.

25. Memorandum, Rita Samuels to JC, May 30, 1973, RG 1-1-5, JC, box 62, GDAH.

26. *New York Times,* October 14, 1973, and January 5, 1974.

27. John A. Kirk, "Martin Luther King, Jr.," in *New Georgia Encyclopedia,* www.georgiaencyclopedia.org; see also Branch, *Parting the Waters,* and *Pillar of Fire;* Garrow, *FBI.*

28. Grant, *Way It Was,* 231; Kent Anderson Leslie, "Lucy Craft Laney," *New Georgia Encyclopedia,* www.georgiaencyclpedia.org.

29. Grant, *Way It Was,* 92, 106, 111–14, 134, 157–59, 286; Stephen Ward Angell, "Henry McNeal Turner (1834–1915)," *New Georgia Encyclopedia,* www.georgiaencyclopedia.org.

30. JC, *Best,* 109; Program for Unveiling the Portrait of Martin Luther King, Jr., RG 1-1-5, JC, box 65, GDAH; news release, August 8, 1974, RG 1-1-5, JC, box 68, GDAH; Bourne, *Carter,* 211.

31. JC, handwritten note for speech in RG 1-1-45, box 12, GDAH; copies in Staff Secretary File, box 260, and Speechwriters File, Nesmith, box 1, both in JCL. Laney's quotation is in *New Georgia Encyclopedia.*

32. Bond to JC, June 19, 1974, enclosing letter from Don T. Dudley, RG 1-1-5, JC, box 17, GDAH.

33. Mays to JC, March 22, 1974, RG 1-1-5, JC, box 21, GDAH.

34. Coretta Scott King to JC, April 2, 1974, RG 1-1-5, JC, box 20, GDAH.

35. Speeches, March 24, April 16, August 1, September 29, 1974, RG 1-1-5, JC, box 20, GDAH.

36. JC note on Memorandum, Rita Samuels to Mary Beazley, April 18, 1974, RG 1-1-5, JC, box 21, GDAH.

37. *New York Times,* July 2, 1974.

38. *Americus Times-Recorder,* April 17, 1974.

39. Telegram, Citizen, Hancock Co., Sparta, to JC, May 13, 1974, RG 1-1-5, JC, box 28, GDAH.

40. May 20, 1974, Executive Minutes, RG 1-10-43, Press Releases, JC, box 4, GDAH.

41. Yvonne Davis to JC, May 9, 1974, JC to Davis, May 15, 1974, RG 1-1-5, JC, box 21, GDAH.

42. JC notes on Yancey E. Martin to JC, May 23, 1974, RG 1-1-5, JC, box 21, GDAH.

43. William G. Moffett III to JC, May 16, 1974, JC to Moffett May 28, 1974, RG 1-1-5, JC, box 2, GDAH.

44. JC to Ben Fortson, June 20, 1974, RG 1-1-5, JC, box 65, GDAH.

45. JC to Mrs. Hollis Austin, July 18, 1974, RG 1-1-5, JC, box 17, GDAH.

46. Samuels, "Increasing Involvement of Black Citizens," RG 1-1-5, JC, box 62, GDAH. See also Tuck, *Beyond Atlanta,* 224, and Bourne, *Carter,* 212–13.

CHAPTER 17

1. Helen Thomas, "Life at the Top," *Atlanta Constitution,* March 13, 1977.

2. RSC, *First Lady,* 91–94; Misc. Interview with RSC, December 21, 1974, 17, 19, JCL.

3. RSC, *First Lady,* 89, 91–94; Misc. Interview with RSC, December 21, 1974, 16, 20, JCL.

4. RSC, *First Lady,* 89, 90, 98, 99, 104, 105, 106, 108, 198; Misc. Interview with RSC, December 21, 1974, 20, JCL.

5. *Americus Times-Recorder,* October 17, 1972; John H. King III to RSC, November 3, 1972, RG 1-1-5, JC, box 43, Peter Bourne to JC, November 14, 1972, RG 1-1-5, JC, box 58, both in GDAH.

6. Press Releases, December 13, 1971, RG 1-10-43, JC, GDAH; RSC, *First Lady,* 100–103; *Atlanta Constitution,* October 4, 1972.

7. GGDP interview with JC, May 1, 1972, 21, GSU.

8. *Atlanta Constitution,* August 8, 1972.

9. *Atlanta Constitution,* August 15, 1971; Cooper C. Clements to JC, November 18, 1971, JC to Clements, December 2, 1971, RG 1-1-5, JC, box 17, GDAH; Simmons, *Rosalynn Carter,* 56–57; Mental Health Activities of RSC, in VF, Carter, Jimmy, Governor (2), JCL; Misc. Interview with RSC, December 21, 1974, 13, JCL.

10. Hall and Bourne, "Indigenous Therapists," 137–42.

11. Jordan to Gary Miller, November 27, 1972, JC to Richard Harden, November 27, 1972, RG 1-1-5, JC, box 60, GDAH.

12. *Atlanta Constitution,* December 14, 1972; Mental Health Activities of RSC, 1971, 1972, VF, Carter, Jimmy, Governor (2), JCL; Larry D. Scott to JC and RSC, May 9, 1973, RG 1-1-5, JC, box 23, JC to Hip Palmour, September 1, 1973, RG 1-1-5, JC, box 28, both in GDAH.

13. Stanley S. Jones, Jr., to RSC, September 24, 1971, Carter Family Papers, box 5, JCL.

14. Misc. Interview with RSC, December 21, 1974, 13, JCL; JC to Jack Watson, April 23, 1973, Watson to JC, April 26, 1973, with Carter's notes, Bobby Rowan to JC, May 4, 1973, all in RG 1-1-5, JC, box 60, GDAH; RSC, *First Lady,* 95.

15. JC to Carl Mahoney, February 23, 1973, RG 1-1-5, JC, box 21, GDAH.

16. Misc. Interview with RSC, December 21, 1974, 13, JCL; JC to Eunice Kennedy Shriver, April 5, 1973, Eunice K. Shriver to JC, April 30, 1973, with Jimmy's note "Ros inf J," and her "R," both in RG 1-1-5, JC, box 54, GDAH; Larry D. Scott to JC, May 21, 1973, RG 1-1-5, JC, box 23, GDAH; "Rosalynn Carter," 3, VF, Rosalynn Carter, box R, JCL. See also Fink, "Jimmy Carter and Georgia: Gubernatorial Politics in Transition" (1986), typescript, 9, VF, Fink, Gary M., JCL, and Rosalynn Carter, *Helping Yourself Help Others,* 25–26.

17. Max Cleland to JC, May 10, 1973, JC to Cleland, May 11, 1973, RG 1-1-5, JC, box 17, GDAH; Carter Speech in Warm Springs, Georgia, August 14, 1973, RG 1-1-45, JC, box 12, GDAH.

18. Richard M. Harden, Report on Mental Health, June 10, 1974, RG 1-1-5, JC, box 59, GDAH; JC to Joseph Jerger, Jr., July 10, 1974, RG 1-1-5, JC, box 41, GDAH; JC to Jack Watson, April 10, 1973, "Mental Health Code," July 11, 1973, boxes 5 and 6, respectively, Carter Family Papers, JCL; RSC, *Helping Yourself,* 25–26.

19. *Atlanta Constitution,* January 18, 1974.

20. *Atlanta Constitution,* January 18, 21, 1972, *Americus Times-Recorder,* January 18, 1974, and *New York Times,* June 6, 1974; JC to Lt. Marcus L. Disbrow, January 18, 1974, RG 1-1-5, JC, box 7, GDAH.

21. Charlenne to JC, January 28, 1974, JC to Charlenne, January 28, 1974, RG 1-1-5, JC, box 17, GDAH.

22. *Seattle Post-Intelligencer,* June 5, 1974.

23. Ibid.

24. *Atlanta Constitution,* October 31, 1971, July 14, 1974; *Americus Times-Recorder,* August 8, 1973, JC to Joe Andrews, April 25, 1973, RG 1-1-5, JC, box 5, Charles Harris to JC, June 21, August 22, 1973, RG 1-1-5, JC, box 30, Tommy Irvin to JC, July 6, 1973, RG 1-1-5, JC, box 55, Schedules for Operation Feedback, August 1973, RG 1-1-5, JC, box 77, JC to Joyce Blackburn, September 5, 1973, RG 1-1-5, JC, box 26, JC to Eugene Moore, July 22, 1974, RG 1-1-5, JC, box 32, all in GDAH.

25. JC to Gerald Rafshoon, August 30, 1973, RG 1-1-5, JC, box 22, GDAH.

26. Governor's Schedule, December 1973, August–December 1974, RG 1-1-5, JC, box 74, GDAH; *Atlanta Journal-Constitution,* August 11, 1974; *Americus Times-Recorder,* October 17, 1974.

27. Misc. Interview with RSC, December 21, 1974, 17–18, JCL.

28. JC to Bob Williford, August 30, 1972, RG 1-1-5, JC, box 5, JC to Mark Huie, July 11, 1973, RG 1-1-5, JC, box 19, JC to Mrs. Richard C. Rubenhoff, August 23, 1974, RG 1-1-5, JC, box 22, all in GDAH.

29. Jeff Carter to Denise Robinson, February 4, 1974, RG 1-1-5, JC, box 29, GDAH.

30. *Atlanta Journal,* August 11, 1974; RSC, *First Lady,* 104; Misc. Interview with RSC, December 21, 1974, 15–16, JCL.

31. *Americus Times-Recorder,* June 29, 1972; JC and RSC to Miss. Allie, September 23, 1972, Carter Family Papers, box 2, JCL.

32. Emily Gordon Dolvin File, box 2, JCL; Gloria Spann to Cloyd Hall, September 6, 1972, Cloyd Hall to Jordan, September 6, 1972, clipping from *American Motorcycle Association News,* all in RG 1-1-5, JC, box 40, GDAH; Hugh Carter, *Beedie and Hot,* 130–32.

33. Sarah to JC, JC to Bert Lance, both February 17, 1972, RG 1-1-5, JC, box 39, GDAH; *Americus Times-Recorder,* June 19, 1972.

34. Sybil and Billy Carter, *Billy,* 63, 64, 67; Stapleton, *Billy,* 83, 102.

35. Lillian to JC, [March 24, 1972], with note from JC to Jordan; Jordan to Mrs. Earl Carter, n.d., RG 1-1-5, JC, box 39, GDAH.

36. Copy of a letter from Bevel Jones to Lillian Carter, May 24, 1973, RG 1-1-5, JC, box 34, GDAH.

37. Don Carter to JC, June 1, 1973, RG 1-1-5, JC, box 2, T. N. Kaul to JC, May 30, 1974, RG 1-1-5, JC, box 53, both in GDAH.

38. Hugh Carter to JC, June 29, 1972, JC to Col. Beardsley, June 30, 1972, both in RG 1-1-5, JC, box 56, B. R. B. Davis to JC, June 29, 1972, JC to B. R. B. Davis, June 30, 1972, JC to Hugh Carter, June 30, 1972, all in RG 1-1-5, JC, box 39, Billy Rees to JC, with Carter's note, January 31, 1972, RG 1-1-5, JC, box 44, Hugh A. Carter to JC, August 6, 1973, with JC's note, L. E. Godwin,

Jr., to Hugh Carter, July 16, 1973, RG 1-1-5, JC, box 70, all in GDAH; *Americus Times-Recorder,*
October 10, 1972.

39. Jennie Greene to JC, November 2, 1972, RG 1-1-5, JC, box 39, Executive Documents,
Press Releases, JC, box 3, March 16, 1972, RG 1-10-43, both in GDAH.

40. JC to Mrs. W. H. Ratledge, November 20, 1972, RG 1-1-5, JC, box 22, GDAH.

41. JC to Bob Sanders, April 19, 1973, RG 1-1-5, JC, box 2, JC to Richard Harden, June 20,
1973, RG 1-1-5, JC, box 60, both in GDAH.

42. English to "Mr. Jimmy," June 24, 1972, with JC note, June 24, 1972, RG 1-1-5, JC, box 39,
GDAH.

43. JC to Leonard E. Foote, August 24, 1972, RG 1-1-5, JC, box 2, Larry Givens to JC, July
31, 1972, Carter to Givens, August 1, 2, 1972, RG 1-1-5, JC, box 12, Jack Crockford to JC, 26,
November 30, 1972, JC to Jack Crockford, December 1, 1972, RG 1-1-5, JC, box 63, Frank H.
Neel to JC, April 2, 1973, RG 1-1-5, JC, box 41, Charles Harris to JC, April 2, 1973, RG 1-1-5, JC,
box 30, all in GDAH; *Macon Telegraph and News,* September 24, 1972.

44. Governor's General Subject File, RG 1-10-125, box 3, JC to Bud Carson, November 25,
1971, RG 1-1-5, JC, box 17, both in GDAH; *Americus Time-Recorder,* January 27, 1972; Bisher,
"South Georgia Carter Boy," 22.

45. JC to Eugene Phillips, July 17, 1972, RG 1-1-5, JC, box 4, JC to John Owings, June 25,
1973, RG 1-1-5, JC, box 36, JC to Mike Shea, November 25, 1973, RG 1-1-5, JC, box 48, all in
GDAH.

46. Bisher, "South Georgia Carter Boy," 22.

47. Bourne, *Carter,* 210.

48. JC to Bill France, May 8, 1972, RG 1-1-5, JC, box 98, GDAH.

49. JC to NASCAR, July 22, 1973, VF, Carter, Jimmy, Governor (2), JCL.

50. Karl Barrett, "Former Governor in Fast Company," *1975 Atlanta 500,* souvenir program,
May 24, 1975, copy in VF, Carter, Jimmy, Governor (2), JCL.

51. State Commission on Compensation to JC, December 8, 1971, RG 1-1-5, JC, box 65,
Jordan to Weldon Adams, August 25, 1972, RG 1-1-5, JC, box 64, both in GDAH; *Atlanta Constitution,* December 16, 1971.

52. JC to Steve Polk, July 25, 1972, RG 1-1-5, JC, box 55, GDAH.

53. JC to Elaine Patterson, May 11, 1973, RG 1-1-5, JC, box 16, GDAH; *Atlanta Constitution,*
May 17, 1974.

CHAPTER 18

1. Bill Shipp, "Governor Bitten By National Bug," *Atlanta Constitution,* April 22, 1971.

2. Kirbo to JC, July 16, 1971, Carter Family Papers, box 3, JCL.

3. Henry Grady, "The New South" (1886), in Escott and Goldfield, eds., *Major Problems,*
2:71–73.

4. Gaughan, "Woodrow Wilson," 771.

5. The literature on the presidencies from Wilson to Carter and their relationship to the
South is legion; a good not-so-brief summary is Leuchtenburg, *The White House Looks South.*

6. *Atlanta Constitution,* May 4, 1971; JC to Don Carter, May 12, 1971, RG 1-1-5, JC, box 50, GDAH.

7. *St. Paul (MN) Pioneer Press,* June 25, 1977, White House Central File, box PP-1, JCL.

8. Quoted in *New York Times,* May 3, 1971.

9. *Americus Times-Recorder,* May 4, 1971, italics added.

10. JC, Speech at Town Meeting, Southern Historical Association Convention, Atlanta, November 5, 1992; author's notes.

11. Bourne, *Carter,* 221; Glad, *Carter,* 205; *Atlanta Constitution,* May 16, 1971.

12. Bourne, *Carter,* 222.

13. *Atlanta Journal,* July 25, 1971; David M. Reid to Hamilton Jordan, August 2, 1972, RG 1-1-5, JC, box 66, GDAH.

14. Press Releases, RG 1-10-43, JC, box 4, Speech before Coastal Plains Regional Commission, December 4, 1972, RG 1-1-5, JC, box 52, both in GDAH.

15. Wallace to JC, December 11, 31, 1970, JC to Wallace, January 8, 1971, all in RG 1-1-5, JC, box 46, GDAH.

16. Glad, *Carter,* 206; *Atlanta Constitution,* May 21, August 17, 1971; JC to Stan Collins, September 1, 1971, Carter Family Papers, box 6, JCL.

17. Press Releases, RG 1-10-43, JC, GDAH.

18. JC to Asa Bennette, May 23, 1972, RG 1-1-5, JC, box 45, GDAH; *Atlanta Constitution,* June 2, 1972.

19. Powell to JC, June 16, 1972, with attached JC notes, RG 1-1-45, Speeches, JC, box 13, and Governor's General Subject Files, RG 1-10-125, JC, box 3, both GDAH; *Atlanta Journal,* June 18, 1972.

20. Powell to T. B. Echols, September 15, 1972, RG 1-1-5, JC, box 43, GDAH.

21. Wallace to JC, June 21, 1972, JC to Wallace, June 26, 1972, both in RG 1-1-5, JC, box 46, GDAH.

22. July 1, 1972, RG 1-1-45, Speeches, JC, box 13, GDAH; *Americus Times-Recorder,* July 11, 1972.

23. Bourne, *Carter,* 214; *Atlanta Constitution,* June 1, 1971; JC to "Mrs. Peterson," August 5, 1971, RG 1-1-5, JC, box 30, GDAH; JC to Mrs. W. G. Sandefu, RG 1-1-5, JC, box 3, GDAH.

24. JC to Dianne Morgan, February 5, 1972, RG 1-1-5, JC, box 5; Press Releases, May 9, 11, 1972, RG 1-10-43, JC, box 3, all in GDAH.

25. Scheer, "Jimmy, We Hardly Know Y'all," 70.

26. JC to Richard Harden, November 29, 1972, RG 1-1-5, JC, box 60, GDAH; Press Releases, March 12, 1973, RG 1-10-43, JC, box 4, GDAH; JC quotation in his letter to Lawrence H. Ray, March 14, 1973, RG 1-1-5, JC, box 42, GDAH.

27. JC to Dianne Morgan, February 5, 1972, RG 1-1-5, JC, box 5, GDAH.

28. JC to Humphrey, January 14, 28, 1971, Humphrey to JC, November 16, 1971, RG 1-1-5, JC, box 53, GDAH.

29. Muskie to JC, May 6, 1971, JC to Muskie, May 14, 1971, Humphrey to JC, September 15, 1971, JC to Humphrey, September 21, 1971, David H. Gambrell to Jackson, December 22,

1970, Jackson to JC, March 4, 1971, RG 1-1-5, JC, box 53, GDAH; *Atlanta Constitution,* March 28, 1971, February 1, 1972; *New York Times,* February 2, 1972.

30. *Atlanta Constitution,* April 27, May 3, 1971; JC note to Jody Powell on copy of O'Neill speech in *Congressional Record,* RG 1-1-45, JC, box 45, GDAH.

31. Kirbo to JC, June 18, 1971, Carter Family Papers, box 3, JCL; *Atlanta Constitution,* June 22, 1971, February 23, 1972.

32. JC to O'Brien, February 8, 1972, O'Brien to JC, February 4, 1972, JC to O'Brien, January 31, 1972, all in RG 1-1-5, JC, box 53, GDAH.

33. Jim Exon to JC, February 27, 1972, JC to Exon, March 6, 1972, RG 1-1-5, JC, box 48, GDAH.

34. Howard Baker to JC, June 5, 1971, RG 1-1-5, JC, box 52, loose leaf binder of papers on UN conference, September 9, 1971, RG 1-1-5, JC, box 74, JC to Claude Pepper, July 8, 1971, RG 1-1-5, JC, box 54, JC to Carlton M. Johnson, July 12, 1971, with attached clipping dated July 25, 1971, RG 1-1-5, JC, box 34, all in GDAH; *Americus Times-Recorder,* April 26, 1972.

35. JC to Rockefeller, November 23, 1971, Rockefeller to JC, December 4, 1971, RG 1-1-5, JC, box 50, both in GDAH.

36. *New York Times,* February 8, 1971; *Americus Times-Recorder,* March 7, 9, 1972; JC to Stuart Eizenstat, March 9, 1972, RG 1-1-5, JC, box 18, JC to Suzette Foster, July 25, 1972, RG 1-1-5, JC, box 40, both in GDAH; Ray Baldwin to JC, January 3, 1972, Carter Family Papers, box 3, JCL.

37. *Atlanta Constitution,* March 17, 1971; Jordan to Neal Boddiford, March 27, 1972, RG 1-1-5, JC, box 45. JC to Mrs. Clyde Page, March 29, 1972, RG 1-1-5, JC, box 11, JC to William F. Haddad, March 13, 1972, Haddad to JC, March 8, 1972, with copy of Kennedy speech attached, RG 1-1-5, JC, box 50, all in GDAH; Bourne, *Carter,* 222–25.

38. *New York Times,* April 8, 1972.

39. Miller Center interview with Jordan, November 6, 1981, 69, JCL; Nathan G. Knight to JC, June 9, 1972, RG 1-1-5, JC, box 11, GDAH; *Atlanta Constitution,* May 4, 6, 24, 1972.

40. Kirbo to JC, June 27, 1972, Carter Family Papers, box 3, JCL.

41. News releases, May 25, 26, 1972, RG 1-10-43, JC, box 3, GDAH.

42. Undated memorandum [May 1972], Jordan to JC, RG 1-1-45, JC, box 13, GDAH; *Atlanta Constitution,* May 26, 27, June 3, 4, 1972. James B. Allen (AL) to JC, May 30, 1972, Lawton Chiles (FL) to JC, June 5, 1972, John Sparkman (AL) to JC, June 7, 1972, RG 1-1-5, JC, box 52, GDAH; Herman Talmadge (GA) to JC, May 30, 1972, Lloyd Bentsen (TX) to JC, June 2, 1972, both RG 1-1-5, JC, box 54, GDAH.

43. Jordan to JC, June 2, 1972, Carter Family Papers, box 3, JCL; *Atlanta Constitution,* June 26, 1972; *New York Times,* June 28, 1972; *Americus Times-Recorder,* June 27, 29, 1972 (quotation in June 29).

44. JC to Wallace, June 26, 1972, RG 1-1-5, JC, box 46, GDAH.

45. *Americus Times-Recorder,* July 1, 6, 11, 12, 1972; Jody Powell to JC, July 1, 1972, RG 1-1-45, JC, box 13, GDAH; Shipp, *Ape-Slayer,* 45; *Atlanta Constitution,* July 11, 1972.

46. *Americus Times-Recorder,* July 11, 1971.

47. Bourne, *Carter,* 225–26.

48. Bourne, *Carter,* 226–27.

49. Bourne, *Carter,* 227; Kaufman, *Jackson,* 157–60, 168–79, 208–10.

50. Bourne, *Carter,* 227–28; Speeches, RG 1-1-45, JC, box 13, Press Releases, RG 1-10-43, JC, Executive, box 3, both in GDAH.

51. Quoted in Bourne, *Carter,* 229.

52. Bourne, *Carter,* 229.

53. Jordan to JC, n.d., Carter Family Papers, box 3, JCL.

54. Bourne, *Carter,* 229; *Americus Times-Recorder,* July 14, 1972.

55. Quoted in Bourne, *Carter,* 228.

56. Jordan to JC, n.d., Carter Family Papers, box 3, JCL.

57. JC to Smith, July 24, 1972, RG 1-1-5, JC, box 23, Duane Riner to JC, July 18, 1972, RG 1-1-5, JC, box 62, both in GDAH.

58. JC to Cecil B. Morris, July 21, 1972, RG 1-1-5, JC, box 2, GDAH.

59. JC to Suzette Foster, July 25, 1972, RG 1-1-5, JC, box 40, GDAH.

60. JC to Bruce Hagan, August 5, 1972, RG 1-1-5, JC, box 50, GDAH.

61. McGovern to JC, August 5, 1972, RG 1-1-5, JC, box 53, GDAH.

62. *Atlanta Constitution,* November 3, 1972; Bourne, *Carter,* 234–35.

63. JC to Jackson, February 20, 1973, Carter Family Papers, box 2, JCL.

64. Governor's Weekly Schedule, January 20, 1973, RG 1-10-125, JC, box 3, GDAH; *Atlanta Constitution,* February 24, 1971.

65. JC to Wiley Wasden, Jr., February 11, 1973, RG 1-1-5, JC, box 2, JC to Nixon, February 14, 1973, RG 1-1-5, JC, box 2, both in GDAH.

66. Press Releases, May 10, 1973, RG 1-10-43, JC, Exec., box 4, GDAH; Robert S. Want, "Impoundment of Water Pollution Control Funds: A Chronology of Events," January 2, 1973, Congressional Research Service, Director of Management and Budget to Spiro T. Agnew, February 5, 1973, *National Journal,* February 17, 1973, 238–42, Georgia Forestry Commission Report, January 10, 1973, JC to Ernie O'Neal with copies to all state agencies, March 8, 1973, Ray Shirley to James T. McIntyre, Jr., March 9, 1973, Jack P. Nix to James T. McIntyre, Jr., March 9, 1973, Shealy McCoy to James T. McIntyre, Jr., March 15, 1973, all in Carter Family Papers, box 6, JCL.

67. David N. Parker to JC, March 12, 1973, RG 1-1-5, JC, box 54, GDAH.

68. *Washington Post,* December 11, 1972.

69. Glad, *Outsider,* 13.

70. *Atlanta Constitution,* November 30, 1972; Jordan to JC, October 24, 1973, Carter Family Papers, box 4, JCL.

71. *Atlanta Constitution,* May 16, 1971; Governor's General Subject Files, RG 1-10-125, JC, box 3, GDAH; *New York Times,* 4, 5, 6, 7, 1972; Memorandum, Hamilton Jordan to JC, n.d. [May 1972], RG 1-1-45, JC, box 13, GDAH; Memorandum, Frank Moore to JC, Mary Beazley, and Madeline MacBean, April 8, 1974, with JC notes, and liquor bill, RG 1-1-5, JC, box 66, GDAH; Bourne, *Carter,* 221.

72. JC, Speech before Southern Growth Policies Board, Atlanta, October 16, 1973, Minutes of the meeting, both in RG 1-1-5, JC, box 76, GDAH; *New York Times,* November 18, 1973.

73. Minutes of the Southern Growth Policy Board, October 17, 1973; speech notes in RG 1-1-5, JC, box 76, both in GDAH.

74. Memorandum, JC to Jim McIntyre and Jody Powell, March 28, 1973, RG 1-1-5, JC, box 64, GDAH; Notebook, 11–39, in Carter Family Papers, box 5, JCL.

75. JC to Eugene Odum, March 29, 1973, RG 1-1-5, JC, box 2, GDAH.

76. United States and Nixon, *Public Papers,* 1973, 301–19; Hakes, *Declaration,* 20–23.

77. Philip Alston to JC, including speech by Chief of Iranian Mission in Washington, D.C., on the Oil Story, July 27, 1973, RG 1-1-5, JC, box 64, GDAH.

78. JC to Rusk, August 22, 1973, enclosing JC to Ted Mock, April 26, 1973, RG 1-1-5, JC, box 2, GDAH.

79. Bourne, *Carter,* 125.

80. JC to Department Heads, May 11, 1973, RG 1-1-5, JC, box 4, GDAH.

81. Harold C. McKenzie, Jr., to JC, August 10, 1973, RG 1-1-5, JC, box 21, GDAH.

82. JC to Agency Heads, August 17, 1973, RG 1-1-5, JC, box 62, GDAH; Lance, *Truth,* 39.

83. Memorandum, JC to State Agency Heads, August 17, 1973, RG 1-1-5, JC, box 62, GDAH; Speech to Seminar on Energy, August 21, 1973, RG 1-1-45, JC, box 45, GDAH; *Americus Times-Recorder,* December 1, 1973.

84. JC, transcript of speech on ETV, RG 1-1-45, JC, box 11, GDAH; John E. Mock to JC, June 5, 1974, with JC handwritten note, RG 1-1-5, JC, box 59, GDAH. Italics added.

85. Press Releases, RG 1-10-43, JC, box 4, JC and RSC to Eugene L. Wyman, December 11, 1972, JC and RSC to Frederick G. Larkin, Jr., December 11, 1972, RG 1-1-5, JC, box 47, all in GDAH.

86. JC to Jackson, February 20, 1973, Carter Family Papers, box 2, JCL.

87. Carter to Johnson, December 18, 1972, White House Central File, box PR-82, JCL.

88. Press Releases, RG 1-10-43, JC, box 4, GDAH.

89. JC to Carl Mahoney, February 23, 1973, RG 1-1-5, JC, box 21, GDAH, italics added.

90. Duane Riner to John Herling, January 24, 1973, RG 1-1-5, JC, box 53, Peter Bourne to JC, February 5, 1973, RG 1-1-5, JC, box 52, both in GDAH; *Congressional Record,* February 15, 1973.

91. Paul Q. Sweeney to Jody Powell, April 6, 1973, William F. Buckley to JC, April 30, 1973, JC to Buckley, May 9, 1973, all in RG 1-1-5, JC, box 50, JC to Mrs. Donald Cathcart, May 1973, RG 1-1-5, JC, box 17, all in GDAH.

92. Jordan to JC, April 20, 1973, with Carter's notes and text of speech, RG 1-1-45, JC, box 13, GDAH.

93. Powell to JC, April 23, 1973, RG 1-1-45, JC, box 13, GDAH.

94. JC, speech notes, May 2, 1973, RG 1-1-45, JC, box 11, GDAH.

95. JC, Speeches, August 8, 1973, RG 1-1-45, JC, box 13, GDAH.

96. JC to Arlene Francis, December 14, 1973, RG 1-1-5, JC, box 50, GDAH.

97. *Atlanta Constitution,* March 7, 1974; *Americus Times-Recorder,* March 15, 1974.

98. Donna K. Smith to JC, April 21, 1974, RG 1-1-5, JC, box 54, GDAH.

99. Lawrence E. Spivak to JC, April 17, 1974, Proxmire to JC, June 3, 1974, both in RG 1-1-5, JC, box 54, GDAH.

100. JC, speeches, January and spring 1974, *Southern Growth and Promise* (pamphlet), all in RG 1-1-5, JC, box 76, GDAH.

101. JC, Speech, July 11, 1974, RG 1-1-45, JC, box 13, GDAH.

102. Schedules for the meeting, August 16–18, 1974, RG 1-1-5, JC, box 74; Governor's Schedule and *Report on Future of the South*, August 1, 1974; Memorandum, Joe Mitchell to JC, August 14, 1974.

103. Tentative Agenda for meeting, August 16–18, 1974, RG 1-1-5, JC, box 76, GDAH; George H. Esser, Jr., to JC, August 20, 1974, JC to Esser, August 26, 1974, both in RG 1-1-5, JC, box 18, GDAH. Pat Derian, who would later serve in Carter's presidential cabinet, was vice president and Raymond H. Wheeler was president of the Southern Regional Council.

104. JC to Lance, January 4, 1973, RG 1-1-5, JC, box 67, GDAH; see also Gerald J. Smith, Sr., "William Few, Jr. (1748–1828)," *New Georgia Encyclopedia*, www.georgiaencyclopedia.org.

105. Harris to JC, April 23, 1971, see also Harris to JC, May 17, 1971, RG 1-1-5, JC, box 30, GDAH.

106. JC to Morton A. Harris, January 28, 1971, RG 1-1-5, JC, box 34; Lipshutz to JC, April 26, May 24, 1971, JC to Lipshutz, May 28, 1971, RG 1-1-5, JC, box 20; William Waronker to JC, May 21, 1971, RG 1-1-5, JC, box 24; Jordan to Moshe Gilboa, October 1, 1971, Gilboa to JC, May 8, 10, 1971, RG 1-1-5, JC, box 19, GDAH.

107. JC, Speech, June 24, 1971, RG 1-1-45, JC, box 13, GDAH.

108. JC, Speeches, June 24, 1971, April 30, 1972, RG 1-1-45, JC, box 13; Press Releases, December 30, April 27, 1971, 1972, RG 1-10-43, JC, box 3; Lipshutz to Gordon R. Sugarman, March 27, 1972, RG 1-1-5, JC, box 23; all in GDAH.

109. Larry S. Pike to JC, August 13, 1973, JC to Brezhnev, June 11, 1973, JC to Nixon, June 11, 1973, Roland L. Elliott to JC, August 13, 1973, RG 1-1-5, JC, box 54, all in GDAH.

110. Miller Center interview with Jordan, November 6, 1981, 69, JCL.

111. *Atlanta Constitution*, November 14, 1974.

CHAPTER 19

1. JC, *Best*, 124.

2. Davis to JC, April 29, 1971, JC to Corbin, May 17, 1971, RG 1-1-5, JC, box 35, GDAH.

3. *Atlanta Constitution*, April 27, 1972; Press Releases, August 31, September 26, December 7, 1972, RG 1-10-43, JC, box 4, Peter C. White to Mary Beasley, September 18, 1974, RG 1-1-5, JC, box 24, both in GDAH.

4. Allen, *Atlanta Rising*, 171–72; Gene Dyson to JC, October 28, 1974, RG 1-1-5, JC, box 67, GDAH.

5. Rusk to JC, July 27, 1971, RG 1-1-5, JC, box 2, GDAH.

6. Press Releases, February 3, March 23, July 5, September 11, 1972, RG 1-10-43, JC, boxes 3, 4, A. E. Manell to JC, January 17, 1972, RG 1-1-5, JC, box 53; JC to Nobuhiko Ushiba, February 13, 1973, RG 1-1-5, JC, box 54, all in GDAH.

7. JC to Rogers, April 20, 1973, Rogers to JC, May 7, 1973, RG 1-1-5, JC, box 54, Plaza to JC, May 6, 1974, JC to Douglas D. Richards, June 10, 1974, RG 1-1-5, JC, box 54, all in GDAH.

8. JC to Rogers, May 11, 1973, RG 1-1-5, JC, box 54, JC to Rusk, August 22, 1973, Rusk to JC, May 10, 1973, October 10, 1972, RG 1-1-5, JC, all in box 2, Carole C. Laise to JC, February 8, 1974, JC to Laise, February 10, 1974, RG 1-1-5, JC, both in box 53, Harry R. Amonoco to JC, April 9, 1974, JC to Amonoco, April 24, 1974, both in RG 1-1-5, JC, box 52, JC to Ashraf A. Ghorbal, October 12, 1972, JC to Nicolas Gonzales-Revilla, June 18, 1974, both in RG 1-1-5, JC, box 53, all in GDAH.

9. Truman to JC, November 19, 1971, RG 1-1-5, JC, box 66, GDAH.

10. JC to A. E. Mahnell, November 22, 1971, RG 1-1-5, JC, box 53, GDAH.

11. JC to Emilio Garrastazu Medici, November 2, 1971, RG 1-1-5, JC, box 66, GDAH.

12. News release, March 2, 1972, RG 1-1-5, JC, box 66, JC to Harold Brockey, April 22, 1972, RG 1-1-5, JC, box 17, both in GDAH; Bourne, *Carter,* 239.

13. *Atlanta Constitution,* April 4, 1972; *Americus Times-Recorder,* April 4, 1972; Press Releases, RG 1-10-43, JC, box 3, JC to Roshe, May 5, 1972, RG 1-1-5, JC, box 54, all in GDAH; JC to Truman, February 29, 1972, Carter Family Papers, box 2, JCL.

14. Phil Garner, "Jimmy Carter in Latin America," *Atlanta Journal and Constitution Magazine,* July 11, 1972; Press Releases, April 6, 1972, RG 1-10-43, JC, box 3, JC, speech before World Mission Conference at North Avenue Presbyterian Church, March 4, 1973, copy in RG 1-1-5, JC, box 18, both in GDAH.

15. Press Releases, April 7, 1972, RG 1-10-43, JC, box 3, GDAH; Garner, "Carter in Latin America," photograph of JC and RSC at graves of southerners in Americana; Frances Cawthon, "Look Away, Look Away," *Atlanta Constitution and Journal Magazine,* March 2, 1974, 19.

16. JC, speech before World Mission Conference, March 4, 1973, RG 1-1-5, JC, box 18, GDAH.

17. Pamphlet, Latin American Trip, April 1972, RG 1-1-5, JC, box 66, GDAH; *Americus Times-Recorder,* April 13, 1972.

18. RSC speech, *Americus Times-Recorder,* October 17, 1972.

19. *Atlanta Constitution,* April 27, 1972.

20. JC to Lauro Cruz, to Jose Rocz, to Walter Rodriques, to Herbert Levy, all June 22, 1972, all in 1-1-5, JC, box 66, GDAH.

21. Preparation booklet (June 1972), 5 and 6, RG 1-1-5, JC, box 74, GDAH.

22. Press Releases, RG 1-10-43, JC, box 4, GDAH.

23. Ibid.; Bourne, *Carter,* 239.

24. Press Releases, RG 1-10-43, JC, box 4, GDAH.

25. For Carter's account of the trip thirty years later, see JC, *Palestine,* 21–35.

26. Press Releases, RG 1-10-43, JC, box 4, GDAH; Moshe Gilboa to JC, May 8, 1971, RG 1-1-5, JC, box 52, GDAH; JC, *Blood of Abraham,* 23–25, 29.

27. JC, *Blood of Abraham,* 24, 25, 28.

28. JC, *Palestine,* 26–28.

29. JC, *Palestine*, 29–31.

30. JC, *Blood of Abraham*, 29–30; Press Releases, RG 1-10-43, JC, box 4, GDAH; JC, *Palestine*, 31–32.

31. JC to Susan Rafshoon, June 14, 1973, RG 1-1-5, JC, box 22, GDAH.

32. JC, *Palestine*, 33–34.

33. JC, speech notes, June 19, 1973, RG 1-10-43, JC, box 13, Lipshutz to JC, February 23, April 30, 1973, JC to Lipshutz, February 28, 1973, all in RG 1-1-5, JC, box 20, I. T. Cohen to JC, June 20, 1973, RG 1-1-5, JC, box 17, all in GDAH.

34. JC, Speeches, April 20, 1974, RG 1-1-45, JC, box 13; Kissinger to JC, April 24, 1974, RG 1-1-5, JC, box 53, all in GDAH.

35. JC, *Palestine*, 35.

36. Peter White to JC, April 30, 1973, RG 1-1-5, JC, box 24, GDAH; Summary of Decisions, April 14, 1973, Brzezinski Donated Materials, box 1, JCL.

37. JC, Speeches, October 18, 1973, RG 1-1-45, JC, box 12, Peter White to JC, April 30, 1973, JC to White [May 1973], RG 1-1-5, JC, box 24, all in GDAH; George Franklin to Gerard Smith, January 20, 1977, box 4, Memorandum of Conversation with Sub-Trilateral Commission, November 30, 1972, Brzezinski to Commission Members, Report on Energy, January 15, 1973, box 7, Memorandum of Conversation with Scotty Reston, February 27, 1973, Summary of Decisions, April 14, 1973, Trilateral Policy Program, August 29, 1973, box 1, Theme for Trilateral meetings, April 3, 1973, box 5, all in Brzezinski Donated Materials, JCL; *Memphis Commercial Appeal*, May 5, 1996; Bourne, *Carter*, 240–41.

38. JC to Brzezinski, December 15, 1973, Brzezinski to JC, December 21, 1973, Brzezinski Donated Materials, box 5, JCL.

39. Brzezinski's article dated January 7, 1974, Brzezinski Donated Materials, box 2, JCL.

40. Minutes of Trilateral Commission Meeting, North America, May 30, 1974, Brzezinski File, box 2, JCL.

CHAPTER 20

1. Miller Center interview with Bell, March 23, 1988, 4–6, JCL; Morris, *Carter*, 191.

2. Quoted in Glad, *Carter*, 210.

3. Quoted in Witcover, *Marathon*, 110.

4. Bourne, *Carter*, 231–36; Miller Center interview with JC, November 29, 1982, 3, JCL; Miller Center interview with Lance, May 12, 1982, 10, both in JCL.

5. Glad, *Carter*, 211–12; Norton and Slosser, *Miracle of Jimmy Carter*, 50–53.

6. Jordan to JC, November 4, 1972, 1976 Presidential Campaign, Campaign Director's Office, box 199, JCL.

7. *Atlanta Journal-Constitution*, May 22, 2008.

8. Jordan to JC, November 4, 1972; see also *New York Times*, July 17, 1976, excerpt in President Ford Committee for Re-election File, box H33, Gerald R. Ford Presidential Library, Ann Arbor, Michigan.

9. Misc. Interview with RSC, December 21, 1974, 18, JCL.

10. JC to Barber, August 7, 1973, RG 1-1-5, JC, box 50, GDAH; Glad, *Carter*, 212.

11. JC to Simpson, February 3, 1972, RG 1-1-5, JC, box 65, GDAH.

12. JC to McKenzie, August 26, 1973, RG 1-1-5, JC, box 21, GDAH.

13. JC to Rickover, September 28, October 19, 1973, Rickover to JC, October 5, 1973, RG 1-1-5, JC, box 54, GDAH.

14. Turner to JC, December 5, 1974, R. H. Smith to Gerald Rafshoon, December 20, 1974, both in Pre-Presidential File, '76 Campaign, Issues, Eizenstat, box 8, JCL.

15. Bourne to JC, October 24, 1973, RG 1-1-5, JC, box 58, GDAH; author interview with Jay Hakes, state coordinator of the 1976 campaign in Louisiana, August 8, 2000, Atlanta.

16. JC to Ms. Audrey Shafer, January 7, 1974, RG 1-1-5, JC, box 1, GDAH.

17. JC to George Woolsey, Jr., June 25, 1974, RG 1-1-5, JC, box 50, GDAH.

18. JC to Pierre Howard, Jr., September 7, 1973, RG 1-1-5, JC, box 12, GDAH; Carter underlined the word "search" twice.

19. Bourne, *Carter*, 212; Simpson, "Carter and Transformation," 78–89; *New York Times*, May 1, 1973; "Democratic National Committee Democratic Campaign Manual" and "Political Report," *National Journal Reports*, September 21, 1974, 1407–17, both in Pre-Presidential File: '76 Campaign, Issues, Eizenstat, box 8, JCL; Jordan to JC, April 24, 1973, Carter Family Papers, box 3, JCL; JC to David Bowen, July 27, 1973, David Bowen Papers, Mississippi State University Library, Starkville.

20. Eizenstat to JC, May 14, 1973, RG 1-1-5, JC, box 18, GDAH.

21. Stuart Eizenstat to JC, May 14, 1974, RG 1-1-5, JC, box 18, GDAH.

22. NARA interview with Stuart Eizenstat, January 1, 1981, 2–3, JCL; Henry Owen to Eizenstat, April 17, 1974, with attachment, Pre-Presidential File, '76 Campaign, Issues, Eizenstat, box 16, JCL.

23. JC to Strauss, May 9, 1973, Strauss to JC, May 7, 1973, RG 1-1-5, JC, box 54, GDAH.

24. Press Releases, RG 1-10-43, JC, box 4, GDAH.

25. "Associations and Organizations of National Scope," Pre-Presidential File, box 13, JCL.

26. Campaign summary book, Pre-Presidential File, box 13; "Confidential to 1974 Democratic Gubernatorial Candidates," Pre-Presidential File, box 14, JCL.

27. Dunham to JC, June 10, 1973, RG 1-1-5, JC, box 47, GDAH.

28. JC, Speech for Naval War College, June 26, 1973, Speeches, RG 1-1-45, JC, box 13, GDAH.

29. JC to Mondale, August 8, 1973, RG 1-1-5, JC, box 53, GDAH.

30. Ibid.

31. Jordan to JC, August 24, 1973, JC to Bill Dodds, September 6, 1973, RG 1-1-5, JC, box 52, JC, Remarks to United Auto Workers, August 1974, Speeches, RG 1-1-45, JC, box 12, all in GDAH, italics added.

32. JC, Speeches, RG 1-1-45, JC, box 13, GDAH.

33. J. Michael Shea to JC, September 27, 1973, Carter to Shea, October 3, 1973, JC to Reuben Askew, September 18, 1973, all in RG 1-1-5, JC, box 48, Margaret Suggs to Jordan and Paul Lutzker, September 19, 1973, RG 1-1-5, JC, box 54, Sen. Lloyd Bentsen to JC, October 3, 1973, RG 1-1-5, JC, box 52, all in GDAH.

34. Jordan to JC, November 26, 1973, RG 1-1-45, JC, box 13, GDAH.

35. JC, Speeches, March, April, May 1974, RG 1-1-45, JC, box 13, GDAH.

36. *Atlanta Journal,* April 28, 1974.

37. Kennedy, *True Compass,* 353.

38. Kennedy's speech supplied by his office and Program of the Law Day Ceremony, RG 1-1-5, JC, box 8, GDAH. There is an ongoing debate over whether the University of Georgia or North Carolina is older; Georgia claims the first charter, North Carolina the first opening. See also E. Stanly Godbold, Jr., "Kennedy, Carter Shared a Similar Vision," *Atlanta Journal-Constitution,* August 30, 2009.

39. Law Day Speech, May 4, 1974, JC, *Government Good as People,* 30–42, italics added.

40. Note attached to text of speech, Speechwriter File, Nesmith, box 1, JCL.

41. JCL interview with Jack Carter, June 23, 2003, 38, JCL.

42. Ibid.

43. Dr. Hunter S. Thompson, "Jimmy Carter and the Great Leap of Faith: An Endorsement with Fear and Loathing," *Rolling Stone,* June 3, 1976, 54–64.

44. Kennedy to JC, May 6, 1974, JC to Kennedy, February 26, 1974, RG 1-1-5, JC, box 53, GDAH; Kennedy, *True Compass,* 353.

45. *New York Times,* June 3, 1974; Bourne, *Carter,* 268; James Exon to JC, May 8, 1974, RG 1-1-5, JC, box 50; JC to Misses Frances and Ruby Bowles, May 28, 1974, RG 1-1-5, JC, box 9; JC, Speeches, May 31, 1974, RG 1-1-45, JC, box 13; Gerard C. Smith to JC, June 10, 1974, RG 1-1-5, JC, box 75; JC to Hedley Donovan, June 11, 1974, RG 1-1-5, JC, box 50; Kennedy to JC, June 6, 1974, RG 1-1-5, JC, box 53; Frank E. Moss to JC, June 11, 1974, RG 1-1-5, JC, box 53, all in GDAH; *Americus Times-Recorder,* June 5, 1974; *Atlanta Journal-Constitution,* June 9, 1974.

46. *New York Times,* July 27, 1974.

47. Bourne, *Carter,* 243.

48. JC to Bert and LaBelle, October 3, 1974, RG 1-1-5, JC, box 26, GDAH.

49. Kennedy to JC, November 6, 1974, RG 1-1-5, JC, box 53, GDAH; Bourne, *Carter,* 246, 248, 253.

50. Miller Center interview with Kirbo, January 5, 1983, 6, JCL.

51. JC to Kennedy, September 25, 1974, RG 1-1-5, JC, box 49, GDAH.

52. *Atlanta Constitution,* December 4, 7, 1974.

53. Bourne, *Carter,* 254–56. See also Damico, "Civil Rights to Human Rights."

54. Quoted in Bourne, *Carter,* 256.

55. Jordan to JC, August 4, 1974, Peter Bourne File, box 1, JCL.

56. Bourne to JC, August 1, 1974, and October 15, 1974, Pre-Presidential File, '76 Campaign, Issues, Eizenstat, box 7, JCL.

57. NARA interview with Zbigniew Brzezinski, February 20, 1981, 4, JCL.

58. G. H. Achenbach to JC, February 6, 1973, JC to Achenbach, February 13, 1973, both in RG 1-1-5, JC, box 41, GDAH.

59. JC to Eugene Gunby, March 25, 1973, RG 1-1-5, JC, box 18; Reagan to JC, March 28, 1973, RG 1-1-5, JC, box 47, GDAH.

60. Goldman, "Sizing Up Carter"; Glad, *Carter,* 176–78.

61. *Miami Herald,* September 7, 1976; Fred Slight to Dave Gergen, September 21, 1976, David Gergen File, box 2, Gerald R. Ford Presidential Library. See also T. McNeill Simpson III, "Appraising the Carter Administration," June 1975, Gary M. Fink, "Perceptions of Jimmy Carter: The Gubernatorial Years," typescript, January 1986, "A State in Action, 1971–1975" (pamphlet), the official account of his "Goals for Georgia" program, all in VF, Carter, Jimmy, Addresses, Governor (2), JCL.

62. Sokol, *There Goes My Everything,* 276–81.

63. Bass and DeVries, *Transformation of Southern Politics,* 146–47.

64. "The Carter Record in Georgia," A. J. Reichley File, box 1, Gerald R. Ford Presidential Library.

65. *Americus Times-Recorder,* December 9, 1974.

66. Bass and DeVries, *Transformation of Southern Politics,* 150.

67. Margaret Shannon, "What's It's Like to Be Governor," *Atlanta Journal and Constitution Magazine,* August 11, 1974, 1, 41, copy in RG 1-1-45, JC, box 13, GDAH.

68. JC, speech in Atlanta, May 7, 1974, RG 1-1-45, JC, box 11, GDAH.

69. *Atlanta Constitution,* November 25, 1974.

70. *New York Times,* December 12, 1974

71. Kenneth Scheibel to JC, October 16, 1974, RG 1-1-5, JC, box 54, JC, handwritten draft of announcement speech, November 21, 1974, Kirbo to JC, November 26, 1974, both in RG 1-1-45, JC, box 13, GDAH; Bourne to JC, August 1, 1974, Pre-Presidential File, '76 Campaign, Eizenstat, box 7, JCL; Jack Burris to JC, September 19, 1974, Eizenstat to JC, November 1, 1974, JC to Jody, individual letters from Stu, Kirbo, Rafshoon, all on December 1, 1974, all in Pre-Presidential File, '76 Campaign, Eizenstat, box 1, JCL; JC to Paul Austin, August 30, 1974, Kirbo to JC, October 22, 1974, both in Carter Family Papers, box 3, JCL; Jack Burris to JC, September 19, 1974, Eizenstat to JC, November 1, 1974, individual notes from JC to Kirbo, Stu, Rafshoon, Jody, all on November 25, 1974, December 1, 1974, Pre-Presidential File, '76 Campaign, Issues, Eizenstat, box 1, JCL; Jerry Rafshoon to JC, December 11, 1974, Pre-Presidential File, '76 Campaign, Eizenstat, box 24, JCL.

72. JC, *Government Good as People;* 43–50; JC, handwritten draft of announcement speech, Pre-Presidential File, '76 Campaign, Eizenstat, box 1, JCL; Bourne, *Carter,* 256–59; JC, handwritten speech in RG 1-1-45, JC, box 13, GDAH, typed copy in Speechwriters File, Nesmith, box 1, JCL.

73. *New York Times,* December 13, 1974.

74. Walter O. Brooks to JC, December 13, 1974, RG 1-1-5, JC, box 60, GDAH.

75. RG 1-10-125, December 12, 1974, GDAH.

SELECTED BIBLIOGRAPHY

ARCHIVAL SOURCES

Jimmy Carter Presidential Library and Museum (JCL), Atlanta

Peter Bourne File
Zbigniew Brzezinski Donated Material
Carter Family Papers
Susan Clough File
Emily Gordon Dolvin Donated Material
First Lady Press File
Tom Gordy File
Richard Harden File
Hamilton Jordan File
Gerald M. Rafshoon Donated Materials
Jody Powell Donated Material
Pre-Presidential File, 1962–74
Speechwriters File
Staff Secretary File
Vertical File
White House Central File
White House Staff Office Files

Carter Library Oral History Project (Interviewee: Jack Carter)
White Burkett Miller Center Jimmy Carter Project (Interviewees: Griffin Bell, Jimmy Carter, Stuart Eizenstat, Hamilton Jordan, Charles Kirbo, Bert Lance, Jody Powell, Gerald Rafshoon)
Miscellaneous Interviews: Rosalynn Carter
National Archives and Records Administration (NARA) Carter/Smith Family Oral History Project (Interviewees: Mary Elizabeth Braunstein, Betty Jennings Carter and Jeannete Carter Lowery, Don Carter, Hugh A. Carter, Sr., Lillian Carter, Rachel Clark, Emily Gordon Dolvin, Allie Smith, Elder Fulford Smith, Jerrold Smith, Murray Lee Smith, Oliver C. Smith, Allethea Smith Wall)
National Archives and Records Administration (NARA) Exit Interview Project (Interviewees: Zbigniew Brzezinski, Stuart Eizenstat)

National Park Service (NPS), Plains Project Oral Histories (Interviewees: Lauren Blanton, Jimmy and Rosalynn Carter, Eleanor Forrest, Ruth Jackson, Maxine Reese, Gloria Carter Spann, Beth Walters)

Columbia University Library, New York

Oral History Research Office Collection (Interviewees: Robert Lipshutz, Michael Straight)

Early County Court House, Blakely, Georgia

Early County Superior Court, Criminal Docket, 1903
Minutes of Early Country Superior Court, 1903 and 1904

Gerald R. Ford Presidential Library, Ann Arbor, Michigan

David Gergen File
Charles McCall File
President Ford Committee for Re-election File
A. J. Reichley File

Georgia Department of Archives and History (GDAH), Atlanta

Biographical Questionnaires
Marion County Ordinary Court, Homestead Book A, 1866–1924
Record Groups (RGs): RG 1-1-3 (Governor's Executive Minutes), RG 1-1-5 (Governor's Correspondence), RG 1-1-8 (Governor's Messages), RG 1-1-45 (Governor's Speeches), RG 1-1-110 (Pamphlets), RG 1-1-111 (Carter clippings), RG 1-10-43 (Press Releases), RG 1-15-64 (Project Director Files), RG 1-15-66 (Reorganization Correspondence), RG 1-15-79 (Assorted news clippings), RG 1-16-120 (Executive Center Publications)
Sumter Country Court of Ordinary, microfilm reels 135–37
Sumter County Superior Court, Grand Jury Minutes, 1872–76, microfilm reels 124–48
Sumter County Tax Digest, 1872
Warren County Tax Digest, 1849

Georgia State University Library (GSU)

Georgia Government Documentation Project (GGDP) (Interviewees: Ellis Arnall, George Busbee, Jimmy Carter, Nathan Dean, Robert F. Flanagan, Hugh Gillis, Lester Maddox, Bobby Rowan, Carl Sanders, George T. Smith, Frank Vandiver)

Lake Blackshear Regional Library, Americus, Georgia

Special Collections

Mississippi State University Library, Starkville

David Bowen Papers
John C. Stennis Oral History Collection (Interviewee: Herman E. Talmadge)

Southern Baptist Historical Library and Archives, Nashville

Southern Baptist History Collection

Manuscript, Archives, and Rare Book Library (MARBL), Robert W. Woodruff Library, Emory University, Atlanta

Morris B. Abram Papers
Ralph McGill Papers
Charles M. Rafshoon Collection
Robert W. Woodruff Papers

INTERVIEWS

Rick Allen
Jimmy Carter
Rosalynn Carter
Morris W. H. Collins, Jr.
Juanita Edmundson
Dan Edwards
Marty Franks
Rod Goodwin
Jay Hakes
O. M. Harrelson
Mary Finch Hoyt
Howard Jones
Billie Larson
Jackie Lassiter
Edmund Muskie
Thomas "Tip" O'Neill
Abraham Ribicoff
John Van Dyke Saunders
Julia Vissotto Saunders
Gary Sick
Scott Singletary
Allie Smith
Rear Admiral James R. Stark (ret.)
Gordon C. Stewart
Stansfield Turner
Cyrus Vance
Mary Whitehead
Annette Wise

VIDEOS

Jimmy Carter. Directed by Adriana Bosch. American Experience Series. Boston: WGBH, 2002.

Citizen Carter. Discovery Education, 1991.

Carter, Lillian. *Press Conference with Miss Lillian Carter.* Special Collections, Mississippi State University Library, Starkville.

The Last Confederates. Produced by Edwin Cohen. Mississippi Public Broadcasting, 1984.

Jimmy Carter: To the White House and Beyond. Produced by Alan Goldberg. New York: A & E Network, 1995.

An American Profile: Robert Strauss, Ambassador-designate to the Soviet Union. Washington, D.C.: C-Span, 1991.

DISSERTATIONS AND THESES

Barnes, Paula Curlee. "Educating the Conscience: Betty Bumpers and Peace Links—A Study of Feminist Peace Work." Ph.D. diss., University of Arkansas, 1996.

Bowden, Elizabeth Gray. "The Gubernatorial Administration of Jimmy Carter." M.A. thesis, University of Georgia, 1980.

Cloonan, Kevin A. "Jimmy Carter and the MX Debate: Passions That Move American Strategy." Ph.D. diss., Claremont Graduate University, 1997.

Cook, Emily Walker. "Women White House Advisors in the Carter Administration: Presidential Stalwarts or Feminist Advocates?" Ph.D. diss., Vanderbilt University, 1995.

Damico, John Kelly. "From Civil Rights to Human Rights: The Career of Patricia M. Derian." Ph.D. diss., Mississippi State University, 1999.

Kramer, Scott. "Struggles of an Outsider: The 1979 Energy Crisis and President Carter's Call for Confidence." B.A. thesis, Princeton University, 1992.

Littlefield, Robert Stephen. "An Analysis of the Persuasion and Coercion Used by the Carter Administration to Promote Human Rights in Argentina, Brazil, and Chile." Ph.D. diss., University of Minnesota, 1983.

Lucella, Mel. "Cyrus Vance's World View: The Relevance of the Motivated Tactician Perspective." Ph.D. diss., Union Institute, New York City, 1996.

Motter, Russell D. "Jimmy Carter's Presidential Style: Energy Policy as a Case Study." M.A. thesis, University of Hawaii, 1992.

Ruechel, Frank A. "The Articulation and Synthesis of Jimmy Carter's Human Rights Policy." Ph.D. diss., Georgia State University, 1991.

Stansfield, Burns F. "Faith and Politics in the Presidency of Jimmy Carter." M.Div. senior paper, Harvard Divinity School, 1988.

Abram, Morris B. *The Day Is Short: An Autobiography.* New York: Harcourt Brace Jovanovich, 1982.

Abramson, Rudy. *The Life of W. Averell Harriman, 1891–1986.* New York: Morrow, 1992.

Adler, Bill, ed. *The Wit and Wisdom of Jimmy Carter.* Secaucus, N.J.: Citadel Press, 1977.

Allen, Frederick. *Atlanta Rising: The Invention of an International City, 1946–1996.* Marietta, Ga.: Longstreet Press, 1996.

——— . *Secret Formula: How Brilliant Marketing and Relentless Salesmanship Made Coca-Cola the Best-known Product in the World.* New York: HarperCollins, 1994.

Anderson, Patrick. *Electing Jimmy Carter: The Campaign of 1976.* Baton Rouge: Louisiana State University Press, 1994.

Anderson, William. *The Wild Man from Sugar Creek: The Political Career of Eugene Talmadge.* Baton Rouge: Louisiana State University Press, 1975.

Angelo, Bonnie. *First Mothers: The Women Who Shaped the Presidents.* New York: HarperCollins, 2001.

Anthony, Carl Sferrazza. *First Ladies,* vol. 2, *The Saga of the Presidents' Wives and Their Power, 1961–1990.* New York: Morrow, 1991.

Arial, Dan, with Cheryl Heckler-Feltz. *The Carpenter's Apprentice: The Spiritual Biography of Jimmy Carter.* Grand Rapids, Mich.: Zondervan, 1996.

Arnall, Ellis Gibbs. *The Shore Dimly Seen.* Philadelphia: Lippincott, 1946.

——— . *What the People Want.* Philadelphia: Lippincott, 1947.

Auten, Brian J. *Carter's Conversion: The Hardening of American Defense Policy.* Columbia: University of Missouri Press, 2008.

Barber, James David. *The Presidential Character: Predicting Performance in the White House.* 4th ed. Englewood Cliffs, N.J.: Prentice-Hall, 1972.

Bartley, Numan V. *Jimmy Carter and the Politics of the South.* St. Louis, Mo.: Forum Press, 1979.

——— . *The New South, 1945–1980.* Baton Rouge: Louisiana State University Press, 1995.

Bass, Jack, and Walter DeVries. *The Transformation of Southern Politics: Social Change and Political Consequence Since 1945.* New York: Basic Books, 1976.

Bell, Griffin. *Taking Care of the Law.* New York: Morrow, 1982.

Biven, W. Carl. *Jimmy Carter's Economy: Policy in an Age of Limits.* Chapel Hill: University of North Carolina Press, 2002.

Black, Earl. *Southern Governors and Civil Rights.* Cambridge, Mass.: Harvard University Press, 1976.

Black, Earl, and Merle Black. *The Rise of Southern Republicans.* Cambridge, Mass.: Harvard University Press, 2002.

——— . *Politics and Society in the South.* Cambridge, Mass.: Harvard University Press, 1987.

——— . *The Vital South: How Presidents are Elected.* Cambridge, Mass.: Harvard University Press, 1992.

Blount, Roy. *Crackers: This Whole Many-angled Thing of Jimmy, More Carters, Ominous Little Animals, Sad Singing Women, My Daddy, and Me.* New York: Ballantine Books, 1982.

Boller, Paul F., Jr. *Presidential Wives: An Anecdotal History.* New York: Oxford University Press, 1988.

Borns, Steven, photographer and ed. *People of Plains, Georgia.* New York: McGraw-Hill, 1978.

Bourne, Peter G. *Jimmy Carter: A Comprehensive Biography from Plains to Postpresidency.* New York: Simon and Schuster, 1997.

Bradbury, M. L., and James B. Gilbert, eds. *Transforming Faith: The Sacred and Secular in Modern American History.* Westport, Conn.: Greenwood Press, 1989.

Branch, Taylor B. *Parting the Waters: America in the King Years, 1954–1963.* New York: Simon and Schuster, 1988.

———. *Pillar of Fire: America in the King Years, 1963–1965.* New York: Simon and Schuster, 1998.

———. *At Canaan's Edge: America in the King Years, 1965–1968.* New York: Simon and Schuster, 2006.

Brinkley, Douglas. *The Unfinished Presidency: Jimmy Carter's Journey beyond the White House.* New York: Viking, 1998.

Brown, Charles C. *Niebuhr and His Age: Reinhold Niebuhr's Prophetic Role in the Twentieth Century.* Philadelphia: Trinity, 1992.

Bryant, James C. *A Gift for Giving: The Story of Lamar Rich Plunkett.* Macon, Ga.: Mercer University Press, 1993.

Brzezinski, Zbigniew K. *Power and Principle: Memoirs of the National Security Advisor.* New York: Farrar, Strauss, Giroux, 1983.

Bumpers, Dale. *The Best Lawyer in a One-lawyer Town: A Memoir.* New York: Random House, 2003.

Burns, James MacGregor. *Leadership.* New York: Harper and Row, 1978.

———. *The Power to Lead: The Crisis of the American Presidency.* New York: Simon and Schuster, 1984.

Califano, Joseph A., Jr. *Governing America: An Insider's Report from the White House and the Cabinet.* New York: Simon and Schuster, 1981.

Callaway, Felix R. *Bloody Links.* Shreveport, La., 1907.

Carlson, Jody. *George C. Wallace and the Politics of Powerlessness: The Wallace Campaigns for the Presidency, 1964–1976.* New Brunswick, N.J.: Transaction, 1996.

Caroli, Betty Boyd. *First Ladies.* New York: Oxford University Press, 1995.

Carroll, Peter N. *It Seemed Like Nothing Happened: America in the 1970s.* New Brunswick, N.J.: Rutgers University Press, 1982.

Carter, Billy and Sybil. *Billy: Billy Carter's Reflections on His Struggle with Fame, Alcoholism and Cancer.* With Ken Estes. Newport, R.I.: Edgehill, 1989.

Carter, Dan T. *The Politics of Rage: George Wallace, The Origins of the New Conservatism, and the Transformation of American Politics.* New York: Simon and Schuster, 1995.

Carter, Hugh Alton, as Told to Frances Spatz Leighton. *Cousin Beedie and Cousin Hot: My Life with the Carter Family of Plains, Georgia.* Englewood Cliffs, N.J.: Prentice-Hall, 1978.

Carter, Jimmy. *Addresses of James Earl Carter, Governor of Georgia, 1971–1975.* Compiled by Frank Daniel. Atlanta: Georgia Department of Archives and History, 1975.

———. *Why Not the Best?* Nashville: Broadman Press, 1975.

———. *A Government as Good as Its People.* New York: Simon and Schuster, 1977.

———. *Keeping Faith: Memoirs of a President.* New York: Bantam Books, 1982.

———. *The Blood of Abraham: Insights into the Middle East.* Boston: Houghton Mifflin, 1985.

———. *Negotiation: The Alternative to Hostility.* Macon, Ga.: Mercer University Press, 1984.

———. *An Outdoor Journal: Adventures and Reflections.* New York: Bantam Books, 1988.

———. *Turning Point: A Candidate, A State, and a Nation Come of Age.* New York: Times Books, 1992.

———. *Talking Peace: A Vision for the Next Generation.* New York: Dutton Children's Books, 1993.

———. *Always a Reckoning and Other Poems.* New York: Times Books, 1995.

———. *Living Faith.* New York: Times Books, 1996.

———. *The Little Baby Snoogle-Fleejer.* Illustrated by Amy Carter. New York: Times Books, 1995.

———. *Sources of Strength: Meditations on Scripture for a Living Faith.* New York: Times Books, 1997.

———. *The Virtues of Aging.* New York: Ballantine, 1998.

———. *Christmas in Plains: Memories.* New York: Simon and Schuster, "2001.

———. *An Hour before Daylight: Memories of a Rural Boyhood.* New York: Simon and Schuster, 2001.

———. *The Nobel Peace Prize Lecture.* New York: Simon and Schuster, 2002.

———. *The Hornet's Nest: A Novel of the Revolutionary War.* New York: Simon and Schuster, 2003.

———. *Sharing Good Times.* New York: Simon and Schuster, 2004.

———. *Our Endangered Values: America's Moral Crisis.* New York: Simon and Schuster, 2005.

———. *Palestine Peace Not Apartheid.* New York: Simon and Schuster, 2006.

———. *Beyond the White House: Waging Peace, Fighting Disease, Building Hope.* New York: Simon and Schuster, 2007.

———. *A Remarkable Mother.* New York: Simon and Schuster, 2008.

———. *We Can Have Peace in the Holy Land.* New York: Simon and Schuster, 2009.

Carter, Jimmy, and Rosalynn Carter. *Everything to Gain: How to Make the Most of the Rest of Your Life.* New York: Random House, 1987.

Carter, Lillian, as told to Beth Tartan and Rudy Hayes. *Miss Lillian and Friends: The Plains, Georgia, Family Philosophy and Recipe Book.* New York: A and W, 1977.

Carter, Lillian, and Gloria Carter Spann. *Away from Home: Letters to My Family*. New York: Warner Books, 1977.

Carter, Rosalynn. *First Lady from Plains*. Boston: Houghton Mifflin, 1984.

———, with Susan K. Golant. *Helping Yourself Help Others: A Book for Caregivers*. New York: Times Books, 1994.

———, with Susan K. Golant. *Helping Someone with Mental Illness*. New York: Times Books, 1998.

Carter, William: *Billy Carter: A Journey through the Shadows*. Marietta, Ga.: Longstreet Press, 1999.

Chafe, William H., Raymond Gavins, and Robert Korstad. *Remembering Jim Crow: African Americans Tell about Life in the Segregated South*. New York: New Press, 2001.

Clark, Henry B. *Serenity, Courage, and Wisdom: The Enduring Legacy of Reinhold Niebuhr*. Cleveland: Pilgrim Press, 1994.

Cleland, Max. *Strong in the Broken Places*. Marietta, Ga.: Longstreet, 2001.

Clifford, Clark, with Richard Holbrooke. *Counsel to the President*. New York: Random House, 1991.

Clowse, Barbara Barksdale. *Ralph McGill: A Biography*. Macon, Ga.: Mercer University Press, 1998.

Clymer, Adam. *Edward M. Kennedy: A Biography*. New York: HarperCollins, 1999.

Coleman, Kenneth, ed. *A History of Georgia*. Athens: University of Georgia Press, 1977.

Collins, Tom. *The Search for Jimmy Carter*. Waco, Tex.: Word Books, 1976.

Cook, James F. *Carl Sanders: Spokesman of the New South*. Macon, Ga.: Mercer University Press, 1993.

Cox, Jack F. *History of Sumter County, Georgia*. Roswell, Ga.: W. H. Wolfe Associates for the Sumter County Historic Preservation Society, 1983.

Crawford, William Lusk, Sr. *Ancestors and Friends: A History and Genealogy*. Dallas, 1978.

Crespino, Joseph. *In Search of Another Country: Mississippi and the Conservative Counterrevolution*. Princeton, N.J.: Princeton University Press, 2007.

Dalleck, Robert. *Lone Star Rising: Lyndon Johnson and His Times, 1908–1960*. New York: Oxford University Press, 1991.

———. *Flawed Giant: Lyndon Johnson and His Times, 1961–1973*. New York: Oxford University Press, 1998.

Davis, Harold E. *Henry Grady's New South: Atlanta, A Brave and Beautiful City*. Tuscaloosa, AL: University of Alabama Press, 1990.

Dawsey, Cyrus B., and James M. Dawsey, eds. *The Confederados: Old South Immigrants in Brazil*. Tuscaloosa, AL: The University of Alabama Press, 1995.

Dees, Morris, with Steve Fiffer. *A Season for Justice: The Life and Times of Civil Rights Lawyer Morris Dees*. New York: Charles Scribner's Sons, 199.

DeRoche, Andrew J. *Andrew Young: Civil Rights Ambassador*. Washington, D.C.: Scholarly Resources Books, 2003.

Dershowitz, Alan M. *The Vanishing American Jew*. New York: Simon and Schuster, 1997.

Dinnerstein, Leonard. *Anti-Semitism in America*. New York: Oxford University Press, 1994.

Dinnerstein, Leonard, and Mary Dale Palsson. *Jews in the South*. Baton Rouge, LA: Louisiana State University Press, 1973.

Drew, Elizabeth. *American Journal: The Events of 1976*. New York: Random House, 1977.

Dumbrell, John. *The Carter Presidency: A Re-evaluation*. Manchester and New York: Manchester University Press, 1993.

Eagles, Charles, ed. *Is There a Southern Political Tradition?* Jackson, MS: University Press of Mississippi, 1996.

Early County in 1976. Blakely, Ga., 1977.

Escott, Paul D., and David R. Goldfield, eds. *Major Problems in the American South, Vol. II: The New South*. Lexington, Mass.: D. C. Heath and Co, 1990.

Evans, Eli N. *The Lonely Days Were Sundays: Reflections of a Jewish Southerner*. Jackson, MS: University Press of Mississippi, 1993.

———. *The Provincials: A Personal History of Jews in the South*. New York: Atheneum, 1973.

Farber, David. *Taken Hostage: The Iran Hostage Crisis and America's First Encounter with Radical Islam*. Princeton, N.J.: Princeton University Press, 2005.

Farrell, John A. *Tip O'Neill and the Democratic Century*. Boston: Little, Brown and Company, 2001.

Fink, Gary M. *Prelude to the Presidency: The Political Character and Legislative Leadership Style of Governor Jimmy Carter*. Westport, Conn.: Greenwood Press, 1980.

Fink, Gary M., and Hugh Davis Graham, eds. *The Carter Presidency: Policy Choices in the Post-New Deal Era*. Lawrence, KS: University of Kansas Press, 1998.

Ford, Betty. *The Times of My Life*. New York: Harper and Row, 1978.

Fowler, James W. *Stages of Faith: The Psychology of Human Development and the Quest for Meaning*. New York: HarperCollins, 1995.

Fox, Richard W. *Reinhold Niebuhr: A Biography*. New York: Harper and Row, 1985.

Frady, Marshall. *Southerners: A Journalist's Odyssey*. New York: New American Library, 1980.

Frederick, R. Karl. *William Faulkner: American Writer*. New York: Weidenfeld and Nicolson, 1989.

Frum, David. *How We Got Here: The 70s, the Decade that Brought You Modern Life (For Better or Worse)*. New York: Basic Books, 2000.

Fuqua, J. B. *Fuqua, A Memoir: How I Made My Fortune Using Other People's Money*. Marietta, Ga.: Longstreet Press, 2001.

Gaddis, John Lewis. *The Cold War: A New History*. New York: Penguin Books, 2005.

Gaillard, Frye. *Prophet from Plains: Jimmy Carter and His Legacy*. With a foreword by David C. Carter. Athens: University of Georgia Press, 2007.

Garrow, David J. *The FBI and Martin Luther King, Jr.: From "Solo" to Memphis*. New York: W. W. Norton and Company, 1981.

Gates, Robert M. *From the Shadows: The Ultimate Insider's Story of Five Presidents and How They Won the Cold War*. New York: Simon and Schuster, 1996.

Gelfand, H. Michael. *Sea Change at Annapolis: The United States Naval Academy, 1949–2000*. Chapel Hill: University of North Carolina Press, 2006.

Gibbons, Tony. *The Complete Encyclopedia of Battleships and Battlecruisers: A Technical Directory of all the World's Capital Ships from 1860 to the Present Day*. London, UK: Salamander Books, Ltd., 1983.

Gibson, Dot Rees, and Dianne Chavers Barfield. *Plains, Ga.: Carter Country, U.S.A.* Waycross, Ga.: Dot Gibson, 1977.

Gilkey, Langdon. *On Niebuhr: A Theological Study*. Chicago, IL: University of Chicago Press, 2001.

Glad, Betty. *Jimmy Carter in Search of the Great White House*. New York: W. W. Norton and Co., 1980.

———. *An Outsider in the White House: Jimmy Carter, His Advisors, and the Making of American Foreign Policy*. Ithaca, N.Y.: Cornell University Press, 2009.

Goolsby, Iva P., et al., comps. *Randolph County, Georgia: A Compilation of Facts, Recollections, and Family Histories*. N.p., 1977.

Gould, Lewis L., ed. *American First Ladies: Their Lives and Their Legacy*. Hamden, Conn.: Garland Publishing Co., 1996.

Grant, Donald L. *The Way It Was in the South: The Black Experience in Georgia*. Edited with an Introduction by Jonathan Grant. New York: Carol Publishing Group, 1993.

Grantham, Dewey W. *The Regional Imagination: The South and Recent American History*. Nashville, TN: Vanderbilt University Press, 1979.

Gray, Macy Bishop. *Through the Years, A Brief Informal Record of Georgia Southwestern College*. Americus, Ga.: Americus Printing Co., 1957.

Gulliver, Hal. *A Friendly Tongue*. Macon, Ga.: Mercer University Press, 1984.

Hakes, Jay. *A Declaration of Energy Independence: How Freedom from Foreign Oil Can Improve National Security, Our Economy, and the Environment*. Hoboken, N.J.: John Wiley & Sons, 2008.

Hardin, Jake. *The Wiley Carter Story*. Avera, Ga., 1977.

Hargrove, Erwin C. *Jimmy Carter as President: Leadership and the Politics of the Public Good*. Baton Rouge, LA: Louisiana State University Press, 1988.

Hart, Gary Warren. *Right from the Start: A Chronicle of the McGovern Campaign*. New York: Quadrangle Books, 1973.

Harter, Eugene C. *The Lost Colony of the Confederacy*. College Station, TX: Texas A & M Press, 2000.

Haugabook, Allene T. *Remembering Plains*. N.p.: Allene T. Haugabook, 1996.

Hefley, James and Marti. *The Church That Produced a President: The Remarkable Spiritual Roots of Jimmy Carter*. New York: Wyden Books, 1977.

Henderson, Harold P. *The Politics of Change in Georgia: A Biography of Ellis Arnall*. Athens: University of Georgia Press, 1991.

Henderson, Harold P., and Gary L. Roberts, eds. *Georgia Governors in an Age of Change: From Ellis Arnall to George Busbee*. Athens, Ga.: University of Georgia Press, 1988.

History of Plains, Georgia. Compiled by Plains Historical Preservation Trust, Inc. Fernandina Beach, Fl.: Wolfe, 2003.

Hutchinson, Duane. *Jimmy Carter's Hometown: People of Plains*. Lincoln, Neb.: Foundation Books, 2003.

Hyatt, Richard. *The Carters of Plains*. Huntsville, Al.: Strode, 1977.

———. *Mr. Speaker: The Biography of Tom Murphy*. Macon, Ga.: Mercer University Press, 1999.

Jenkins, Philip. *Decade of Nightmares: The End of the Sixties and the Making of Eighties America*. New York: Oxford University Press, 2006.

Jones, Charles O. *The Trusteeship Presidency: Jimmy Carter and the United States Congress*. Baton Rouge: Louisiana State University Press, 1988.

Jordan, Hamilton. *Crisis: The Last Year of the Carter Presidency*. New York: Putnam, 1982.

———. *No Such Thing as a Bad Day: A Memoir*. With a foreword by Jimmy Carter. Marietta, Ga.: Longstreet Press, 2000.

Jordan, Vernon, Jr. *Vernon Can Read: A Memoir*. New York: Public Affairs, 2001.

Kaufman Burton I., and Scott Kaufman. *The Presidency of James Earl Carter, Jr*. 2nd ed. rev. Lawrence; University Press of Kansas, 2006.

Kaufman, Robert G. *Henry M. Jackson: A Life in Politics*. Seattle: University of Washington Press, 2000.

Kaufman, Scott. *Rosalynn Carter: Equal Partner in the White House*. Lawrence: University Press of Kansas, 2007.

Kennedy, Edward M. *True Compass: A Memoir*. New York: Twelve, 2009.

Killian, Lewis M. *White Southerners*. Rev. ed. Amherst: University of Massachusetts Press, 1985.

King, Martin Luther, Sr., with Clayton Riley. *Daddy King: An Autobiography*. With a foreword by Benjamin E. Mays and with an introduction by Andrew J. Young. New York: Morrow, 1980.

K'Meyer, Tracy Elaine. *Interracialism and Christian Community in the Postwar South: The Study of Koinonia Farm*. Charlottesville: University Press of Virginia, 1997.

Kotkin, Stephen. *Armageddon Averted: The Soviet Collapse, 1970–2000*. New York: Oxford University Press, 2002.

Kucharsky, David. *The Man from Plains: The Mind and Spirit of Jimmy Carter*. New York: Harper and Row, 1976.

Kuhn, David Paul. *The Neglected Voter: White Men and the Democratic Dilemma*. New York: Palgrave Macmillan, 2007.

Lamis, Alexander P. *The Two-party South*. 2nd ed. New York: Oxford University Press, 1990.

Lance, Bert, with Bill Gilbert. *The Truth of the Matter: My Life in and Out of Politics*. New York: Summit Books, 1991.

Lance, LaBelle, with Gary Sledge. *This Too Shall Pass*. New York: Bantam Books, 1978.

Lasky, Victor. *Jimmy Carter: The Man and the Myth*. New York: Richard Marek, 1979.

Lea, James F., ed. *Contemporary Southern Politics*. Baton Rouge: Louisiana State University Press, 1988.

Lee, Dallas. *The Cotton Patch Evidence*. New York: Harper and Row, 1971.

Lesher, Stephen. *George Wallace: American Populist.* New York: Addison-Wesley, 1993.

Leuchtenburg, William E. *In the Shadow of FDR: From Harry Truman to Ronald Reagan.* Ithaca, N.Y.: Cornell University Press, 1983.

———. *The White House Looks South: Franklin D. Roosevelt, Harry S. Truman, Lyndon B. Johnson.* Baton Rouge: Louisiana State University Press, 2005.

Lewis, Finlay. *Mondale: Portrait of an American Politician.* New York: Harper and Row, 1980.

Love, Robert W., Jr. *History of the U.S. Navy.* Vols. 1 and 2. Harrisburg, Pa.: Stackpole, 1991.

Maddox, Robert L. *Preacher in the White House.* Nashville: Broadman Press, 1984.

Martin, Harold H. *A Good Man…A Great Dream: D. W. Brooks of Gold Kist.* Atlanta: Gold Kist, Inc., 1982.

———. *Ralph McGill, Reporter.* Boston: Little, Brown, 1973.

Marton, Katai. *Hidden Power: Presidential Marriages That Shaped Our Recent History.* New York: Pantheon Books, 2001.

Mattson, Kevin. *"What the Heck Are You Up To, Mr. President?" Jimmy Carter, America's "Malaise," and the Speech That Should Have Changed the Country.* New York: Bloomsbury, 2009.

May, Rollo. *The Courage to Create.* New York: Norton, 1975.

Mazlish, Bruce, and Edwin Diamond. *Jimmy Carter: An Interpretative Biography.* New York: Simon and Schuster, 1979.

McLellan, David. *Unto Caesar: The Political Relevance of Christianity.* Notre Dame, Ind.: Notre Dame University Press, 1992.

McMorrow, Fred. *Jimmy: The Candidacy of Carter.* New York: Whirlwind, 1976.

Michael, Deanna L. *Jimmy Carter as Educational Policymaker.* Albany: State University of New York Press, 2005.

Miller, William Lee. *Yankee from Georgia: The Emergence of Jimmy Carter.* New York: Times Books, 1978.

Morris, Charles R. *A Time of Passion: America, 1960–1980.* New York: Penguin Books, 1986.

Morris, Kenneth E. *Jimmy Carter: American Moralist.* Athens: University of Georgia Press, 1996.

Muravchik, Joshua. *The Uncertain Crusade: Jimmy Carter and the Dilemmas of Human Rights Policy.* Lanham, Md.: Hamilton Press, 1986.

Neustadt, Richard E. *Presidential Power and the Modern Presidents: The Politics of Leadership from Roosevelt to Reagan.* New York: Free Press, 1991.

Norton, Howard. *Rosalynn: A Portrait.* Plainfield, N.J.: Logos International, 1977.

Norton, Howard, and Bob Slosser. *The Miracle of Jimmy Carter.* Plainfield, N.J.: Logos International, 1976.

Oberdofer, Don. *The Two Koreas: A Contemporary History.* Reading, Mass.: Addison-Wesley, 1997.

O'Brien, William Patrick. *Special History Study: Jimmy Carter National Historic Site and Preservation District, Georgia.* N.p., 1991.

O'Neill, Tip, with Gary Hymel. *All Politics Is Local, and Other Rules of the Game.* Holbrook, Mass.: Bob Adams, 1994.

Oren, Michael B. *Six Days of War: June 1967 and the Making of the Modern Middle East.* New York: Oxford University Press, 2002.

Patterson, James T. *Brown v. Board of Education: A Civil Rights Milestone and Its Troubled Legacy*. New York: Oxford University Press, 2001.

———. *Restless Giant: The United States from Watergate to Bush v. Gore*. New York: Oxford University Press, 2005.

Pendergrast, Mark. *For God, Country, and Coca-Cola: The Unauthorized History of the Great American Soft Drink and the Company that Makes It*. New York: Macmillan, 1993.

Pierard, Richard V., and Robert D. Linden. *Civil Religion and the Presidency*. Grand Rapids, Mich.: Academic Books, 1988.

Pippert, Wesley G., comp. *The Spiritual Journey of Jimmy Carter*. New York: Macmillan, 1978.

Podhoretz, Norman. *Why Are Jews Liberals?* New York: Doubleday, 2009.

Polmar, Norman, and K. J. Moore. *Cold War Submarines: U.S. and Soviet Design and Construction*. Washington, D.C.: Brassey's, 2002.

Polmar, Norman, and Thomas B. Allan. *Rickover: Controversy and Genius*. New York: Simon and Schuster, 1982.

Powell, Jody. *The Other Side of the Story*. New York: Morrow, 1984.

Preston, Antony. *Battleships of World War I: An Illustrated Encyclopedia of the Battleships of All Nations, 1914–1918*. Harrisburg, Pa.: Arms and Armour Press, 1972.

Quandt, William B. *Camp David: Peacemaking and Politics*. Washington, D.C.: Brookings Institute, 1986.

Rabhan, David. *Conscious Coma: Ten Years in an Iranian Prison*. With a foreword by President Jimmy Carter. Mexico Beach, Fl.: Dream Catcher, 2004.

Radcliffe, Donnie. *Simply Barbara Bush: A Portrait of America's Candid First Lady*. New York: Warner Books, 1989.

Reston, James. *Deadline: A Memoir*. New York: Random House, 1991.

Ribuffo, Leo P. *Right Center Left: Essays in American History*. New Brunswick, N.J.: Rutgers University Press, 1992.

Roberts, Nancy. *Southern Ghosts*. Garden City, N.J.: Doubleday, 1979.

Rockefeller, David. *Memoirs*. New York: Random House, 2002.

Rockwell, Theodore. *The Rickover Effect: The Inside Story of How Admiral Hyman Rickover Built the Nuclear Navy*. New York: Wiley, 1992.

Rowan, Bobby. *Georgia's Modern Day Legislature: A Personal History of Georgia's Politics, 1962–1998*. Pine Mountain, Ga.: Main Street Printers, 1999.

Rozell, Mark J. *The Press and the Carter Presidency*. Boulder, Colo.: Westview Press, 1989.

Rubenzer, Steven J., and Thomas R. Faschingbauer. *Personality, Character, and Leadership in the White House: Psychologists Assess the Presidents*. Washington, D.C.: Brassey's, 2004.

Rusk, Dean as Told to Richard Rusk. *As I Saw It*. New York: Norton, 1990.

Sachar, Howard M. *A History of the Jews in America*. New York: Knopf, 1993.

Sanders, Randy. *Mighty Peculiar Elections: The New South Gubernatorial Campaigns of 1970 and the Changing Politics of Race*. Gainesville: University Press Of Florida, 2002.

Schneller, Robert J., Jr. *Breaking the Color Barrier: The U.S. Naval Academy's First Black Midshipmen and the Struggle for Racial Equality*. New York: New York University Press, 2005.

Schulman, Bruce J. *The Seventies: The Great Shift in American Culture, Society, and Politics.* New York: Free Press, 2001.

Schulman, Bruce J., and Julian E. Zelizer, eds. *Rightward Bound: Making America Conservative in the 1970s.* Cambridge, Mass.: Harvard University Press, 2008.

Shipp, Bill. *The Ape-slayer and Other Snapshots.* Macon, Ga.: Mercer University Press,1997.

Short, Bob. *Everything Is Pickrick: The Life of Lester Maddox.* Macon, Ga.: Mercer University Press, 1999.

Simmons, Dawn Langley. *Rosalynn Carter: Her Life and Work.* New York: Fell, 1979.

Simons, Howard. *Jewish Times: Voices of the American Jewish Experience.* Boston: Houghton Mifflin, 1988.

Smith, Gaddis. *Morality, Reason, and Power: American Diplomacy in the Carter Years.* New York: Hill and Wang, 1986.

Sokol, Jason. *There Goes My Everything: White Southerners in the Age of Civil Rights, 1945–1975.* New York: Knopf, 2006.

Spirz, Bob. *Dylan: A Biography.* New York: Norton, 1989.

Stapleton, Ruth Carter. *Brother Billy.* New York: Harper and Row, 1978.

——— . *The Gift of Inner Healing.* Waco, Tex.: Word Books, 1976.

St. John, Jeffrey. *Jimmy Carter's Betrayal of the South.* Ottawa, Ill.: Greenhill, 1976.

Strong, Robert A. *Working in the World: Jimmy Carter and the Making of American Foreign Policy.* Baton Rouge: Louisiana State University Press, 2000.

Stroud, Kandy. *How Jimmy Won: The Victory Campaign from Plains to the White House.* New York: Morrow, 1977.

Tall, Jeffrey. *Submarines and Deep-Sea Vehicles.* San Diego: Thunder Bay Press, 2002.

Talmadge, Herman E. *Talmadge: A Political Legacy, A Politician's Life.* Atlanta: Peachtree, 1987.

Teel, Leonard Ray. *Ralph Emerson McGill: Voice of the Southern Conscience.* Knoxville: University of Tennessee Press, 2001.

Thomas, Dylan. *The Collected Poems of Dylan Thomas, 1934–1952.* New York: New Directions, 1957.

Thomas, Kenneth H., Jr. *The Rock House: McDuffie County, Georgia.* Atlanta, 1974.

Thompson, Hunter S. *Fear and Loathing on the Campaign Trail—'72.* New York: Warner Books, 1985.

——— . *The Great Shark Hunt.* New York: Ballantine Books, 1979.

Truman, Margaret. *First Ladies.* New York: Random House, 1995.

Tuck, Stephen G. N. *Beyond Atlanta: The Struggle for Racial Equality in Georgia, 1940–1980.* Athens: University of Georgia Press, 2001.

Turner, Stansfield. *Secrecy and Diplomacy: The CIA in Transition.* Boston: Houghton Mifflin, 1985.

Tyler, Patrick. *A Great Wall: Six Presidents and China.* New York: Public Affairs, 1999.

United States. *Public Papers of the Presidents of the United States, Jimmy Carter: 1977–1981.* 9 vols. Washington, D.C.: Government Printing Office, 1977–81.

United States. *Public Papers of the Presidents of the United States: Richard Nixon: Containing the Public Messages, Speeches, and Statements of the President, 1973.* Washington, D.C.: Government Printing Office, 1975.

Vance, Cyrus. *Hard Choices: Critical Years in America's Foreign Policy.* New York: Simon and Schuster, 1983.

Wallace, Robert B., Jr. *Dress Her in White and Gold: A Biography of Georgia Tech and the Men Who Led Her.* Atlanta: Georgia Tech Foundation, 1969.

Walton, Hanes, Jr. *The Native Son Presidential Candidate: The Carter Vote in Georgia.* New York: Praeger, 1992.

Walters, Beth, comp. *A History of Plains, Georgia, 1885–1985.* Americus, Ga.: Gammage Print Shop, n.d.

Watson, Robert P., and Anthony J. Eksterowicz, eds. *The Presidential Companion: Readings on the First Ladies.* 2nd ed. Columbia: University of South Carolina Press, 2006.

Wells, Della Wager. *George Waldo Woodruff: A Life of Quiet Achievement.* Macon, Ga.: Mercer University Press, 1987.

———. *The First Hundred Years: A Centennial History of King and Spaulding.* Atlanta: King & Spaulding, 1985.

Wilkie, Curtis. *Dixie: A Personal Odyssey through Events That Shaped the Modern South.* New York: Scribner's 2001.

Williford, William Bailey. *Americus through the Years.* Atlanta: Cherokee, 1975.

Witcover, Jules. *Marathon: The Pursuit of the Presidency, 1972–1976.* New York: Viking Press, 1977.

———. *Party of the People: A History of the Democrats.* New York: Random House, 2003.

———. *The Year the Dream Died: Revisiting 1968 in America.* New York: Warner Books, Inc., 1997.

Woodward, C. Vann. *The Burden of Southern History.* 3rd ed. Baton Rouge: Louisiana State University Press, 1993.

———. *Tom Watson, Agrarian Rebel.* 1938; Reprint, New York: Oxford University Press, 1963.

Wooten, James T. *Dasher: The Roots and the Rising of Jimmy Carter.* New York: Summit Books, 1978.

WPA Writer's Program. *A Guide to the United States Naval Academy.* New York: The Devin-Adair Co., 1941.

Young, Andrew. *An Easy Burden: The Civil Rights Movement and the Transformation of America.* New York: HarperCollins, 1996.

ARTICLES

Allen, Henry. "Just Plains Folk." *Washington Post/Potomac* (August 15, 1976).

Battelle, Phyllis. "Jimmy and Rosalynn: Living Well Is the Best Revenge." *Woman's Day* (June 16, 1987).

Bergren, D. Jason. "'I Had a Different Way of Governing': The Living Faith of President Carter." *Journal of Church and State* 47, no. 1 (winter 2005): 46–56.

Bisher, Furman. "The South Georgia Carter Boy." *Georgia Magazine* (January 1972).

Bonafede, Dom. "No One Tries to Roll Over Jordan in the White House." *National Journal* (April 16, 1977): 580–84.

———. "Charles Kirbo: The President's One-Man 'Kitchen Cabinet.'" *National Journal* (July 22, 1978): 1152–56.

Boney, F. N. "Georgia's First President: The Emergence of Jimmy Carter." *Georgia Historical Quarterly* 72, no. 1 (spring 1988): 119–26.

Bourne, Peter G. "Jimmy Carter: A Profile." *Yale Review* 72, no. 1 (autumn 1982): 126–40.

Bowden, Mark. "Among the Hostage-Takers: The Iranian Students Twenty-five Years Later." *Atlantic* (December 2004): 76–96.

Brill, Steven. "Jimmy Carter's Pathetic Lies." *Harper's* (March 1976): 77–88.

Brinkley, Douglas. "A Time for Reckoning: Jimmy Carter and the Cult of Kinfolk." *Presidential Studies Quarterly* 29, no. 4 (December 1999): 778–98.

———. "Bringing the Green Revolution to Africa: Jimmy Carter, Norman Borlaug, and the Global 2000 Campaign." *World Policy Journal* 13, no. 1 (spring 1996): 53–63.

———. "Jimmy Carter's Modest Quest for Global Peace." *Journal of Foreign Affairs* 74, no. 6 (November-December 1995): 90–100.

———. "The Rising stock of Jimmy Carter." *Diplomatic History* 20, no. 4 (fall 1996): 505–29.

Brooks, Jennifer E. "Winning the Peace: Georgia Veterans and the Struggle to Define the Political Legacy of World War II." *Journal of Southern History* 66, no. 3 (August 2000): 563–604.

Brzezinski, Zbigniew. "White House Diary, 1980." *Orbis* 32, no. 1 (winter 1988): 32–48.

Callaghan, Karen J., and Simo Virtanen. "Revised Models of The 'Rally Phenomenon': The Case of the Carter Presidency." *Journal of Politics* 55, no. 3 (August 1993): 756–64.

Carter, Jimmy. "The Geneva Initiative: A Promising Foundation for Peace." *Israel Journal of Politics, Economics, and Culture* 2, no. 9 (2004): 9–11.

———. "Human Rights: The Real Cost of War." *Mediterranean Quarterly* 3, no. 2 (spring 1992): 1–7.

———. "The Challenge of Education for Health in America's Schools." *Journal of School Health* 60, no. 4 (April 1990): 129.

———. "The Greatest Human Rights Crime: War." *Emory International Review* 17, no. 1 (spring 1990): 16.

———. "The Third World Is Not a Hopeless Place." *New Age Journal* 7, no. 2 (March 2001): 52.

———. "The United States and the Advancement of Human Rights around the World." *Emory Law Journal* 40, no. 3 (summer 1991): 723–30.

"The Carter Boys *Speed* Fertilizing," *Cotton: The Magazine of Advanced Technology for Large Scale Producers* (January 1969): 14–15.

Chambers, John Whiteclay, II. "Jimmy Carter's Public Policy Ex-Presidency." *Political Science Quarterly* 13, no. 3 (fall 1998): 405–61.

Chancey, Andrew S. "'A Demonstration Plot for the Kingdom of God': The Establishment and Early Years of Koinonia Farm." *Georgia Historical Quarterly* 75, no. 2 (summer 1991): 321–53.

Chanley, Virginia A. "The First Lady as Presidential Advisor, Policy Advocate, and Surrogate: Rosalynn Carter and the Political Role of the First Lady." *White House Studies* 1, no. 4 (fall 2001): 549–64.

Clotfelder, James. "Populism in Office, or Whatever Happened to Huey Long?" *New South: A Quarterly Review of Southern Affairs* 28, no. 2 (spring 1973): 56–61.

Cobb, Charles, et al. "Jimmy Carter's Roots." *National Enquirer* (March 15, 1977): 47–48.

Cogan, Charles G. "Desert One and Its Disorders." *Journal of Military History* 67, no. 1 (January 2003): 201–16.

Coombs, Orde. "The Hand That Rocked Carter's Cradle." *New York* (June 14, 1976): 40–43.

Darling, Lynn. "'Passionless Presidency' and the Insider's Dilemma: James Fallows Defends His 'Honorable' Criticism.'" *Washington Post* (April 25, 1979).

Drew, Elizabeth. "A Reporter at Large: In Search of a Definition." *New Yorker* (August 27, 1979): 45–73.

Driemen, John. "Jimmy and Rosalyn." *Good Housekeeping* (January 1992): 100–101, 170, 172–73.

Edwards, George C., III. "Exclusive Interview: President Jimmy Carter." *Presidential Studies Quarterly* 38, no. 2 (March 2008): 1–13.

Elowitz, Paul H. "Three Days in Plains." *Journal of Psychohistory* (fall 1977): 175–99.

Elzy, Martin I. "Camp David Accords Set Model for Lasting Peace, Piece by Piece." *Austin (TX) American-Statesman* (September 17, 2003).

Fardella, Enrico. "The Sino-American Normalization: A Reassessment." *Diplomatic History* 33, no. 4 (September 2009): 545–78.

Fallows, James. "The Passionless Presidency." *Atlantic Monthly* (May and June 1979).

Fontham, Elizabeth T. H., and Pelayo Corres. "Epidemiology of Pancreatic Cancer." *Surgical Clinics of North America* 69, no. 3 (June 1989): 551–67.

Forsythe, David P. "U.S. Foreign Policy and Human Rights." *Journal of Human Rights* 1, no. 4 (December 2002): 501–21.

Gaughan, Anthony. "Woodrow Wilson and the Rise of Militant Interventionism in the South." *Journal of Southern History* 55, no. 4 (November 1999): 771–808.

Glad, Betty. "Contributions of Psychohistory." In *Handbook of Political Psychology,* edited by Jeanne N. Knudson. San Francisco: Jossey-Bass, 1973.

Godbold, E. Stanly, Jr. "Dusty Corners of the Mind: Jimmy Carter's Poetry." *Studies in the Literary Imagination* 30, no. 1 (spring 1997): 107–17.

Goldman, Peter. "Sizing Up Carter." *Newsweek* (13 Sept. 1976).

Gorman, Siobhan, and Sydney J. Freedberg, Jr. "Carter and Turner on Intelligence Reform." *National Journal* (October 9, 2004): 3080–82.

Green, Joshua. "Better Luck This Time." *Atlantic* (July-August 2009): 78–86.

Grob, Gerald N. "Public Policy and Mental Illness: Jimmy Carter's Presidential Commission on Mental Health." *Milbank Quarterly* 83, no. 3 (2005): 425–56.

Hall, Arthur L., and Peter G. Bourne. "Indigenous Therapists in a Southern Black Urban Community." *Archives of General Psychiatry* 28, no. 1 (January 1973): 137–42.

Holifield, E. Brooks. "The Three Strands of Jimmy Carter's Religion." *New Republic* (June 5, 1976): 15–17.

Jensen, Faye Lind. "An Awesome Responsibility: Rosalynn Carter as First Lady." *Presidential Studies Quarterly* 20, no. 4 (fall 1990): 769–75.

Kaufman, Victor S. "The Bureau of Human Rights during the Carter Administration." *Historian* 61, no. 1 (fall 1998): 51–65.

Lisby, Gregory C. "Trying to Define What May Be Indefinable: The Georgia Literature Commission, 1953–1973." *Georgia Historical Quarterly* 84, no. 2 (spring 2000): 72–97.

Lynn, Katalin Kadar. "The Return of the Crown of St. Stephen and Its Subsequent Impact on the Carter Administration." *East European Quarterly* 34, no. 2 (summer 2000): 181–209.

McMath, Robert C., Jr. "Jimmy Carter: A Southerner in the White House?" In *The Adaptable South: Essays in Honor of George Brown Tindall*, edited by Elizabeth Jacoway, Dan T. Carter, Lester C. Lamon, and Robert C. McMath, Jr. Baton Rouge: Louisiana State University Press, 1991.

Murphy, Reg. "The New Jimmy Carter." *New Republic* (February 14, 1976): 14–17.

O'Conner, Charles S. "The Politics of Industrialization and Interracialism in Sumter County, Georgia: Koinonia Farm in the 1950s." *Georgia Historical Quarterly* 89, no. 4 (winter 2005): 505–27.

Osborne, John. "Carter Talk." *New Republic* (September 25, 1976): 15–20.

Pastor, Robert A. "The Carter Administration and Latin America: A Text of Principle." In *United States Policy in Latin America: A Quarter Century of Crisis and Challenge*, edited by John D. Martz. Lincoln: University of Nebraska Press, 1988.

Pfluger, Friedbert. "Human Rights Unbound: Carter's Human Rights Policy Reassessed." *Presidential Studies Quarterly* 19, no. 4 (fall 1989): 705–17.

Price, Reynolds. "Family Stories: The Carters of Plains." *Time* (January 3, 1977): 26, 29.

Randolph, Eleanor. "The Carter Complex." *Esquire* (November 1977): 166–84.

Raymond, John, Jack Wilkinson, Selby McCash, Erv Cuevas, and Prentice Palmer. "Jimmy Carter: A Midterm Report." *Georgia Magazine* 16, no. 7 (February 1973).

Ribuffo, Leo P. "God and Jimmy Carter." In *Transforming Faith: The Sacred and Secular in Modern American History*, edited by M. L. Bradbury and James B. Gilbert. Westport, Conn.: Greenwood Press, 1989.

———. "Jimmy Carter and the Ironies of American Liberalism." *Gettysburg Review* 1, no. 4 (fall 1988): 738–49.

———. " 'Malaise' Revisited: Jimmy Carter and the Crisis Confidence." In *The Liberal Persuasion*, edited by John Patrick Diggins. Princeton, N.J.: Princeton University Press, 1997.

Rosati, Jerel A. "Jimmy Carter, a Man before His Time? The Emergence and Collapse of the First Post-Cold War Presidency." *Presidential Studies Quarterly* 23, no. 3 (summer 1993): 459–76.

Rozell, Mark J. "Carter Rehabilitated: What Caused the 39th President's Press Transformation?" *Presidential Studies Quarterly* 23, no. 2 (spring 1993): 317–30.

Ruechel, Frank A. "Politics and Morality Revisited: Jimmy Carter and Reinhold Niebuhr." *Atlanta History* 37, no. 4 (winter 1994): 19–31.

Safran, Clair. "The Women in Jimmy Carter's Life." *Redbook* (October 1976): 82, 84, 92, 94.

Sanders, Randy. " 'The Sad Duty of Politics': Jimmy Carter and the Issue of Race in His 1970 Gubernatorial Campaign." *Georgia Historical Quarterly* 76, no. 3 (fall 1992): 612–38.

Scheer, Robert. "Playboy Interview: Jimmy Carter." *Playboy* (November 1976).

———. "Jimmy, We hardly Know Y'All." *Playboy* (November 1976).

Schmitz, David E., and Vanessa Walker. "Jimmy Carter and the Foreign Policy of Human Rights: The Development of a Post-Cold War Foreign Policy." *Journal of Diplomatic History* 28, no. 1 (January 2004): 113–43.

Shannon, Margaret. "A President in the Family." *Atlanta Journal and Constitution Magazine* (January 16, 1977): 8–9, 19–23.

———. "What It's Like to Be Governor." *The Atlantic Journal-Constitution*, April 11, 1974: 1, 41.

Sheehy, Gail. "Ladies and Gentlemen, The Second President—Sister Rosalynn." *New York* (November 22, 1976): 50–59.

Sheppard, Peggy. "The Man from Plains." *Georgia Magazine* 4 (December 1970): 16–19.

Simpson, T. McNin, III. "Jimmy Carter and the Transformation of Southern Politics, 1953–1987." In *Contemporary Southern Politics,* edited by James F. Lea. Baton Rouge: Louisiana State University Press, 1988.

———. "Restyling Georgia Courts." *Judicature* 59, no. 6 (January 1976): 282–87.

Smith, Kathy B. "The First Lady Represents America: Rosalynn Carter in South America." *Presidential Studies Quarterly* 27, no. 3 (summer 1997): 540–67.

Spann, Willie Carter, with Burton H. Wolfe. "The Other Carter." *Hustler* (May 1977): 49–54.

Stein, Kenneth W. "My Problem with Jimmy Carter." *Middle East Quarterly* 14, no. 2 (spring 2007): 1–8.

Strong, Robert A. "Recapturing Leadership: The Carter Administration and the Crisis of Confidence." *Presidential Studies Quarterly* 16, no. 4 (fall 1986): 636–50.

Terry, Janice J. "The Carter Administration and the Palestinians." *Arab Studies Quarterly* 12, no. 1/2 (winter–spring 1990): 153–66.

Thomas, Kenneth H., Jr. "Georgia Family Lines." *Georgia Life* (winter 1976).

———. "Georgia Family Life." *Georgia Life* (winter 1980).

Thompson, Hunter S. "Jimmy Carter and the Great Leap of Faith: An Endorsement with Fear and Loathing." *Rolling Stone* 214 (June 3, 1976): 54–64.

Tyler, Patrick. "The (Ab)Normalization of U.S.-Chinese Relations." *Foreign Affairs* 78, no. 5 (September-October, 1999): 93–123.

Walker, Breck. " 'Friends, but Not Allies'—Cyrus Vance and the Normalization of Relations with China." *Diplomatic History* 33, no. 4 (September 2009): 579–613.

Wall, James M. "Jimmy Carter: Doing Work That Speaks for Itself." *Christian Century* 107, no. 17 (November 1990): 515–16.

————. "Jimmy Carter: Finding a Commonality of Concern." *Christian Century* 107, no. 18 (December 1990): 555–56.

Wested, Odd Arne. "Secrets of the Second World: The Russian Archives and the Reinterpretation of Cold War History." *Diplomatic History* 2, no. 2 (spring 1997): 259–71.

Wilkie, Curtis. "Blessed is the Peacemaker: The Resurrection of Jimmy Carter." *Boston Globe Magazine* (August 12, 1990).

Williams, Miller. "A Conversation with Jimmy Carter." *Image: LA Journal of the Arts and Religion* 24 (fall 1999): 61.

Wills, Brian S. "Georgia History in Pictures: D. W. Brooks: Gold Kist's Goodwill Ambassador." *Georgia Historical Quarterly* 74, no. 3 (fall 1990): 487–502.

Wills, Garry. "The Underestimation of Jimmy Carter." *Notre Dame Magazine* (summer 1985): 18–21.

————. "The Plains Truth: An Inquiry into the Shaping of Jimmy Carter." *Atlantic* (June 1976): 49–54.

INDEX

Crowe, Carl E., 98–100
Cutler, Lloyd, 264

Davis, A. D., 22–23
Delta Airlines, 147, 165, 179, 181
Democratic National Committee, 265
Democratic National Convention of 1968, 141,
    144, 224, 230–235
Democratic National Convention of 1972,
    230–232
Department of Human Resources, 180,
    182–183, 187
Derian, Pat, 266, 320n103
Dolvin, Emily Gordy (Aunt Sissy), 25, 48, 120,
    170, 193, 219
DuBois, W. E. B., 23
Dukakis, Michael, 259
Dylan, Bob, 198, 219, 263

Eagleton, Thomas, 235–236
Egypt, 148, 246, 252
Eisenhower, Dwight D., 161, 225
Eizenstat, Stuart, 144, 169, 243, 258–259,
    267, 270
Emory University, 84, 122, 146
energy crisis, 237–239, 250, 252, 270
English, Millard, 220
ERA (Equal Rights Amendment), 192, 213,
    216, 217

Faulkner, William, 7–8, 80, 226
Few, William, 243
Firing Line, 241
Fitzpatrick, Mary Prince, 173, 213, 219, 243
Flint River, 97, 105
Floyd, James H. "Sloppy", 269
Food and Agriculture Act of 1965, 113
Ford, Betty, 198
Ford, Gerald R., 165, 198, 265
Forrest, Rembert, 23, 39
Forrester, Beverly W., 189
Forrester, E. L. "Tick," 76–77
Fortson, Ben, 96, 171, 181, 184, 186, 209
Fortson, Warren, 95, 98–99, 104, 107,
    112, 186

Fuller, Millard, 123, 194
Fuqua, J. B., 100, 102, 147, 172

Gambrell, David, 98, 119, 122, 124, 145, 165,
    175–176, 189, 200, 255
Gaston, Hugh, 90, 136, 183
Geer, Peter Zack, 101
George, Walter F., 76
Georgetown, GA, 96, 98–99
Georgia Association for Mental Health, 151
Georgia Crop Improvement Association, Inc.,
    83, 100
Georgia Heritage Trust Commission, 196–197,
    207
Georgia Institute of Technology, 47–48, 52, 62,
    111, 146, 222
Georgia Lockheed Corporation, 48, 200
Georgia Planning Commission, 134
Georgia Power Company, 85, 179, 238, 257
Georgia Southwestern College, 43, 46, 94, 107,
    117–118, 146, 154, 189, 193–194, 213
Georgia State College for Women, 29, 32, 55,
    58, 60, 73
Georgia Tech. *See* Georgia Institute of
    Technology
Georgia World Congress Center, 200, 245
Ghana, 246
Gillis, Hugh, 161, 164, 177, 184, 188
Gills, Jim, 154, 156, 159, 161, 163, 167, 182, 188
Girardeau, John, 122
Goals for Georgia, 179–180, 189, 239
Goldwater, Barry M., 109, 115, 123
Gone with the Wind, 172
Gordy, Bessie Lillian. *See* Lillian Gordy Carter
Gordy, James Jackson ("Jim Jack",
    grandfather), 11–12, 15, 40
Gordy, Mary Ida Nicholson
    (grandmother), 11
Gordy, Tom (uncle), 26, 46–47, 64–65
Grady, Henry, 224
Graham, Billy, 135, 192, 208
Great Depression, 7, 15, 29–30, 80, 195, 225
Griffin, Caron, 173, 219. *See also* Chip Carter
Griffin, Marvin, 93–94, 109, 153, 163, 170, 180,
    182, 185